T0354503

# Whose Children Are We?
# The future that awaits us

*The prayer of the Our Father*
*and the Christian roots of life, family, and society*

## STEFANO TARDANI

Preface by Mgr. Giovanni D'Ercole

WESTBOW
PRESS®
A DIVISION OF THOMAS NELSON
& ZONDERVAN

Original Italian Edition
*Figli di chi? Quale futuro ci aspetta*
© Àncora, Milano

*Author*: Stefano Tardani
*Translated by*: Raffaela Merlini
*Editorial support*: Denise Biscossi, Susanna Ciriello, Maria Francesca Rescio

WestBow Press books may be ordered through booksellers or by contacting:

WestBow Press
A Division of Thomas Nelson & Zondervan
1663 Liberty Drive
Bloomington, IN 47403
www.westbowpress.com
1 (866) 928-1240

ISBN: 978-1-5127-4589-4 (sc)
ISBN: 978-1-5127-4588-7 (e)

Library of Congress Control Number: 2016909799

Print information available on the last page.

WestBow Press rev. date: 08/29/2016

*Who is wise enough to understand these things?*
*Who is intelligent enough to know them?*
*Straight are the paths of the LORD,*
*the just walk in them,*
*but sinners stumble in them.*

*Bible.* Hosea 14:10

# Contents

# Preface

The economic and financial crisis that is sweeping the world, particularly in highly-developed countries, forces us all to sit up and take note that we are coming to the end of an era, the easy era of low cost happiness, a marketable happiness without principles, ideals and values. Happiness is viewed as the fulfilment of every whim or desire, a right and a pleasure never to be denied. In the frantic search for this happiness, often illusory, the culture of manic consumerism has brought in its wake a sense of frustration that has driven many – often young people without values – to flee to artificial paradises which turn out to be a real hell of sadness and death. Drugs and violence, to name just a few examples, are symptoms and not causes of the widespread malaise among young people. If one tries to understand more, if one examines this satiated and dissatisfied postmodern society in depth, one senses a growing restlessness and vacuum in the soul of many. People have everything, yet it is not enough! People are sad! Why? What is missing?

If one wishes to be an honest and attentive listener to the "cry of life" rising up from the present generation, it is not enough to be satisfied with a purely superficial analysis of the crisis marking the family today, by now almost dismantled by a concentric attack on all sides. It is not enough just to find fault with the decline of institutions that seem to have lost any connection with the wealth of our heritage of values; one cannot passively stand back and watch the virtual suicide of our traditions that have made the Christian West, especially our country, Italy, a beacon of civilization and far-sighted spirituality. There is a general crisis, the crisis of Western civilization.

Is everything going wrong? Are we on the verge of a global catastrophe made more evident by extensive telecommunication and information networks enveloping the globe? It is right to wonder but not to let ourselves become pessimistic in an atmosphere of indifference and resignation. This is both dangerous and useless. Even if everything seems to be falling apart, we should not give up. Indeed, this is the time to rise to the challenge and, through hope, give renewed stimulus to those who risk drowning in a stormy sea. But in order to hope it is necessary to turn to the source, to start afresh from the 'certainties' of life, and to rediscover the ever ancient and ever present news that dwells within the heart of man, within every human person. This is the time when hope must be dared, when it must be pursued, boldly and consciously, by those who are prepared to stake everything so as not to be lost. It is up to everyone who feels within them this desire for life to strive to build a new humanity "before the silver thread snaps, or the golden bowl is cracked, or the pitcher shattered at the fountain, or the pulley broken at the well-head" (Qo 12:6).

Whoever takes up this book by Don Stefano Tardani with its catchy title, *Whose Children Are We? The future that awaits us* is plunged into the whys and wherefores, and the hardships of our time, and must allow themselves to be led to wonder about the most intimate and radical reasons for the humanitarian defeat that many are now bitterly forced to acknowledge. Humanity is adrift like a boat tossed in the ocean of history without a sound rudder and an experienced helmsman. Consciously and often recklessly, our generation, but also the previous one, have gradually rejected the embrace of God, arrogantly seeking to create a human brotherhood without Him. However, this denial of God, this crisis of authority, and the ideological rejection of any form of rules, have produced a generation of lost and frightened children, ill at ease, just like 'sheep without a shepherd'. However, not everything is lost. Indeed, the current crisis is a useful and providential opportunity to start afresh, to be reborn and build new prospects for life and progress. Without God man is lost. With Him nothing is impossible. Don Stefano correctly points out: "It is in a sincere relationship with God that there grows a sense of good and the true meaning of life".

In the pages of this volume, the attentive reader will examine with the enthusiasm and curiosity that is characteristic of anyone who allows himself to become engrossed in the plot of a novel, the human and spiritual path traced by the author that enters the self and enables it to open up to the 'you' with whom we are constantly called upon to relate. The reader will note, as he makes his way through this book, an invitation and inducement to assume responsibility to build, together with any person of good will, a society that has as its horizon of action the common good and happiness of all. In fact, the construction of the family and social 'we' presupposes awareness and desire for good that we can rediscover.

How? What then is the secret? To fully enjoy our existence, we cannot rule out God. Indeed, constant contact with Him should be maintained. It is necessary to learn to pray. How topical is prayer! "It is in prayer – observes Don Stefano – that our love for God and for humanity grows". Jesus taught the apostles to pray, He prayed with them. In the prayer *par excellence* – the *Pater Noster* – He taught them to call God by the name of Father. In this prayer, we find the summary and framework for any other way of praying. It is a prayer that embraces life and moulds the heart to filial tenderness. This is the reason that the *Our Father* has become the school of life for every Christian community. Today more than ever, it is a prayer to be rediscovered and translated into life.

In this book, Don Stefano, gathering the fruit of his pastoral and catechesis experience with engaged couples and families, traces a formative path modelled on the *Our Father*. In my view this is a particularly effective choice. Browsing through these pages we can see the intermingling of doctrine and experience, the Word of God and human research, perennial Church teaching (especially the Magisterium of Papal teaching subsequent to Vatican Council II, and in particular that of John Paul II and Benedict XVI) and the findings of science that investigates the secrets of the human soul. Each invocation of the *Our Father* is a gradual and further deepening of self-discovery – knowledge of self – in search of the truth of good. What has been experienced in years of serious pastoral work within the *Movimento dell'Amore Familiare* (Movement of Family Love), Don Stefano presents here in a systematic manner for the benefit of everyone.

This is a useful journey, and is especially recommended for families, the vital cells of society that make up the mystical body of the Church. A path of formation, but also a concrete proposal for the sanctity of everyone. Whoever claims to be a non-believer or considers himself to be distant from the practice of the faith will not feel excluded from the blueprint for life that this book presents. Rediscovering the Christian roots of our society is useful to all those who are part of a world that has been formed in two millennia by the rich cultural and spiritual heritage of the Gospel.

No tree can continue to live and produce fruit if it is detached from its roots. The author's purpose is to show us that the prayer of the *Our Father* helps us to return to our roots and therefore enables us to build the future with renewed hope.

Thanks are due to the author and his staff for having prepared this text which I gladly recommend to priests and educators, parents and teachers, as well as to young people looking for the real meaning of their existence. In this text the truth of the Gospel, illuminated by the Teaching of the Church and the testimonies of the Saints, is presented and gathered together in seventeen chapters, the result of studies and experience using an anthropological research method. Here one can note something very interesting for a new evangelization which involves us all. It is a useful contribution to the deepening of the pastoral plan of the Italian Bishops Conference for this decade dedicated to educating new generations in the faith: 'Educating to the good life of the Gospel'. The text translated into a number of languages may serve a new evangelization in other countries. The perspective in which we move is clear right from the introduction. "When confusion is rampant – writes Don Stefano – it is truly necessary to take up again the light of Gospel wisdom. The prayer of the *Our Father*, also known as 'The Lord's Prayer', is truly the summary of the whole Gospel. We then realise that its words actually contain the blueprint for our lives and our survival: the wisdom and beauty not only of the human being and the family but also of the way of life in society". In short, it is necessary to return to God and talk to Him not as a remote and omnipotent creator of our destiny, but as a tender and loving Father. God is Father, our Father.

MGR. GIOVANNI D'ERCOLE
BISHOP OF THE DIOCESE OF ASCOLI PICENO (ITALY)

# Introduction

'In the beginning', every reality in history is revealed through its manifestation and, with ever greater clarity, through its development. At the 'start', for example in the case of a plant seed or even at the beginning of a human embryo life, there is not only the very fact of its existence but inherent too is how it exists and matures.

When human progress and development are undermined by the confusions and contradictions of modern day life, when man sees himself superseded and 'downgraded' by the existence of what he has produced, the wisest choice is to return to the 'beginning'. In this, like the 'Source', there lies not only the beginning of life, but also the mystery, the sense of life: it is here that we find the foundation and the roots of human life, the family and society.

And this is exactly what John Paul II taught in many of his catecheses, especially those on human love, which seek to answer the many questions of the world today: "They are asked by single persons, by married and engaged couples, by young people, but also by writers, journalists, politicians, economists, demographers, in sum, by contemporary culture and civilization. I think that among the answers that Christ would give *to the people of our times* and to their questions, often so impatient, *fundamental would still be the one* he gave to the Pharisees. In answering these questions, Christ *would appeal first of all to the 'beginning'*"[1].

The problem of culture and life today mainly seems to concern the thematics of 'deep roots'. Regardless of the many groundbreaking initiatives in our postmodern era enabling progress in every field towards new and further boundaries, what is becoming increasingly clear to everyone is the 'inconsistency' of this 'tower', this 'power' of the city of man, this kind of giant with feet of clay referred to in the Bible[2]. Indeed, even economic empires are collapsing and the very

---

[1] *Magisterium.* John Paul II, *Man and Woman He Created Them. A Theology of the Body,* Pauline Books & Media, Boston, MA 2006, p. 219 (see also text no. 1 in Appendix).
[2] *Bible.* Cfr. Book of the Prophet Daniel 2:27-45.

same financial crises are one of the signs of imbalance and inequity in the 'system', which as a result of its increasingly global and complex administration risks 'collapsing' and backfiring on human life.

Indeed, above all it is the foundation that seems to be missing in much of the culture and vision of life today.

There come to mind the words of the Gospel, when Jesus speaks about the house built *on rock*, in other words based on true security which is God, and the other house built *on sand*, i.e. built on opportunism, false security, lies, and foolishness. As Jesus says in the Gospel: "And everyone who listens to these words of mine but does not act on them will be like a fool who built his house on sand. The rain fell, the floods came, and the winds blew and buffeted the house. And it collapsed and was completely ruined."[3].

Today we are witnessing the inner ruin of people, families and society. The greatest values have been lost or are in the process of being lost, or worse still, are being transformed. There is no desire to see the roots of life and Christian culture. There is therefore a gradual downward slide into cultural chaos, 'subculture' and 'cultural dictatorship'. We are witnessing a process of rampant relativism, materialism and massive confusion with regard to values. This is reflected in the turmoil of family and social life. On one hand people lament about the lack of meaning of life while on the other hand every effort is made to conceal the true points of reference and tenable certainties. Jesus tells us in the Gospel of the great temptation that, today as ever, pollutes life and culture: 'mammon', money, wealth, power and worldly pleasures. Jesus cautions us: "You cannot serve God and mammon."[4].

Owing to increased cultural and economic wealth, knowledge, and human possibilities, the world in its development is turning still more its gaze and heart towards the power and illusory fascination of 'mammon'. The whole of humanity and each and every individual conscience are constantly having to choose between God and 'mammon', between God the Father, on the one hand, and wealth, power and worldly pleasures, on the other.

One wonders, will Christians, together with the many people of good will, succeed in bringing personal and social life back to the paths of God the Father and to the paths of true love, restoring a face of humanity and fraternity to our world? If, indeed, on the one hand the power and number of available means are ever increasing, and on the other the values of conscience and spirit are diminishing, what will become of our lives? And if the 'power' to be well off, 'mammon',

---

[3] *Bible*. Gospel of Matthew 7:26-27.
[4] *Bible*. Gospel of Luke 16:13.

becomes the idol, the direction, and the goal of human existence, substituting the will of God the Father, what will become of our human reality?

In short, in a world that wants to live as though God did not exist, sooner or later man and consequently the family will lose the meaning of life, their truest dignity and deepest values. There will then arise in the human soul a sense of nostalgia, distrust and frustration and finally also one of indifference to everything and everyone, but also an interior suffering, like a void, an absence of well-being, that the satisfactions of the body and the rewards of life cannot fill. This is why Jesus Christ, Son of God and Son of man, in the light of the *Our Father* accompanies us and introduces us to the mystery of human life, its bases and its roots.

These pages on the prayer of the *Our Father*, which Jesus has taught and given to us, offer the opportunity for a great rediscovery of the mysterious face of God and the precious face of man. It is a journey through the words of the *Our Father*, explained phrase by phrase. They give us renewed hope and strength, providing us with the light of wisdom, and the truth of life, revealing to us the mystery of God, together with the deepest values of human life and the Christian roots of our life and actions. By the expression 'Christian roots' we refer to the deep roots of human life which we define as 'Christian' since it is Christ who revealed their truest and most mysterious reality, and it is always He who guides us to them, so that we may find again the fullness of life already here on earth.

One must then ask: what 'I' is at the basis of our relationships? Why are they increasingly more complex and less authentic? And why has confusion come about gender identity? What is the basis of the family? What kind of society are we building? These are some of the questions on which the prayer of the *Our Father* opens up horizons and gives us true and extraordinary answers. It will then be clear why the words of the *Our Father* act as 'the compass' for our life and our existence.

When confusion is rampant, it is truly necessary to take up again the light of Gospel wisdom. The prayer of the *Our Father*, also known as "The Lord's Prayer"[5], is truly the summary of the whole Gospel[6]. We then realise that its words actually contain the blueprint for our lives and our survival: the wisdom and beauty not only of the human being and the family but also of the way of life in society. The prayer of the *Our Father* reveals profound wisdom, of which there is so much need today, and that we can only ask of God.

---

[5] *Magisterium*. Cfr. *Catechism of the Catholic Church*, no. 2765.
[6] *Magisterium*. Cfr. *Catechism of the Catholic Church*, no. 2761.

Otherwise man, in search of himself, confused by the 'new lights' that dazzle and divert him, so often ends up going off track, being deceived and deceiving. This is what is happening now. Man, in losing sight of God and the mystery of God, also loses himself and his own personal identity; he loses the power to establish, in the truth and love, a family that can withstand the passage of time and, though using all his resources, including technological ones, loses the ability to build a society in which there is true good and well-being for everyone.

These pages are a great opportunity to unearth the answers to the main problems of personal, family and social life. The profound explanation, word after word, of the magnificent prayer that the Lord has taught us, marks out a great path to renew ourselves in mind and heart, and to unearth those answers that we would otherwise never find. Indeed, it was Jesus Christ who delivered and entrusted them to us in the *Our Father*.

Christianity has something great and valuable to offer everyone, Christians and non-Christians alike. It is up to us to find it again, to rediscover and spread this news through a renewed work of evangelization. It is still the Gospel, but presented in a novel way with a faith that does not disregard but includes the reality of the world. And that is what I am about to do in these pages, trusting in the wisdom of God.

This text was developed from a series of catecheses on *The Prayer of the Our Father*, held in Rome in 2010: here, transcribed and enlarged, they are offered to the reader in an easy and spontaneous style, maintaining the expressive effectiveness of conversational meditation.

It is necessary to point out that in this text the *Prayer of the Our Father* may be indicated in italics in its abbreviated form, i.e. *Our Father*, while Our Father in normal print refers to God the Father. The citations in footnotes are always repeated in full for clarity and convenience.

I have also felt it useful to enclose quotations in three major categories: Bible, Magisterium and Tradition. The word *Bible* is an easier term with which to refer the reader to the complete books of the Old and New Testament which make up the Holy Scripture.

The term *Magisterium* refers to the Documents of Papal Teaching, the successor of Peter the Apostle, and of the Bishops in communion with him, without making any further distinction between the ordinary and the extraordinary Magisterium.

Although a distinction should be drawn between the Apostolic Tradition itself and the various 'traditions' through which the Apostolic Tradition is expressed, the term *Tradition* is used here to indicate some particularly significant sources for our discussion, inspired by the Tradition and the Magisterium of the Church: being at the beginning of the citation, they appear with a capital 'T'.

The quotations from the Holy Scripture are derived from the *New American Bible, revised edition* (2010).

In writing this book I have considered many texts and references also of other sciences but, given the sensitive and challenging nature of the subject, I have preferred not to specifically mention them, choosing instead to refer to official sources of Christian faith.

The Reader will find in the Appendix an interesting and useful collection of extracts from the Magisterium, especially enlightening for further study.

I wish to extend my grateful thanks to the laity who have contributed to the original Italian edition of this book: in particular, Gabriella Briganti, Alessandro Di Stasio, Laura Lenzi, and all those who have supported its circulation.

I also wish to thank Mgr. Giovanni D'Ercole for his invaluable Preface.

My gratitude goes to the translator of this English edition for producing a very accurate and faithful rendition of the Italian original text, and to those who have generously worked on the French, German, Polish and Spanish translations for forthcoming publication, as well as the Arabic and Chinese ones.

Last but not least, I thank my parents for their example of faith, generous 'yes' to the Lord, and love of life, my family, the many families in the Movement, and the many friends with whom I've learnt to observe and understand.

To readers I truly hope that these pages will be a gift for their lives.

To all my sincere thanks.

# 1

# Father

If we look around we can see a pluralism of ideas and opinions but also a lot of confusion. We are witnessing a succession of generations that ignore one another, in a discontinuous pursuit of values that eventually cancel one another out. We are witnessing great disillusions, especially in what should be the most stable environment, i.e. the family, the place *a priori* for affection, the love of man and woman and the blossoming of human life. It is here that the warmth and certainty of being loved, listened to and supported should reign supreme. This, unfortunately, as we know only too well is often not the case. Despite the remarkable progress achieved by human civilization in many fields, it is often difficult to live, and sometimes even to survive. Moreover, the milestones attained run the risk of being nullified.

It is not always easy to listen to a constructive dialogue between husband and wife, and likewise a serious and constructive dialogue of parents with their children. While they are little, dialogue is relatively straightforward, but as children grow up, situations change, particularly when they start going to school and discover friendships, the Internet, *social networks*, and everything else that follows.

Engaged couples also start off with big dreams and projects, but nonetheless fear that something is going to unexpectedly pop up and undermine their happiness. So, even if couples and families are happy and succeed in various ways to overcome life's difficulties, there lurks a degree of uncertainty. Lovers, even if they are sure of their love, perceive some 'voids' within themselves and harbour great questions. Somehow, these are the nightmares of today's world. To escape, some lapse into a state of indifference. Once it was not so. Life was more stable and perhaps also simpler.

What is happening? We need to ask ourselves this question if we wish to be members of society, able to carry life forward and deliver it to new generations. What life are we building together? What messages are we handing down to children and young people? What is happening

1

to the family? What is changing in the people around us? One of the things that invites reflection is the figure of the father.

Something is changing. Slow but continuous, this change is also at times rapid and unexpected.

In the *Our Father,* Jesus gives us secrets as never revealed before. The *Our Father* can be compared to a flash of lightning, a penetrating light in the darkness of night. Perhaps we are in the habit of saying the prayer of the *Our Father*. But if we consider the words carefully, and see them in silhouette, we become all the more aware of today's situation, and we begin to understand many things! Jesus has given us this prayer, indeed He has handed it to us. If we do not want to be completely lost, it is here that we must unearth not only the deep mystery of our life but also our way of life.

Most of the experiences and considerations I am going to describe here are those that I recount every year to engaged and married couples: many have thanked me, even after many years, for their validity and the good that such teachings have brought about in their lives and in their love, many of them have moved closer to the truth, others have undergone a deep conversion to Christianity. Even agnostics and atheists have found their relationship with God. These powerful messages are born of prayer, study, and experience.

So, let us now embark upon this new journey in the prayer and words of the *Our Father.*

The text of the *Our Father* is to be found in two Gospels: *Matthew 6:9-13* and *Luke 11:2-4*. The most detailed and complete version is the one in the Gospel of Matthew. This is the text taken from the *New American Bible, revised edition* (2010):

> "This is how you are to pray:
> Our Father in heaven,
> hallowed be your name,
> your kingdom come,
> your will be done,
> on earth as in heaven.
> Give us today our daily bread;
> and forgive us our debts,
> as we forgive our debtors;
> and do not subject us to the final test,
> but deliver us from the evil one".

In the chapters that follow, we will refer to the more traditional and more commonly known wording of this text.

## God Abba

"This is how you are to pray: Our Father...". Well, perhaps we do not pay much attention but the first word Jesus gave us, in the original Hebrew, Aramaic and Greek texts, is 'Father'. In addressing God with the title 'Father', Jesus used a common term but in an entirely new and extraordinary way; nobody would ever have used it or imagined its use in relation to God.

Jesus, in teaching us to turn to God, uses a word nobody would have used towards Almighty God: *'Abba'*. This Aramaic word is an expression of familiarity, used by a child addressing his father, equivalent to our usage of 'papa', 'dad', and 'daddy' today. It is a term of endearment that children use when speaking to or about their fathers.

Therefore, the Jews used this term within the family as an expression of intimacy. In the Old Testament the title of God as Father is used to refer to the people of Israel[1], as God the Father of the nation, creator of his people through the Alliance. However, the term 'Father' is not understood in our personal sense. Children like adults could not call God in a personal way, much less so using an Aramaic term such as 'Abba', 'papa', completely void of any solemnity! For this reason, addressing God as 'Father' could not have been an invention of the disciples or the apostles of Jesus who were Jews; it was not an invention of the Church.

The apostles would never have been able to take such an initiative on their own. In fact, no God-fearing Jew could or would have done so. No one would have given voice to such an expression in relation to God unless God himself had revealed and granted it. Only Jesus, the Son of God, could have expressed himself in this way, revealing God as Father! Moreover, He takes this amazing initiative, placing us within his confidence – his alone – with the You of God, his Father. This fact does not exist in any other religion. This is a fact and a gift revealed by Jesus Christ and brought into the world through the Church. The pagan world with its polytheistic vision could never have invented it.

Thus, in Islam, this word to address God does not exist. Muslims call God Allah. In the Koran there are at least 99 ways to express and to name Allah but the term 'Father' is not among them. They include 'The Creator', 'The Lord', etc. Great and beautiful terms, it is true, but what is missing is the term which Jesus Christ revealed to us, drawing us close to the fatherhood of God, to the point of being able to call on him as 'Father'.

---

[1] *Bible*. Cfr. Book of Deuteronomy 32:6; Book of the Prophet Malachi 2:10.

Nobody could have done something like this. Without Jesus, we would never have been able to really know God the 'Father'. It is only Jesus who said that God is substantially 'Father' in himself. This, as He has revealed to us, is precisely because of his Trinitarian reality. Jesus, throughout his life, continually showed his intimate proximity to the Father[2]. Only Jesus of Nazareth, the Word made flesh, made man in the womb of the Virgin Mary by the work of the Holy Spirit, only Jesus 'true God and true Man', has been able to bring this news for us: to reveal the true face of God and bring us into the heart of God the Father so as to call on him as 'Father'. Knowing the Face of God is the most beautiful and sublime gift that we could have received from Jesus, an enormous gift, changing perspectives and behaviour, leading us to the 'roots of our life'.

The news that Jesus has brought us is extraordinary and fundamental for humanity. It therefore follows that if it is of such importance, we must begin to understand it well, because here lies the secret, the very secret of Jesus Christ. When, after having profoundly found God, I converted from a superficially lived Christianity to a living Christianity, one of the things that fundamentally struck me was precisely this extraordinary revelation that Jesus has brought to the world. In the *Our Father* we have the secret of Jesus Christ but we also have the secret of our life. How is it possible to survive on earth? What are we? How do our lives, our relationships, our families, and our society function? Let us be careful. Someone will try to take the *Our Father* away from us: first hiding and then removing the roots, slowly and in such a way that hardly anyone will notice.

And yet, the word 'Abba' is so new and powerful that no one can have the *Our Father* set aside – as many would like to by sowing seeds of indifference and ignorance. These people make themselves wiser than everyone, while in fact "they became fools"[3], and as the Book of Wisdom says, "they did not know the hidden counsels of God"[4]. Indeed, it is only by knowing God's secrets that we can know our secret. It is only by knowing their parents' secret that children can understand their own secret.

We may have prayed the *Our Father* many times but perhaps we have not properly understood its meaning, its import. Many also have their own idea of God, far from the reality with which He has revealed himself, an idea that has been imagined or dictated by negative

---

[2] *Magisterium.* Cfr. Joseph Cardinal Ratzinger, *The God of Jesus Christ. Meditations on the triune God,* Ignatius Press, San Francisco, 2008 (text no. 2 in Appendix).
[3] *Bible.* Letter to the Romans 1:22.
[4] *Bible.* Book of Wisdom 2:22.

conditioning, i.e. the wrong idea. God is not just the Creator. Moreover He is neither, as some philosophers say, the 'Immobile Engine', nor God 'Architect', as understood by the Masons, nor a non-personal generic 'Divine', present in us and in the world, as the New Age movement would have us believe in taking up the concept of Buddhism.

Those who have left Christianity, without a deep knowledge of it, sense a 'fundamental nostalgia' within them. Indeed, saying that God is Father is much greater than saying anything else. We must not let the gift of God the Father shrink and diminish, since Jesus saw to revealing and giving it to us. "For this is the will of my Father, that everyone who sees the Son and believes in him may have eternal life, and I shall raise him [on] the last day"[5]. "Now this is eternal life, that they should know you, the only true God, and the one whom you sent, Jesus Christ"[6].

**Why it is so important**

All this makes us understand that first and foremost God is Father. But what does this mean? There are two fundamental truths that change our life.

The first concerns God, God is One and certainly the Only One. He, however, is not alone in himself. How can we say that, though subsisting and unique, 'God is not alone'? For Jews, God is One, and also for us Christians God is One and also for Muslims who call him Allah, God is One. But we know that 'God is not alone'. In what sense? He is not alone because God is Father. How does one become a father? A man is a father in the same way any woman is a mother because they have a child.

So, the fact that God is Father means that God is Father of the Son, who is the Word, Eternal with him, 'generated' by him and likewise God. As the Credo says: "God from God, Light from Light, true God from true God, begotten, not made, consubstantial with the Father"[7]. Jesus says in the Gospel: "The Father and I are one"[8]. This is extraordinary: the Son is One with the Father in the communion of Love, in the Holy Spirit, the Spirit of Power, Truth and Love. And it is to the Holy Spirit, the gift of the Risen Jesus, that Christians turn to so as to have light on the mystery

[5] *Bible*. Gospel of John 6:40.
[6] *Bible*. Gospel of John 17:3.
[7] *Magisterium*. Nicene Creed (http://www.usccb.org/beliefs-and-teachings/what-we-believe/index.cfm., accessed in July 2014); cfr. Henricus Denziger & Adolfus Schönmetzer (eds.), *Enchiridion Symbolorum*, Verlag Herder KG, Freiburg im Breisgau 1965, pp. 66-67.
[8] *Bible*. Gospel of John 10:30.

of God[9], as they do when they invoke him with the words of the prayer *Veni, Creator Spiritus*: "Oh, may Thy grace on us bestow the Father and the Son to know; and Thee, through endless times confessed, of both the eternal Spirit blest". God has revealed that He is a Communion of Love. God not only loves, but 'God is Love'[10]: Community of Love. One God in a Communion of Love of three Persons[11]. Jesus reveals to man the true face of God and the true face of man[12].

Unearthing the roots of true faith also leads us to unearth the roots to our life. In the mystery of God, Jesus brings us the mystery of life[13] and the mystery of Communion[14]. This revelation is of extraordinary strength, because it enables us to understand that in God there is the secret we seek both of life and relationships. The couple search for this secret: how to stay together, despite their differences, male and female, each with their own way of being?

Sometimes, alternative behavioural patterns and other ways of being are sought. For many, mass standardisation, i.e. dampening and ironing out differences and contrasts, would seem to be the solution, while others prefer the freedom to multiply the variants of human nature itself as much as possible. In this way, the sense and meaning of human life are twisted. Where the creativity of man seeks to push beyond and overcome any boundary without God, human nature itself will no longer appear to express any rule, neither biological nor moral.

What is forgotten is that God is not only Creator but also Father, and has entrusted mankind with a part of creation to preserve and develop its meaning. He has entrusted this especially to man and woman where, most of all, there is found the ability and responsibility for a free, loving and conscious collaboration with God the Father. It would appear that by culpably ignoring God the Father, any natural order can be subverted and modified at will. But in doing so, nature ends up in chaos and life in madness.

And in society? In the end, we must ask ourselves: what is the sense of globalization? It has within itself at the same time the dynamics of uniformity and those of plurality. To avoid the chaos and the cancer

---

[9] *Bible*. Cfr. Letter to the Ephesians 1:17-18.
[10] *Bible*. Cfr. First Letter of John 4:8.
[11] *Bible*. Cfr. First Letter to the Corinthians 12:4-6; Second Letter to the Corinthians 13:13. *Magisterium*. Cfr. *Catechism of the Catholic Church*, nos. 253-255. *Tradition*. Cfr. St. Athanasius (295-373), *The Letters of Saint Athanasius concerning the Holy Spirit*, translation with introduction and notes, by C.R.B. Shapland, Epworth Press, London 1951, pp. 137-138 (text no. 3 in Appendix).
[12] *Magisterium*. Cfr. Vatican Council II, Pastoral Constitution *Gaudium et Spes* no. 22.
[13] *Bible*. Cfr. Gospel of John 14:6.
[14] *Bible*. Cfr. Gospel of John 14:23.

of madness it is necessary to go to the foundations, to the roots of life and, in particular, to the roots of human life. Therefore, for many aspects, the dominant theme of culture has shifted from a social one, which nonetheless remains essential, to that of life and private life, which is crucial. Jesus Christ has in himself the solution to what, for us and for all mankind, is a major problem: the secret of how to be together in our diversity, how to reconcile the multiplicity of rights with the essentiality of duties. How can people live together in society, how can they freely bring together apparently conflicting diversities? How can the arrogance and violence of some be prevented from prevailing over others? Certainly, this is by no means easy. But if we want to remain *human* it is not enough to be free; to be united also in a family it is not sufficient to agree upon what is 'useful'. God must have in himself, precisely because He is One but not alone, the keystone, 'the secret to the co-presence of diversity'. This is the formula that is also being sought to a greater or lesser extent in all fields. This is why the Bible warns us: "Unless the Lord build the house, they labor in vain who build"[15].

In our times we have to get used to having a capacity for greater depth so that 'the mystery that unites' may be revealed to us: how we can live well and live together, and not as prisoners of the 'useful', the 'immediate', and the 'ephemeral'. In approaching and understanding the *Our Father* we will find this secret, and this secret will gradually become increasingly clear. It will be clearer to many people, to parents and to many young people, who do not see the road leading to this capacity for communion both in social and family relations, between man and woman, and brothers and sisters. It will be much clearer to everyone what to do so that humanity does not turn into inhumanity. In this sense, the *Our Father* is a path of liberation for humanity. But for this we have to go in depth, to the 'roots of life', where biology and sociology 'touch' with the mystery of God.

**What we are more**

This introduces us to the second fundamental reality which is made manifest in the extraordinary and beautiful Word: 'Father'. This is of great importance to us because it reveals and reminds us of our secret.

When you pray, Jesus said, pray thus: 'Father', 'Our Father'. Jesus Christ has come to extend to us, 'by grace', that which is 'by nature' his relationship with God, his Father. He is the Son in a unique way, divine

---

[15] *Bible.* Book of Psalms, 127:1.

7

'by nature', the same being as the Father. We are children 'by grace' of God, and by participation in the life of Jesus: we are 'children in the Son'. Now, if Jesus has us turn to God calling him 'Father', it means that we are essentially 'children' and 'his children'.

Do we truly realise what this fact means? Let us try to understand it a little better.

There are many ways of being. There are those who are single. There are those who are husbands, wives, fathers, mothers, grand-parents, brothers, sisters, nieces, nephews, cousins, uncles, aunts or friends, and many other ways. These are all ways of being different: each person has his own way and everyone has more than one. Now, what is the way of being that is common to all human beings? There is one, and only one, which is the same for everyone and we all have it in a radical way.

It can be observed that we are people and we all have the same human dignity. This is our value. But on what is the value of human dignity based, i.e. that of every man and every woman? What is the real thing, and not just an idea? I do not mean a cultural superstructure, which any school of thought may build up or knock down. What is the fact by virtue of which personal human dignity is the same for all of us, and that cannot possibly be misinterpreted?

It is this: we are all *'children'*. This is common to all of us human beings. Even in the many ways in which we are different we are all and always 'children'. Children, in the truest sense, are those who have received life and have not given it to themselves. This fact is the same for all 'sons and daughters'. It is this that defines us and it is the same for everyone! That which makes us equal is 'being children' and this is the basis of our human dignity. Everything else is an addition. All other attributes are added: cousins, relatives, friends, brothers in law, sisters in law, uncles, aunts, co-workers, labourers, businessmen and so on.

In being children, two truths immediately emerge. The first is that someone has given us life. You cannot give life to yourself! Who is a child? One who finds life in his hand. Therefore, being children means that we have received life from someone. All of us have received life. Our life rests on this gift that is its base. Clearly, we must also see what we make of life... But this is something else. And so as not to be deceived and not to get everything wrong in life, it is necessary to get down to the roots, to the 'roots of life'.

The amazing thing that God reminds us of in the prayer of the *Our Father* is that we are his children! We are his children, not children of the earth... the stars... test tubes... machines... but of a Father that is God! And, if we are his children this means that God the Father reflects and sends back to us our truth as a reflection: it means that we find life in our hand, that life is granted, that it is our precious reality, that someone wanted us to have it, that someone has thought of us, that someone loved us and wanted us, that someone expects something from our life, from the lives of each one of us. Our greatest freedom is that of being ourselves, through and through, in being children of God the Father: there is no greater freedom.

But being a 'child' also involves a second truth: I cannot invent everything myself, I must already have a matrix within me in my biological, mental, emotional, sexual, psychological and spiritual mechanism. We have something within us, a 'how'. We are made in a certain way, because together with the gift of life that we received, we were also given the way of life. This way of life we call 'being human'. Our love for words such as 'papa', 'father', as well as 'mum', 'mother' shows a great fascination, often betrayed by the misdeeds of parents or the great shallowness of our world. Therefore, on closer consideration, the first word of the *Our Father*, 'Father', reveals our 'being sons and daughters', our root, our secret which is our hidden life that must be made manifest.

We then have to ask ourselves the question: have we received human life together with the revelation about its meaning and its root? Have parents shown more of themselves to children, or have they shown this deeper reality of life? Have they really revealed this great truth to children that is the root of life, and that exists 'before' the parents themselves? In what sense 'before'? Before, because it is not the parents who made the model of the child, it is not the parents who created human life: they have just received it! Since they too are children... .

Once, an expectant mother responded to my compliments and good wishes: "Is it me who should be congratulated? It is all due to God, He does everything". And she was right! Yes, a mother finds this life as a tremendous gift, whole and entire, she welcomes it, carries it in her womb, nourishing it with love and the substance of her blood. The root of being children does in fact come *before* parents. This is why they are called children. All the other things we build or do are called 'things' and not 'children'. Instead, the child is someone that parents receive as a pre-existing reality because everything is already there in the gift, in the human embryo, in the yes of God the Father and in the yes of the parents to life.

The *Our Father* leads us to the profound mystery of our life that passes through our parents, but which is before our parents. Indeed, parents have not invented life, neither theirs nor that of their children: they have just accepted it! They should not hide the real root of every life: the Father of everyone, the Father of life, of every life. In fact, the root of every life is not the love of the parents. Their love, in sexual union, is the condition, it is not the life of their son or daughter.

True parents, who do not betray God the Father and their mission, know how to reveal this 'mystery' to their children. Other parents who do not know this mystery or conceal and hide it from their children, actually betray them. How many injustices and how much violence is suffered by children! What little 'humanity' so many children have had to suffer! However, there are also the many generous and heroic acts of countless fathers and mothers. Today as ever, the greatness and poverty of parents is intertwined in the history of each individual.

Life passes through that of parents, whether they are good or bad, but it cannot stop at them, it must go beyond... 'to the roots of life'. Conversely, by fleeing from our past and charging ahead, under the illusion of being able to be better fathers or mothers without being truly 'children', we will only succeed in further damaging our already wounded life. It takes courage to be a real, authentic man or woman: I would say that it takes courage to be children, to rediscover the beauty and greatness of our *mystery*, often hidden or defaced by suffering and the lies served up by life which stick in our memory.

Here, I intentionally use the word *'mystery'*. It is neither taboo nor the domain of ignorance. Mystery is the space of the Truth. Mystery is what represents us the most: more than science and technology. These can be an aid for man but cannot be considered an absolute. Instead, mystery is something that belongs to us and represents us, it is not what we do not know, it is not ignorance. Instead, it is what we know about ourselves and from which we come, since it is greater than us: so we know it because it belongs to us and has been revealed; we know it as something upon which we are based, like a 'root'; and, at the same time it attracts us as the 'meaning and purpose' of existence. For us, the mystery is not the ignorance of those who do not know and therefore have blind trust, instead it is the awareness of those who do know and therefore have confidence.

Calling God 'Father' leads us back to that great mystery of peace and communion that God lives and, at the same time, also refers us to that mystery of beauty and grandeur of each one of us, just as God the Father wants, and wanted, everyone's life to be. With God, life takes on a different light and another colour. Without him, everything becomes dark and absurd.

The human secret of the root lies in God the Father. Certainly much of human fatherhood has betrayed the divine mandate to 'be the image and transparency' of God the Father. Denying God the Father and distancing him from the hearts and lives of people is the most serious and foolish mistake that the consumer society or any ideology can do!

We cannot be good, meaningful and active in doing good, if we are not what we are at the root! The greatest thing that we can do 'to be' is to rediscover the beauty and the preciousness of this great mystery of being children.

If we adults find what we are in depth, then everything else will come right for new generations. But unless we fully know this, the whole of life will be like chasing after the wind, and also, unfortunately, a constant tripping up in a vortex of errors and disappointing compromises.

In the next chapter we will see what is truly 'ours', what we cannot do without and, conversely, the surrogates, i.e. those which are misleadingly presented as 'ours', but in actual fact do not belong to us, and deceive us, so that we go off the right track and destroy our life.

# 2
## Our Father
### *Our Father*

We now come to the second word which is truly extraordinary: the word 'our' referring to God the Father. Jesus could also have taught us to say: "Father, who art in heaven", or "Almighty Father", "God Creator of the universe", or any other appellation. However, by including this second word, the mystery of God our Father is revealed to us!

'Our' is a particular word, one that is full of meaning. 'Our' is what belongs to us: our life, our body, our feelings, our thoughts. 'Our' connotes something intimate that belongs to us and constitutes us. On a deeper level, 'our' implies a relationship that expresses a reciprocal belonging, telling us that 'God the Father is really ours'. We use the word 'our', for example, when we love: couples say 'our love', 'our home', 'our children'.

'Our' reveals something profound, it is a reality that touches us in our innermost being! Saying 'Our Father', as Jesus taught us, shows that there must be something that is his, but also belongs to us, that is ours but also belongs to him. This is something to which we have not given sufficient thought. That there is God, that He is far away... and that He is the Creator, this we can understand. But that He is 'ours' and we 'his' and that we belong to each other; this is the tremendous gift that Jesus has brought to us. As we shall see shortly, this is a new and profound revelation.

Our human reality is that 'of being children of God the Father'. "See what love the Father has bestowed on us that we may be called the children of God. Yet so we are. "[1], Scripture tells us.

Pope Emeritus Benedict XVI in his book *Jesus of Nazareth*, when commenting on the *Our Father* with regard to the paternity of God writes: "Every human being is unique, and willed as such by God. Every

---

[1] *Bible*. First Letter of John 3:1.

individual is known to him. In this sense, by virtue of creation itself man is the 'child' of God in a special way, and God is his true Father. To describe man as God's image is another way of expressing this idea. (...) Above all, though, Jesus is 'the Son' in the strict sense – he is of one substance with the Father. He wants to draw all of us into his humanity and so into his Sonship, into his total belonging to God. (...) We are not ready-made children of God from the start, but we are meant to become so increasingly by growing more and more deeply in communion with Jesus. Our sonship turns out to be identical with following Christ. (...) We see that to be God's child is not a matter of dependency, but rather of standing in the relation of love that sustains man's existence and gives it meaning and grandeur. (...) Jesus alone was fully entitled to say 'my Father', because he alone is truly God's only-begotten Son, of one substance with the Father. By contrast, the rest of us have to say 'our Father'. Only within the 'we' of the disciples can we call God 'Father', because only through communion with Jesus Christ do we truly become 'children of God'"[2].

Our most beautiful mystery is this: being children through the grace of Jesus Christ, the Son of God. It was for this that God himself became man in Jesus of Nazareth. As Saint Irenaeus wrote: "For this end, the Word of God was made man, and He Who is the Son of God, Son of Man, that man blended with God's Word, and receiving the adoption, might become the Son of God"[3]. So "He the Word of God Which dwelt in man, and was made Son of Man, that he might inure man to receive God, and God to dwell in Man: – according to the good pleasure of the Father"[4]. By becoming man, the Son of God has made it possible for us to become the 'children of God', 'partakers of the divine nature': "Through these, he has bestowed on us the precious and very great promises, so that through them you may come to share in the divine nature, after escaping from the corruption that is in the world because of evil desire"[5].

Here, then, we are far from the distorted and alienating ways of understanding man as are sometimes heard: flower children, children of joints, children of the stars, children of selfishness and interest, children of error, children of science and technology, digital children, children

---

[2] *Magisterium*. Benedict XVI, *Jesus of Nazareth*, Doubleday, New York 2007, pp. 138-141.
[3] *Tradition*. St. Irenaeus bishop of Lyons (130-202), *Against Heresies*, translated by J. Keble, James Parker and Co., London, Oxford and Cambridge 1872, pp. 281-282.
[4] *Tradition*. St. Irenaeus bishop of Lyons (130-202), *Against Heresies*, translated by J. Keble, James Parker and Co., London, Oxford and Cambridge 1872, pp. 285-286.
[5] *Bible*. Second Letter of Peter 1:4.

of wealth, and in the end... children of themselves, children of no one! Modern man does not want to depend on anybody. The men and women of today want to be free and independent. Certainly, God the Father wants our emancipation and our freedom, otherwise we would not be able to love in a mature way. However, He does not want us to be deceived about freedom and independence.

What has happened? What distortion has penetrated society and people's minds? In one way or another, someone has sought to remove our root which is Our Father so as to make us become orphans! Orphans of God the Father! Without meaning, without a history, without past and future. Why? To make people weaker, to make way for someone else. Hiding or removing our roots eliminates the future; it means making us weak and confused. Think about it: isn't this the reason for so many shortcomings and so much weakness in people today? For so much boredom? Is it not true that we see so many young people in the wild pursuit of sounds, noises, emotions, feelings and experiences that, although fascinating, are consumed in a minute? This is why we witness such great disorientation: people feel empty and bewildered. Here then is the reason for sinking into the virtual and alienating world, the world of drugs and sex without a face, without a future, and without true love.

There is so much good in the extraordinary potential of young people, provided, however, that they are not deceived hiding the roots of their life, without which, sooner or later they too will sadly wither.

In conclusion, we have something of ours that belongs to us but which, if hidden from consciousness or denied and trampled upon, creates a sense of emptiness within that causes people to suffer and go off track. Let us not lose our Father, the deepest root, the mystery of our lives. Many, taken up with their material well-being or self-elation, or scandalized by the evils in the world, have ceased to listen to and recognise the living God.

How has this loss of our 'Father' come about, the secret of our life, our development and our origin? There are many attacks on this front. Each country may want to find evidence of this in its own history. Here, we will look at just two examples in our past: *the case of Freud* and that of the *French Revolution*.

**The case of Freud**

If we want to look for some sign in the culture and history of Europe, we could cite, for example, *the case of Freud*, the father of psychoanalysis, the great discoverer of the subconscious. A doctor, he was born in 1856 and died in 1939. He described a mechanism whereby the child, since a very young age, by being closely tied to the mother wants to exclude the father, i.e., the famous Oedipus complex. There is then the so-called 'killing of the father' through exclusion, as if it were necessary for the growth of human beings, for their emancipation, to detach themselves and 'kill the father'. This 'killing', not physical but of the heart and the mind, is allegedly not only useful but necessary in order to acquire independence. Although it is a metaphor, Freud's 'patricide' theory has left its mark in culture. According to Freud, God the 'Father' is the image of the feared and hated father-master who is then killed.

Several textbooks state that this 'killing', traumatic to a greater or lesser extent, is in some way necessary for separation, not only from the mother's body but also from the father and his 'oppression'. We should not forget that Freud always had to come to terms with the sick reality of his patients: this was his point of departure, i.e. divided, broken, suffering, sick beings; he did not start off from the good of a balanced and healthy human being. It should also be added that Freud did not manage to track down the energies of the human spirit, while his disciple Jung broadly interpreted them as 'psychical expressions'.

The fundamental idea of 'survival', 'by necessarily trampling', is something we find much in our lives and in our society, in the generational clash on the one hand, and in the vacuum of values on the other. All draped and covered by the word 'freedom' that often hides ignorance and presumption, or perhaps the desire of man who feels a prisoner and would like to 'be saved' but does not know from whom. Of many young people with their contradictions, of their struggle for a free life, it was said: "It's their age, it's their age... it is something that will pass and they will come back". Not true! And they did not come back. It is not at all easy for them to return to abandoned values and to the faith. We are seeing a kind of trap or psycho-affective labyrinth whereby people are often imprisoned in themselves and in their thoughts, blocked to the point of not being able to get out of themselves, to seek and know any truth by reason of everyone's distrust of everything; it is as if a veil has dropped over them and covered their hearts. In fact, it is life that is sick. A return to values and faith requires a healing journey of life itself.

**What is ours?**

The parents' oppression or abandonment of children on the one hand, and the adaptation of children or their abandonment of parents on the other, leave serious wounds in both. Disappointment leads to selfishness and apathy and thus independence and escape. It is here that 'the killing of the father', is made manifest, the killing first of fatherhood then motherhood; in short, the killing of something that is precious, but that has been overshadowed and overlooked. Similarly, our values and roots have also been abandoned and with these roots our secret, that of God our Father.

The question that must be asked is: in bringing them into the world, have parents truly revealed to their children the mystery of their lives which goes well beyond biology? Have they generated bodies or the mystery of life? I believe that this is the fundamental point: we have forgotten our Father, above all, the 'our'. Consequently, parents have looked upon children as 'their property' filling them with their dreams and imposing their way of life. Or vice versa, not being able to consider them as 'their property', feeling themselves as perhaps more 'friends' than parents, they have abandoned them to their fate, without showing them the good, some rules, and an intelligent freedom, which has sense, purpose, and a root.

These fathers have forgotten the 'our' as Jesus has taught us to address God in the prayer of the *Our Father*! Indeed, only God the Father is 'truly our': they, parents, children, all of us belong to this reality, this mystery of God the Father. By ignoring God, the Source of life, that which is 'really our', existence shatters into countless 'properties', to be either used in a selfish way, or irresponsibly left to themselves, and in any case to be always lived in an inhuman and misleading way.

This is why Jesus tells us in the Gospel: "Call no one on earth your father; you have but one Father in heaven"[6]. This means that there is only one Father, God, and all human fathers can and should show themselves to be fathers by revealing rather than concealing that God is Father. No father can take his place. Yet, this is something we have forgotten. And if human fathers have their children call them as such, they should be aware that there is a common Father from whom all fatherhood comes, both natural and spiritual.

The greatest example we have is that of Saint Joseph, the husband[7] of the Blessed Virgin Mary and putative[8] father of Jesus, who accomplished this throughout his life in recognising the mystery of God which enveloped him. For his loyalty, "God has put him at the head of his family"[9] as "Guardian of the Redeemer"[10] and as "Patron of the Universal Church"[11].

---

[6] *Bible*. Gospel of Matthew 23:9.
[7] *Magisterium*. Cfr. John Paul II, Apostolic Exhortation *Redemptoris custos* (1989) no. 18.
[8] *Magisterium*. Cfr. John Paul II, Apostolic Exhortation *Redemptoris custos* (1989) no. 27.
[9] *Magisterium*. Cfr. John Paul II, Apostolic Exhortation *Redemptoris custos* (1989) no. 8.
[10] *Magisterium*. Cfr. John Paul II, Apostolic Exhortation *Redemptoris custos* (1989) no. 1.
[11] *Magisterium*. Cfr. John Paul II, Apostolic Exhortation *Redemptoris custos* (1989) no. 1.

## Silence – word of Saint Joseph

Perhaps some of our readers will sometimes wonder why there is no word of Saint Joseph, the putative father of Jesus, reported in the Gospel, unlike the Virgin Mary, his spouse, who has left us three interventions in the Gospel: the Magnificat[12], the speech to the Son on finding him in the Temple[13], and her exhortation at The Marriage Feast of Cana[14] which marks the beginning of miracles and manifestation of Christ.

Every point in the Gospel is full of deep meaning. The Virgin Mary, who receives Christ the Saviour, is the image of the Church, of the humanity that welcomes him with faith and love, and receives him in the reality of life. Her three interventions reported in the Gospels are the expression of our humanity and the Church on receiving Jesus, a gift from the Father.

The Magnificat is the proclamation of *faith*, the fulfilment of the promises of God and the joy of certain hope. The second intervention of Mary, the one in the Temple, in which she shows her concern when addressing the Son, expresses the need for humanity to understand God, and to adapt to him so that the *hope* of his presence and hence religion is not an escape from reality, but a responsible choice. The third intervention of Mary, the one at the Wedding Feast of Cana, shows the capacity of the Church and every Christian, to cooperate in the work of God's *love* in communion with him.

These are the three moments that mark the growth of every faithful soul, and that of the whole Church, of which Mary is model and image. This entails, if we so desire, the ever increasing experience that God gives us of the three theological virtues: faith, hope and charity. Mary the Most Holy Mother of God reminds us as Mother what we are and what we can become. Whereas Saint Joseph represents all spouses and natural or adoptive fathers of which he is the model and image. He is the transparency of the mystery of God the Father and lives his role perfectly: symbolically his word is not that of a man who speaks of himself, it is not just 'any word', but the Word of God and of his plan.

This is why there is no word enunciated by Saint Joseph in the Gospels, not because he was silent or dumb, but because his human word is the entire Bible in that it is the Word of God. Here he reveals the message, which is that of any loyal 'father', of being in gestures and words the *'transparency'* of every Word of God, the Pastor and head of

---

[12] *Bible*. Cfr. Gospel of Luke 1:46-55.
[13] *Bible*. Cfr. Gospel of Luke 2:41-52.
[14] *Bible*. Cfr. Gospel of John 2:1-12.

the family. Just a single word of his reported in the Gospel would have obscured rather than revealed this message that is so important and valuable for us all.

## The 'before' parental

What we are investigating leads us to consider a primary and fundamental aspect.

The Apostle Paul writes: "For this reason I kneel before the Father, from whom every family in heaven and on earth is named"[15]. If one is a father or mother, if there is a paternity or maternity, this is because there is God the Father. In fact, none of us has invented life, life is not a discovery or scientific conquest, being a human person is a gift that comes from above. Therefore, it is not medicine, not even biology, science or technology that make us human persons: it is a gift from God our Father. The great human resources found in science and technology can make life more human as long as they do not deny or conceal the root of our life, that is God our Father.

That's why God vindicates the truth, yes, vindicates it! God has his rights. This, too, is something we have forgotten! He is the Source of all justice. We talk about everyone's rights but we forget *God's rights*. Jesus warns us in the Gospel: "repay (...) to God what belongs to God"[16], who is Father, our Father. Let's really think about this: Jesus warns us not to call anyone 'father' on earth except in truth, not to deceive anyone, but to reveal to each one their own secret.

It is necessary to understand the meaning of the Gospel in the faith with which it was faithfully written. It is clear that if one is a father or mother it is not because they have given life to their children, because life has already been received: life does not begin with him or her. This is what Jesus means when He says "you are all brothers. Call no one on earth your father; you have but one Father in heaven."[17]. In fact, every father and every mother carry this mystery within them: they, rather than generating 'their children', 'receive them' in the same way that they too 'have received' their lives.

No one, then, is truly father or mother in the absolute sense: otherwise children, not being able to find in their parents the 'reason' for their life, or barely putting up with a life stemming from human caprice or error (of their parents), in their search for independence are tempted

---

[15] *Bible.* Letter to the Ephesians 3:14-15.
[16] *Bible.* Gospel of Matthew 22:21.
[17] *Bible.* Gospel of Matthew 23:8-9.

to base their lives, arrogantly and foolishly, within themselves, so as not to succumb to the 'non sense' of their origin.

Therefore, without God our Father, parents suffocate their children or abandon them to themselves. In turn children despise and, in their hearts, 'kill' their parents, abandoning or exploiting them. Only Our Father, our common Father has us love and respect life to the full, that of the children and that of the parents, thus overcoming respective claims that life 'belongs to me' which can go to the point of destroying it by obscuring its meaning and history.

Only by living and demonstrating the mystery of God our Father, mystery of Love and Life, which is *before* that of the parents, will children not have to 'kill' anyone and will grow in truth and love, truly free and human. This reality of our life – which 'precedes' our birth, the relationship with parents and creation itself – is attested by Holy Scripture when Saint Paul says: "Blessed be the God and Father of our Lord Jesus Christ, (...) as he chose us in him, before the foundation of the world, to be holy and without blemish before him"[18]. The question then arises: have parents, and in particular Christian ones, shown their children the secret of their life? Indeed, there is a secret to be passed on: the life of children is *before* that of their parents. In this *before* there is all the goodness of God the Father towards us and all our preciousness. True parents must recognise this and show, defend, and love it. They must neither invent nor create it with material goods.

We need to better understand this profound truth of the *before*[19] and clearly understand the news that Jesus has brought, so necessary for human progress. Indeed, over the centuries man has always looked for possible forms of social life and, to prevent getting lost, has a constantly growing need to find his mystery, his true roots.

**Common Father**

'Our' meets this need since it also indicates a *second aspect*, it also means that it is common. In our times we have to unearth the *Our Father*, understand it anew, make it clear to ourselves: there is an Our Father, a common Father. The Father that Jesus Christ revealed to us is not just any common 'generic' father as some might think. He is 'that Father' to whom Jesus has brought us back with the gift of his sacrifice and the gift of the Holy Spirit[20].

---

[18] *Bible*. Letter to the Ephesians 1:3-4.
[19] *Bible*. Cfr. Book of the Prophet Jeremiah 1:5.
[20] *Magisterium*. Cfr. Joseph Cardinal Ratzinger, *The God of Jesus Christ. Meditations on the triune God*, Ignatius Press, San Francisco, 2008 (text no. 4 in Appendix).

I believe that Jesus has given us the key to life in the prayer of the *Our Father*. In fact, if God is the common Father both of fathers and children, it follows that parents are not the masters but the witnesses of life: a transparency of the mystery of life that comes from God the Father. If children see this, going beyond their loved ones and grandparents, they will have a great appreciation of themselves and of life. They will sense and understand the preciousness and freedom of life that is spontaneous and free, a responsible gift to both them and their parents since there is *a common mystery* that links the generations. Parents have everything to gain if, faithful to the Lord, they are transparent ministers, showing love, care, intelligence and sensitivity towards this mystery, which comes from God our Father, our common Father.

This secret reveals the reality of our lives: on the one hand it helps parents to have a true balance of love and respect for the lives of their children, and on the other hand it helps children to have a healthy respect for the life received and a feeling of gratitude for life, which has come to them from God through their parents. Conversely, by hiding the truth of the common Father we maim the being of parents in relation to their children and the being of children in relation to parents. So, conflict is easy, to the extent of denying earthly fathers and even the mystery of life: "Finally I've got my own life! I'm leaving! It's my life, I'll do what I want with it!" And so, in turn the children also come to the denial of conjugal life, of love, and even of the lives of their children and grandchildren; hence, the tearing of the social fabric that brings us the drama we have today of abortion. Even in Europe, abortion is becoming the main cause of death, more common than cancer or stroke. Human Life International speaks of 40 million abortions throughout the world every year!

'Our Father', 'the common Father' is the tremendous reality that parents must convey to their children, and that children must acknowledge and also carry within them. I believe that it is only if we return to this fundamental truth, that life will be truly respected. Otherwise, life will remain cheated, camouflaged, abandoned, raped. Sooner or later, the death that is carried in the heart will also become the death of abandoned, abused, or aborted children. It is along this path that a 'culture of death' has developed.

Jesus reminds us: "You cannot serve God" that is Father, "and mammon"[21]. 'Mammon'[22] is wealth and self-interest, living a life without a deep sense of the mystery of the given life; 'mammon' is hoarding, using life in a foolish way. 'Mammon' grows in personal and social life by cutting away more and more at the roots of the relationship with the 'Our Father which art in heaven' and consequently with the 'others' who have become *strangers*.

Many are those who have themselves called 'father' in many things: the father of science, the father of a magazine, the father of this or that discovery... all fathers! But we have forgotten the common Father, God our Father and, sooner or later, 'mammon' makes itself apparent and imposes itself upon us. Either we choose God the Father, the foundation, the source of life and communion, or we become slaves to wealth, pleasure, political power, as well as insane needs and alienating rights resulting in madness and the destruction of human life. The new 'atomic bomb' that can destroy humanity is man himself who, in his madness, forgets who he is.

We should reflect on this fact.

In rediscovering God, our Father, our common Father, man and woman overcome their conflict of diversity to meet in the mystery of love and life from which they both originate.

With the Our Father, the common Father, the Father of all, parents and children overcome the generational conflict that sets the past against the future.

Similarly, by rediscovering the only common source that is God who is above everyone and for everyone, peoples and nations can learn to walk together, rediscovering what we all have in common, namely not economic and interlocking utilitarian interests that end up in the exploitation of some by others, thereby constantly widening the gap between the rich and the poor, but rather the biggest reality, that is God the Father from whom we come and to whom we return. In fact, we are accountable to him for every action and choice before his kingdom of love and justice.

What we are saying does not fossilize the different positions held by believers and non-believers, on the contrary it makes it more possible to bring about human relations that today are at the basis of the two

---

[21] *Bible*. Gospel of Luke 16:13.
[22] *Bible*. Cfr. Gospel of Matthew 6:24. The term "mammon" appears both in the Gospel of Matthew 6:24 and in the Gospel of Luke 16:13. **Translator's Note**: The *New American Bible, revised edition* (2010) explains that "mammon is the Greek transliteration of a Hebrew or Aramaic word that is usually explained as meaning 'that in which one trusts'", i.e. the accumulation of riches, wealth and power.

most important needs: knowing how to comprehend and understand each other, even 'that which is different', and knowing how to achieve harmonious coexistence despite diversity, and without the loss of personal identity.

Nowadays, to avoid slipping into the trap of trivial reductionism, parity in the couple means accepting and viewing differences as complementary. However, this is by no means easy. It is by pursuing the truth in the roots that this difficult process is made possible. This is the opposite of what some would like to do by evading the search and love for truth, and thinking that the solution for peaceful coexistence is to be found only in 'social habit', that, over time, is supposed to become encoded in the DNA. As if citizens were 'empty bags' that society has simply to fill. According to this view there would be no root to unearth and man would be the fruit of the social way of thinking. How unjust this view is in relation to each person can be seen today with ever greater clarity, since in the end the person is deprived of any true identity and human dignity.

Man and woman must not forget and lose sight of the gift of 'life' that is *before*, given since the *'beginning'*, which cannot therefore be just the result of the environment. Indeed, the social environment will be respectful to the extent that this reality, that is the human being in his roots, is recognised. Personal and social dignity must be entwined and respectively enriched without changing or destroying the human face, whose foundation is in the 'mystery' of the 'roots' of human life. Consequently, the human fraternity of all mankind is also 'ours'!

**The case of the French Revolution**

The second example of the attack on the mystery of our life precisely concerns fraternity; we see it in European history in the unfolding of the French Revolution in 1789. In modern world development, alongside the various political revolutions taking place in different countries, we are also witnessing economic, biotechnological and sexual revolutions that are undermining the stability of love and human life itself.

Like all revolutions, even those dictated by the ideals of justice and progress always carry within themselves something distorted, which then has to be downsized to prevent inevitable exaggerations and errors, i.e. their fruits, becoming apparent with the passing of time. How much violence, how much shedding of blood, how much injustice in the history of peoples and nations! Nonetheless we can see, for example, three great principles arising out of the French Revolution: *liberté, egalité, fraternité*.

Liberty, equality, fraternity. Now, if we look at the historical process, we can see that the values of freedom and equality have been adopted in the language of politics and political culture, to the extent of being included in the Constitutions of States. For the other term, that of *fraternity*, it has been quite a different matter. In fact, great presumption was shown in taking the best of what was present in Christian culture and history, but cutting out their root: removing God the Father.

In the Encyclical Letter *Caritas in Veritate* (Charity in truth), on the point concerning the lack of brotherhood as cause of underde-velopment, Benedict XVI wrote: "Will it ever be possible to obtain this brotherhood by human effort alone? As society becomes ever more globalized, it makes us neighbours but does not make us brothers. Reason, by itself, is capable of grasping the equality between men and of giving stability to their civic coexistence, but it cannot establish fraternity. This originates in a transcendent vocation from God the Father, who loved us first, teaching us through the Son what fraternal charity is"[23]. So, equality is achieved by making diverse people alike, whereas fraternity unites diverse people: in fact, brothers are diverse from one another, and are brothers just because they have the same father.

Otherwise, by setting aside this fraternity, there is the prospect of constant conflict or leveling, a depersonalizing and overpowering uniformity. We see this in many situations. Something is always lost along the way when the roots are hidden! Rediscovering God the Father leads us back to rediscovering not only how to survive on earth but also how to have peace among peoples and for each person. This is the peace that Jesus has brought us, the peace that Jesus has brought to all humanity: "Peace I leave with you; my peace I give to you. Not as the world gives do I give it to you"[24]. It is his peace. Without God our Father, *tHis* peace is not possible.

We have forgotten our Father! It is necessary to rediscover our Father, the great mystery that Jesus has given us in the prayer of the *Our Father*. In this prayer, which gives us wonderful indications, there is the greatest treasure for our survival.

God has given the prayer of the *Our Father* to all generations, but perhaps we have not fully grasped its true import. It is only because we have the same Father that we can be brothers, as Jesus tells us: "and you are all brothers"[25]. The expression 'brothers' assumes vigour with Christianity: it is Christians who have called each other 'brothers'

---

[23] *Magisterium.* Benedict XVI, Encyclical Letter *Caritas in veritate* (2009) no. 19.
[24] *Bible.* Gospel of John 14:27.
[25] *Bible.* Gospel of Matthew 23:8.

in Jesus Christ. So much good is present in the world and so many Christians are generously committed to sustaining so many good social works.

Benedict XVI, in Encyclical Letter *Spe salvi* (Saved in hope) dealing with the Christian faith-hope transformation in modern times, recalled the need to construct real progress[26]. It is necessary to come out! Indeed, there are many areas where human life is being wasted and thrown away. This should be food for thought: how many mistakes, how much apathy, how much emptiness!

**The cocktail**

What humanism are we building? What humanity are we delivering to future generations? To my mind, rather than with humanism, we are dealing with an 'atheistic humanism', one that does not go to the root of things, that does not recognise its deeper roots, and in the end becomes a pseudo-humanism!

Where then is the ambiguity? Because there is an ambiguity: laicists – not laity but the laicists in the sense of the many 'well-meaning' false Christian people who claim to be Christians but are not faithful to Jesus Christ – use the technique of taking the best from Christian culture, while removing the roots, with the presumption that everything will then hold up in a vacuum. They do not realise that the tree needs its roots to yield good fruit, nor do they realise that they are acting in the interests of others that lurk in the darkness of evil. This is the process of dechristianisation and secularization that prefers to fight Christianity not overtly but by "reducing it" to a set of ideological values or utopian ideals, aiming thus to turn it into what we might call *'christianism'*, i.e. a Christianity without Christ. In this way, an attempt is made to cut God out from the human considering him as 'useless'. This operation is often conducted through the trick of the 'cocktail of values without roots', so as to be accepted by the world, and ultimately to have the world move forward without God. Unbeknown to most people, there are those working to 'dismantle' the Christian faith. In their desire to 'reduce' it to any human faith, they seek to turn it into any belief with no foundation in reality[27].

From the Gospel, from our Christian history, and from our Christian Europe, values and fragments of truth have been taken, combined together, and then suspended in a vacuum without roots! The Christian

---

[26] *Magisterium*. Cfr. Benedict XVI, Encyclical Letter *Spe salvi* (2007) no. 22 (text no. 5 in Appendix).

[27] *Bible*. Cfr. First Letter of John 1:1-4.

values of freedom, equality and fraternity have been adopted, but without God that is the Source. Likewise Christ is wanted, but without the Church, the Gospel, but without Christ, parents without our Father, children without fathers, and by carrying on in this direction machines will be wanted to make children without father or mother. It is not sufficient to demand values if the foundation, i.e. God our Father, is removed.

We believe that this is the great conceit in the world today. Without foundations it is not possible to live well or in the end even to live: it is an ugly illusion.

There has been the presumption of cutting off life from our roots, causing us to lose our awareness that we are children of God and that only as such are we brothers. So, we call each other in a number of different ways: friends, companions, colleagues and so on, but referring to each other as brothers is becoming increasingly difficult without the root of our Father. Children, too, have ended up receiving their names from those of objects or animals, while the terms husband, wife, spouse, and tomorrow 'children', the keywords of our lives, are put evermore aside, emptied of their meaning and then replaced.

Who will free us from this historical and cultural intrigue, namely losing the profound mystery of our lives, our true identity, the awareness of the roots to our individual, family and social life? The answer lies in the third 'word'. Amazingly, the secret of our existence has been delivered by Jesus in the *Our Father*: the third 'word' of the *Our Father* gives us the key to escape this intrigue, this confusion of lies and the chaos of today. We shall see it in the third chapter.

# 3

# Who art in heaven
## *In heaven*

We have already seen that true fatherhood is only that of God, and whoever is a father or mother, a real parent, is a transparency of this great mystery, of this great power that God has so desired to deliver to human life and to human love, that of man and woman. To forget this is to forget our roots.

So, what can we do to get out of this mixture and confusion of contradictory values and choices that are to be found a little everywhere? How is it possible to shed ourselves of the moral relativism that infects everyone? Do Christians really have something to offer others? And how can they break free from a sense of inferiority that has penetrated many, to the extent that to feel accepted and welcomed in society they tend to forget and hide the fact that they are Christians and that they have received a 'gift' for society?

There is a subculture which is becoming increasingly widespread through the work of laicists, namely 'right-thinking' phoneys, false or weak Christians, who have collected and blended all those aspects that could be pleasant and beneficial to all, arrogantly hanging good and bad fruits from a tree without roots!

How is it possible to build a sustainable future without unearthing the roots? So, how then is it possible to find the roots of existence in your own life, in your marriage, in your love and also in the future of our society? This is the research we are conducting in this book through the study and examination of the phrases in the Our Father.

Man, in fact, is naturally open to transcendence so that faith and reason can communicate. Man needs an intelligent[1] reading of faith. This emerges when taking a closer look at the prayer of the Our Father.

---

[1] *Magisterium.* Cfr. Benedict XVI, *Interview with journalists during the flight to Portugal.* Apostolic Journey to Portugal (May 11, 2010) (text no. 6 in Appendix).

We realise that God is really intelligent and knows what to do! He is the Source of every intelligence. Jesus could have taught us to simply say 'Our Father' before continuing with the prayer[2]. But no, instead He inserts the clause "who art in heaven". Why? Because every now and then humanity longs for other fathers, leaving behind and abandoning the fundamental and foundational paternity, which is that of God. Mention is made of our fathers, our ancestors, the father of this or of that, inventors, creators, patrons, founders, benefactors, dictators, etc. It is a fact that these personal and social realities, sometimes meaningless, are experienced as an 'empty space' being filled, and can thus attract and engage: then, unknowingly, you become a little like what you respect and love, without realising that all these 'fathers', without reference to God the Father, sooner or later become 'masters' or tyrants. Without God the Father it is, to some extent, easy to become slaves to whatever it is you appreciate.

It is at this point that 'mammon' emerges. Jesus offers us the choice[3]: either God who shows himself as Father in a relationship of love and hence freedom, or a bond with power and wealth that fascinate us and that we make ours, but that take us and make us similar to slaves. True fathers like true benefactors do not usurp the place of God, they recognise him, leaving the sole primacy to him.

In this world, wisdom needs to be rediscovered. Science with knowledge and technology provide us with the means, give us power, but for the human being knowledge, wisdom, power and wealth are not enough, for even with these man is lost. Not even experience and lessons learnt from history suffice. The world needs wisdom which we specifically ask for in the prayer of the Our Father. Jesus has taught us to say Our Father who art in heaven. This is the way to rediscover the wisdom that the world so desperately needs. Let us see why.

What does "who art in heaven" mean? It certainly does not mean "who art in the sky". In fact, to say 'in heaven' is by no means the same as saying 'in the sky' in the sense of among the clouds or in the air.

'In heaven' means something else: beyond the skies, beyond the sky and what we can see with our eyes, 'beyond' and 'above' all that exists and is perceived through our senses or that which we can imagine. This mode of existence is what we call heaven, divine, spiritual, unlike the earthly, material, terrestrial one.

The term 'in heaven' expresses the fact that God is transcendent, and beyond everything. He is above nature and is not to be confused

---

[2] *Bible*. Cfr. Gospel of Matthew 6:9-13.
[3] *Bible*. Cfr. Gospel of Luke 16:13.

with nature which he has created[4]. He is something else, God transcends and greatly surpasses all creation.

At this point some expressions come to mind which make me smile as, although they are apparently innocuous, they actually convey a false way of speaking of God as if God were in nature. Jesus did not say Our Father who art in the woods... in the mountains... in the universe... but "who art in heaven"!

Here one thinks, for example, of the vision of the divine in the New Age and in Buddhism. It is a great temptation for man to see God in what he likes and aspires to, even silence, the interiority, and the spiritual, and to confuse God, a personal reality and Father, with the divine.

When on April 12, 1961, the Soviet astronaut Yuri Gagarin made the first space flight around the earth this was an extraordinary and momentous event that made its mark in history. On his return, he was quoted as saying: "I was up there, I did not find anything, God is not in the sky". What did he think he would find in the sky: an old man with a beard? It seems strange that a man with such a scientific background, an astronaut, could say something like that! What comes to mind is the atheistic and materialistic subculture, or that of a facile and superficial vitalistic spiritualism.

It is a great deception to think of levelling out and pruning all the differences, so as to gain greater consensus and sustain a more prosperous economy. It is in fact a wild and false reductionism that penetrates culture and people's lives. If we want to find the truth in reality we have to be able to see and understand distinctions and differences with a new found maturity.

If God has opened up so much through the words of the *Our Father*, if He leads us to trust in him and reveals to us that our root is that of 'God our Father who art in heaven', it means that God the Father is distinct from and superior to nature, and that we are his children because He has us call him 'Father'.

## What makes us human

So, if we are children of the One that is 'heavenly', we have something of his. We are certainly made of something terrestrial, of earth, but we are not made only of matter, we are also made of something of his, something that does not come from the earth, from dust, from the life of animals. This is who we are. Saying "Our Father who art in heaven"

---

[4] *Magisterium*. Cfr. *Catechism of the Catholic Church*, no. 370.

means that we have a soul; this is something we have forgotten! This fundamental and precise reality forms the basis of human dignity and should not be concealed! It must be said to children, to young people. If we do not forget what we are and what God wants of us, we are filled with joy and happiness and given strength and true equilibrium.

We have solely relied on our intelligence, believing and imagining that God was up there and we were down here. But these words of the *Our Father* tell us something else and bring us back to the truth about ourselves. Benedict XVI, when reflecting on the *Our Father* in his book *Jesus of Nazareth*, reminds us that: "Through him, and only through him, do we come to know the Father. And in this way the criterion of true fatherliness is made clear. The Our Father does not project a human image onto heaven, but shows us from heaven – from Jesus – what we as human beings can and should be like"[5].To understand this we have to go more in depth.

We possess something that is of 'heaven', something that is of God our Father. Unless this is stated and taught, unless this is the real foundation of our culture, then what we say is deceptive and superficial, the misleading fruits of human life, 'empty fruits' of a tree without roots. All human teaching is thereby diminished, culture deprived, and life deceived: the new generations do not understand how creation truly functions, while distrust, careerism, and social climbing make their victorious entry. Even the teaching of Christian children is compromised. They no longer understand what the Church is and what marriage is. Human life and Christian life lose their meaning when man loses his foundation and sense of things. This 'non-comprehension' is the blindness of those who prefer to be blind, of those who seek to deny the presence of the spirit in man and of God's gifts in history. The words of the Psalmist come to mind: "The gods neither know nor understand, wandering about in darkness, and all the world's foundations shake"[6].

I think this is the real *taboo* in society today. People are afraid to speak of it: they do not want to recognise the reality of the spiritual soul and of God "Our Father who art in heaven". They cannot speak about this because they require that God and religion be considered as something intimate, indeed so personal as to be no longer recognised. This is where the persecution begins.

Yet, if we think about it, this is a gift for all men and women, human beings are made up of both body and spirit; this is the basis of our 'human dignity'. Saint John Paul II in a *Message addressed to the participants of the Plenary Assembly of the Pontifical Academy of Sciences*

---

[5] *Magisterium.* Benedict XVI, *Jesus of Nazareth*, Doubleday, New York 2007, p. 137.
[6] *Bible.* Book of Psalms 82:5.

in 1996 stated: "the human individual cannot be subordinated as a pure means or a pure instrument, either to the species or to society; he has value per se. He is a person. With his intellect and his will, he is capable of forming a relationship of communion, solidarity and self-giving with his peers. (...) even more, man is called to enter into a relationship of knowledge and love with God himself, a relationship which will find its complete fulfilment beyond time, in eternity. All the depth and grandeur of this vocation are revealed to us in the mystery of the risen Christ (cfr. *Gaudium et Spes*, 22). It is by virtue of his spiritual soul that the whole person possesses such a dignity even in his body (...) theories of evolution which, in accordance with the philosophies inspiring them, consider the spirit as emerging from the forces of living matter or as a mere epiphenomenon of this matter, are incompatible with the truth about man. Nor are they able to ground the dignity of the person"[7].

If we call God Father using such an intimate and personal term as *'Abba'*[8] (in Hebrew), as Jesus taught us – and no other religion does so – going so far as saying "Our Daddy who art in heaven," this means that we recognise ourselves in the depth of this extraordinary dimension, it means that we belong in some way to this 'heavenly' world, to the world of God, having within us, as Vatican Council II reminds us, a "divine germ"[9].

But let's take a closer look at this extraordinary fact.

A son is a 'son' because he has something of his father and his mother, he has something of his parents otherwise how would he be their son? He is similar to his parents and understands them. God our Father who is in heaven has created us for love and with love. As Saint Catherine says in her *Dialogue of Divine Providence*: "What reason had You for creating man in such dignity? The inestimable love with which You saw Your creature in Yourself, and became enamored of him, for You created him through love, and destined him to be such that he might taste and enjoy Your Eternal Good"[10].

And again, Saint Bernard, commenting on the Song of Songs, says: "when God loves, he desires nothing but to be loved, since he loves us for no other reason than to be loved, for he knows that those who love him are blessed in their very love". This is because "love is sufficient for

---

[7] *Magisterium*. John Paul II, *Message to the Participants in the Plenary of the Pontifical Academy of Sciences* (22 October 1996).
[8] Cfr. Chapter 1.
[9] *Magisterium*. Cfr. Vatican Council II, Pastoral Constitution *Gaudium et spes*, no. 3.
[10] *Tradition*. Saint Catherine of Siena (1347-1380), *The Dialogue of Saint Catherine of Siena*, translated by Algar Thorold (http://www.ewtn.com/library/SOURCES/CATHDIAL.HTM, accessed in July 2014).

itself; it gives pleasure to itself, and for its own sake. (...) it is its own purpose"[11].

Having God, 'for love', made humans 'children', can they then only relate with the earth? To become worms and dust? And to endure all the efforts and toil of living only to die? It is really rather little. What would be the point? If God has created us as 'children' there should be a particular power and capacity within us to relate to God, otherwise we would not have had the opportunity to call him 'Father'.

So when Jesus teaches us to pray addressing God with the words "Our Father who art in heaven", He tells us that God is transcendent, pure spirit and that we too are not just made of earth, of 'dust' but also of 'heaven', of spirit: our father is not only the human one, but we all have a common Father who is in heaven.

**Search for the traces**

As 'children of God' and having been delivered the *Our Father*, we have to look for *the signs of the spirit*, of 'heaven', present in us, in our reality. We must look for the traits and manifestations of our spirit using our intelligence to understand who we are and how we are made, in the same way as biology does in DNA research.

These signs are concealed by the subculture; a false culture that has every interest in concealing such signs as it does not want God as interlocutor, but instead wants the power and the life that is incumbent only to him. So, let's look for the *distinctive features* of the spirit that the subculture has hidden and so well covered that, as a result, a certain amount of effort is required to hunt them out.

**Man's constituent dimensions**

Man has fundamentally four constituent dimensions.

Looking at reality, first of all we see the full physical, biological, and material dimension, that of the body (*soma* in Greek). We can identify this through various sensations: cold, heat, pleasure, pain, and so on. We can also see that, like animals, we have a certain sensitivity, emotions, affections and feelings: this is the psychical dimension that exists, to a certain extent, also in animals. We perceive it as interiority and 'sense' it even if we do not see it in the way we see and touch material things like the body. This second dimension we perceive through emotions and

---

[11] *Tradition*. St. Bernard of Clairvaux (1090-1153), *Sermons on the Song of Songs*, Book II, no. 83, 4-6, (http://www.pathsoflove.com/bernard/songofsongs/sermon83. html, accessed in July 2014. Text no. 7 in Appendix).

feelings that are 'finer' and cannot be measured using a yardstick or weighing scales. They have, nonetheless, a great influence on the lives of human beings. They animate the entire psychical world of 'feelings': joy, pain, love, anger, fear, courage and so on. It is the 'interior' dimension of the soul (*psychè* in Greek).

We also have another mode of capturing reality, different from the experience we have through 'sensations' and 'feelings', which expresses itself with great freedom. We always use it, but perhaps not always with sufficient care. It is the construction of thought, it is our thinking (*nous* in Greek), which, though within certain limits, is extraordinarily free. For example, an animal such as a dog when it is shown sausage meat, sees and necessarily 'thinks' of the sausage meat. Humans 'think' but do not necessarily equate thought to the vision of an object. We can be cold and think of a warm place when for example we want to go on holiday. We have the freedom to structure thought so we can avoid matching thoughts with bodily sensations, or even with feelings. This, given our conditioning, allows us to think, albeit within certain limits, in a critical and free way.

But we need to recognise that we also have another dimension: that of the spirit (*pneuma* in Greek), of the human soul which is spiritual. What makes us people – and animals are not people – must necessarily be the specific reality that we have, i.e. the spirit. Every human reality in its nature and body reveals 'meanings' and above all is rich in 'sense'. Therefore, the reality that most distinguishes us as 'human persons' is this dimension that we have variously called heavenly, divine, the spiritual soul or the spirit.

We should never forget this essential truth, the most intimate and extraordinary, nor should we allow it to be taken away from us. It is our greatest identity and at the same time it is the secret of our 'human' way of existing. But how does it make itself manifest?

**Spirit as a personal identity**

In the Bible, in the Book of Genesis, it is written: "then the LORD God formed the man out of the dust of the ground and blew into his nostrils the breath of life, and the man became a living being"[12].

God 'shapes' and creates man with 'dust' and mud, and blows into his nostrils his *'ruah'*, the 'breath of life'. This is the spirit, in Hebrew *'ruah'*, in Greek *'pneuma'*, in Italian *'spirito'*, the spiritual soul. This is what God seeks to tell us with the direct creation of man: God has put

---

[12] *Bible*. Book of Genesis 2:7.

something of his, something mysterious, which belongs to him and makes us human people. The Lord "fashions the human spirit within"[13]. God has 'blown' his breath so that man might breathe and live. God uses this vital expression in the Bible because without breathing one dies, the breathing of air, even if it is not visible to the eye, is essential for life.

So "the man became a living being"[14] through the gift of the spirit. For this we are his children. The root of our human dignity is God the Father and the secret of human existence is his spirit. For this reason Benedict XVI wrote in *Jesus of Nazareth*: "man can be understood only in light of God, and (...) his life is made righteous only when he lives it in relation to God. But God is not some distant stranger. He shows us his face in Jesus. In what Jesus does and wills, we come to know the mind and will of God himself. If being human is essentially about relation to God, it is clear that speaking with, and listening to, God is an essential part of it"[15]. The crisis of humanity, the family and society is the crisis of the sense of God, of 'his image' that is in each one of us, and therefore is also a crisis of personal prayer.

But what is this 'dust of the ground', this 'mud' with which God created man? We do not know what it is, but what we do know is that God took something and turned it into a human being, i.e. into a being with a soul, the spirit that makes men and women live as 'persons'.

Some scientists see a connection between an animal, in particular the monkey, and the human being. However, this does not mean that the monkey has become a human being, as evolutionists would mistakenly like to believe. For this reason the Church does not recognise the theory of evolution as a true doctrine, since it denies the greatness of the human being endowed with a spirit and thus created directly by God. In addition to the doubts surrounding evolution – which remains an unproven scientific theory – there are some missing links in the 'development of the species'. Thus, there is an unjustified leap that cannot validate the theory put forward by evolutionists. Could it be the qualitative leap referred to in the Bible with the direct creation of man and woman by God? There are, on the other hand, scientists who categorically deny any link between human development and the monkey.

Whatever the case, the being derived from the monkey would not be a human being; there is a definite qualitative leap between

---

[13] *Bible*. Book of the Prophet Zechariah 12:1. Cfr. Book of Genesis 6:3, Ecclesiastes 12:7; Job 27:3; 34:14s.

[14] *Bible*. Book of Genesis 2:7.

[15] *Magisterium*. Benedict XVI, *Jesus of Nazareth*, Doubleday, New York 2007, p. 128.

the animal and the human person. Evolutionism and naturalism – by which man's existence is explained by natural laws without any reference to God – have taken foothold in culture. As a result, this has greatly obscured the religious dimension of man. Such a reduction in the vision of man has invaded culture which knows less and less how to reconstruct 'man'. However much scientists continue to discuss the biological origins of man while failing to agree on the origins of the species, one thing remains certain: the power of the mind, thought and will (intelligence that thinks and will that decides), and consciousness (value judgment as to good and evil), which are exclusive to the human species, cannot be derived from the purely material and biological plane, unlike the brain which is their instrumental organ.

Intelligence, will, and consciousness are of spiritual origin: capacities of the human spirit, the gift of God, Creator and Father. It is properly the reality of the spirit in man that is the foundation of his greatest dignity, his capacity for freedom and love. The *Catechism of the Catholic Church*, valid throughout the world, states: "The human person, created in the image of God, is a being at once corporeal and spiritual. (...) Man, whole and entire, is therefore *willed* by God"[16]. Man is a whole being. God came to save his whole life. "The Church teaches that every spiritual soul is created immediately by God – it is not 'produced' by the parents – and also that it is immortal: it does not perish when it separates from the body at death, and it will be reunited with the body at the final Resurrection"[17]. "Endowed with a spiritual and immortal soul, the human person is 'the only creature on earth that God has willed for its own sake'. From his conception, he is destined for eternal beatitude"[18]. "Of all visible creatures only man is 'able to know and love his creator'. He is 'the only creature on earth that God has willed for its own sake', and he alone is called to share, by knowledge and love, in God's own life. It was for this end that he was created, and this is the fundamental reason for his dignity"[19]. "Lᴏʀᴅ, my God, you are great indeed!"[20] says the Psalmist. How small we are before God! Yet, how much He loves us!

---

[16] *Magisterium. Catechism of the Catholic Church*, no. 362.
[17] *Magisterium. Catechism of the Catholic Church*, no. 366.
[18] *Magisterium. Catechism of the Catholic Church*, no. 1703, cfr. no. 1711.
[19] *Magisterium. Catechism of the Catholic Church*, no. 356.
[20] *Bible*. Book of Psalms 104:1.

## Spirit as personal relatedness

In the Bible, again in the Book of Genesis, God reveals to us in another passage that He wanted to create man 'in his image and likeness'. "Then God said: Let us make human beings in our image, after our likeness"[21]. "God created mankind in his image; in the image of God he created them; male and female he created them"[22]. In the New Testament, Paul the Apostle expresses this as follows: "May the God of peace himself make you perfectly holy and may you entirely, spirit, soul, and body, be preserved blameless for the coming of our Lord Jesus Christ"[23]. Consequently, the 'image of God' is in man, in this 'celestial' element, that is, the divine, the spirit that is immersed in the body and sexuality of both the male and female being, and that founds the relational capacity of freedom and love in its first social base, i.e. in the family.

It needs to be recognised that sexual experience in which the spiritual dimension is ignored is destructive sex; it loses its human dimension and is less authentic than animal sexuality. Animals follow their sexual instinct. While man, although endowed with instinct, has something else: he has the freedom of the gift, he has intentionality, and a whole wealth of spiritual energies that are to be experienced in sexuality and not alienated. The widespread commercialisation of sex encourages *paraphilia*, so that in a sexual encounter 'the other' is considered not for 'who he is' but for 'one's own needs' with an obvious lack of the oblative dimension, as in the case of the hysterical, the narcissist and the borderline.

When the spiritual dimension is ignored or indeed trampled on, sexuality does not function as it should, since it was created in the truth of the image of God and needs this image, that comes from God, to be nurtured. He is love, truth, freedom and goodness.

Also the human spirit created by God is substantially love, truth and freedom and hence goodness: it is the image of God. Ultimately, man is capable of looking for "truth and goodness"[24], in one word, of 'loving'.

If this 'image' is suffocated or disfigured, human sexuality becomes sick. In fact, its distortions, malfunctions and sickness are for all to see. While the sexuality of animals keeps to the path of instinct, that

---

[21] *Bible*. Book of Genesis 1:26.

[22] *Bible*. Book of Genesis 1:27.

[23] *Bible*. First Letter to the Thessalonians 5:23.

[24] *Tradition*. Cfr. Edith Stein (1891-1942), *Finite and eternal being: an attempt at an ascent to the meaning of being,* translated by Kurt F. Reinhardt, Washington Province of Discalced Carmelites, ICS Publications, Washington, DC 2002, pp. 311-312 (text no. 8 in Appendix).

of human beings deviates, is disoriented and cheapened, losing its meaning and significance. This is because it is founded, as God created it, on a reality that is not seen but exists. This reality is of a spiritual nature: it is 'the spirit' that God wanted to give men and women by creating them 'in his image, man and woman'. Therefore, in the physical and psychical reality of sexuality as also in human thoughts and sentiments, we are 'animated', and in some way sustained and directed by its human foundation that in everyone is the human spirit, with its spiritual energies.

Only in this way can sexuality remain 'free', a sign of love and of goodness. These spiritual energies are expressed 'in the truth' of 'male' and 'female', and not just in any way. Indeed God has also created this world with a 'how' that is shown in order, wisdom and also beauty. This is why the homosexual vision cannot be the same as that of the heterosexual, as attested to by the Bible and stated in the *Catechism of the Catholic Church*[25]. Here, we also express the right approach to love and understanding that we must have towards everyone. It should be added that only the sexuality that knows how to listen to the truth of the spirit can be 'free' of deception, and can become a sign of love and goodness capable of understanding God who wanted and created it. It is therefore easy to understand that true sexuality and authentic religion cannot remain separate but help each other in expressing their meaning. It is often the case that a chaotic sexual life, whether heterosexual or homosexual, goes hand in hand with an equally confused, if not misled, life of faith.

Forgetting or concealing the spiritual dimension and its most profound truth from human sexuality means deceiving man and woman, and deceiving the new generations! The same can be said when the spiritual dimension in thought and culture is similarly forgotten or neglected.

## The night of the spirit

Under the pressure of various interests, and starting with the linguistic and cultural practice, the word *pneuma* has been quietly and deviously eliminated in teaching, not only in universities but also at all levels in every kind of school as well as in all texts: they have deleted the word *pneuma* as referring to the reality of the spirit given to man by God. 'The night of the spirit' comes about when man chooses deception

---

[25] *Magisterium.* Cfr. *Catechism of the Catholic Church*, nos. 2357-2359 (text no. 9 in Appendix).

and fraud instead of God: "And it was night"[26] the Gospel reminds us on the subject of Judas. In today's globalization 'the night of the spirit' runs the real risk of becoming 'the night of the world'.

But how has it been possible to eliminate this fundamental term? It has been simple. Initially, studies on the psyche left the field open to the specific dimension of the spirit (*pneuma*) but, in time, the particular use of each of these two words occurred less and less, to the point that they were totally assimilated. In this way the *psychè* (psyche) was transformed into *the soul* and everything became 'psychical'. Consequently, from a cultural point of view, we have lost our deepest dimension: the spiritual soul, the spirit, and with it, too, the recognition of the objective capacity of the relationship with God.

And if all our inner reality becomes just 'psychical', then our way of thinking is deformed: there is no longer the true and not true, the false. There is no longer a way to discern good from evil, because the psyche on its own leaves most of the space to the subject; everything becomes experience and sensible perception. Even the conscience becomes solely psychical. Good psychologists, who also have the faith, can in some way bring the two dimensions together and combine them, and this is a truly commendable practice. But this reunification process is no longer so straightforward; it is not so easy, indeed it is not taught and it cannot be taught. At the end of the day, there are few people able to do this synthesis in a personal way so as to effectively recognise the dimension of the spiritual soul.

Thus, the spread of this scientific culture on the psyche and the mind has become dominant to the extent of entirely 'replacing' the spiritual and religious dimension, leaving no recognised space for the spirit and the reality of God. Under the thrust of this reductive concept, religion too has been increasingly relegated to a pre-scientific field, and almost totally absorbed by the 'customs and traditions' of other sciences, such as cultural anthropology and sociology.

Meanwhile, advances have been made by new discoveries in the chemical and pharmacological fields as applied to the human psyche and mind. In this way, there has been an increasing shift in favour of the only capacity to recognise human reality: the biological-material. Ultimately, we have been moved to an ethical materialism in which what is *readily useful* counts the most; by now disconnected from any other value. This can increasingly be seen in the fields of medicine and communications, economics and politics.

Consequently, by increasingly forgetting or neglecting our spiritual dimension, God the Source of life has been forgotten; the truest root

---

[26] *Bible.* Gospel of John 13:30.

of our existence. As a result, the world is becoming more and more materialistic, naturalistic and atheist, and is going into the hands of slavery to 'mammon' and the new human dictators who take their place on the world stage.

Man is losing himself all the while falling into a precipice since he is searching but fails to find himself: where is his freedom? Never before had freedom been so much spoken about as in the twentieth century. And, quite rightly, even now we want to affirm it. But let's think about it, what are its foundations? Perhaps there is freedom in matter? Perhaps in physics there is freedom? Perhaps in biology there is freedom? Perhaps in chemistry? But then who is it who really believes in freedom? If the reality of the spirit is denied – where the freedom that God wanted us to have can only reside – then isn't promising freedom perhaps a trick, if its actual possibility is denied?

Many would like to believe in values and lean on them as they would on crutches, but by now they lack their foundation, they lack roots, and everything revolves around subjectivism. And here is the chaos and ethical relativism whereby one opinion is worth as much as another, and the reason why it is possible to state a concept or a choice and immediately afterwards the opposite. Nowadays, there is the predominance of what is known as 'weak thought', thought that is not well-formed and which 'cannot say more'. The lack of certainty, both in thought and in the stability of feelings, shows that every aspect of the human being reflects the fact that the real dimension of the spirit given by God to the human being has been concealed. Truth and consciousness can return man back to himself. For consciousness to be once again more human, more secure, less 'psychical' and less easy to manipulate, we need to illuminate it not only with awareness but above all with the reality of the spirit. The prayer of the *Our Father* enables us to do precisely this.

## The manifestations of the spirit in man

But how can one find the reality of the spirit in man? Where can we detect its presence in our way of thinking, acting and perceiving? Where are the *signs* of its presence in man? Let us intelligently conduct an in-depth search for these signs of the human spirit, signs of the real existence of the spiritual soul, namely the human spirit that comes from God.

38

Let us take a look at our roots with a magnifying glass. We are able to[27].

Four of these "signs" and manifestations of the spirit in man are discussed here.

*First 'sign'.* The infinite in us.

We have physical perceptions through the body, and by using words and conventional signs, we interpret reality, defining and measuring it. We can say that a certain thing, for example, is not a meter (1 m) in width but half a meter (50 cm), and so on. Therefore by using conventional words and mathematical symbols we endeavour to convey an interpretation of the reality we see or perceive in various ways.

Proceeding carefully along this path of reasoning, we can see that a small symbol, a rotated eight (8), ($\infty$) meaning 'infinity', has been used in all computers and with this we have also been able to get to the moon; an extraordinary fact. Whereas, for example, the words 'unlimited' or 'hypothetical' are quite different in meaning.

These words do not create any problems because we experience them and they are clear to us who use them. But in this case, it is different: we are speaking of 'infinity'!

Note this word 'infinite'. How can one read the infinite, how can one say that something 'is' 'infinite' as if we could identify and measure it? We have no device to measure that something 'is' 'infinite'. Yet we affirm that the infinite is real! Yes, real, not hypothetical. But from where do we have this certainty? Moreover, where does the infinite exist in such a real way that we can measure and state with certainty that it is infinite? That a thing can be defined by us as 'unlimited', 'indefinite' or 'hypothetical' yes, we can experience it, it falls within our limits. But how do we measure when it concerns the 'infinite'? Where do we take the measure of the infinite to measure and say that a reality is truly infinite and that the infinite exists? What we are considering is a very strange concept! Yet, we all affirm it as real and certain! How do we do it? Only the infinite can measure the infinite!

---

[27] *Magisterium. Catechism of the Catholic Church*, no. 36: "'Our holy mother, the Church, holds and teaches that God, the first principle and last end of all things, can be known with certainty from the created world by the natural light of human reason'. Without this capacity, man would not be able to welcome God's revelation. Man has this capacity because he is created 'in the image of God'. (Gn 1:27)"; no. 33: "The *human person*: with his openness to truth and beauty, his sense of moral goodness, his freedom and the voice of his conscience, with his longings for the infinite and for happiness, man questions himself about God's existence. In all this he discerns signs of his spiritual soul. The soul, the 'seed of eternity we bear in ourselves, irreducible to the merely material', can have its origin only in God".

From where do we take the 'measure' of the infinite? My answer is: from the world of the soul, from the world of the spirit that God has given us. The measure of the infinite stems from the world of the soul: thus 'we have' the ability to recognise it as existing and real! The thought of the infinite and the ability to read it as 'infinite' in a real way cannot come from the world of finite nature but from the world of the Infinite, from God, through the presence within us of the 'spirit' that God has given us as 'his image'.

This is a sign that we have something of the infinite in our small human reality which comes 'from heaven', i.e. from the world of the spirit, namely from "God our Father who art in heaven".

There are some realities that the spiritual soul transmits directly to our brain, and among these there is the reality we have called 'infinite'. We think of the 'infinite' in a real and not in a hypothetical way, affirming it in mathematics! How is it that these sciences fail to see their roots in the Infinite of God!

*Second 'sign'.* Freedom.

We can clearly see that freedom is to be found in all generations: it is in the heart of each and every person and cannot be suppressed in the human being.

Freedom dwells within us, freedom is a need: freedom is a going beyond. We love free things and despise what is not free. We are all characterized by the experience of freedom.

Two people who are fond of one another must feel free and under no constraints. The same need is felt by a baby so much so that if he learns that his mother and father did not freely accept him but were forced to, is no longer happy. You can therefore see that we reason with the measure of freedom: that which is true, beautiful, and good must also be free. Thus, within us, we are, in some way made of 'freedom'.

This dimension does not exist in any machine or in any animal, even though animals also want to be left free. Freedom belongs to our human world and is a particular way of existing, like that of God; the only difference being that God is absolutely free and wanted to make us "in his image". Therefore, we 'resemble' God who is "our Father who art in heaven". We are made of a freedom for the good. We cannot do without freedom, we are not ourselves unless we do good freely and without obligation, as we can only love and exist if we are free: indeed, "by virtue of his soul and his spiritual powers of intellect and will, man is endowed with freedom, an 'outstanding manifestation of the divine image'"[28].

*Third 'sign'.* The consciousness of being.

---

[28] *Magisterium. Catechism of the Catholic Church*, no. 1705.

Let's look at how a child expresses himself. He is not aware of either freedom or the spiritual soul, but he is made of soul, goodness, and eternity. Once a mother told me about her small child who had asked how he was born. On the mother replying that she had kept him within her and then he had come to the light with great joy, the child asked: "Where was I before?".

Why is it that a child asks, "Where was I before"? What is 'before' for him? Why did he think of the before? So a child thinks of the before his being! Would an animal ask where was I before? In what place was I before? A child yes! Our beloved animals do not ask this question, they do not have the deep reality of the spirit with its awareness, while we humans do. The story of this mother and her four-year-old child tells us something.

It is not a physical, psychological or emotional question; it is to do with the soul: it is the spirit in man, it is that eternity which is made up of the freedom to exist beyond time and space. This inner eternity gives us an awareness of the passage of time, of the before and the after... This too is freedom!

The mother told me that the child calmed down when she replied, "You were in the heart of God". It was only then that the child stopped asking questions. Why did he stop and not continue to ask other questions, such as how he arrived here? Why did he stop there, in the heart, in the intention, and the love of God?

No one had spoken to the child of the soul, but the sign of the spirit emerged in him since we are all made in this way, of spirit, and we come from God the Father. This is our root and it is extraordinary! Not even a computer has the perception of time of this four-year-old child. This is because the perception of time is not given by the passage of time recorded in the memory such as that of a computer. An electronic memory can only indicate to us the before and after a given time, as a given point. In man, it is not a matter of 'a point', and this is why the machine does not have the 'awareness' that man has. An animal may have the memory of an experience impressed in its mind, but it does not have the perception that man has of the 'passing' of time. The human person has the perception of the before and after with respect to the 'perception of the present' which in the human being is given by the presence of the spiritual soul, his spirit. In the human being, be it a child or an adult, the perception of time is given by the spirit. This is the reality which gives us the present, the 'being', the awareness of 'being now', and it is this present that can measure the past and the future, being always present to itself.

It is this 'being now' that forms the basis of human awareness and of time: this 'being' is properly the foundation of our life which is the image

41

of God, which is Absolute *par excellence*. The 'being in the present' that we live through time, can also be perceived by us from beyond and above time, flowing as past and future.

This is why the child asked: "Where was I before?". Replying: "You were not here, you had never existed before" and "One day you shall die and be no more" means deceiving him, denying him his human dignity, that which renders him a human being, his spiritual soul. This is one of the first confusions that the 'reductive' world of atheist or agnostic subculture can give him today.

*The fourth 'sign'*. The search for happiness.

The presence of the spirit is also shown in us in this way. Why do we want happiness? Have we ever seen it? Have we ever had it? But we all look for it!

Where does this longing come from? Why do we look for happiness, even if we know that it is not within our power to have it, or that we shall never find it and that nobody has the key to give it to us. Why is it that first we search for it through affection, then through gifts, then money, then the body, then through something else, and so on? It is a continuous lifelong search! Everybody is digging away, looking for this great treasure: there are those who grasp at something and those who grasp at someone, there are those who cling on to the past and those who cling on to the future. Happiness is sought by everyone. If we think about it, if it were not already within us, we would not search for it! We would not search with such persistence unless it were something we had already seen or known.

Why do we look for water? Because we are made of water. Why do we look for love? Because we are made of love. So why do we look for happiness? Where does this longing come from? Isn't it perhaps so that much of our suffering and tears come about because of the harsh reality that is in such stark contrast to the happiness we all seek? Among the causes of suffering – for example the suffering of two young people who loved each other and have broken up – shouldn't the reality of the spirit which is in the flesh be considered? However, this fact is not seriously taken into consideration by the dominant culture which only values desire as a cause of suffering. But what lies behind desire? Isn't there also the reality of the human spirit? The world of human sciences has made great steps forward, and they have hugely developed. However, just like their founders, they have almost totally ignored the reality of the human spirit. Psychotherapy textbooks would have to be rewritten, and psychoanalysis given a new turn.

Animals are content but human beings are constantly in search... of heaven. Human life has a truth: happiness. Everyone has this need within them which drives them in the search for it and also for well-being. It is this longing that drives us to love, but which also makes us suffer. To find happiness, to respond to this inner need it is necessary to unearth its deep root, namely the soul. This is because happiness does not belong to the earth, it does not belong to chemical, physical or biological conditions. It belongs to another world, to the world of the spirit, to the world of God. It is for this reason that Saint Augustine said: "Our heart is restless until it rests in you"[29].

Our humanity which is made of earthly 'dust' but also of 'heavenly' reality, of spirit, seeks happiness. This we shall only have by finding where we come from, i.e. from "God our Father who art in heaven". The world that does not want God and is enslaved to mammon seeks to deny this longing, by suffocating and inhibiting it in the hope of no longer suffering from nostalgia for God and heaven.

But in doing this, one becomes more and more inhuman. The world tells us that we are condemned to never finding happiness and should look instead for pleasure and satisfactions. In the "Our Father who art in heaven", Jesus points out to us the path so that we will not be deceived. The human spirit is 'made' of freedom, the infinite, and happiness, namely of love. It is made of truth and light. In this way everything becomes clearer: this is why we rejoice, cry, suffer, battle, this is why we want to be happy. We long for beautiful and good things!

The spiritual dimension in man, his spirit, is not a fairy tale or a myth. Neither is it learnt: it is not a cultural superstructure, but can be discovered in our nature.

We ask ourselves: if it is so important, if the human spirit, the spiritual soul is the *secret* of our life, why then does it elude us? Why do we conceal it from the new generations? Why have we allowed this secret concerning our roots to be forgotten? If it is so important, if it is the secret to our human life, then we should ask ourselves: what can we do not to forget it and not to be deceived by allowing it to be taken away?

Here is the solution. The fourth phrase in the *Our Father* shows us how to get out of this great danger into which many people fall, urged on also by the civilization of wealth and consumerism. How is it possible to stably remain on the secret of one's existence and give a human face to the family and society, without falling into the trap of dangerous camouflages? This we will see in the fourth chapter.

---

[29] *Tradition.* Cfr. Saint Augustine (354-430), *Confessions and Enchiridion*, newly translated and edited by Albert C. Outler, Westminster Press, Philadelphia 1955.

# 4

# Hallowed be thy name

*Hallowed be your name*

In the last chapter we saw that we have the profound gift of the spirit. It is this which makes us human beings; full of enthusiasm, life, and creativity even if there are so many problems, expectations, fears and deep running tensions. This is because we have an inner background that does not solely consist of our history or our sensibility but is brought about through the extraordinary dimension of the human spirit within us that sets us apart from animals and makes us people. This gift does not come from the earth but from God, from the very moment of conception, and determines the respect and love for all human beings of every age from the beginning of life until natural death. This characteristic is the foundation for the 'dignity of the human person'.

## When the spirit darkens

An atheist and materialist State, or even a laicist one, pursues a vision of life 'without God and without soul': an atheist is a man without God, a materialist, who only recognises the material life and denies the existence of the spirit. Therefore, without the spirit, the attainment of the 'useful', even when it conflicts with the truth and life, becomes the norm, the means and the end. This is the basis for the madness that history has all too often shown us! The Gospel brings to the world the supremacy of the spirit which reconnects us to God.

In the Pastoral Constitution *Gaudium et spes* (Joy and Hope) Vatican Council II showed its concern by reminding us that atheism "must be accounted among the most serious problems of this age, and is deserving of closer examination"[1].

---

[1] *Magisterium*. Vatican Council II, Pastoral Constitution *Gaudium et spes* no. 19 (text no. 10 in Appendix).

Unfortunately, if, as only too often happens, the reality of the spirit is forgotten or neglected, we find ourselves in a situation where, almost without realising it, human identity is suffocated, going so far as speaking of rights such as that of abortion which has by now become an open sore: a crime that cannot be recognised as a right. The fact that in our society it has assumed the configuration of an acquired right constitutes a form of moral degradation: a false conception of man which reduces him to an object. A people that kills its own children cannot be considered wise!

Saint John Paul II, in the Encyclical letter *Evangelium vitae* (The Gospel of life) drawing on the conciliar document of *Gaudium et spes* (n. 51), reiterates that abortion is to be considered, "together with infanticide, as an 'unspeakable crime'"[2], and in the same Encyclical Letter, at no. 73 defines abortion together with euthanasia as "crimes" where he says: "Abortion and euthanasia are thus crimes which no human law can claim to legitimize. There is no obligation in conscience to obey such laws; instead there is *a grave and clear obligation to oppose them by conscientious objection*. From the very beginnings of the Church, the apostolic preaching reminded Christians of their duty to obey legitimately constituted public authorities (cf. Rom 13:1-7; 1 Pet 2:13-14), but at the same time it firmly warned that 'we must obey God rather than men' (Acts 5:29)"[3].

How has it come about that, together with the dimension of the human spirit, man has forgotten these truths, so as to transform the crime of abortion into a 'right'? In this Encyclical, the Pope denounced the idea that was being circulated, namely that in order to be tolerant and democratic one must do away with moral rules. On the basis of this false premise, the consciences of many Christians and Catholics have been stifled, as have those of many men and women of good will which have similarly become dormant. At no. 70 with regard to 'ethical relativism' John Paul II states: "There are those who consider such relativism an essential condition of democracy, inasmuch as it alone is held to guarantee tolerance, mutual respect between people and acceptance of the decisions of the majority, whereas moral norms considered to be objective and binding are held to lead to authoritarianism and intolerance.

But it is precisely the issue of respect for life which shows what misunderstandings and contradictions, accompanied by terrible practical consequences, are concealed in this position.

It is true that history has known cases where crimes have been committed in the name of 'truth'. But equally grave crimes and radical

---

[2] *Magisterium.* John Paul II, Encyclical Letter *Evangelium vitae* (1995) no. 58.
[3] *Magisterium.* John Paul II, Encyclical Letter *Evangelium vitae* (1995) no. 73.

denials of freedom have also been committed and are still being committed in the name of 'ethical relativism'. When a parliamentary or social majority decrees that it is legal, at least under certain conditions, to kill unborn human life, is it not really making a 'tyrannical' decision with regard to the weakest and most defenceless of human beings? Everyone's conscience rightly rejects those crimes against humanity of which our century has had such sad experience. But would these crimes cease to be crimes if, instead of being committed by unscrupulous tyrants, they were legitimated by popular consensus?"[4].

Absolutely not! They could never be legitimised! What the Pope denounces comes about when the spiritual dimension is forgotten or ignored. Together with the clouding of the conscience, that is the fruit of negating the human spirit, there follows a lengthy list of other evils, such as dishonesty, blackmail and theft, gangsterdom and crime, exploitation in the work place including that of minors, pornography, prostitution and sexual abuse.

Young people and new generations are particularly sensitive to this. Benedict XVI addressed young people in Glasgow with the heart of a pastor when he said: "I urge you to lead lives worthy of our Lord (cf. Eph 4:1) (...). There are many temptations placed before you every day – drugs, money, sex, pornography, alcohol – which the world tells you will bring you happiness, yet these things are destructive and divisive. There is only one thing which lasts: the love of Jesus Christ personally for each one of you. Search for him, know him and love him, and he will set you free from slavery to the glittering but superficial existence frequently proposed by today's society. Put aside what is worthless and learn of your own dignity as children of God. (...) I pray that many of you will know and love Jesus Christ and, through that encounter, will dedicate yourselves completely to God, especially those of you who are called to the priesthood and religious life"[5].

But today what space is really given to the spirit to combat the evils in man and society? As in the case of euthanasia, isn't the presence of the spirit in a human life forgotten when that very life is thrown out as if it were an object of no further use to anyone? Grave injustices and new wars are spoken of: indeed reference is made to the 'culture of death' that is being quietly developed to sustain and legitimise vested interests. In short, many lies have emerged and are being spread not only in our societies, not only in Italy and in Europe, but everywhere in the world, to a greater or lesser extent, so that our most important

---

[4] *Magisterium*. John Paul II, Encyclical Letter *Evangelium vitae* (1995) no. 70.
[5] *Magisterium*. Benedict XVI, *Homily at Holy Mass in Bellahouston Park, Glasgow*. Apostolic Journey to the United Kingdom (16 September 2010).

and radical dimension is forgotten, namely the human spirit. As a result its Source, the truth and the love of God our Father, is also forgotten.

So, if the gift of the spirit – that is, the gift which qualifies us as human beings capable of recognising the true face of God "Our Father who art in heaven" and also the true precious face of every human being – is so important, how can this dimension be recovered? Who can help us? First and foremost we have to evaluate whether the other three dimensions, i.e. body, mind and psyche, which each one of us carries within and which we have examined in the previous chapter, can help us to come into contact with our deepest personal reality, namely the spirit.

Let's start with the body. The body has its drives, sensations, and needs. It is certainly the spirit that animates the body, but at first glance the spiritual dimension in the body is not so obvious.

In our thought, in our mind which is the second dimension, there is certainly the work and action of the spirit. But thought risks being a prisoner of itself. Indeed also ethical relativism shows itself through so-called 'weak' thought. In human thought, which appears to be so enlightened, this fact is missed: namely, that it is free thought and this freedom is not inherent to organic matter. Searching for self-reference in itself, thought remains a prisoner of itself without producing a critical attitude, which is properly that of free thought.

Let's think about this: in thought we have the freedom to think! However, by claiming to be self-referential, with no link to God, and by not acknowledging the value of the truth, thought often back-slides on itself, without wishing in any way to go beyond itself. This is why, in the end, it does not give us any security: if it were humble it would show us the spirit, but since it is easily filled up with itself, in what is called arrogance, it remains proud of itself, and sooner or later says: "it is only an opinion...". It thus remains prisoner of an individualistic and relativistic thought and, in the end, also fearful of becoming lost. This is the basis of agnosticism. Human thought without God is proud or base, and is therefore necessarily foolish[6].

Let's ascertain whether in the third dimension, the psyche, we can find something to assist us in fully grasping the reality of the spirit.

The psychical dimension, that of emotions, is animated by the spirit and is capable of making good choices, feeling good things, and choosing love with passion. However, emotion can also be directed towards a variety of opposite reactions, such as destruction and hate: thus, it is fundamentally ambiguous. So, neither does this approach enable us to immediately identify with certainty the spiritual dimension in the human being.

---

[6] *Bible.* Cfr. Gospel of Luke 12:16-21.

In actual fact, the human spirit is immersed in each of the three dimensions; corporeal, mental and psychical. Each of these dimension present in every human being cannot show us the spirit in itself, which, by its own nature, is greater than the other dimensions; so, who can 'help' our spirit? Seen from this perspective, why is it of such importance that Jesus included in the *Our Father* the request "Hallowed be thy name"? What does this mean for us and what change does it bring about in our personal history? This is what we have to find out.

In other words, we are looking for something that can reveal to us the profound reality of our spirit. How can we make the extraordinary reality of our spirit emerge in a living, luminous and clear manner? Who can nurture it?

We need to ask ourselves: if the human spirit is the most profound and richest reality we have, what is more radical than this root? If the human spirit is the root, the secret to our human existence that makes us God's children and makes us love with our bodies, think with our minds, love with our hearts, what is there that is more radical, that can illuminate and maintain our root, our spirit, alive?

It is a good question. What is more radical than the root within us which is the spirit and which makes us human beings? There is only one answer: the Source of our human spirit, God the Father.

Indeed, in order that we realise the precious nature of the human spirit, we cannot base ourselves on a smaller power, however important, beautiful or magnificent it may be, as is each of the other three dimensions, i.e. body, thought, affectivity *(psyche)*. Instead, we should base ourselves on a greater reality than our root: God, the Source of our spirit.

It is something we could never have imagined. In the *Our Father*, Jesus has put as first and foremost this request so that we do not slip back into either of the two dramatic consequences: on one hand, atheism[7] and agnosticism, namely the forgetting, the consignment

---

[7] In support of atheism some have used mathematical and physical thinking, with particular reference to Heisenberg's Uncertainty Principle and Gödel's Theorem. On closer examination, precisely the same arguments, vice versa, show the reversal of their findings and the mathematical logical possibility to affirm the extreme dimension of the human spirit. The error that is often made is to identify the product of thought with the logical-mental processes that produce it. Indeed, the logical process of human thought always presupposes the *absolute* in any relative or absolute assertion. Not even "chance" explains the existence of the world, and much less so explains its "order". To exist, (mathematical) thought and (physical) reality are in agreement in necessarily presuming the Absolute without which we could neither think in a coherent manner nor exist in a logical manner. However, another study is needed to deal with these issues.

to oblivion of the most profound reality of the mystery of God and his face; and, on the other hand, relativism and materialism, with the consequent tragic situation of man that no longer knows who he is. Having denied the dimension of his spiritual soul, man himself thus becomes an object, an almost insignificant reality, manipulable and vulnerable. And this is especially true of the poorest people.

For this reason Jesus has put "Hallowed be thy name" as the first petition in the prayer of the *Our Father:* only in this way can we manage to have a perception and a deep maturity of our reality, the secret of our person, that of the dimension of the human spirit. The Scripture says: "Among human beings, who knows what pertains to a person except the spirit of the person that is within? Similarly, no one knows what pertains to God except the Spirit of God. We have not received the spirit of the world but the Spirit that is from God, so that we may understand the things freely given us by God"[8].

Our spirit needs the relationship with God so that we can recognise and feel it in us. This is by virtue of the fact that without him we do not exist and would never have existed. Only God can reveal to us our most profound secret, our spirit created in his image and likeness[9]. He is the Source of our mystery; He is the restoration, the 'water' that feeds our spirit, but also our 'mirror' that reveals to us who we are[10]. No other reality can reveal this to us, neither human nor spiritual, there is no surrogate, and as we shall see later on, no yoga, New Age, Gnosticism, esotericism or spiritualism: this would be just another deceit. Only transcendent God, the living God, God the Father can tell this to us and enable it to mature within us. But how?

The petition "Hallowed be thy name" means saying to God that we have understood, that we acknowledge him as the one and only God and we openly say that He is the Holy One.

In this regard, there is an interesting comment by Saint Cyprian on the *Lord's Prayer* when he writes: "Hallowed be thy name. Not that we ask for God that He may be hallowed in our prayers, but that we beseech Him that His Name may be hallowed in us. By whom, indeed, could God be hallowed Who is Himself the Hallower?"[11].

---

[8] *Bible*. First Letter to the Corinthians 2:11-12.
[9] *Bible*. Cfr. Book of Genesis 1:26.
[10] *Magisterium*. Cfr. Vatican Council II, Pastoral Constitution *Gaudium et spes* no. 22.
[11] *Tradition*. St. Cyprian (210-258), *St. Cyprian on the Lord's Prayer. An English Translation, with Introduction*, by T. Herbert Bindley, Society for promoting Christian knowledge, London 1914, p. 38.

So, it is not that we pray that God be sanctified but that He be sanctified within us, namely that our spirit may recognise God, so as to be able to enter into communion with God who is the Holy One.

What does Holy One mean? In the Hebrew text the word used is 'kadoš'[12] and means that God is separated from every other reality, that He is the only one, that God is different from nature, and beyond what we can imagine. Holy means extraordinarily, unimaginably unique, separate, distinct. We say it at Holy Mass: "Holy, Holy, Holy Lord God of hosts..."[13]. In this way we state and affirm that God is Holy. To remain truthful people, that do not deceive and do not let themselves be deceived, we need to state that God is Holy, that "Hallowed be his name" in us. God is so Holy and Unique that proclaiming the truth can only be good for us. If we do not give *worship to God*, our spirit does not receive the light, it does not receive the confirmation: it is as if we put our spirit below ground. For this reason Jesus taught us in the *Our Father* to come out, to acknowledge and develop this dimension and thereby rediscover our relationship with God the Father.

What we believe is not the effect of our thought, since God is beyond our thought: we can understand God, but He is always beyond us, He is immensely greater, He "the Holy One"[14] as we are told in the Bible: "For my thoughts are not your thoughts, nor are your ways my ways"[15].

In the same way we express the dimensions of the body, sentiment and thought, we have to express and acknowledge our spiritual dimension. Where do we recognise it most? When we pray and say: "Hallowed be thy name". The soul finds expression not only in the body and its functions, in sentiment and its manifestations, in thought and its faculties, but in a particular way also in the dimension of prayer. It is only if and when we pray that we are human persons in touch with our roots. For this reason the first request that we put before Jesus in the *Our Father* is "Hallowed be thy name". God does not ask for himself: He does not need our prayers and our praise. God asks prayer for us, to rediscover ourselves and not to lose our way!

This fact is highly important because our spiritual dimension matures through the recognition that God is the Holy One, that there

---

[12] *Bible*. Cfr. Book of the Prophet Isaiah 6:3; Book of Numbers 20:13; Book of Revelation 16:5.

[13] Cfr. Liturgy of the Holy Mass, Preface, Roman Missal (www.liturgies.net, accessed in July 2014).

[14] *Bible*. Cfr. Book of Psalms 22:4; Book of the Prophet Hosea 11:9; Book of Revelation 4:8.

[15] *Bible*. Book of the Prophet Isaiah 55:8.

is no other, that He himself is the One and Only, distinct, and not to be confused with creation. This changes our life because it 'touches' our roots; God is able to nurture us. If we do not pray we become lost, we lose sight of our mystery and our roots.

As we shall see later on, this relationship with God, which is 'to worship God', changes the reality of people in the sphere of sexuality, the family and society. It is through meeting God in prayer that our human capacities change by opening up to God the Father and to our neighbour. True worship rendered to God opens the heart to brothers. Benedict XVI reminded us of this during his trip to Santiago de Compostela: "One cannot worship God without taking care of his sons and daughters; and man cannot be served without asking who his Father is and answering the question about him. The Europe of science and technology, the Europe of civilization and culture, must be at the same time a Europe open to transcendence and fraternity with other continents, and open to the living and true God, starting with the living and true man. This is what the Church wishes to contribute to Europe: to be watchful for God and for man, based on the understanding of both which is offered to us in Jesus Christ."[16]

God is not the fruit of our thought or needs, God is not something we can project or invent. Many of those who criticise religion consider God as basically 'created' by man, a projection of himself! Even many writers and philosophers, psychologists and psychiatrists have interpreted the reality of prayer as if the search for God were simply dictated by human needs and fears. This way of thinking reflects a truly infantile vision of the Christian religion, and is the reason why many atheists believe that living without faith is a choice which is both courageous and adult. At this point, it is necessary to see if Christians have always presented a true image of the faith[17].

It is for this reason that God wants us to take his extraordinary, mysterious and unique name seriously. When Moses asked God his name, God gave the name 'YHWH'[18] which is written only with consonants. It is 'inexpressible' because the mystery of God cannot be 'possessed' by any of our knowledge, and maintains the secret of

---

[16] *Magisterium.* Benedict XVI, *Homily at Eucharistic Celebration on the occasion of the Compostelian Jubilee Year at Plaza del Obradoiro at Santiago de Compostela* (6 November 2010).

[17] *Magisterium.* Cfr. Benedict XVI, *Homily at Chrism Mass* (21 April 2011) (text no. 11 in Appendix).

[18] *Bible.* Cfr. Book of Exodus 3:14. **Translator's Note**: In the *New American Bible, revised edition* (2010) the term appears only in the explanatory note. Throughout the text, the word LORD (in small capital letters) indicates that the Hebrew text has the sacred name Yhwh.

the identity of God. Basically, it means that 'God is He who is'. We have to clearly understand: not He who has life, like us who have had life, but He who Is, the Absolute Being, Absolute Life. In other words, God has his identity and does not want to be confused, misunderstood or invented. God is 'jealous' of his Name[19] because He keeps, in his Name, his mystery to give it, in the truth of himself, to man.

The name of God expresses the respect of that which God truly is, not how we want to invent him, not how we would like him to be; in that case, He would no longer be as He is. "Hallowed be thy name" has us say not only that God exists but that He 'exists as He is'.

When I met the Lord in depth, my life changed and I was struck to find his appeal in the Bible: "think of the LORD in goodness, and seek him in integrity of heart"[20]. If we truly want to meet and understand him, God requires us to think of him with proper sentiments and thoughts. He is not satisfied that we just believe He exists.

Each one of us wants to be recognised for what we are and with our proper identity. This fact, so characteristic for us, is dictated by the spiritual dimension. For this reason everyone is rightly attached to their identity and name. All the more so God who is God wants to be acknowledged, respected, and prayed to in his extraordinary, formidable and mysterious, but also close reality, since He has delivered to us the intimacy of the prayer: "Our Father who art in heaven, hallowed be thy name".

**Development of the spiritual dimension**

To the extent that we recognise God, we choose him and we move to his reality, our spiritual reality increases, becomes tangible; our deep spiritual reality surfaces and becomes light.

In us, everything must develop, even the spiritual dimension. The spirit develops through the relationship with God which is the Source of life and of our being.

As pointed out by Pope Emeritus Benedict XVI, this is the reason why religion, its reality and the consequent right to religious freedom are so important[21]. It is equally important to be able to see where it is threatened[22] particularly with regard to the service that religion offers

---

[19] *Bible.* Cfr. Book of Exodus 34:14; Book of the Prophet Ezekiel 39:25.
[20] *Bible.* Book of Wisdom 1:1.
[21] *Magisterium.* Cfr. Benedict XVI, *Message for the Celebration of the XLIV World Day of Peace* (8 December 2010) (text no. 12 in Appendix).
[22] *Magisterium.* Cfr. Benedict XVI, *Address to Members of the Diplomatic Corps* (10 January 2011) (text no. 13 in Appendix).

in the formation of young people. The Pope reminds teachers that the teaching of the Roman Catholic religion is particularly useful for the development of humanity in young people and for society: "Thanks to the teaching of the Catholic religion, school and society are enriched with true laboratories of culture and humanity in which, by deciphering the significant contribution of Christianity, the person is equipped to discover goodness and to grow in responsibility, to seek comparisons and to refine his or her critical sense, to draw from the gifts of the past to understand the present better and to be able to plan wisely for the future"[23].

It is therefore necessary to keep up the right to religious freedom and religious feasts. "Observe the sabbath day – keep it holy" the third of the Ten Commandments tells us[24]. God rests on the seventh day[25] and wants us, like him who is Father, to do the same. It was the Sabbath day of rest that with the resurrection of Jesus has become the Sunday day of rest. Why does God call us to this 'sanctification'?

Because by working every day we get used to organising and developing through our work the resources of the reality that surrounds us, of physical matter and everything that human ingenuity has produced and produces. In this way we become the originators of everything, and in the end we feel that we are 'the masters' of creation, the world and even of life! In this way we succeed in deceiving ourselves about the world and about ourselves. Indeed, through work we see a result in our hands that is always smaller than us, and that certainly cannot tell us who we really are: through the work of his hands and his ingenuity the man without God becomes ever less man losing himself behind the idols he himself has built. Only if we stop looking at 'our creations' and raise our eyes to God, will we not lose sight of God our Father, and also of ourselves, our truth, and our mystery which is above creation and belongs to God. We are reminded of this in the *Our Father* when we pray "Hallowed be thy name".

For this reason God the Father cautions us with the third Commandment: "Observe the sabbath day – keep it holy". It is as if our conscience tells us: "Recognise in the Feast Days that God is Holy. Make them Holy! You cannot just look at what you do, you also need to see what God has done for you! This is what puts you straight on the mystery of your life, not the objects that you produce or manipulate, nor the things you acquire". For this it is essential that we do not lose our relationship with God. Thus, the importance of Holy Mass on the

---

[23] *Magisterium*. Benedict XVI, *Address to the Catholic religion teachers* (25 April 2009).
[24] *Bible*. Cfr. Book of Deuteronomy 5:1-22.
[25] *Bible*. Cfr. Book of Genesis 2:2-3.

Lord's day: the greatest contact we have with God, in which we can see who we are and how we are infinitely loved by him. "This is the day the LORD has made; let us rejoice in it and be glad"[26].

Contact with God reactivates and gives the breath of life to the mysterious dimension of our human person, namely to the mystery that makes us people: the reality of our spirit. It is necessary to tell this to children and young people, and not to hide it from them!

If this contact with the living God were not essential the Lord would not have given us the third Commandment, and Jesus would not have put the first request of "Hallowed be thy name" in the *Our Father.* The same dominical precept 'serves us'. We must be able to say: "God, Holy is your name". This happens in the Celebration, in the contact with the Word of God, in the Church sacraments, and in the Holy Mass in a full and complete way.

This is communion and union with God, and outflows in the adoration of God[27] and in love for one's neighbour[28].

Only in this way does man acquire his greatest value. "Taste and see that the LORD is good; blessed is the stalwart one who takes refuge in him"[29]. How wonderful to be before God with love! Could there be anything greater?! This was how Benedict XVI addressed young people on the occasion of his Apostolic Journey to Madrid for the XXVI World Youth Day: "God is looking for a responsible interlocutor, someone who can dialogue with Him and love him. Through Christ we can truly succeed and, established in him, we give wings to our freedom. Is this not the great reason for our joy? Isn't this the firm ground upon which to build the civilization of love and life, capable of humanizing all of us?

Dear friends: be prudent and wise, build your lives upon the firm foundation which is Christ. This wisdom and prudence will guide your steps, nothing will make you fear and peace will reign in your hearts. Then you will be blessed and happy and your happiness will influence others. They will wonder what the secret of your life is and they will discover that the rock which underpins the entire building and upon which rests your whole existence is the very person of Christ, your friend, brother and Lord, the Son of God incarnate, who gives meaning to all the universe.

---

[26] *Bible.* Book of Psalms 118:24.
[27] *Magisterium.* Cfr. Benedict XVI, *Homily Solemnity of the Sacred Body and Blood of Christ* (22 May 2008) (text no. 14 in Appendix).
[28] *Magisterium.* Cfr. Benedict XVI, *Address on visit to the Cathedral of Santiago de Compostela.* Apostolic Journey to Santiago de Compostela and Barcelona (6 November 2010) (text no. 15 in Appendix).
[29] *Bible.* Book of Psalms 34:8.

He died for us all, rising that we might have life, and now, from the throne of the Father, He accompanies all men and women, watching continually over each one of us"[30].

Christian spirituality has some beautiful pages on the intimate relationship with God. Here are some examples. The first is by Saint John Vianney: "See my children; the treasure of a Christian is not on the earth, it is in Heaven. Well, our thoughts ought to be where our treasure is. Man has a beautiful office, that of praying and loving. You pray, you love – that is the happiness of man upon the earth. Prayer is nothing else than union with God. When our heart is pure and united to God, we feel within ourselves a joy, a sweetness that inebriates, a light that dazzles us. In this intimate union God and the soul are like two pieces of wax melted together; they cannot be separated. This union of God with his little creature is a most beautiful thing. It is a happiness that we cannot understand.

We have not deserved to pray; but God, in his goodness, has permitted us to speak to Him. Our prayer is an incense which He receives with extreme pleasure. My children, your heart is poor and narrow; but prayer enlarges it, and renders it capable of loving God. Prayer is a foretaste of Heaven, an overflow of paradise. It never leaves us without sweetness."[31].

Another beautiful page that can help us to understand the beauty of loving Jesus is that written by Saint Alphonsus Liguori: "All holiness and perfection of soul lies in our love for Jesus Christ our God, who is our Redeemer and our supreme good. It is part of the love of God to acquire and to nurture all the virtues which make a man perfect.

Has not God in fact won for himself a claim on all our love? From all eternity He has loved us. And it is in this vein that He speaks to us: 'O man, consider carefully that I first loved you. You had not yet appeared in the light of day, nor did the world yet exist, but already I loved you. From all eternity I have loved you.' Since God knew that man is enticed by favours, he wished to bind him to his love by means of his gifts: 'I want to catch men with the snares, those chains of love in which they allow themselves to be entrapped, so that they will love me.' And all the gifts which He bestowed on man were given to this end. He gave him a soul, made in his likeness, and endowed with memory, intellect and will; He gave him a body equipped with the senses; it was for him that He created heaven and earth and such an abundance of things. He made

---

[30] *Magisterium.* Benedict XVI, *Address at Welcome Ceremony with young people for XXVI World Youth Day.* Apostolic Journey to Madrid (18 August 2011).
[31] *Tradition.* Saint John Vianney (1786-1859), *Catechism on Prayer* (http://saints.sqpn.com/stj18010.htm, accessed in July 2014).

all these things out of love for man, so that all creation might serve man, and man in turn might love God out of gratitude for so many gifts.

But He did not wish to give us only beautiful creatures; the truth is that to win for himself our love, He went so far as to bestow upon us the fullness of himself. The eternal Father went so far as to give us his only Son. When He saw that we were all dead through sin and deprived of his grace, what did He do? Compelled, as the Apostle says, by the superabundance of his love for us, he sent his beloved Son to make reparation for us and to call us back to a sinless life.

By giving us his Son, whom he did not spare precisely so that He might spare us, He bestowed on us at once every good: grace, love and heaven; for all these goods are certainly inferior to the Son: He who did not spare his own Son, but handed him over for all of us: how could He fail to give us along with his Son all good things?"[32].

New generations are entitled to know and be guided in the extra-ordinary wealth of Christianity, the gift of Jesus to humanity. Loving means not deceiving: for this there is need for the profound revelation of 'what we are and what God is', since this really changes life, on condition however that we take it seriously. It is not true that contact with God 'is of no use, and that it doesn't change anything'. This is the great heresy in the world today: thinking that God is useless! This is what brings about scepticism and religious indifference, and then empirical atheism which together with materialism, relativism and naturalism, is becoming increasingly more widespread. Conversely, being close to God, Jesus entrusts us with the same light! Benedict XVI recalled this in the beautiful message addressed to young people during his Apostolic journey to Germany[33].

So as not to lose God, our Father who art in Heaven, we must look for, proclaim and praise his name as the One and Holy One! We must do this to also avoid becoming confused with other human fatherhoods or being the slaves of idols, the surrogates of religion. Since if we remove or hide the secret of our life we enter the deepest chaos and the greatest injustice. Consequences arise, the surrogates to religion which is what many want. It is the usual method: first, they trample on values and their meaning; then, in the vacuum thereby 'produced', other values are progressively made to emerge, with the pluralism of opinions and

---

[32] *Tradition*. Saint Alphonsus Liguori (1696-1787), *On the love of Christ, Liturgy of the Hours, Office of Readings for the Feast of St. Alphonsus Liguori* (http://www.liturgies. net/saints/alphonsusliguori/readings.htm, accessed in July 2014).

[33] *Magisterium*. Cfr. Benedict XVI, *Address at Prayer vigil with the young people at the trade fair grounds of Freiburg im Breisgau*. Apostolic Journey to Germany (24 September 2011) (text no. 16 in Appendix).

rights; finally, they take the place of what they had previously opposed. This devilry can be seen so frequently in history.

If we fail to give the spiritual dimension, the spiritual soul, its space, its recognition, and its *habitat*, which is the infinite heart of God, its perfection and its love, its great mystery with which it seeks to embrace us and allow us to breathe, what will happen to the human spirit? The human spirit is a reality. It is necessary to open our eyes: either it returns to God in prayer and love or it is fed with evil surrogates that are chiefly superstition, magic, witchcraft, and spiritualism, even going so far as satanism.

## Evil surrogates

If the soul does not encounter the reality of God, then it looks for a surrogate. This is the reason why religious truth is one of the greatest and most delicate realities that exist for the life of human beings, and is not to be trivialised, as so often done by the mass media enslaved to the power of 'mammon' and the ideology of the time. The Church is at the service of the truth and freedom of man "who is the only creature on earth which God willed for itself "[34].

*Superstition* is the first surrogate trap that the human spirit comes across when the soul distances itself from God. The soul attaches itself to things: it lacks breath, the breath of God, and so it relies on horoscopes, moving glasses, pendulums, stones, palmistry, fortune tellers and so on. Faith in God is replaced by faith in the power of objects that become increasingly important and ultimately idols. Superstition replaces the great relationship between our soul and God. This is the great sin of idolatry[35]. In the end, this soul is 'stunted' and no longer hears God, it is paralysed and evil diffuses inside and around it, instilling within it a vision that is increasingly malefic and short-sighted.

The second surrogate is *magic*, with its practitioners. Magic is expanding with impunity: books are circulated among children and young people, also outside school and unknown to parents. Many, as with drugs, fall victim. The difference being that this is the drug of the spirit. There is no difference between black magic and white magic; it is not the good or evil end that can justify it, it is always wrong, and using it is harmful. The means is always wrongful and impure since it contaminates the spirit of man bringing evil to it and to others. This is the great sin of magic and witchcraft which the Bible speaks of[36]. Magic

---

[34] *Magisterium*. Vatican Council II, Pastoral Costitution *Gaudium et spes* no. 24.
[35] *Bible*. Cfr. Letter to the Galatians 5:19-21.
[36] *Bible*. Cfr. Letter to the Galatians 5:19-21.

brings about a fundamental disturbance and manipulation of reality through trust in the occult powers of other forces, and of certain occult energies. People who practise it and those that follow it have lost their good spiritual energy in the relationship of trust, obedience to and love for God the Father, preferring to place their trust in these sub-energies, perhaps not realising how much these are connected to the work of the devil (witchcraft). The use of magic and occult forces also brings about confusion and some profound changes in those that practise them. These people remain entangled in evil, blocked and incapable of doing good, remaining in darkness and confusion. The good energies of the spiritual soul are curbed and made subservient.

In the end, unless 'the name of God is sanctified', idols are praised: gurus and spectacular signs can even appear as miraculous. Only spiritual forces can overcome man. There can also be the influence of Satan, the devil, aided not just by occult forces but also by spiritual entities rebellious to God. With these instruments of power the devil seeks to distance man from God, from his Glory, from his goodness, and from complete obedience and trust in him. Over and above big scandals, superstition and magic are two means that Satan uses to distance men from God and the Catholic Church that fights against him.

But where does Satan aim if not at the third surrogate form, namely witchcraft, spiritism and satanism with its satanic sects?

The most serious forms of *spiritual perversion* are represented by: *witchcraft*, namely the manipulation of matter through forces rebellious to God; *spiritism*, that claims to enter a relationship with the spirits that God does not want as it is harmful; and finally *satanism*. With *satanism* the devil seeks to increasingly establish his power, and to this end can make use of men who become his slaves! In these situations, under the satanic proposals of blackmail, death and deceptions of which the Bible speaks in both the Old and New Testament, people with their souls come to hate the light, the truth, the goodness, the love of God, and fall into rebellion and flight from God. In the end they become prisoners of the darkness and death they love.

Only the infinite mercy of God can enable them to get close again to the Love overcoming all the evil of Satan that they have accepted. But as we shall see later on, the drama is consumed in the absence of repentance and refusal of love, indeed their hating it. The faithful should know more about this world of terrible realities, i.e. the spiritual evil that is not seen because it is hidden from the sight of superficialists and naturalists, those who should have the humility to learn from the Church.

With these three surrogates, that are the opposite of true religion, it is impossible to live: inner joy, the happiness of the love and light of

God's kingdom is lost and without realising it a false kingdom is slowly built, the prelude to hell. In the workplace, in the home, in the family and above all in the hearts of young people, adults and the elderly, taken over by superstition, materialism and utilitarianism, what is being built is not the kingdom of truth, goodness and love that God has entrusted to us, but rather something quite different. And this results in us making all the wrong choices of life!

Hence, we must ask ourselves: how is the kingdom of God made and how does it function? This concerns that kingdom for which Jesus has us pray for in the second petition of the *Our Father*: "Thy kingdom come" which we shall see in the next chapter. It is then that a light is projected into our lives.

# 5

# Thy Kingdom come (I)
## *Your kingdom come*

The three progressive forms of degeneration in the religious relationship with God, that we saw in the last chapter, constitute the most harmful surrogate gaining ground nowadays, causing malaise in the spirit of countless people, also through the bad use made of the media and internet. In the absence of a healthy relationship with the living God, our Father, men too will end up 'using' each other, building a world that is no longer our world, the one that God wants for us. Through not following God the Father but, as Jesus calls him, "the ruler of this world"[1], the devil, men create what can be defined as a *principality*: a form of surrogate kingdom, an abnormal, monstrous 'principality', a concentrate of corruption which imprisons man and leads him to his greatest suffering. This is the beginning of hell. In the end, Jesus "hands over the kingdom to his God and Father, when he has destroyed every sovereignty and every authority and power"[2].

## Subjected to temptation

How, despite temptation, can we avoid entering the *principality's* vortex of corruption? We cannot but be tempted since we exercise freedom having within us the spiritual soul, the spirit! We have within us a greater power than that of the body which dies; greater than the psyche and affectivity which can disturb us, bringing joy or perturbation; greater than our mind which thinks on the basis of its cultural conditioning. This is why Jesus has inserted this beautiful second petition, "Thy Kingdom come" in the *Our Father.*

---

[1] *Bible.* Gospel of John 12:31.
[2] *Bible.* First Letter to the Corinthians 15:24.

After acknowledging and praising God with "Hallowed be thy name", Jesus immediately has us direct our spiritual power to the relationship with God, indicating a space on which to build so as to give value to our life. He immediately entrusts us with the prayer of the kingdom, which is of such immense importance to us in our life, since it is us who are the builders, workers and inventors of our lives. Indeed, given that our spirit is in the image of God the Creator, what do we make of all the power we have been endowed with? We can build the kingdom of God! Continuing to look deeper into the revelation contained in the *Our Father* we can see that in this prayer Jesus has presented us with the fundamental mystery of our human life and society. It is all in this prayer, it is all in the *Our Father*!

Let's then continue our in-depth study of the reality of the kingdom which will occupy us for two chapters: this chapter on the personal and family dimension, and the next chapter on the social dimension.

**Builders of the kingdom: personal and family dimension**

The petition "Thy Kingdom come" should not be understood in the sense that we need to 'encourage' God that his kingdom may come. God is not undecided. The kingdom of God comes in any case! Since it is He who commands; He has truly and clearly shown this in the Bible, in both the Old and the New Testaments. Jesus gave evidence of this: after they killed him, He resurrected from the dead. It is God who commands! It is as well to recall here the words of Jesus: "This is why the Father loves me, because I lay down my life in order to take it up again. No one takes it from me, but I lay it down on my own. I have power to lay it down, and power to take it up again. This command I have received from my Father"[3]. Power as well as his love are part of his kingdom. This is why we have to ask for it as a gift in the prayer to the Father. The kingdom is his! We should reveal this programme to children, adolescents, and young people since they are not aware nor mindful of this plan. We speak to them about building their future, their careers, interests, work, home, marriage, etc. And the kingdom? There is a vacuum, indeed a chasm, in educational values.

What then is the deeper meaning of the request "Thy Kingdom come"?

Perhaps this is what has really been forgotten: that it is God's kingdom and it has been entrusted to us to build it together with Jesus. In some way we can and should cooperate *so that it comes*. This is what

---

[3] *Bible*. Gospel of John 10:17-18.

Jesus has us ask him, so that we do not lose sight of the fact that it is God's, but that it is also for us and that we have to build it together with him. As Benedict XVI points out in his book *Jesus of Nazareth* when commenting on the request of "Thy kingdom come" in the *Our Father*: "Where God is absent, nothing can be good. Where God is not seen, man and the world fall to ruin. This is what the Lord means when he says to 'seek first his Kingdom and his righteousness, and all these things shall be yours as well' (Mt 6:33). These words establish an order of priorities for human action, for how we approach everyday life"[4].

But how is this kingdom made and how does it function, this kingdom of which Jesus speaks in a new way on innumerable occasions in the Gospel? When Jesus stands before Pilate who questions him on the kingdom, He replies: "My kingdom does not belong to this world"[5]. It is then that Pilate, the representative of the political and military power of Rome and Caesar, asks him: "Then you are a king?". Jesus answers: "You say I am a king. For this I was born and for this I came into the world, to testify to the truth. Everyone who belongs to the truth listens to my voice". And Pilate asks him: "What is truth?"[6].

In this way the surrogate of the kingdom is made manifest in Pilate, i.e. the 'principality' that does not want and does not seek the truth. What Pilate lacks is *love for the truth*, and he actually denies it when he asks: "What is truth?". This is why he does not defend the truth! Therefore Pilate, having asked Jesus the question, stops speaking; it is here he breaks off his dialogue and leaves... while this should have been the very moment to pursue the dialogue! Human power, 'mammon', uses the truth or denies it, according to its usefulness in any given situation, as the truth in itself is of no interest to it. In this way it denies all God's kingdom, all the work of Jesus. The clash between God's kingdom that Jesus brings into the world – "for this I came into the world, to testify to the truth"[7] – and the political power of Pilate concerns the problematic issue of the truth[8]. The truth is the centre of God's kingdom: the truth of God and the truth of man.

From careful examination it appears that it is precisely the point of the truth which is nowadays being attacked by *ethical relativism*; the latter having been denounced on numerous occasions by the Church. However, it is not just in our time, the truth has always been

---

[4] *Magisterium*. Benedict XVI, *Jesus of Nazareth*, Doubleday, New York 2007, p. 145.
[5] *Bible*. Gospel of John 18:36.
[6] *Bible*. Gospel of John 18:37-38.
[7] *Bible*. Gospel of John 18:37.
[8] *Magisterium*. Cfr. John Paul II, Encyclical Letter *Veritatis splendor* (1993) no. 84 (text no. 83 in Appendix).

profoundly betrayed and persecuted. It is then that righteousness is eclipsed and there reigns the arrogance of evil which seeks to establish its 'principality'. The essential fact that we are dealing with is that the truth is denied when man seeks to live 'without the kingdom of God' or to 'substitute the kingdom of God'. This is what is denounced by the Church, and it is for this reason that the Church is being fought and persecuted in various ways[9].

In the Gospel, referring to the kingdom that the Jews were waiting for Jesus also says: "the kingdom of God is among you!"[10]. In some ways the kingdom of God seems invisible to the eye but it exists and is present. On one hand Jesus states that it is not of this world, but on the other hand He announces that it is already "here among you". How can this be explained? Ultimately, the kingdom is Jesus himself who together with the Father has come to deliver his divine reality. The kingdom is God's being-Lord, it is his lordship[11].

The kingdom of God that Jesus brings us is a way of existing in perfect and profound communion with God the Father: it is the life of God in the fullness of freedom, truth and love. It is the kingdom of God for the *renewed man* namely for *the truth of the whole man* and for *the communion of all men*. That is why we pray in our hearts, lives, thoughts and actions that "Thy Kingdom come": the kingdom is the way of already living as children of God on this earth through Christ. Where Christ reigns, there is his kingdom with his love and wisdom.

The Church that follows Christ brings his kingdom into the world: it can only propose it with truth, faith and charity. It cannot impose it. Saint John Paul II in his first Encyclical Letter *Redemptor hominis* (The Redeemer of man) recalled that "The Church's fundamental function in every age and particularly in ours is to direct man's gaze, to point the awareness and experience of the whole of humanity towards the mystery of God, to help all men to be familiar with the profundity of the Redemption taking place in Christ Jesus"[12].

Hers is a universal task for the service of the whole of humanity. We are reminded of this in the Letter addressed by Benedict XVI to the Church in the Popular Republic of China: "to remind you of what Pope John Paul II emphasized so strongly and vigorously: the new evangelization demands the proclamation of the Gospel to modern man, with a keen awareness that, just as during the first Christian millennium the Cross was planted in Europe

---

[9] *Bible*. Cfr. Book of Genesis 3:15.
[10] *Bible*. Gospel of Luke 17:21.
[11] *Magisterium*. Cfr. Benedict XVI, *Jesus of Nazareth*, Doubleday, New York 2007, pp. 55-56 (text no. 17 in Appendix).
[12] *Magisterium*. John Paul II, Encyclical Letter *Redemptor hominis* (1979) no. 10.

and during the second in the American continent and in Africa, so during the third millennium a great harvest of faith will be reaped in the vast and vibrant Asian continent. (...) Let China rest assured that the Catholic Church sincerely proposes to offer, once again, humble and disinterested service in the areas of her competence, for the good of Chinese Catholics and for the good of all the inhabitants of the country. (...) The Catholic Church which is in China does not have a mission to change the structure or administration of the State; rather, her mission is to proclaim Christ to men and women, as the Saviour of the world, (...) the Church in her teaching invites the faithful to be good citizens, respectful and active contributors to the common good in their country, but it is likewise clear that she asks the State to guarantee to those same Catholic citizens the full exercise of their faith, with respect for authentic religious freedom"[13].

In substance the Church fulfils and will always fulfil its task, namely that of bearing witness to Jesus, his life and his kingdom in the world: a kingdom of truth and life, a kingdom of holiness and grace, a kingdom of justice, love and peace[14].

With these seven words we can express the seven characteristics of the kingdom of God. Recognising the kingdom of God means recognising God as Father. Jesus warns us: "You cannot serve God and mammon"[15].

God the Father is Father of his kingdom. But if we do not allow this kingdom to enter our lives and our families, if we do not bring it about, then this means we are serving the kingdom of 'mammon', it means that our objective is our wealth and not God, our egoism and not love. At the end of our lives, we shall reap what we have sown: "Do you not know that the unjust will not inherit the kingdom of God? Do not be deceived; neither fornicators nor idolaters nor adulterers nor boy prostitutes nor sodomites nor thieves nor the greedy nor drunkards nor slanderers nor robbers will inherit the kingdom of God"[16]. What is the relationship between us and the kingdom of God? Let's take a closer look.

First God created the universe, as attested in the Bible, in the first chapter of Genesis: we call the universe 'Creation' because with this term we recognise that it was created by God.

Many, not wishing to recognise God the Creator, have replaced the term 'Creation' with 'nature': so the power of 'mammon', with the

---

[13] *Magisterium*. Benedict XVI, *Letter to the Bishops, Priests, Consecrated Persons and Lay Faithful of the Catholic Church in the People's Republic of China (27 May 2007)*.
[14] *Tradition*. Cfr. The Feast of Christ the King: From the ROMAN MISSAL, 3rd edition (http://www.catholictradition.org/Christ/cking-feast2.htm, accessed in July 2014).
[15] *Bible*. Gospel of Luke 16:13.
[16] *Bible*. First Letter to the Corinthians 6:9-10.

expansion of selfishness and irreligiosity, seeks to take an ever tighter grip. Gradually, as man distances himself from God the Creator, he loves increasingly less, and increasingly less does he respect what God has entrusted to him; for this reason egoism and the fears that accompany it become more widespread and the world's serious environmental problem worsens.

In fact God, with love and wisdom, has entrusted man "in our image, after our likeness"[17] with the management of Creation and this kingdom is for man! "God blessed them and God said to them: Be fertile and multiply; fill the earth and subdue it. Have dominion over the fish of the sea, the birds of the air, and all the living things that crawl on the earth"[18]. God is then pleased: "God looked at everything he had made, and found it very good"[19]. Creation and the whole of the universe are not needed by God. They speak to man of the existence of God and his power, as "ever since the creation of the world, his invisible attributes of eternal power and divinity have been able to be understood and perceived in what he has made"[20].

But there is something in the creation of the universe that is closer to God: the creation of the human being. God wished to create on earth in man, male and female, something of his kingdom, and this constitutes the way of existing of the human being that regards man but also God, the couple but also the life of other human beings.

## The 'human' as 'entrusted'

What do we mean when we say 'the human'? It means 'entrusted', in the sense that is closer to humility than arrogance: the human is not something that has been invented by man, woman, science, culture, a power, or any form of energy. It is God that has created the life of the human being, it is not us who have created it. It remains a gift. Family, sex, life have not been invented by us but are a creation made in his image and likeness of which God is 'jealous' and which He has entrusted us with great care. The first creation closest to God is hence the family made up of the man, woman and the gift of life that is born from it.

Only love understands love, and this is even more true with regard to God. Indeed, the more we love him the more we understand him, and the more we understand him the more we love him: it is so true! God wants the unity of love: the love for him and the love for creatures, and

---

[17] *Bible*. Book of Genesis 1:26.
[18] *Bible*. Book of Genesis 1:28.
[19] *Bible*. Book of Genesis 1:31.
[20] *Bible*. Letter to the Romans 1:20.

primarily those that bear 'his image'. "You shall love the Lord, your God, with all your heart, with all your soul, and with all your mind. This is the greatest and the first commandment. The second is like it: You shall love your neighbor as yourself"[21].

The kingdom of God grows through the family and children. The *Catechism of the Catholic Church* emphasises this value: "'The intimate community of life and love which constitutes the married state has been established by the Creator and endowed by him with its own proper laws... God himself is the author of marriage'. The vocation to marriage is written in the very nature of man and woman as they came from the hand of the Creator. Marriage is not a purely human institution despite the many variations it may have undergone through the centuries. (...) Although the dignity of this institution is not transparent everywhere with the same clarity, some sense of the greatness of the matrimonial union exists in all cultures. 'The well-being of the individual person and of both human and Christian society is closely bound up with the healthy state of conjugal and family life'"[22].

Love always includes the care of the person loved; it is protection, understanding, interest for the other and wisdom. "God who created man out of love also calls him to love the fundamental and innate vocation of every human being. For man is created in the image and likeness of God who 'is himself love' (1 Gv 4, 8:16). Since God created him man and woman, their mutual love becomes an image of the absolute and unfailing love with which God loves man. It is good, very good, in the Creator's eyes. And this love which God blesses is intended to be fruitful and to be realised in the common work of watching over creation: 'And God blessed them, and God said to them: Be fruitful and multiply, and fill the earth and subdue it' (Gn 1:28)"[23].

Life is an extraordinary journey from being children to being married and then parents, mothers and fathers, in the 'image' of God who is Father. This is not just a development but a development that is 'a safekeeping', so that life may develop and grow in its true sense and meaning and not be destroyed. It concerns the 'safekeeping' of the *human*, namely what God has entrusted to 'humanity', something precious that is not to be manipulated or concealed! Driven by ambition for a progress that is all his own but above all by the aims of 'mammon', man seeks to disrupt human life by transforming it increasingly from a 'gift' of God and love to a *product* of science and technology. But man is greater than science! How much greater is reality than what man

---

[21] *Bible*. Gospel of Matthew 22:37-39.
[22] *Magisterium. Catechism of the Catholic Church*, no. 1603.
[23] *Magisterium. Catechism of the Catholic Church*, no. 1604.

discovers with science. It is here that I would like to raise a question: "Is marriage between two people that love one another a 'gift' of their love or a 'product' of their sex?! Then why does a child have to be a 'product' of technology and not a 'gift' of their love?".

Therefore the family is a gift of God to be understood, loved, cherished, and kept safe[24]. This is why human love and the family need God and his 'closeness'. Through human love and children there thus develops the kingdom of God. It is not imposed, it is proposed to the love and responsibility of human beings... This is a beautiful reality which bestows great dignity to the family and to the love that nourishes it.

Conversely, by distancing himself from God, the human being loses the kingdom. Where have we lost the kingdom of God? Right there in the couple. How and why is the similarity that brings us closer to God the Creator and Father made manifest in the couple? Mathematics can help us to understand.

Let's take the example of a couple that loves one another: a he and a she that are joined together in love, with dedication to raise a beautiful family, to be just one heart, one body, in short a perfect couple. But even if they are joined together, they will never be and will never make 'one' since one plus one is always two! $1+1=2$. In this way the union as a mathematical sum is always two. Indeed, God in the Bible never defines marriage as a pair. Materialism and hedonism have created the image of a he and a she that simply join together, but in this way the two never constitute a proper couple: but rather a *pseudo* couple'!

We should not then be amazed if couples break up, because in this way they never function well! God has not created them in this way.

The secret of the couple is found in the Bible since the human couple is a particular creation of God. It is for this reason that the creation God has entrusted us with functions solely in a certain harmony and in a certain equilibrium of forces, and God, throughout the Bible, calls upon man to listen to him. The beginning of life is, as biology tells us, a particular combination. The harmony of the universe as studied in physics is a particular combination of elements, and if we were to change one or half of it nothing would be as it is, we would have another world. The world rests on a sense, an order that numbers can describe to us. Like Creation, but even more so, the human couple is a particular creation of God which only functions in one way: it cannot be maimed, manipulated or changed, since otherwise the kingdom is

---

[24] *Magisterium.* Cfr. Benedict XVI, *Homily at Holy Mass with dedication of the Church of the Sagrada Familia and of the Altar.* Apostolic Journey to Santiago de Compostela and Barcelona (7 November 2010) (text no. 18 in Appendix).

lost and 'mammon' takes over in human love and in the couple. This is what 'mammon' seeks to achieve by providing a banal culture of the ephemeral and immediate utility. It is then that the *human* vanishes and *love* is lost.

To love it is necessary to understand! This is the intelligence of faith of which the Church speaks! Intelligence is required to understand the truth, and an even greater love is required to love it. In reality, those who do not love the truth do not even love themselves. It is in the truth that we find God and his kingdom, since as Jesus tells us: "you will know the truth, and the truth will set you free"[25].

At this juncture we can ask ourselves how the couple functions. The *'pseudo* couple' will always make 1+1=2 but never one (1), a marriage, a family, since marriage is not brought about by a sum of people and two attracting bodies, it is made in the 'image of God' and God is not a sum, He is, as Jesus revealed to us, One in Three Persons.

**Formula for true love and marriage**

What then is, so to speak, 'the marriage formula'? Here we have to go into detail; here much enlightenment and knowledge of God is needed.

In general, upon reflection, people think: "In fact, if nothing changes in our life together and each of us remains indifferent we are not a couple. It is therefore necessary to meet somewhere halfway and change a little so as to please each other". Thus, by experiencing the attraction of love, the two come to a compromise, and by so doing they shrink, become smaller, each becoming like a half to make 1/2+1/2=1. But it is not possible to create unity in the human by adding 'half plus half', even if the sum makes 'one', as love cannot be a diminution of the person: *reduction does not work*, not even in love! It does not hold! God does not want 'half plus half' between and among human people! Indeed, today many people think that this is the reality of love and the family, going so far as to despise it by claiming that "marriage is the tomb of love" or by making simplistic judgements: "it is better not to get married", "one is better off on one's own", "isn't it enough to stay together as long as it lasts?". They do not know what love is! They are distrustful because they have distanced themselves from the mystery of the human being.

Who believes in love? Very few since "love is of God"[26] and to love is like entering God's kingdom. It may sometimes be the case that

---

[25] *Bible.* Gospel of John 8:32.
[26] *Bible.* First Letter of John 4:7.

although love is sought, there is greater belief in the *pseudo* couple than in love and the family. It is therefore quite natural that the family breaks down, since it is not wanted the way it is, even though God has made it! God has created it in another way, but families today are particularly tried and tested, being assailed by materialistic, hedonistic and atheistic pressures.

Let's continue the search: in what other way can one find unity in the love of man and woman? And what could be its 'formula'?

If we cannot be diminished to form a couple, perhaps an alternative way could be 'one day for each', putting each one aside on alternate days? This is totally out of the question, even if 0+1=1 and vice versa 1+0=1. Also in this way, love would not work given the equal and constant dignity of man and woman. Since love involves the whole person it is not only a big but also delicate commitment, and has its laws. Consequently, when there is conflict, this can lead to destruction: 1−1=0. It then becomes necessary for the couple to separate in order to survive, to rediscover themselves through effort and suffering: 1÷1=1.

What then is the formula for true love? The love between man and woman that builds a marriage and brings about the kingdom of God functions in this way, 'one per one': 1×1=1. This is the only way.

The beautiful apostolic letter *Mulieris dignitatem* (Dignity of the woman) by Saint John Paul II affirms: "In the 'unity of the two' man and woman are called from the beginning not only to exist 'side by side' or 'together', but they are also called *to exist mutually 'one for the other'*"[27]. "Man and woman were made 'for each other' – not that God left them half-made and incomplete: He created them to be a communion of persons, in which each can be a 'helpmate' to the other, for they are equal as persons ('bone of my bones...') and complementary as masculine and feminine. In marriage God unites them in such a way that, by forming 'one flesh' (Genesis 2:24), they can transmit human life: 'Be fruitful and multiply, and fill the earth' (Genesis 1:28). By transmitting human life to their descendants, man and woman as spouses and parents cooperate in a unique way in the Creator's work"[28].

The world lacks the secret of love; it is only God that has it, and it is what Christianity bears witness to, and is presented in the Bible. One per one, one; 1×1=1, i.e., the formula of true good love, a love that lasts in marriage and builds with God. But we have to understand this formula well: it is not enough to be just 'one for the other' in order to be happy. It would be infantile to think so! Even two thieves... can get

---

[27] *Magisterium.* John Paul II, Apostolic Letter *Mulieris dignitatem* (1988) no. 7.
[28] *Magisterium. Catechism of the Catholic Church*, no. 372.

on very well, helping and being supportive to each other. It is not true that in the couple it is enough just to be accomplices.

In actual fact there are *two conditions* for the formula to be effective. The *first condition* is that each of the two 'is for the other and vice versa'; a commitment on the part of just one of the two is not enough. There has to be a commitment on the part of both of them. The *second condition* is that it is necessary to be whole. 'Whole' stands for 'intact'. Indeed, if a person is not 'intact' in truth, good and love and is, let's say in mathematical terms, 0.8, the couple will not function well: $1 \times 0.8 = 0.8$ in the same way that $0.8 \times 1 = 0.8$. Discounts are not possible! If one is 'a little less' than 1, he/she will 'lower' and humanly impoverish the entire family.

Let's look at another hypothesis. In the case where one of the two could be considered as having a 'higher' value than 1, for example 1.3, our family would show, given the inequality among its members, the presence of a dangerous surplus, i.e. an imbalance: $1.3 \times 0.9 = 1.17$ (in our case 0.17 with respect to 1). This would act as an impetus for one or the other to get out of the faithful relationship of the couple.

Therefore, loving also means being able to assess one's own integrity in truth and goodness in order not to cause harm to the other, and allow the couple the integrity and fullness represented by 'one' (1). This means that loving and caring arouse not only the good of loving but also *wanting the good* for each other! Both the love and the good that each in the couple can bring to the other must be verified possibly through a life path. And this is what is proposed[29] to the many couples who attend the 'Family – Little Church' Centre of the Movement of Family Love (*Famiglia Piccola Chiesa – Movimento dell'Amore Familiare*), where all that is described in this book has been experimented with excellent results. Certainly to achieve all this, the sciences of the mind and the body are not enough; those of theology and the spiritual soul are also needed.

To marry well, people and couples must find truth and goodness, and become, as far as is possible, *authentic and intact*! Entering the kingdom of life and love is demanding, and as Jesus reminds us in the Gospel: "How narrow the gate and constricted the road that leads to life. And those who find it are few"[30]. Both sloth, i.e. laziness of the soul, one of the seven deadly sins, and narcissism, typical of the many distorted personalities in the world today, do not render a good service to love, and nor does religious indifference or secularism. One wonders: who really wants to heal and improve themselves in order to love? Who feels the joy and the love to improve their life, to heal from deficiencies

---

[29] Cfr. Chapter 8.
[30] *Bible*. Gospel of Matthew 7:14.

and shortcomings, because they want to marry well and so serve God and his kingdom better?

**The pen game**

Another convincing example of what we are describing is what I have called 'the pen game'. In Figure 1 'the hut' of the *pseudo* couple is represented: the two, male and female (M and F pen respectively; colour images are available at figlidichi.altervista.org), are 'tilted' by life and burdened by defects, they like each other and, attracted, they love each other and come together even sexually (point c). The tilt which defines angle (a) and angle (b) shows 'the angle of the pathology' (a) and (b), i.e. of the needs and shortcomings due to spiritual or psychical dysfunctions. Thus, almost without realising it, the two come together in a love that 'interlocks' them, given that in this love they are mutually supportive, they often justify themselves by concealing each other and defending this position which gives them some security. Plane (d) represents the weight of life with its responsibilities and expectations: it is difficult for them 'to be married forever!' or 'to have children!' They fear that their hut will cave in and collapse.

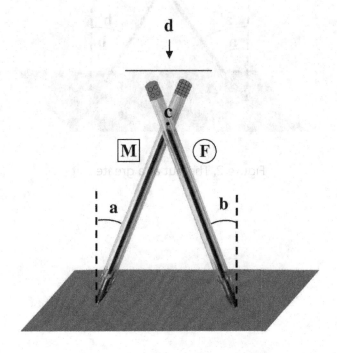

Figure 1. The hut

Figure 2 highlights that, in any given case, the tilt of angles (a) and (b) may be greater or lesser or different from each other. These couples give rise, nonetheless, to *huts* which are more or less 'tilted', more or less unstable, also because the weight (d) of life expands, 'increases', and is more greatly felt in proportion to the angles of the pathology (a and b) and (a' and b'). So, the more he and she are 'tilted' the more the couple feels the *weight* (d) of the responsibility of life, not least that of marriage, often 'seeking refuge' in *cohabitation*.

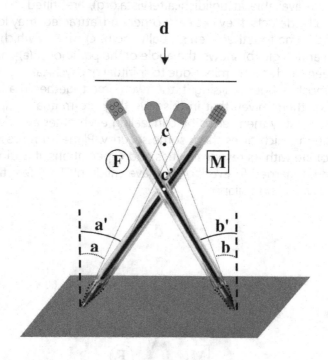

Figure 2. The hut at a greater tilt

In Figure 3 the couple's *home* is represented. The more a person is set on the roots of truth and goodness found in God, that is the Source, the more he or she will emerge without compromise or deviations.

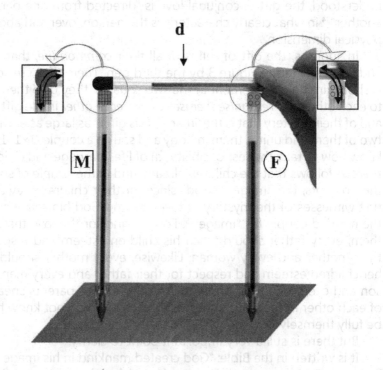

Figure 3. The home

Here both he and she are one (1) and one (1), authentic and intact. Their identity and positivity does not give rise to dangerous encounters and misunderstandings. Their distance shows their specific identity and diversity: there is no confusion and there is mutual appreciation between the man and the woman. Their love is not just in their sexual union, it is not just in one part of the body (point c in Figures 1 and 2); vice versa, in their love there passes their entire lives which they give as *a sincere and total gift from one person to another*[31]. A 'total' gift is understood here in the sense that it engages the whole person and for the whole of life in the giving of him/herself, forever. And this is its value, not because it is a possession, but because it is an expression of the 'gift', i.e. of the love of God that is forever. In fact, "directed from one

---

[31] *Magisterium.* Cfr. Vatican Council II, Pastoral Constitution *Gaudium et spes,* no. 24 d, nos. 48-49.

person to another" their love "involves the good of the whole person"[32]. The expression "a sincere gift of himself"[33] indicates the truth of the heart that loves and the will that wants to love without duplicity. Thus understood, the gift in conjugal love is "directed from one person to another"[34] in what clearly characterizes the person, over and above the physical dimension.

In spouses, the gift of self is of all their *common life*, that of him and her, depicted in Figure 3 by the third pen. Their gift in reciprocity is shown in the enlargement in the two squares: they give themselves to each other and *recognise themselves and each other* in the gift of self and of their mystery that is the 'image'. This gift is as large as each of the two of them and unites them in body and soul in a couple (1×1=1). They know how to take the responsibility (d) of life, marriage and children. It thereby follows that the children already find in the couple of spouses, their parents, the 'image of God', since for their children they are the first witnesses of the mystery of love, life and God himself, who gave the married couple his "image"[35]. For this and for the love that unites them, every father should teach his children esteem and respect for their mother and every woman. Likewise, every mother should teach her children esteem and respect for their father and every man. Every son and every daughter are entitled to have both parents speak well of each other in the truth, otherwise the children do not know how to be fully themselves.

But there is still a very important point to clarify.

It is written in the Bible: "God created mankind in his image; in the image of God he created them; male and female he created them"[36]. And it is precisely from this 'image of God' that there arises in man and woman the ability to love[37] and the 'likeness' to God[38]. But here, in this verse of the Bible, the couple seems to consist of two beings, male and female, and at first glance one cannot see 'how' they are in the 'image' of God.

On closer analysis, we realise that in this Bible sentence there is the mystery of the Triune God: Three persons, Father, Son and Holy Spirit in

---

[32] *Magisterium*. Cfr. Vatican Council II, Pastoral Constitution *Gaudium et spes*, no. 49.
[33] *Magisterium*. Cfr. Vatican Council II, Pastoral Constitution *Gaudium et spes*, no. 24.
[34] *Magisterium*. Cfr. Vatican Council II, Pastoral Constitution *Gaudium et spes*, no. 49.
[35] *Magisterium*. Cfr. John Paul II, Letter to Families *Gratissimam sane* (1994) no. 11 (text no. 19 in Appendix).
[36] *Bible*. Book of Genesis 1:27.
[37] *Magisterium*. Cfr. John Paul II, *Man and Woman He Created Them. A Theology of the Body*, Pauline Books & Media, Boston, MA 2006, p. 180 (text no. 20 in Appendix).
[38] *Magisterium*. Cfr. John Paul II, Apostolic Letter *Mulieris dignitatem* (1988) no. 7 (text no. 21 in Appendix).

one God. This fact changes everything: indeed, if they were only 'two', male and female, if the human was made only of two dimensions, the male and female, only the *pseudo* couple' would be possible and not the couple 'in the image' of God! So, since God is Triune, where does the third dimension appear in the above-mentioned sentence from the Bible?

## The image in the two sexes

The *third dimension* in the human is precisely in the 'image of God'. This, in males and females, makes it possible for the man and the woman to be in love 'one for the other in a human way', making a reciprocal gift of their person. To be one, 'one flesh', that is, a 'conjugal person', three are needed. We human beings, in our profound reality, live with a mystery that is the image of God. The couple is given by that mysterious *per* (×) which is the image of God, capable of love as "the sincere gift of self"[39], capable of doing good and not just to feel comfortable together like two simple accomplices, as is sometimes suggested by the world that knows neither God nor the human.

Therefore, man and woman carry within them the image of God not only as individuals but even more so in their "communion between persons"[40], whose first fruit is a mutual revelation in which the woman reveals the man and the man the woman. The human couple, who 'comes' from God and follows him, works this way. On this subject[41] we have the precious catechesis on human love by Saint John Paul II published in the book *Man and Woman He created Them*.

Conversely, if the 'image', the spiritual dimension that is inscribed in sexuality, is covered or deformed, the man and the woman do not live the mystery of self-giving in the image of God, of self-giving in the unity of the couple, but they mate – while it lasts! – in the use of the difference between the sexes. In this way, a *'pseudo* couple' is brought about rather than the couple that God wants. In fact, if there are two different genders, the *male* and *female*, who can join them? Perhaps need, lack, exchange, caprice, or rather something that is similar in both? And if they are different, what is *similar* in the male and female?

A *common element* is needed to unite them, not an aspect but something that makes them great, that makes them be what they are,

---

[39] *Magisterium*. Vatican Council II, Pastoral Constitution *Gaudium et spes*, no. 24.
[40] *Magisterium*. Cfr. *Catechism of the Catholic Church*, no. 383.
[41] *Magisterium*. Cfr. John Paul II, *Man and Woman He Created Them. A Theology of the Body*, Pauline Books & Media, Boston, MA 2006, pp. 163, 182, 185-186 (text no. 22 in Appendix).

that is equal to their great personal mystery. It is the mystery which is common in both, the 'image and likeness' that is a gift of God, and founds their equal dignity as persons as well as the ability to love and the reciprocal self-giving of male and female. It is wonderful to be male, and it is wonderful to be female, experiencing the great value of one's gender and accepting oneself in the complementarity of the common mission. "Respect for the human person considers the other 'another self'. It presupposes respect for the fundamental rights that flow from the dignity intrinsic of the person"[42]. Only this spiritual dimension allows love in freedom and responsibility for mutual benefit, that is as children of God.

The beauty and grandeur of the human being, through sexuality, makes the man fall in love with the woman and vice versa, but not for a sexual or emotional need that comes and goes. Not for a need due to loneliness or possessiveness! The kingdom of God begins with the couple; if the couple is how God made it, it must show three dimensions. The kingdom of God stems from the couple, the family, which is the fundamental nucleus of society. The kingdom of God is something great and powerful that God has put within each one with the creation of the spiritual soul.

If families show this 'image', this third dimension, then it will be more obvious that the couple and the family are manifestations of God's kingdom. If it is hidden, the couple automatically falls into the trap of possession, that is, into the schemes of economic and political powers, and of private selfish interests. The family, therefore, is based on a mystery of love and truth that Jesus has us ask for in the *Our Father*: "Thy Kingdom come".

It is here that premarital sex and 'cohabitation' show their weakness, and rather than being a preparation for love, they often become an escape from true good and responsible love, even if this is what is sought and aspired to through such experiences. So 'trying out' seems to be the easiest thing to do, in fact more often than not it would appear to be considered an 'entitlement'. In reality, an attempt at 'cohabitation' is chosen as if it were something one could try out... Yet life is not something you can try out, and neither can you try out the sincere and ever-lasting gift of self, for any test has a duration, it is neither total nor 'forever', and therefore would bear greater resemblance to a loan. In the test of cohabitation there lacks the fullness which characterises the choice of marriage.

Likewise, a mother or a father cannot try out being a parent, either you are or you are not. You can try out 'things' but not the lives of

---

[42] *Magisterium. Catechism of the Catholic Church*, no. 1944.

human beings. Otherwise, these are reduced to mere objects. Of course, in acknowledging the greatness and beauty of human love, the couple must be guided to overcome reductive temptation and opt instead for entirety and fullness, adequately preparing themselves for marriage not only before but also afterwards so as to avoid becoming lost.

Unfortunately, couples sometimes get stuck in 'a love that stagnates' in a vacuum of routine, to the point that it becomes meaningless. Unfortunately, so many loves are lost because they do not allow themselves to be healed by the 'Mystery' of Love whose root is in God! How many wounds are human beings able to inflict upon each other without ever thinking of seeking a cure. According to the mindset of the world, it is considered normal for love to burn itself out and just be one experience after another, like a 'thing' that is consumed.

But can the world ever know love if it runs far away from the Source of Love that is God? At most it will be able to know the 'erotic', but not the fullness of human love which necessarily also includes the spiritual dimension and the religious relationship with God.

Today, those who marry well are those that have found the mystery of love, truth and the kingdom. The first thing that engaged couples and spouses should do is to understand the kingdom of God that dwells within them. They must find the mystery of their love, not just love! Human love alone is not sufficient to save us! If human love alone were sufficient, and more specifically 'erotic' love alone, Jesus Christ would not have come to earth to save us!

Jesus saves spouses and unites them in him: then they will join "in the Lord"[43] because their love, blessed and sanctified by Jesus with the sacrament of Marriage, belongs to his kingdom, being consecrated in him and grafted in God the Source of Love. It is then that human love is capable of being not only true and good but also beautiful, the "fairest love" as Saint John Paul II called it[44].

And this is what Jesus came to bring us, the kingdom of God. To love and marry, this must somehow be recognised. It is not sufficient that the two love one another humanly, they must love the Love. It is not sufficient for them to be joined, they must love their mystery: that of the common 'image' which makes them capable of loving, and that of Christ which unites them. It is not enough that they love their family, they must pray to God the Father that "Thy Kingdom come"; in this way human love is saved! In order for human love to hold up it must find its mystery, its roots in the spirit, in God's plan and in love for God: the

---

[43] *Bible*. Cfr. Letter to the Ephesians 5:25-33.
[44] *Magisterium*. Cfr. John Paul II, Letter to Families *Gratissimam sane* (1994) no. 13 (text no. 23 in Appendix).

house, as Jesus says, must be built on rock[45]. This is the mystery that belongs to Christianity and that Jesus came to reveal to all humanity, as we are also reminded in the Letter to Families of Saint John Paul II: "Yet there is no true love without an awareness that God 'is Love' – and that man is the only creature on earth which God has called into existence 'for its own sake'. Created in the image and likeness of God, man cannot fully 'find himself' except through the sincere gift of self. Without such a concept of man, of the person and the 'communion of persons' in the family, there can be no civilization of love; similarly, without the civilization of love it is impossible to have *such a concept of person and of the communion of persons*. The family constitutes the fundamental 'cell' of society. But Christ – the 'vine' from which the 'branches' draw nourishment – is needed so that this cell will not be exposed to the threat of a kind of *cultural uprooting* which can come both from within and from without. Indeed, although there is on the one hand the 'civilization of love', there continues to exist on the other hand *the possibility of a destructive 'anti-civilization'*, as so many present trends and situations confirm"[46]. It is therefore a question of being aware of the new scope of value that the family has today.

## Virginity, a sign of love for God

As Jesus says in the Gospel, in building the kingdom, there is also the role of *virginity for the kingdom of heaven*[47]. This "is an unfolding of baptismal grace, a powerful sign of the supremacy of the bond with Christ and of the ardent expectation of his return, a sign which also recalls that marriage is a reality of this present age which is passing away"[48]. Pope Emeritus Benedict XVI on his Apostolic Journey to France urged young people to trust in Christ on giving their lives: "Do not be afraid to give your life to Christ! Nothing will ever replace the ministry of priests at the heart of the Church! Nothing will ever replace a Mass for the salvation of the world! Dear young and not so young who are listening to me, do not leave Christ's call unanswered"[49].

---

[45] *Bible*. Cfr Gospel of Matthew 7:24-27.
[46] *Magisterium*. John Paul II, Letter to Families *Gratissimam sane* (1994) no. 13.
[47] *Bible*. Cfr Gospel of Mattew 19:12.
[48] *Magisterium*. *Catechism of the Catholic Church*, no. 1619.
[49] *Magisterium*. Benedict XVI, *Homily at Holy Mass Notre Dame, Esplanade des Invalides, Paris*. Apostolic Journey to France on the occasion of the 150th Anniversary of The Apparitions of the Blessed Virgin Mary at Lourdes (13 September 2008).

**A mystery in common**

Both vocations live a common mystery that they proclaim through life:

*When two human beings, a man and a woman*
*come together with the love of God*
*to build their future*
*the "Family – Little Church" is born.*
*This is the gift of the Sacrament of Marriage.*

*When in the Church a man or a woman*
*full of love for God offer themselves to Him*
*to find themselves in the absolute of God*
*they announce the Church of the future,*
*what they will be and what the world will be tomorrow.*
*This is the gift of celibacy for the kingdom of heaven.*

*When the human and the Divine Spirit*
*come together in harmony*
*for the sake of God and the good of man*
*the Church and familiarity with the mystery are born.*
*And this creates the communion in Christian spouses*
*and in consecrated persons.*

It is already some years ago that using these words I pointed out the 'common mystery'. "Both the sacrament of Matrimony and virginity for the Kingdom of God come from the Lord himself. It is He who gives them meaning and grants them the grace which is indispensable for living them out in conformity with his will. Esteem of virginity for the sake of the kingdom and the Christian understanding of marriage are inseparable, and they reinforce each other"[50]. Virginity for the kingdom of Heaven, in fact, opens up to joy and hope so that everyone, especially the family and the world, remembers the ultimate goal of human life, the future to which God calls humanity: love in God for the eternal wedding of the Lamb, the Divine Bridegroom[51].

'The Christian meaning of love and marriage' as well as 'virginity for the kingdom of Heaven' are needed in the world and in the heart of every man to give full meaning to human life as transparency of the mystery of God, and to cooperate fully with him. Spouses and consecrated people

---

[50] *Magisterium. Catechism of the Catholic Church*, no. 1620.
[51] *Bible.* Cfr. Book of Revelation 19:7-9.

enlighten each other, saying and teaching something of themselves to each other so that true love is their common language, and when one sees love one learns to love.

We must hand down to future generations the beauty of the kingdom of God present in our human reality, in virginity offered to God for their brethren as in marriage and the Christian family: finding and showing that sexuality, family and life are part of the kingdom of God. Christians must be more forthright and let all this be seen with greater clarity, not only for themselves, but also for their children and their friends. 'Mammon' with its powers is building its couples and society differently! 'Mammon' does not want God and the things of God, it does not care that the family does not function as it should, because it wants to pervert it, to be like a new invention, distancing it far from God. This is called theft. We shall see this again later on: taking the things of God but without God; taking the reality of man and woman but without their mystery; ripping out everything of God from the kingdom of God to turn it into the 'principality'. This is the *upheaval* we are witnessing today.

What we can and should do is to propose Christ and his Gospel to the world, in freedom and truth. Not in a covert manner but in the way Jesus wants. The world needs light, the wisdom and beauty of God. In the new evangelization it will be necessary, then, not only to propose new anthropological ways but also to propose new experiences of spirituality, beauty and mysticism that touch the human heart. To us, obedient to Jesus Christ, servants of the Lord and the Lord's friends, the children of God, there lies the task of finding the preciousness of what Jesus has entrusted to us and is ours, delivering it in truth, humility and charity to the younger generations: to the many young men and women who seek him, as we are made for the kingdom of God and not for the *traps* laid by 'mammon' leading to the precipice. With Jesus, true God and true man, 'between heaven and earth' there is a light that makes its way to us.

# 6

# Thy Kingdom come (II)
## *Your kingdom come*

In the previous chapter we saw what Jesus means when He teaches us to pray using the words: "Thy Kingdom come" and how He himself is ultimately identified with the kingdom of God which is being progressively established, in an unexpected way, through the love and freedom of man. New eyes are needed to realise this, a certain sensibility of heart and mind.

Above all it is important to realise, as was seen in the previous chapter, that his kingdom has come, and is with us now. Yet, Jesus gave us this prayer: "Thy Kingdom come". Certainly, not that it 'may come' in heaven where He already is and dwells. What Jesus wants is that this kingdom becomes ever more established on earth, where, with our collaboration it may grow, until the day on which He, as He has promised, returns in glory: "But when the Son of Man comes, will he find faith on earth?"[1].

Vatican Council II reminds us that "The Lord is the goal of human history, the focal point of the longings of history and of civilization, the centre of the human race, the joy of every heart and the answer to all its yearnings. He it is Whom the Father raised from the dead, lifted on high and stationed at his right hand, making Him judge of the living and the dead. Enlivened and united in his Spirit, we journey toward the consummation of human history, one which fully accords with the counsel of God's love: 'To re-establish all things in Christ, both those in the heavens and those on the earth' (Ephesians 1:10). The Lord Himself speaks: 'Behold I come quickly! And my reward is with me, to render to each one according to his works. I am the Alpha and the Omega, the first and the last, the beginning and the end' (Revelation 22:12-13)"[2].

---

[1] *Bible.* Gospel of Luke 18:8.
[2] *Magisterium.* Vatican Council II, Pastoral Constitution *Gaudium et spes* no. 45.

The kingdom of God begins in individuals where truth, freedom, love, and goodness reign. It is then shown in the couple and in the family inasmuch that they are the 'image of God', transparencies of the love and the 'gift from one person to another'; consequently the kingdom is also present in society. Jesus has come to establish his kingdom first and foremost in individuals and then in the couple and family bringing the light and the profound truth. Indeed, the first miracle that Jesus performed was at the Wedding Feast of Cana[3]. This is the way the kingdom of God comes: putting to right, healing, and highlighting the just relationship that God wants not only with us but also between man and woman, that is, in the couple and family, opening it up anew to the gift of human life. This is what Jesus teaches us in the *Our Father* when He has us ask: "Thy Kingdom come".

## Builders of the kingdom: the social dimension

But the scope of the kingdom of God also extends to the city of men, to that other dimension which is the social dimension. It is the family that is the core of society, and these two pillars – i.e. family and society – are interconnected. The family is not just of a private nature, it is also a vital resource for society[4].

In the *Our Father* Jesus not only teaches us to ask that "thy Kingdom come", but He also asks that 'we prepare' for his return by taking part in the building of his kingdom. This is something we have to pray and ask the Father for since it is a gift of God, and it "does not belong to this world"[5]. In asking the Father, Jesus is also teaching us to want, work for, and love the kingdom so that it might grow and spread, in this way lovingly preparing for his return. Indeed, love requires participation: love is not imposed, love is built. This is an expression of the love of God for us: we are called to his vineyard to work, with intelligence, alongside him in building his kingdom in truth, justice and peace. However, faith and meekness, humility and courage are also needed, and precisely because it is of God, the kingdom of God is not extended through the use of violence[6]. Here we should also remember, as indicated in the *Catechism of the Catholic Church*, that the right to personal defence

---

[3] *Bible*. Cfr. Gospel of John 2:1-11.
[4] *Magisterium*. Cfr. John Paul II, Apostolic Exhortation *Familiaris consortio* (the family bond) (1981) nos. 42-45.
[5] *Bible*. Gospel of John 18:36.
[6] *Magisterium*. Cfr. Benedict XVI, *Jesus of Nazareth. Holy week: from the Entrance into Jerusalem to the Resurrection*, Part two, Ignatius Press, San Francisco 2011, p. 15 (text no. 24 in Appendix).

or the legitimacy of a defensive war is one thing[7], while violence is something else.

How does the kingdom of God grow and spread? Through our growth. As the kingdom grows within us, it also grows through us in two fundamental ways: in the building of families and in the building of society. God has created two realities that are particularly his: first, the couple, 'male and female able to love and give life to the image of God, the family', and then the social reality, the Church, the people of God[8], the family of families. It was Jesus that established the Church when He said to Peter, "you are Peter, and upon this rock I will build my church, and the gates of the netherworld shall not prevail against it"[9]. Jesus calls it "my church" stressing that it is 'his', created by him. The faithful belong to it, too[10]. It is his and He guarantees it. The Church is here to serve the kingdom of God, not herself. The Church serves Our Father and is at the service of the Gospel and the kingdom of Jesus Christ in the world[11].

## The relationship between Church and kingdom

The relationship between the Church and the kingdom of God is of paramount importance to all. Vatican II has already reminded us: "From this source the Church, equipped with the gifts of its Founder and faithfully guarding his precepts of charity, humility and self-sacrifice, receives the mission to proclaim and to spread among all peoples the Kingdom of Christ and of God and to be, on earth, the initial budding forth of that kingdom"[12]. So the Church serves and is the beginning of the kingdom. As regards lay people Vatican Council II states: "But the laity, by their very vocation, seek the kingdom of God by engaging in temporal affairs and by ordering them according to the plan of God. (...) They are called there by God that by exercising their proper function and led by the spirit of the Gospel they may work for the sanctification of the world from within as a leaven. In this way they may make Christ known to others, especially by the testimony of a life resplendent in faith, hope and charity. Therefore, since they are tightly bound up in all types of temporal affairs it is their special task to order and to throw

[7] *Magisterium.* Cfr. *Catechism of the Catholic Church*, nos. 2263-2267; 2302-2317.
[8] *Magisterium.* Cfr. *Catechism of the Catholic Church*, no. 782.
[9] *Bible.* Gospel of Matthew 16:18.
[10] *Bible.* Cfr. Gospel of John 21: 15-17.
[11] *Magisterium.* Cfr. Benedict XVI, *Jesus of Nazareth. Holy week: from the Entrance into Jerusalem to the Resurrection,* Part two, Ignatius Press, San Francisco 2011, pp. 100-101 (text no. 25 in Appendix).
[12] *Magisterium.* Vatican Council II, Dogmatic Constitution *Lumen Gentium* no. 5.

light upon these affairs in such a way that they may come into being and then continually increase according to Christ to the praise of the Creator and the Redeemer."[13].

"Consequently, even when preoccupied with temporal cares, the laity can and must perform a work of great value for the evangelization of the world. (...) still it remains for each one of them to cooperate in the external spread and the dynamic growth of the Kingdom of Christ in the world"[14]. This is a great task! It is not just a matter of praying but collaborating with him to accomplish what we ask for in prayer.

But what form does this task take for Christians, i.e. the task of building the kingdom of God and the city of men? This question is considered in the beautiful text *Gaudium et spes* which establishes some very important points: "Hence, while earthly progress must be carefully distinguished from the growth of Christ's kingdom, to the extent that the former can contribute to the better ordering of human society, it is of vital concern to the Kingdom of God. For after we have obeyed the Lord, and in His Spirit nurtured on earth the values of human dignity, brotherhood and freedom, and indeed all the good fruits of our nature and enterprise, we will find them again, but freed of stain, burnished and transfigured, when Christ hands over to the Father: 'a kingdom eternal and universal, a kingdom of truth and life, of holiness and grace, of justice, love and peace'. On this earth that Kingdom is already present in mystery. When the Lord returns it will be brought into full flower"[15].

We can therefore say that the kingdom of God is already present but not yet fully developed and manifest. Its manifestation will take place with the return of Jesus Christ on earth. But what Jesus recommends is to persevere in the living faith that knows how to wait for his return: "But when the Son of Man comes, will he find faith on earth?"[16]. It can help to remember that we are not alone and we are not working in vain: in heaven there is his kingdom which is prepared for us[17]. Jesus extends it on earth and does so through those who believe in him and love him.

## The kingdom and new education

What we really need to ask ourselves is this: have we really understood and borne witness to the news of the Father's kingdom, announced and brought to us by Jesus? To what extent have Christian

---

[13] *Magisterium*. Vatican Council II, Dogmatic Constitution *Lumen Gentium* no. 31.
[14] *Magisterium*. Vatican Council II, Dogmatic Constitution *Lumen Gentium* no. 35.
[15] *Magisterium*. Vatican Council II, Pastoral Constitution *Gaudium et spes* no. 39.
[16] *Bible*. Gospel of Luke 18:8.
[17] *Bible*. Cfr. Gospel of Matthew 25:34-36; Second Letter of Peter 3:13-14.

parents believed this news and handed it down to future generations? To what extent have we been faithful to the task of a truly Christian education in our schools? Pope Paul VI in the Declaration *Gravissimum educationis* (Declaration on Christian Education)[18] drew attention to this need in a time of secularization. What values are being taught to our young people? Spiritually and emotionally healthy parents are aware of the evils that affect the children and young people of today.

For many children and young people, 'transformed' into children of the 'technological age', the *virtual* can take on such importance as to become 'true' thereby replacing what is 'real'! In this way, the human spirit, having lost its roots through the virtual, no longer turns to God the Father, and leaves the field free for the spirit and fantasy of *omnipotence*. This has created and creates many misfits, 'phonily truthful' people, inauthentically spontaneous people, or respectable 'mad people'.

The 'virtual world' is not a defect of technology but could become – like all idols – a dangerous escape for the human mind, when detached from its true roots that are founded in God. How many people have realised that a true 'youth revolution' is in progress, as the young have been enabled to build 'their' world without the significant educational contribution of parents and adults? In the past, parents, grandparents, the school and church were left the role of educating the younger generations. This role has gradually 'passed' to the 'world', and today in particular to the 'virtual world', the one which children and young people find the most *fascinating and true*, the one that can be most easily constructed with their imagination without the need for God or adults. Technological and economic energies are 'sold' for this subtle silent revolution, driven by financial interests! While with the cultural revolution some of the roots of reality and truth have been forgotten and covered up, with the 'virtual' revolution categories of human thought concerning reality and truth are easily and completely ignored. This is having an impact on life and human relationships that as a result are being denigrated.

Benedict XVI recalled the importance of devoting all necessary energy for the great task of education that has nowadays become a true 'educational emergency'[19]. In his message "Educating young people in justice and peace" given on the occasion of the XLV World Day of Peace

---

[18] *Magisterium.* Cfr. Vatican Council II, Declaration *Gravissimum educationis* no. 8 (text no. 26 in Appendix).

[19] *Magisterium.* Cfr. Benedict XVI, *Letter to the Faithful of the Diocese and City of Rome on the Urgent Task of Educating Young People* (21 January 2008) (text no. 27 in Appendix).

he stated: "Education is the most interesting and difficult adventure in life. Educating – from the Latin *educere* – means leading young people to move beyond themselves and introducing them to reality, towards a fullness that leads to growth. (...) parents are the first educators. The family is the primary cell of society; 'it is in the family that children learn the human and Christian values which enable them to have a constructive and peaceful coexistence. It is in the family that they learn solidarity between the generations, respect for rules, forgiveness and how to welcome others'. The family is the first school in which we are trained in justice and peace. (...) Peace, however, is not merely a gift to be received: it is also a task to be undertaken. In order to be true peacemakers, we must educate ourselves in compassion, solidarity, working together, fraternity, in being active within the community and concerned to raise awareness about national and international issues and the importance of seeking adequate mechanisms for the redistribution of wealth, the promotion of growth, cooperation for development and conflict resolution. 'Blessed are the peacemakers, for they shall be called sons of God', as Jesus says in the Sermon on the Mount (Mt 5:9)"[20].

In this message the Pope also addresses the young: "Dear young people, you are a precious gift for society. (...) Do not be afraid to make a commitment, to face hard work and sacrifice, to choose the paths that demand fidelity and constancy, humility and dedication. Be confident in your youth and its profound desires for happiness, truth, beauty and genuine love! (...) Be aware of your potential; never become self-centred but work for a brighter future for all. You are never alone"[21].

The family is therefore the place of the gift, the place of gratuitous and free participation where love must grow in the humanity of the children. This educational and cultural commitment is of great relevance today for Christians and all people of good will. Saint John Paul II also stressed its importance and the urgency of the educational mission of parents[22]. Together with any necessary updating in the field of education, it is in prayer that we can draw on new wisdom and courage for the education and welfare of the young. However, recognition must be given to the great commitment of many parents who generously and joyfully carry out their difficult task of education. It is they who bear

---

[20] *Magisterium*. Benedict XVI, *Message for the Celebration of the XLV World Day of Peace* (8 December 2011) no. 5.

[21] *Magisterium*. Benedict XVI, *Message for the Celebration of the XLV World Day of Peace* (8 December 2011) no. 6.

[22] *Magisterium*. Cfr. John Paul II, Apostolic Exhortation *Familiaris consortio* (1981) nos. 36-41.

witness to courage and wisdom in preparing the younger generations to live in hope and be committed in the social sphere, too.

Today culture needs the truth and love of the Gospel and all our energy in the field of education to make known the beauty of the Gospel and Christian life. Let's recall the appeal made by Pope Emeritus Benedict XVI when he addressed the young on the occasion of the XX World Youth Day: "With Mary, say your own 'yes' to God, for He wishes to give himself to you. I repeat today what I said at the beginning of my Pontificate: 'If we let Christ into our lives, we lose nothing, nothing, absolutely nothing of what makes life free, beautiful and great. No! Only in this friendship are the doors of life opened wide. Only in this friendship is the great potential of human existence truly revealed. Only in this friendship do we experience beauty and liberation'. Be completely convinced of this: Christ takes from you nothing that is beautiful and great, but brings everything to perfection for the glory of God, the happiness of men and women, and the salvation of the world"[23]. This is what we ask God when we pray in the *Our Father*: "Thy Kingdom come". God is for life.

The people of God are the people of hope[24] and the people of life[25]. Saint John Paul II addressed the most urgent appeal to the people of life and for life: "To all the members of the Church, the people of life and for life, I make this most urgent appeal, that together we may offer this world of ours new signs of hope, and work to ensure that justice and solidarity will increase and that a new culture of human life will be affirmed, for the building of an authentic civilization of truth and love"[26].

**Functions of State and Church**

What is the scope of action in society for the faithful who are also citizens of a State?

At this point a distinction certainly needs to be made and we must be well aware of the respective roles of State and Church. "The Church, by reason of her role and competence, is not identified in any way with the political community nor bound to any political system. She is at once a sign and a safeguard of the transcendent character of the human

---

[23] *Magisterium.* Benedict XVI, *Address at Papal Welcoming Ceremony on the Poller Rheinwiesen bank in Cologne on the occasion of XX World Youth Day* (18 August 2005).
[24] *Magisterium.* Cfr. Benedict XVI, *Message for the XXIV World Youth Day* (22 February 2009) (cited text is reported in Conclusion).
[25] *Magisterium.* Cfr. John Paul II, Encyclical Letter *Evangelium vitae* (1995) no. 77; no. 101 (text no. 28 in Appendix).
[26] *Magisterium.* John Paul II, Encyclical Letter *Evangelium vitae* (1995) no. 6.

person. The Church and the political community in their own fields are autonomous and independent from each other. Yet both, under different titles, are devoted to the personal and social vocation of the same men. The more that both foster sounder cooperation between themselves with due consideration for the circumstances of time and place, the more effective will their service be exercised for the good of all. For man's horizons are not limited only to the temporal order; while living in the context of human history, he preserves intact his eternal vocation"[27].

There is a rightful distinction between Church and State and other forms of civil communities: an independence between them but not a separation as some would like. It is a matter of spheres which, though necessarily distinct and independent, are always related because they concern man. Autonomy is achieved while respecting the fundamental rights of the whole man.

Modern Western States, originating in the most part from the French Revolution and the Enlightenment, have frequently preserved democracy through a deformed laicity of politics and the secularization of society, but have done so without considering the dimension of the human spirit, transcendence and religion. Indeed, they have pursued a kind of breakup and divorce between the social man and the inner man, between the social nature understood as objective and the private nature understood as subjective, keeping them separate and unrelated. The deleterious consequences of such a schism are there for all to see in today's so-called modern countries. In order to foster a just and modern independence of roles and powers there was no need to perpetuate a doctrine of break up and separation. Such an approach belongs more to a past marked by misunderstandings and fears than to a maturation of history in this third millennium where, in many fields, independence can be experienced not in separation but in interrelationship.

However, a further observation is necessary to bring about the healthy development of social forces in the field. To humanize the world it is not possible to wait for the proper relationship between politics and economics, between State and market to come about. In the more or less conflictual dialectics existing between the labour model and the liberal model, the third model, the corporatist one, should be allowed to emerge. This concerns the relationship among individuals able to humanize resources, with the family, the basic cell of society, as its fundamental reality. Unfortunately, nowadays the family is instead fought over as an object to be exploited both by political and market forces. The positive reality of the family as a proactive subject still needs

---

[27] *Magisterium.* Vatican Council II, Pastoral Constitution *Gaudium et spes* no. 76.

to gain awareness of its social role together with other corporatist realities, i.e., Associations, Movements, Groups, Communities. This means considering the family and family Associations as social entities with which other political forces and the market must confront. Indeed, society, which is made up of people, needs to live *its tridimensionality.*

As long as this third model is not included in the dialogue, it will be impossible to achieve a healthy balance of forces capable of building a better and more just world. In order for politics and economics to be truly at the service of man, their operators must learn to listen to and respect the 'human'. It is the value and stature of this 'human', precious in the eyes of God, that the Church aims to love, serve and defend.

## To Caesar what is Caesar's and to God...

Some, far from the Church, have fallen into the trap of a clear-cut separation, as they have ill-interpreted the words of Jesus: "Then repay to Caesar what belongs to Caesar and to God what belongs to God"[28]. Certainly, Jesus did not intend a clear-cut separation. Indeed, in another passage from the Gospel, replying to Pilate on his question concerning political power, He states: "You would have no power over me if it had not been given to you from above"[29]. The government authorities to which Pilate lays claim – Jesus tells him – come to him not from Caesar but ultimately from 'above': there is therefore a relationship between earth and heaven and heaven and earth, between the social and the religious component. We must not allow ourselves to be misled by those who, using the Gospel, wish to completely separate the two dimensions, i.e. the human and the divine, to then make the earth another kingdom... Therefore, the truth envisages the distinction and reciprocal independence and autonomy but not the separation between the social reality of the State and the religious reality of the Church as if they were two distant non-communicating worlds. Indeed, a State that supports laicity in opposition to religion cannot be considered neutral or even democratic. It is then that the just 'laicity' of the State is transformed into profane 'laicism' and a just autonomy into an unjust one.

The function of the State is to foster and develop the *common good in justice*, whereas the function of the Church is to contribute to the search for the truth through the revelation and pursuit of *true good* and *true justice.* The Church offers us this highly important background of revelation and in-depth knowledge of the truth: of true good and true

---

[28] *Bible.* Gospel of Matthew 22:21.
[29] *Bible.* Gospel of John 19:11.

justice. Benedict XVI in his Encyclical Letter *Deus caritas est* (God is love) emphasises in a truly illuminating manner the difference between the functions of the State and Church: "The two spheres are distinct, yet always interrelated. (...) The Church cannot and must not take upon herself the political battle to bring about the most just society possible. She cannot and must not replace the State. Yet at the same time she cannot and must not remain on the sidelines in the fight for justice. She has to play her part through rational argument and she has to reawaken the spiritual energy without which justice, which always demands sacrifice, cannot prevail and prosper. A just society must be the achievement of politics, not of the Church. Yet the promotion of justice through efforts to bring about openness of mind and will to the demands of the common good is something which concerns the Church deeply"[30].

So, on one hand the Church cooperates in the work of nurturing and expanding the kingdom of God on earth, and on the other, by calling the faithful to true values, she helps to build and sustain the true good of the city of men, doing her utmost for the good and best of everyone. Unfortunately, some prejudices slow down the service that the Church offers society[31]. In serving God, the great support that the Church offers man and society is that of communicating the divine life and at the same time contributing towards the humanisation of life and human relationships[32].

The *Social Doctrine of the Church*[33] is the collection of teachings in the light of the Gospel for the edification of society in the service of the good, true and right progress of the city of men. This is invaluable in order to embody the Gospel in the changing history of man. It is truly important to realise how much and in what manner the Lord, through the Church, wants to build the kingdom of God, spreading it on earth and among nations, through the participation of all men, offering the meaning, power, and light of the Gospel message with complete freedom of conscience, also to the city of men, in the search for progress and development. Conversely, throughout history, isolation or individualism, and the pride or arrogance of 'having no

---

[30] *Magisterium.* Benedict XVI, Encyclical Letter *Deus caritas est* (2005) no. 28. Cfr. Vatican Council II, Pastoral Constitution *Gaudium et spes* no. 36.

[31] *Magisterium.* Cfr. Benedict XVI, *Homily at Holy Mass on the occasion of the Compostelian Jubilee Year, Plaza del Obradoiro, Santiago de Compostela.* Apostolic Journey to Santiago de Compostela and Barcelona (6 November 2010) (text no. 29 in Appendix).

[32] *Magisterium.* Cfr. Vatican Council II, Pastoral Constitution *Gaudium et spes* no. 40 (text no. 30 in Appendix).

[33] *Magisterium.* Cfr. Pontifical Council for Justice and Peace, *Compendium of the Social Doctrine of the Church* (2004).

need for God' have often shown the weakness of a limited functional vision that betrays true human progress and the longing for happiness of human beings.

## A joint task

Significantly, Benedict XVI, in the Encyclical Letter *Caritas in veritate*, reminded the world that "the *earthly city* is promoted not merely by relationships of rights and duties, but to an even greater and more fundamental extent by relationships of gratuitousness, mercy and communion. Charity always manifests God's love in human relationships as well, it gives theological and salvific value to all commitment for justice in the world"[34]. Without these relationships it is impossible and illusory to build a world with a human dimension.

In this regard the Encyclical again states: "In the course of history, it was often maintained that the creation of institutions was sufficient to guarantee the fulfilment of humanity's right to development. Unfortunately, too much confidence was placed in those institutions, as if they were able to deliver the desired objective automatically. (...) Moreover, such development requires a transcendent vision of the person, it needs God: without him, development is either denied, or entrusted exclusively to man, who falls into the trap of thinking he can bring about his own salvation, and ends up promoting a dehumanized form of development. Only through an encounter with God are we able to see in the other something more than just another creature, to recognize the divine image in the other, thus truly coming to discover him or her and to mature in a love that 'becomes concern and care for the other'"[35].

What wealth of humanity! This is what it means to introduce the charity and wisdom of the Gospel into the social structure and environment. The Gospel criss-crosses an enormity of problems and decisions, joys and sorrows, hopes and struggles, aspirations and struggles in the world. Ultimately, peace is maintained among men in love, truth, and justice: this is why there is a need for God's love. As Benedict XVI recalls in his book, *Jesus of Nazareth* "only the man who is reconciled with God and with himself can establish peace around him and throughout the world"[36].

---

[34] *Magisterium* Benedict XVI, Encyclical Letter *Caritas in veritate* (2009) no. 6.

[35] *Magisterium*. Benedict XVI, Encyclical Letter *Caritas in veritate* (2009) no. 11.

[36] *Magisterium*. Benedict XVI, *Jesus of Nazareth*, Doubleday, New York 2007, p. 85 (text no. 31 in Appendix).

## Manifestations of the kingdom

In building the kingdom *attention to the weakest*[37] is a priority concern and the most heartfelt one, being the most threatened: the conceived but yet unborn are the weakest and most defenceless, followed by those who have been marginalised in life, namely the elderly living under the fear of suppression – euthanasia being proposed as a free right, when it is nothing short of suppression and self-destruction. A modern, secular society is said to involve the exercise of these new rights over the life of the conceived and to one's own voluntary death, whose legitimacy is supported by invoking human values such as, for example, the dignity of the woman, the right for every man or woman to live a normal and comfortable life, and 'freedom of conscience'. This, however, hides the underlying deceit, namely the creation of a way of thinking which is against man and against humanity, a sort of love for a 'mad culture'. Indeed, the consequences of the great social and economic pressure created by these so-called 'social rights' are overlooked. There is a kind of 'cultural' manipulation and dictatorship, a grip which first takes hold of many people's consciences, causing them to fall dormant, and then proceeds to increasingly direct their choices in social and health structures, creating a less human world; one that is not as free and not as beautiful. Unbeknown to millions of people, choices in economics, politics and law 'passed' as *useful and democratic* are often allied. Whereas, what is really useful and democratic is the struggle for a greater human empowerment of consciences and for information capable of opposing the subtle deceit of 'mammon'.

The work of evangelization which the Church carries out today is becoming increasingly vast since it takes on the entire dimension of human and social life. In this way, the Gospel is also being spread through the Gospel of life[38]. Justice, peace and development are constituent elements of the announcement that the Church makes: proclamation of the same is not tantamount to taking direct political action, but to entering the social conscience of citizens, politicians, technicians and economists, and the consciousness of nations, thereby creating world awareness. One only has to think of the serious and yet unresolved problems afflicting the lives of millions of people, such as hunger and famine in poorer countries, drug-trafficking wars, the exploitation of women and children, and terrorism.

---

[37] *Magisterium*. Cfr. Benedict XVI, Encyclical Letter *Caritas in veritate* (2009) no. 15 (text no. 32 in Appendix).
[38] *Magisterium*. Cfr. John Paul II, Encyclical Letter *Evangelium vitae* (1995) no. 6.

## Opening up to the Transcendence

To overcome these evils and work for the good there must not be only the political will but also an awakening of the human conscience, and good will together with the power of the Holy Spirit and faith. Pope Paul VI in his famous *Speech to the United Nations* made during his Apostolic Journey in 1965 showed great foresight when he urged: "this edifice which you are constructing does not rest upon merely material and earthly foundations, for if so, it would be a house built upon sand; it rests above all on our own consciences. The hour has indeed struck for 'conversion', for personal transformation, for interior renewal. We must get used to thinking of man in a new way; and of men's life in common in a new way; in a new way, too, of the paths of history and the destiny of the world, in accordance with the words of Saint Paul, 'to put on the new man, which has been created according to God in justice and holiness of truth' (Ephesians 4:23). The hour has come for a halt, a moment of contemplation, of reflection, almost of prayer; a moment to think anew of our common origin, our history, our common destiny. Today, as never before, in an era marked by such human progress, there is need for an appeal to the moral conscience of man. (...) In a word, then, the edifice of modern civilization must be built upon spiritual principles; the only principles capable not only of supporting it but also of enlightening and animating it. And these indispensable principles of superior wisdom must be founded this, as you know, is our belief upon faith in God"[39].

The Church, as Jesus desires, is at the service of the kingdom of God, in truth, freedom and love to serve the whole man and every man. Pope Emeritus Benedict XVI in the Encyclical Letter *Caritas in veritate* reaffirmed the centrality of this truth and our commitment to achieving it: "Precisely because God gives a resounding 'yes' to man, man cannot fail to open himself to the divine vocation to pursue his own development. The truth of development consists in its completeness: if it does not involve the whole man and every man, it is not true development. This is the central message of *Populorum Progressio*, valid for today and for all time. Integral human development on the natural plane, as a response to a vocation from God the Creator, demands self-fulfilment in a 'transcendent humanism' which gives [to man] his greatest possible perfection: this is the highest goal of personal development"[40]. There

---

[39] *Magisterium*. Paul VI, *Pope Paul's Address to United Nations General Assembly* (4 October 1965) (http://www.christusrex.org/www1/pope/UN-1965.html, accessed in July 2014).
[40] *Magisterium*. Benedict XVI, Encyclical Letter *Caritas in veritate* (2009) no. 18.

is therefore affirmed the need for the *development* of the whole man, not just his intelligence, body, or sentiments but also his spirit: unless the *whole man* is considered there is no true development and it is not true service and love for humanity! It is precisely this vision that has characterised and inspired countless acts of selfless and heroic altruism on the part of men and women of the Church and missionaries who have given themselves entirely for the good of humanity. Countries and cultures would do well not to forget this so as to draw on new energies.

If progress is not for *everyone*, for each and every individual person and the whole person, then it is only for the selfish benefit of someone who, in the end, will turn out to be a tyrant! True development with its need of truth and charity cannot be solely entrusted to technological evolution, the production of wealth, or the application of human ingenuity. An integral development 'of the whole man' requires something else, namely openness to the transcendent, i.e. to God.

Religious indifference and government systems can stifle and weaken this spiritual wealth which is a gift for society[41]. Indeed, atheism is against the authentic development of people and peoples. There are also those who, through the mass media, organise and push for religious indifference among minors! And this is not all. When economic or cultural assets are exported, very often a reductive form of man, of his spiritual dimension and destiny is also exported. What is hidden is that which founds man in the dignity of his human person and in his link to God the Father.

**Love for truth and life**

For this, a new commitment on the part of Christians is needed in the world of work, politics, culture and education. We must understand, love and want the kingdom to come: not just wait for it but prepare for it with our Christian contribution, the contribution of everyone. Together with proactive action based on the Gospel, the Church must also warn against the temptation to listen to 'new messiahs'. From the so-called *false messianisms*, that deceive many people's expectations and invade culture and the market, we must keep our distance. It is these messianisms that today are presented with deceptive 'charm' even to the very young.

Also the world of economics and finance pushes towards creating new needs and expectations along with promises to satisfy them, often working on the sensations, emotions and expectations of young people,

---

[41] *Magisterium*. Cfr. Benedict XVI, Encyclical Letter *Caritas in veritate* (2009) no. 29 (text no. 33 in Appendix).

children and adolescents, kindling false mirages. Today, this increasingly concerns hedonistic type mechanisms[42], fuelled by the idol of money. The great *monster* of finance, markets and the world economy is now revealing the extent of its profound flimsiness.

In contrast, the kingdom of God that we ask for in the prayer of the *Our Father* is the kingdom of love and respect for every reality because God is Father. This is what distinguishes the kingdom of God from the work of 'mammon'. Nonetheless there are those who fight against the Christian faith and the values of the Gospel[43]. Indeed there are those who are giving a helping hand to 'Herod'[44] in building his kingdom! 'Herod', goes round canvassing, so to speak, in search of votes. Nowadays, he too has had to adapt to the times and disguise himself... Today there is democracy and it is necessary to respect the rules, at least as long as people are watching! The various rotating 'Herods' also take their turn at playing and sitting at the table of rules; they benefit from the rules but nonetheless they are always 'Herod'. Each of them seeks goodwill and political votes. Votes for their own 'kingdom', giving rights that do not exist and we know cannot exist, and using lies and injustice to create peace. When we build society we must therefore be careful that rights and obligations are just, i.e. true and good, and do not contradict the 'truth' of life. We must remain lucid and ensure that the human dimension does not solely consist of relationships based on respect and justice but also on gratuitousness, mercifulness and communion.

Today, we must also beware of the ways of thinking which are loaded with a veneer of spirituality and appear as valid truths for everyone, like that of the *New Age*. Its interpretation of life and the world with its contribution of yoga techniques is proliferating in many ways, creeping into culture and passing unnoticed by many people: reference is made to a spiritual dimension which is actually vague and superficial but fills all worldly realities, whereby God seems to be everywhere. In this way nostalgia for God and the 'distance' from him appear to be filled. And yet, it is to be noted that in the New Age vision, no mention is made of the kingdom, a leader, the Lord, or a saviour. The figure of Jesus Christ is reinterpreted and radically distorted. The existence of a spiritual world is accepted but without the existence of God; God the Creator and Father. Even when reference is made to God as father and every reality is assigned to him including that of man, in actual fact everything is

---

[42] *Magisterium*. Cfr. Benedict XVI, Encyclical Letter *Caritas in veritate* (2009) no. 17 (text no. 34 in Appendix).
[43] *Bible*. Cfr. Second Letter to the Thessalonians 3:1-2.
[44] *Bible*. Cfr. Gospel of Matthew 2:1-23.

conceived of as a reflection, a spiritual 'emanation' of God, so that He ceases to be Creator.

Let us distrust spiritual surrogates that seem harmless but instead, upon close examination, are fundamentally atheist or spiritually wrong![45] The proliferation of alternative ideologies, sects and gurus reflects the confusion in the spiritual ambit as well as the unanswered needs of the human spirit. In the light of failure to stifle Christianity through materialism on one hand and spiritualism on the other, attempts are made to transform it by distorting it completely. In the Encyclical *Spe salvi*, Benedict XVI makes an interesting observation on Kant's *The End of All Things*[46] concerning the kingdom of God and the case that one day Christianity may no longer be loved. But since God was made man on earth, his reply to man that seeks him has become certain: man calls with faith and love and God replies. In this way, as Jesus points out to us in the *Our Father*, his kingdom manifests itself.

How much and how great is that which Jesus has entrusted us! How much the world needs Christianity, Christians, and Christ in our midst! Christianity is the true gift, the most magnificent, precious and extraordinary gift of God the Father for humanity. Let's not leave the various 'Herods' free, let's not make way to the dominance of 'mammon', thinking it is sufficient to believe in God. Jesus has taught us to ask the Father that 'his kingdom' may come, and to build it with him in humility and truth. First and foremost it is the 'kingdom of truth': we must love the truth. Who is it that falls and is lost? He who does not love the truth. Who is it that supports the various 'Herods' throughout history? He who does not love the truth. Whoever loves the truth loves God and every man, and whoever loves God loves his kingdom since it is the kingdom of love and justice, and is the kingdom for us. Jesus reminds us of this in the Gospel: "Come, you who are blessed by my Father. Inherit the kingdom prepared for you from the foundation of the world"[47].

Good is diffusive. When one truly has God within him, in his inner life, people notice: good does good around itself, and as the Gospel tells us, "the light shines in the darkness"[48]. The Christian must not live as if he had an inferiority complex. A living faith is called love, it is called service to the world, it is called truth that frees and comforts. The world needs this so as not to progressively fall into the hand of alienation and

---

[45] *Magisterium*. Cfr. Pontifical Council for Culture, *Jesus Christ the Bearer of the Water of Life. A Christian reflection on the "New Age"* (2003).
[46] *Magisterium*. Cfr. Benedict XVI, Encyclical Letter *Spe salvi* (2007) no. 19; no. 23 (texts nos. 35 and 36 in Appendix).
[47] *Bible*. Gospel of Matthew 25:34.
[48] *Bible*. Gospel of John 1:5.

evil. Praying the *Our Father* has taught us both to cultivate this love for our neighbour, so that this world grows in the direction of the kingdom of God, and to ask for the wisdom of God the Father for families, and for the true development of society and the whole of humanity.

## At the centre of social development

Today, what is the central propeller for authentic social development? Is it perhaps development in communications and economic well-being, economic and technological power, understood by the world as 'mammon'? No. It is life itself, considered in its intrinsic meaning and value. Everything that is built is of no use if it is then lost and destroys human life! The heart and core of human life lies precisely in the family. In the Encyclical letter *Caritas in veritate*, Benedict XVI particularly emphasized this fact: *"Openness to life is at the centre of true development.* When a society moves towards the denial or suppression of life, it ends up no longer finding the necessary motivation and energy to strive for man's true good. If personal and social sensitivity towards the acceptance of a new life is lost, then other forms of acceptance that are valuable for society also wither away. The acceptance of life strengthens moral fibre and makes people capable of mutual help. By cultivating openness to life, wealthy peoples can better understand the needs of poor ones, they can avoid employing huge economic and intellectual resources to satisfy the selfish desires of their own citizens, and instead, they can promote virtuous action within the perspective of production that is morally sound and marked by solidarity, respecting the fundamental right to life of every people and every individual"[49].

Going against life means going against true human development! Against the true development of the world: not just of a country, city or nation but of the world, that indivisible unit of all humanity. One cannot stand back and remain idle. A new moral conscience is needed. This also concerns the problem of *ecology* since nature and life are interconnected in the responsibility entrusted to man by God the Creator. The prayer of the *Our Father* has us ask God the Father that his kingdom comes, this we must work for with the respect that creation deserves[50], as it is the work of the Father donated to us.

The world advances with its discoveries and conquests, but needs light and love; the world itself needs to find its identity also in globalisation. This is why humanity needs to see its future, at least to

---

[49] *Magisterium.* Benedict XVI, Encyclical Letter *Caritas in veritate* (2009) no. 28.
[50] *Magisterium.* Cfr. Benedict XVI, Encyclical Letter *Caritas in veritate* (2009) no. 51 (text no. 37 in Appendix).

glimpse the sense of it: it needs God, truth, hope and clarity, but it also needs to join forces in dialogue with everyone. Christians must stay in the forefront of research, not behind, they must not passively accept it but seek to understand it and propose solutions, pointing out the road forward for true humanity and true development. This is the extraordinary task of Christians and the whole of the Church in working together for the development of civilisations[51].

It is also for this that a *reasoned faith* is needed that is of help to the world. A faith that has not been reasoned and fails to have an impact on life would display a chasm between faith and life. In the eyes of some people a symptom of such a schism could be a serious personal conflict, while for others a scandal. However, it could also be the symptom of a serious illness which needs courage to be faced, overcoming that separation between thought and reality similar to a form of 'schizophrenia'.

## There are crosses and crosses

In building the kingdom special attention should also be paid to human suffering. Our human reality is deeply marked by much suffering. The greatest consolation for those who suffer is to know that it will end. The Christian, like the good Samaritan, is particularly close, through charity, to those who suffer[52], and it is true that every sufferance and every pain finds its sense and value in Christ as they are united in the redemption of Christ, and God himself "will wipe away all tears from their eyes"[53]. God is on the side of our tears. Christian faith is and will always be of help and comfort to the sick and the suffering, also in understanding the will of God with regard to every cross He asks us to carry compared to another one that He does not give us. In fact, as Jesus reminds us in the Gospel, it is necessary to take up *one's own cross*[54]. Knowing how to recognise it is not easy.

However, it so happened that when the aids and means of medicine became means of relief and cure, able to combat sickness as God allows us and asks us to do, many then put God aside. I believe that it is here that part of the secularisation process began. Every suffering having been conquered and overcome through scientific progress and the help of God, we have forgotten the 'Christian' suffering of those that suffer

---

[51] *Magisterium.* Cfr. Benedict XVI, Encyclical Letter *Caritas in veritate* (2009) no. 74 (text no. 38 in Appendix).
[52] *Bible.* Cfr. Gospel of Luke 10:33.
[53] *Bible.* Book of Revelation 7:17; cfr. Letter to the Colossians 1:24.
[54] *Bible.* Cfr. Book of Mark 8:34.

because they are *faithful* to Jesus Christ and follow him on his Cross. Not all suffering is equal. "For it is better to suffer for doing good, if that be the will of God, than for doing evil"[55].

Suffering *for the kingdom of God* is a kind of suffering that is not to be fled from, but embraced, since it stems from faithfulness to the love of God, for God, and for one's neighbour. It does not come about by reason of the limits of nature from which everyone wishes to escape. Certainly, we also experience these limits and infirmities[56] with love and faith, giving witness to 'the comfort' of faith as God is "for us"[57]. It is the love of the Lord that consoles and gives strength, as Saint Paul recalls in the Letter to the Romans: "What will separate us from the love of Christ? Will anguish, or distress, or persecution, or famine, or nakedness, or peril, or the sword? (...) No, in all these things we conquer overwhelmingly through him who loved us. For I am convinced that neither death, nor life, nor angels, nor principalities, nor present things, nor future things, nor powers, nor height, nor depth, nor any other creature will be able to separate us from the love of God in Christ Jesus our Lord."[58].

The certainty of his love sustains man in all the ups and downs of life, even the most difficult and painful, since God is faithful to his promises and remains close to those who belong to him, as Saint John Chrysostom says: "Numerous are the waves, and great the tossing of the sea, but we have no fear of going down, for we stand upon the rock. Let the ocean rage as it will, it is powerless to break the rock. Let the waves roll, they cannot sink the bark of Jesus. Tell me, what should we fear? Death? *To me to live is Christ and to die gain.* Is it exile perchance? *The earth is the Lord's, and the fullness of it.* Is it confiscation of property? We brought nothing with us into the world, and it is clear that we can take nothing away with us. I despise what the world fears, and hold its good things in derision. I do not fear poverty, nor do I desire riches. I am not afraid of death; I do not pray to live, if it be not for your good. This is why I speak of what is now taking place, and exhort your charity to be of good cheer"[59].

[55] *Bible*. First Letter of Peter 3:17.
[56] *Bible*. Cfr. Second Letter to the Corinthians 12:9-10.
[57] *Bible*. Cfr. First Letter of Peter 2:21.
[58] *Bible*. Letter to the Romans 8:35, 37-39.
[59] *Tradition*. Saint John Chrysostom (349-407), *Homily by Saint John Chrysostom before he went into exile* (http://www.todayscatholicworld.com/homily-chrysostom.htm, accessed in July 2014).

Indeed, the very attachment to earthly power and goods is truly ridiculous, and as Saint Francis reminds us: "For people lose everything they leave behind in this world"[60].

## God's love is more powerful

What does God's love do for us? According to Holy Scripture: "We know that all things work for good for those who love God, who are called according to his purpose. For those he foreknew he also predestined to be conformed to the image of his Son, so that he might be the firstborn among many brothers. And those he predestined he also called; and those he called he also justified; and those he justified he also glorified."[61].

With the extraordinary gift that God gives to him, the Christian already lives 'in the glory' of God: he already lives in beatitude and peace. He experiences so much of the 'love' of God that he also wants to be 'for God', for his kingdom and for his will, with the love and in the love of Jesus Christ, and embraces with a sense of responsibility also the suffering that follows, going so far as loving his enemies. "But to you who hear I say, love your enemies, do good to those who hate you, bless those who curse you, pray for those who mistreat you."[62]. Here we must remember the many religious and Christian lay men and women, i.e. martyrs and saints who have given witness to their great love for God by going so far as giving up their own lives.

Christianity is the most serious fact that exists: "We did not follow cleverly devised myths when we made known to you the power and coming of our Lord Jesus Christ, but we had been eyewitnesses of his majesty"[63]. A *martyr* is the witness of Christ, it is he who, for faith and love, bears witness to Christ with the gift of his own life, his death being inflicted by others and never by himself. The martyr by undergoing death, offers his life to God to bear witness to him, giving it with love for others; a martyr is never one who takes his own life and that of others, like those who blow themselves up to bear witness to their own idea or belief. The latter give death, not life, through voluntarily sacrificing their own life and taking it from others against their will. Contrary to what is sometimes said, such a person cannot be called a martyr. Therefore,

---

[60] *Tradition*. St. Francis of Assisi (1182 ca.-1226), *St Francis' Letter to all the Faithful (2nd Version)* (http://totus2us.com/vocation/saints/st-francis-of-assisi, accessed in July 2014).
[61] *Bible*. Letter to the Romans 8:28-30.
[62] *Bible*. Gospel of Luke 6:27-28.
[63] *Bible*. Second Letter of Peter 1:16.

the martyr is not a person who sacrifices his own life for an ideal, but someone who bears witness to Someone else, even at the cost of undergoing death for this. The Christian martyr is also capable, with the help of God, to give life to those who bring about his death. He believes in the living God that is Love capable of renewing life after death[64].

To work for the kingdom of God, that Jesus has us ask for in the *Our Father*, it is necessary to return to God, to the God of truth and joy, security and salvation: it is necessary to 'convert'. *Conversion* is effectively a turning back and basically fulfilling *three passages:* from the lie to the truth; from theft to honesty, restoring to God what is his and to men their dignity; from the death of self and of others to eternal life. The description of the conversion of Zacchaeus in the Gospel is symbolic[65].

The conversion process is gradual as is the accompanying capacity to build good in society for the kingdom of God. At first God is sought for 'our good', to feel well; it is the first conversion whereby God is recognised as God and Jesus as the Saviour of man.

Growing in the relationship with him and 'knowing' his love, the Christian opens up with trust and makes himself available to serve God with all his heart and with all his life, 'to live for him': this is the second conversion when God bursts in with his beauty and goodness dragging the whole man to the communion of love with him and in confident trust. We can think of many saints and of how the kingdom of God and the social good for an infinite number of persons have grown around them! There are countless examples of saints, men and women, young people and adults who have shown through their lives that God is the only true good and the root of our humanity.

I can cite for example a passage from the letters of Saint Maximilian Kolbe, who offered himself to save the life of the father of a family at Auschwitz concentration camp: "It is sad for us to see in our own time that indifferentism in its many forms is spreading like an epidemic not only among the laity but also among religious. But God is worthy of glory beyond measure, and therefore it is of absolute and supreme importance to seek that glory with all the power of our feeble resources. Since we are mere creatures we can never return to him all that is his due. The most resplendent manifestation of God's glory is the salvation of souls, whom Christ redeemed by shedding his blood. To work for the salvation and sanctification of as many souls as possible, therefore, is the preeminent purpose of the apostolic life. Let me, then, say a few words that may show the way toward achieving God's glory

---

[64] *Bible*. Cfr. Letter to the Hebrews 11:17-19.
[65] *Bible*. Cfr. Gospel of Luke 19:1-10.

and the sanctification of many souls. (...) God alone is infinitely wise, holy, merciful, our Lord, creator, and Father; he is beginning and end, wisdom and power and love; he is all. Everything other than God has value to the degree that it is referred to him, the maker of all and our own redeemer, the final end of all things. It is he who, declaring his adorable will to us through his representatives on earth, draws us to himself and whose plan is to draw others to himself through us and to join us all to himself in an ever deepening love. (...)

Let us love our loving Father with all our hearts. Let our obedience increase that love, above all when it requires us to surrender our own will. Jesus Christ crucified is our sublime guide toward growth in God's love.

We will learn this lesson more quickly through the Immaculate Virgin, whom God has made the dispenser of his mercy.

It is beyond all doubt that Mary's will represents to us the will of God himself. By dedicating ourselves to her we become in her hands instruments of God's mercy even as she was such an instrument in God's hands" [66].

Truly, there is a hidden heroic *sanctity* that only God sees, also in the lives of many lay men and women who work in the world, spouses and parents, children and young people, elderly and sick. It is always the love of God that calls and knocks on the human heart[67] for a free and total response. There are bishops and priests, deacons, consecrated people and sisters who with undwindling love dedicate their holy lives to God and for the good of humanity. We can think of countless men and women of good will, also of other religions, that spread good around them to build a better world.

But where does one start to build the kingdom of God and a 'true humanity' a gift for everyone? Who to listen to? The voices are many, confused and conflicting... In the *Our Father* Jesus points out to us what to do; so that we may not lose our bearings, Jesus has given as a compass. This, we shall see in the next chapter.

---

[66] *Tradition*. St. Maximillian Kolbe (1894-1941), *From a letter of Maximilian Mary Kolbe, Liturgy of the Hours, Office of Readings for the Feast of St. Maximilian Kolbe* (http://www.liturgies.net/saints/kolbe/readings.htm, accessed in July 2014).
[67] *Tradition*. Cfr. St. Therese of Lisieux (1873-1897), *History of a Soul: The Authobiography of St. Thérèse of Lisieux with Additional Writings and Sayings of St Thérèse* (http:// www.catholicbible101.com/St.%20Therese%20Story%20of%20a%20soul. pdf, accessed in July 2014. Text no. 39 in Appendix).

# 7

# Thy will be done

## *Your will be done*

In the *Our Father* Jesus not only teaches us to pray that God's kingdom comes but also goes on to teach a very important request which shows the link between man and the divine.

How can the kingdom of God be built? How can the kingdom of God be brought about, a kingdom that is not of this world but is present and unique and is not to be confused with 'Herod's' or other human kingdoms? Where to begin? In answer to this, Jesus includes an essential phrase which is very close to his heart: "Your will be done", i.e. the will of the Father. This is found at the centre, at the most profound point, let's say at the *'heart'* of the *Our Father*. Jesus reminds us: "Not everyone who says to me, 'Lord, Lord,' will enter the kingdom of heaven, but only the one who does the will of my Father in heaven"[1]. The *Commentary on the 'Our Father'* by Saint Francis of Assisi[2] is most significant.

And it is precisely the understanding of this 'will' that develops the relationship with God, in which not only the game of life of individuals is played but also, as we shall soon see, that of the history of the world.

Also in the commitment to build the city of men, how is the kingdom built? Where is the kingdom of God affirmed? We'll discover in these extraordinary words that we have been given a condition that is both beautiful and essential.

Why is it that Jesus has to point *this road* out to us to build the kingdom of God the Father? Why is it that our will fails to take the road to the kingdom? God has created his image in man and woman in

---

[1] *Bible.* Gospel of Matthew 7:21.
[2] *Tradition.* Cfr. St. Francis of Assisi (1182 ca.-1226), *The Writings of Saint Francis of Assisi. Translated from the Critical Latin Edition*, edited by Fr. Kajetan Esser, O.F.M., Franciscan Archive, 2000 (http://www.franciscan-archive.org/patriarcha/opera/preces.html, accessed in July 2014. Text no. 40 in Appendix).

goodness and in the freedom of love, so why is it so difficult to follow the will of God? What has happened?

## No myth

God shows this to us in the Bible, in the third chapter of the Book of Genesis. Here an essential aspect is highlighted: the meeting between Satan and the consequent covering up of God's image, a contamination that has marked the human heart, mind and body. Here, there is shown the first dramatic impact with evil which marks a turning point in history.

God has chosen to reveal this in the Bible, which is an inspired book; we must take him seriously! To start with, the first eleven chapters of Genesis are written in a unique linguistic style, which we should not mistake as an untruthful, arbitrary or mythical language, i.e. one that does not communicate anything to our scientific mentality. Instead, we have before us eleven inspired chapters, as are the other books of the Bible, written in an aetiological language that underscores the value of our relationship with God.

The image of the serpent is clearly a figurative allusion, a symbol. Above all, the serpent makes no noise and keeps itself well-hidden. This is why it is difficult to discover Satan as he conceals his work and is sly. Jesus defines him as "the father of lies"[3], the one that generates lies and deception. Secondly, the image of the snake has a double meaning; it can be used to refer to both the male and the female, also in the psychoanalytic sense: in a certain way it represents ambiguity and variability. This does not mean that original sin is of a sexual nature, as if the sexual dimension represents evil as opposed to the divine reality which is spiritual. On the contrary, as we shall see, the evil of original sin, which is spiritual, has entered the image of God inherent in sexuality, diverting it from its proper order.

In fact, the image of the snake was already present in the language at that time. Evidently, God wants to tell us something that is fundamental in the impact between the human being, man and women, and this being, the Evil One, Satan, the tempter that is able to undermine personal balance, not only within the couple but also on a social level.

In the biblical text, Satan turns first to the woman as it is she who is capable of generating life. By blocking or 'disturbing' Eve, he consequently disturbs and, thus, marks all future generations. The evil of the snake that bites and injects 'poison' helps us in understanding this dramatic impact.

---

[3] *Bible*. Gospel of John 8:44.

Eve is perfect, created by God from man, with the same personal dignity, having within her a feminine image of God[4]. How does Satan enter into dialogue with her and draw her to evil? By using a highly important key word: *truth*, something that the subculture conceals because it fears it. Satan uses this word to enter into a relationship but then hides and contradicts it.

The first question that Satan asks Eve is: "Did God really say, 'You shall not eat from any of the trees in the garden'?"[5]. Satan makes use of the opening up of Eve's soul to the truth. Eve, created in the image and likeness of God, believes and lives in the full 'truth'. Pilate will say to Jesus: "What is truth?"[6]: the corrupt world hides the truth and as soon as it catches sight of it, ignores it, tramples on it or *manipulates it for its own purposes* as it 'does not love the truth'.

At first, Evil does not appear to be so negative or ugly as to cause fear, but is disguised; to reach out to man and woman, their families and their children, it uses 'tools' which are, so to say, 'normal', and images that correspond to apparent good. Yet, in this good, it injects the 'poison' to distort and pervert them; this is Satan's technique.

Satan, *the deceiver*, first appears as one who is close to the truth, but then cleverly introduces the lie: "Did God really say, 'You shall not eat from any of the trees in the garden'?"[7].

Before this falsehood how does Eve reply? She is amazing! She does not reply: "It's not true," as we would expect. In fact, if it were a myth, Eve would have replied with an essential and circumscribed phrase: "yes" or "no, it is not like that". Eve, however, does not respond in this way. Eve responds in an extraordinary manner, which would never occur to anyone. It is a unique text of its kind, totally different from all the other ancient texts and even more so from the world of myths. This shows that it is an inspired text: here also non-believers may discover and see a gift, a sign that comes from God. The Bible has not only been written by men, with their human intelligence, but also under the special guidance of the Holy Spirit, the Spirit of Truth.

As we were saying a unique text: indeed, Eve does not know the lie – we do. Therefore, Eve does not say, "no, you are saying something that is not true". Eve repeats exactly what God has said, she is so united with God, her whole self is so completely in the truth – her way of living being according to God – that she answers exactly in the way that God has told her, and repeats only the Word of God. Falsehood has not yet

---

[4] *Bible.* Cfr. Book of Genesis 1:26-27.
[5] *Bible.* Book of Genesis 3:1.
[6] *Bible.* Gospel of John 18:38.
[7] *Bible.* Book of Genesis 3:1.

entered her: "The woman answered the snake: We may eat of the fruit of the trees in the garden; it is only about the fruit of the tree in the middle of the garden that God said, 'You shall not eat it or even touch it, or else you will die.'"[8]. Eve answers perfectly. However, it is here that Satan intervenes and reveals what he is: the *perverter*. We can see in the biblical message how Satan injects his mendacious 'poison': heavy words that God wants us to understand so as to open ourselves up to the need for salvation.

It is here that the potent 'poison' of the lie is about to enter: Satan tells her: "You certainly will not die!"[9]; in other words saying that the Word of God 'is not true at all!'. Satan, the father of the lie, inverts the truth and the life, perverting them, and claims that the Word of God is untrue so as to put himself in God's place, as the bearer of truth and freedom! Eve begins to vacillate. Everything about her, as in Adam, has been made in the most profound truth, in the image of God, in love. The lie begins to enter her, to enter the image of God, to contaminate her and to produce its effects. Eve, listening passively, becomes weak and confused.

Eve then receives the second injection of 'poison' and the drama of what is about to happen is obvious. The Evil One adds: "God knows well that when you eat of it your eyes will be opened and you will be like gods, who know good and evil"[10]. The devil speaks ill of God, attributing God with deceit and envy, perverting the image of the true face of God in the woman's heart! In this way, Satan seeks to put himself in God's place to take possession of creation. It is here that the deceived Eve begins to decide to rebel against God and commit the *original sin*. "The woman saw that the tree was good for food and pleasing to the eyes, and the tree was desirable for gaining wisdom. So she took some of its fruit and ate it; and she also gave some to her husband, who was with her, and he ate it"[11].

Some still subscribe to this deception of Satan – who is very sly – thinking that by 'knowing good and evil' it is possible to be 'like God'; thus foolishly identifying knowledge, which is a great power, with God himself. This is just a short step away from viewing God as the human projection of the full power of knowledge, and from believing that, with science and culture, God is no longer needed! However, it is here that two basic realities are overlooked.

---

[8] *Bible*. Book of Genesis 3:2-3.
[9] *Bible*. Book of Genesis 3:4.
[10] *Bible*. Book of Genesis 3:5.
[11] *Bible*. Book of Genesis 3:6.

The first is that it is not possible 'to be like God' since God is the One and Only.

The second is that 'knowing or experiencing good and evil' is a human characteristic since man 'finds' good and evil as a fact and interprets it. Indeed, the satanic phrase 'knowing good and evil' at verses 4 and 5 referring to the *fruits* – here the deception and the lie – deliberately omits the word *tree* which instead is present in the Word of God: "the tree of the knowledge of good and evil"[12]. 'The tree' implies the roots which are in God and therefore cannot be identified with knowledge, i.e., with the fruits that are the knowledge of good and evil. The truth of the 'tree' cleverly hidden from Eve by Satan expresses the sovereignty of the One and Only God, the source not only of Life but also of Truth and Goodness.

## The consequences we do not want to see

It must be understood that this 'poison', as the distortion of truth and aversion to God, is in contradiction with the human being 'created in the image of God'. It penetrates the body, mind, brain, and sexuality. It makes itself manifest and is transmitted from generation to generation.

It affects the nervous system, the autonomic nervous system, it affects the way we function: original sin is not only consumed in human nature, but is also transmitted through it; in this way it is handed down through the generations. Lies and rebellion have penetrated man and the idea of God is no longer whole and intact: the truth given to us in the light becomes camouflaged and seeks darkness. As a result of the satanic lie, the will which was directed to good, truth, love, life and justice rebels against God and brings about the isolation of the human being, who then seeks refuge in a happiness which does not exist, leading to the death of himself, his brothers and the destruction of the world.

For this reason man will die and lose the kingdom and life even though he is made in the image and likeness of God. Indeed, everything becomes deformed: love becomes selfish; without trust in God the future becomes a source of anguish; intelligence without the light becomes confused, uncertain or arrogant; fear and madness make their appearance, and eventually man is seen fleeing from God: "When they heard the sound of the LORD God walking about in the garden at the breezy time of the day, the man and his wife hid themselves from the LORD God among the trees of the garden"[13].

---

[12] *Bible*. Book of Genesis 2:9.
[13] *Bible*. Book of Genesis 3:8.

The perversion that distorts our relationship with God distorts the relationship between man and woman and consequently between people. In them the divine image is covered by the lie that has been accepted as 'truth'! They cover themselves, wary now of the truth, love and good will: "Then the eyes of both of them were opened, and they knew that they were naked; so they sewed fig leaves together and made loincloths for themselves"[14]. Human life, distancing itself from the glory of God who is Father, becomes a search for human glory that threatens all, going so far as the crime of Cain who kills the just Abel, his own brother[15]. In this way man is capable of death and self-destruction.

Therefore, the will of humans is infected by falsehood and rebellion against God and a lack of fraternal love, becoming instead one of indifference and hatred. Original sin was the sin against God who is Love. Satan has deceived love and reduced it to a false convenience.

We have here the beginnings of 'mammon'. God wants us to return to him who is Father, He who is the Highest Good of Love, our Homeland and our future. Precisely because God is Love, and his kingdom, heaven, is love there is only one way back: the way of love, namely that our will freely returns to him in love. Love accords with freedom, but love also implies, at least within certain limits, a dependence which love itself freely dictates.

Modern humanity wants love but does not want to be tied and dependent because it is afraid of losing its freedom, and fears having to depend on something or someone. This is why freedom today is emptying itself of love to the point of becoming a freedom without meaning and without anyone. After sin, freedom and love are divided in the human heart: so sometimes we may think that those who want freedom cannot love, because they are afraid of dependency, and those who want to love fear the freedom of the beloved who might flee away... A return to God is needed in order that freedom and love might meet in the heart of man and woman, so that they return to each other.

## The work of Jesus

This is why the kingdom of God, before imposing itself through power, comes in truth, freedom and love. To this end, Jesus, the Son of God, by coming on earth, brings the truth to our confused minds and speaks well of God; He speaks of God's love and shows us all the Good that God has prepared for each one of us and for humanity. When you hear God spoken ill of that is sin, original sin that permeates history, and

---

[14] *Bible*. Book of Genesis 3:7.
[15] *Bible*. Cfr. Book of Genesis 4:1ff.

walks alongside us. Hence, we need to experience again the positivity and goodness of God to go back to the truth of God and to believe in his love for us.

This is why Jesus brings the truth of God's love and shows us how we function, the truth of how we exist; he teaches us again, through his love and the work of his grace, to put to rights that which Satan has put and wants awry, perverse, without the meaning that God has given it in creation.

Jesus is the 'Saviour', the sole Saviour of each and every man and woman and all men, as Pope Benedict XVI reminded us in his Christmas message to the city and the world: "Come to save us! This is the cry raised by men and women in every age, who sense that by themselves they cannot prevail over difficulties and dangers. They need to put their hands in a greater and stronger hand, a hand which reaches out to them from on high. Dear brothers and sisters, this hand is Christ, born in Bethlehem of the Virgin Mary. He is the hand that God extends to humanity, to draw us out of the mire of sin and to set us firmly on rock, the secure rock of his Truth and his Love (cf. *Ps* 40:2). (...) He was sent by God the Father to save us above all from the evil deeply rooted in man and in history: the evil of separation from God, the prideful presumption of being self-sufficient, of trying to compete with God and to take his place, to decide what is good and evil, to be the master of life and death (cf. *Gen* 3:1-7). This is the great evil, the great sin, from which we human beings cannot save ourselves unless we rely on God's help, unless we cry out to him: *"Veni ad salvandum nos!"* – Come to save us!"[16].

The first reality that we have to change in order to return to God is our will, which has been tainted by the satanic lie and rebellion against God. Jesus takes us by the hand into the truth and urges us to pray: "Thy will be done", the will of God. He teaches us to return, with love and trust, to the will of God the Father, and thereby to his kingdom. We had never felt this within us in such a way: only Jesus is able to indicate to us how to go back, with love and trust, to the will of God the Father, He who is in intimate relationship with the Father, He who is the 'face' of the Father, He who on earth comes to do the Father's work, to do everything with love for the Father. Jesus teaches us to trust him as 'Abba, Father' and urges us to ask with love in the prayer: "Thy will be done". We had lost the will of God and with this we had also lost the love and communion with him, the kingdom and eternal life. To enter the kingdom, to participate in the life of the kingdom of God, there is no alternative but to renew our love for the will of the Father. And that's all. It is a word, a relationship, and it is the only wisdom and the only

---

[16] *Magisterium.* Benedict XVI, *Urbi et Orbi Message.* Christmas 2011.

salvation for each and every individual and for the whole of humanity, the only 'gift of ours' that we can give to God.

God created man 'in his own image, male and female' because it is in sexuality that the gift and mystery, the transparency and manifestation of God's love in human love should shine forth. Human sexuality – i.e. the mysterious place from which life is born, where baby boys and girls are born and hence the future of humanity – is, according to God's plan, the place where the image of God is to be found, and not the place of the flight from God! Life has been deformed by sin: after sin, humans and the world need to be purified, and it is no longer possible to love as before, because humans and the world have become ambiguous like the heart of man and woman. In fact, human life, in affectivity as in sexuality, seduced by worldly priorities and secularization, has lost much of the presence of the spirit and hence the transparency that the image of God brings within it and that God has entrusted to us. As Saint John the Apostle tells us in his first letter: "Do not love the world or the things of the world. If anyone loves the world, the love of the Father is not in him. For all that is in the world, sensual lust, enticement for the eyes, and a pretentious life, is not from the Father but is from the world. Yet the world and its enticement are passing away. But whoever does the will of God remains forever"[17].

Our will, the mind, the heart, the human body are disorientated since they are 'infected' by evil. Our will and our deepest energies must *focus anew*. This is accomplished by Jesus through the truth, his love and the grace of the Holy Spirit. It is then that the will of God the Father becomes our will and our will becomes that of the Father, i.e. peace of the heart and entrance into the kingdom of God. To do this Jesus brings us the Truth, the fundamental truth that we have lost. The world, on the contrary, stops at the pluralism of many partial truths, which, though perhaps useful, are more akin to opinions. In fact, *reduced man* can only have 'opinions', with their confused sum total providing the wealth of knowledge.

*Enriching pluralism* made up of positions, ideas and free member-ship, and completely disconnected from any search for the roots of absolute truth, is another trick of our time, a way to downgrade any 'truth' and thereby any authority. Indeed, such pluralism, not based on the search for 'truth', becomes the soul of individualism and division among men. In the end, through relativism it leaves space solely for 'mammon' and material interests that unite individuals in their needs. On the other hand, to bring about unity, it is equally not possible to assert a 'fanatic' dogmatism of the truth, the soul of authoritarianism,

---

[17] *Bible*. First Letter of John 2:15-17.

which is ultimately imposed as an ideological dictatorship. Pluralism is a great value, if combined with a love for the truth and the good of man.

Both positions, the one that is relativistic and, in the end, individualistic, and the other that is despotic and authoritarian, are light years away from Christianity and the faith of the Church, since neither represent goodness for people or society. The faith of the Catholic Church is not something ideological, i.e. dependent on an *a priori* doctrine. Moreover the term 'catholic', which *per se* means 'universal', is synonymous with truth, seriousness and generous commitment for the good of the world.

In solely pursuing scientific truth and in thinking thus to protect its freedom, the 'secular' world finds itself trapped in the ideology of the moment, under the pressure of economic plans, particularly those of 'mammon'. Today, for instance, it is fashionable to consider anything useful as good, and anything that is not instant and useful as bad.

Jesus tells us: "I am the way and the truth and the life. No one comes to the Father except through me"[18].

"But when the Son of Man comes, will he find faith on earth?"[19]. Jesus refers to his faith, the faith He has brought on the earth, the faith 'of God'. He does not refer to the 'natural faith' of men, to that aspiration with which we can turn to God who is on high and gives us a hand to deal with the difficulties and fears of life. We must not despise this 'human' faith but at the same time we cannot hide the faith 'of God' as revealed in Jesus Christ.

Science gives us a new sense of security; this too is a gift from God. But the faith 'of God' is superior to science. The common factor is the human spirit, without which there would be no aspiration on the part of man and no search for God. Without the presence in man of his spirit, the spiritual soul, there would not be the ability to do science with intelligence and freedom of thought, neither would there be the ability to meet God and welcome him in freedom and love.

Tolerance, love for mankind, for all men, and the ability to share resources and human talent for good, all stem from the common dimension of the human spirit where 'the image of God' resides. This is the way of peace. Saint John Paul II reminds us that "To seek and teach the truth effectively is indeed a great mission (...) You are called to place the great patrimony of truth at the service of man. Truth itself becomes the service of love and unity. In the acceptance of the truth there open up possibilities of love. (...) Each discipline has of course its autonomy,

---

[18] *Bible*. Gospel of John 14:6.
[19] *Bible*. Gospel of Luke 18:8.

but all disciplines converge towards the good of man in accordance with the truth of his nature"[20].

It is not by 'reducing' the truth and increasingly aligning the meaning of 'truth' with that of 'opinion' that peace is brought about. On the contrary it is by finding together, with respect for all, the truth of what we are, starting from what constitutes us. *Opinionism* is a false road, which alienates men and does not prepare the way for peace and justice nor for love among human beings. The search for spiritual truth builds unity, respect and human solidarity. *Opinionism* humiliates the human being because thought is only needed to the extent it serves a purpose. So in the end, economic action and power appear to be more useful, and this is the path of 'mammon'. So by putting aside the search for truth recommended by Jesus: "the truth will set you free"[21], the door has been opened to power with a view to establishing other types of tyranny, such as that of the 'useful'. These range from those in the economic and political fields to those of a pseudo-spiritual or spiritualistic nature.

Freedom of thought must get to the truth, otherwise man cannot build anything, and freedom will prove to be useless. Since the mystery hangs over us, the real truth is always humble. Mystery is our home, but only the truth enables us to dwell in it. That is why we need the revelation of life. The human being needs not only to develop his life, but also the revelation about the truth of his life.

Unlike animals we do not need just a biological life, we also need the profound revelation so as to understand what it is of life that makes us human. What will our future be? Who are we? Why do we live on earth? And then, why is there death? How is it overcome? We ask so many questions because we have the kingdom within us. It was for this that Jesus came; He came to give us the answer, because we are made for and aspire to the kingdom. Jesus has opened the doors of heaven to us, but already here on earth He comes to us so that we do not die deceived or lost.

On countless occasions, I have seen the intuition of the kingdom of love and the mystery of life transpire in the love between man and woman; it is something they feel. But I have also seen them fall back upon themselves, fall back into the ego and become lost. Jesus Christ is needed, alone we are unable to 'live well' in the mystery of who we are.

---

[20] *Magisterium*. John Paul II, *Address to the Representatives of All Australian Institutions of Higher Learning, Sydney* (26 November 1986).
[21] *Bible*. Gospel of John 8:32.

Jesus has opened the kingdom so that we may not only enter it but also dwell there: "Remain in my love"[22], He tells us. Without Jesus Christ we would remain outside. Jesus comes to meet each of us to direct us to the will of the Father, to return 'inside' the communion with him and to full Life. God gives us the truth, but we must offer our will to God so that it may increasingly conform in truth and freedom to his. This is crucial! By doing the will of God, our lives are filled with joy and meaning. This is the most to which every man and woman can truly aspire, since it is only with God that we can seriously build, as Jesus says in the Gospel: " Whoever is not with me is against me, and whoever does not gather with me scatters"[23]. As Pope Benedict XVI reminded us in his message delivered in various languages to over two million young people at the XXVI World Youth Day in Madrid, the Church constantly points out the search and love for the will of God, which alone can fill the human heart and our human history[24].

The kingdom of God is built with God's will and our will, with ours and his. First, it is built in the soul of the person, the image and likeness of God, and then in the couple, the family and society.

We need to ask ourselves why is it so difficult for the human will to choose God's will? Why isn't it instantly easy to do it? Why is the human being so attracted by evil, by wrong, and deviation with the result that everything is perverted? Why is it that the mystifier, the Evil One plays around with human passions? Why does the will choose evil? How is all this possible if we come from God?

By the power of the human spirit that moves away from God, it is possible to choose and do evil, hating the light of truth and rejecting the love of God. This is the 'sin' and the tragedy of humanity.

Indeed, as John tells us in the third chapter of his Gospel, Jesus speaks of this to Nicodemus. Here Jesus speaks of the heart of God and the heart of the world: He compares the two, showing how they are different and where sin comes from. "For God", says Jesus "so loved the world that he gave his only Son, so that everyone who believes in him might not perish but might have eternal life"[25]. This is *the heart of God:* God loves the world so much that He gives, notice the expression, 'gives' his Only Son, his heart, his life, his kingdom.

---

[22] *Bible*. Gospel of John 15:9.

[23] *Bible*. Gospel of Matthew 12:30.

[24] *Magisterium*. Cfr. Benedict XVI, *Angelus at Cuatro Vientos Airport*. Apostolic Journey to Madrid on occasion of XXVI World Youth Day (21 August 2011) (text no. 41 in Appendix).

[25] *Bible*. Gospel of John 3:16.

Now what then is the *heart of man*? "And this is the verdict, that the light came into the world, but people preferred darkness to light, because their works were evil. For everyone who does wicked things hates the light and does not come toward the light, so that his works might not be exposed"[26]. In other words, so that what he has stolen is not taken away. It is in fact a theft: instead of acknowledging the truth, the love of God and his kingdom, and, in love, participating in what belongs to God as He has offered us, the spiritual power of man and woman strives to take everything of this life for themselves.

In this dynamic, people love darkness more than light, "because their works were evil"[27]. What works are these? They are the works by which they seize things for themselves rather than discovering them as 'gifts' received from God, as his and entrusted to us.

Evil makes us use the good things that are of God as if they were 'ours', taking possession of them to bring about 'the principality' rather than the kingdom of God. Human will is contaminated by Satanic lies and rebellion against God in such a way that, whether realising it or not, it appropriates what is God's by theft. Man does not even care and is totally disinterested about this as his heart is elsewhere: he only considers himself and his love for himself! And he does not even want this theft to be discovered. A bad momentary deception. "For everyone who does wicked things hates the light and does not come toward the light, so that his works might not be exposed. But whoever lives the truth comes to the light, so that his works may be clearly seen as done in God"[28]. Indeed, he who does the truth does the works of God, fulfils the works that are his, and is happy that these are shown because they are 'done in God': this is true, and he 'does' the truth and builds the kingdom of God and not his 'own'.

**The two systems**

No doubt there are different ways to live this conflict. Jesus in the parable of the "prodigal son"[29], also known as the "merciful father", gives the example of the relationship between a father and two sons. In the two brothers we can recognise the different reaction of Jews and Gentiles to the good news brought by Jesus. However, I deem it appropriate to consider this parable in the light of our social reality *vis-à-vis* the kingdom.

---

[26] *Bible* Gospel of John 3:19-20.
[27] *Bible*. Gospel of John 3:19.
[28] *Bible*. Gospel of John 3:20-21.
[29] *Bible*. Cfr. Gospel of Luke 15:11-32.

In this parable, Jesus tells of two sons: the first is close to the father, it seems he understands his father, but in reality he does not care about anything, he does not understand his father's heart, and when the father welcomes the youngest son who has repented and come back, he does not even want to enter the house, despite the loving invitation of the Father towards him. So, this is a son who seems to believe in the father who, in this parable, represents God. He seems to be obedient and do the will of the Father, but in reality, despite being close to the Father, has learnt nothing of the heart of God the Father. He is closed within himself, in his privileges and rights that closeness to the Father has given him.

In his Father's house he uses the properties of the Father ('religious practices'). He uses the Father's house, but deep down he only thinks of himself and his rights, and is only too ready to take offense. He aims to fulfil himself, and when the Father does something extraordinary following his own heart, he does not understand him and rebels, remaining outside his heart and house!

Therefore, it is possible to be close to God, believe in God, subscribe to religion and go to Church, but in an *extraneous* way, not according to the heart of God. One may desire the freedom of the Church and also the work of the Church, the work of God, but without living according to the heart of God. This is a warning to us all. It is possible to administer the Father's holy things but without his heart[30]!

The other son, the younger one, says to the Father: "Father, give me the share of your estate that should come to me"[31]. He talks blatantly about his own rights, offending the father perhaps without realising it. The father divides the inheritance between the two sons and he, taking 'his', leaves, slamming the door behind him... He is not interested in the will of his father, he is not in the least interested in his father, he is only interested in his own rights and freedom. He claims the goods of his father, wanting to enjoy them in freedom but without the Father whom he has abandoned. What he thinks is his actually belongs to his Father, but he considers it to be his by right! He squanders it all with prostitutes, and throws away his life, having pursued his rights to the brink of death. "And he longed to eat his fill of the pods on which the swine fed, but nobody gave him any. Coming to his senses he thought, (...) 'I shall get up and go to my father'"[32]. It is only then that he decides to return to the Father expressing his repentance.

---

[30] *Bible*. Cfr. Gospel of Luke 13:25.
[31] *Bible*. Gospel of Luke 15:12.
[32] *Bible*. Gospel of Luke 15:16-18.

On reflection, the two sons represent, both in a wrong way, two different attitudes that remind us of *capitalism* and *liberalism* on one hand, and *Marxism* and *communism* on the other. The first son seeks security, demanding it from God; the other wants freedom and adventure in life, demanding it far from God. Neither of the two sons live according to the will of the father; neither the eldest who remains close to the Father, formally but without loving him, nor the youngest who goes 'to live' far away from the Father without recognising and without loving him. Neither children understand and love the Father. He will come out for both children to meet them. In essence, the two sons represent two horizontal systems that throughout history collide, oppose, run after and overlap each other. It must be said that many aspects of these two systems as represented by the two brothers, when put together, have historically given shape to *laicism*, that comes from the term 'lay' but implies a degeneration. In addition, there is *atheism* that does battle by denying the vertical relationship with God, and basically leaves an empty place for someone else to fill... In these solely human and horizontal systems what is really sought is that which seems to be 'ours'.

## What is 'ours'

Jesus Christ reveals that 'ours' is only that which is 'for God', and therefore much more. Jesus shows us the Cross, uniting within it the horizontal and vertical dimension, the reality of man and the reality of God. Jesus restores, thus, *the rights of God*. Even God has his rights. We can remember how Jesus cast the merchants out of the temple saying to them: "It is written, 'My house shall be a house of prayer, but you have made it a den of thieves.'"[33]. In fact, it is a theft, perpetrated both by those who can stay close, seeking comfort and adapting themselves, and by those that contest and leave, going far away. At the basis of the various systems, when God is missing, there is always selfishness disguised as well-being and altruism.

The only truly alternative way is to enter the will of the Father and understand that all realities are his: his is love, his is happiness, his is the life of human beings, his is intelligence, and his is science, as too is the ability for progress. His is the world, and we are part of it since we are in the kingdom of truth, freedom and love. In this way, Jesus brings back the will of the Father to us on earth and brings us back on track 'to that which is for God' because only this is 'truly ours' and no one can

---

[33] *Bible*. Gospel of Luke 19:46.

take it from us. It is then that we can find ourselves in God as brothers, and build a more just world for everyone. This is why Jesus tells us to first seek the kingdom of God and his justice, and promises us that the other things we need "will be given (...) besides"[34]. The sooner we recognise the rights of God the sooner we recognise ours: a universal brotherhood, but one centred on God, on the relationship with God the Father in Jesus.

Only 'what is for God' is truly ours and for all of us. What is truly 'ours' is that which belongs to the Father because we are his children. The rest is theft, deceptive and momentary! And what are the rights of God? These are worth repeating. The rights of God are those of truth, freedom and love. And only by entering the will of God do they belong, as a gift, also to us.

This is what Jesus taught us on earth, and He wants us to teach children to look to the Father: "Thy kingdom come and Thy will be done". For the kingdom of God can only come in this way, i.e. by finding the will of the Father and adapting ourselves to it every day in freedom and love for our good, the good of the family and the good of all mankind. This is what the *Our Father* teaches us.

Only by loving God's will do we find God as Father: to love God is to love his will. Sometimes we hear people say regretfully: "It is the will of God!". Thank goodness we do the will of God! What's better than his? Loving the kingdom of God means loving his will. Loving our religious life, our family life, our work, and our social development is to love his will. Loving humanity so that it becomes one family of God's children, means loving his will. We love the will of the Father: "Thy will be done" as we pray in the *Our Father*. What sweetness, depth, and beauty! Only light and love in the freedom and truth of our hearts and our work as children of God for the true good of everyone.

But why has Jesus added "on earth as it is in heaven"? Would it not be sufficient to say, "Thy will be done"? Jesus has left us another essential phrase for our lives that we need to understand well. Many are those people, as history has sadly shown us, who, either to silence their own consciousness or to bend those of others, are tempted to refer to 'God's will'. Indeed, we need this further clarification that we must not ignore, and which we will see in the next chapter.

[34] *Bible*. Gospel of Luke 12:31.

117

# 8

# On earth as it is in heaven (I)
## *On earth as in heaven*

We have seen that the third petition in the *Our Father* not only is to be found half-way through this prayer but it also constitutes its very *'heart'*, since it is in rediscovering our love for the will of God the Father that we find the signs of his presence, and together we can develop his kingdom as well as our ability to build it. This changes our life and alters the construction of society.

So why does Jesus add a further phrase in the *Our Father:* "on earth as it is in heaven"? Isn't it enough to say "Thy will be done"? Doesn't this phrase cover everything? Let's start off with considering this interesting question.

Perhaps we have sometimes heard it said: "What can we do? Let God's will be done!". If we think about it, this is a very superficial way of looking at things. If even parents bear such bad witness to their love for the will of God, how will their children do God's will with lucidity and love? How can you seek, understand, and love the will of God if you despise it? It cannot be dealt with like this. What idea of God the Father would a non-believer or a member of another religion have? Is it then true that the will of God is always the one we suffer or in any case not the one we would freely do? Let's take a closer look at this aspect.

**How to know it?**

A fundamental theme that runs through the entire Bible is precisely the search for the will of God, and how to recognise and understand it.

The assumption, as Holy Scripture tells us, is that we have a soul, the human spirit, the divine image with which we can enter into communion with God.

It seems useful to recall some considerations offered by Pope Emeritus Benedict XVI on the possibility of understanding the logic of

God, his plan and his will. When commenting on the prayer of the *Our Father* in *Jesus of Nazareth*, he writes: "The essence of heaven is oneness with God's will, the oneness of will and truth. (...) we pray that it may be on earth as it is in heaven – that heart may become 'heaven'. (...) man has knowledge of God's will in his inmost heart, that anchored deeply within us there is a participation in God's knowing, which we call conscience. (...) this participation in the Creator's knowledge, which he gave us in the context of our creation 'according to his likeness', became buried in the course of history. It can never be completely extinguished, but it has been covered over in many ways (...). Because our being comes from God, we are able, despite all of the defilement that holds us back, to set out on the way to God's will"[1]. The first way to know the will of God is precisely the sanctuary of the *conscience.*

With the gift of the spiritual soul, the image with which God has created the human being, each one of us can 'set out on the path' to God, certain that he will be able to understand him since He wants to be known, certain that he will be able to understand what God asks of him because God is our Father. The second way to get to know the will of God is to listen to and meditate his Word, the *Bible.*

Along with consciousness and the gift of the Holy Scriptures, the third way of knowing the will of God the Father is *Jesus* himself, his Son. He tells his disciples that bring him food, "My food is to do the will of the one who sent me and to finish his work"[2]. The being of Jesus is being at one with the will of the Father[3]. This is the secret of the life of Jesus. "See; I come with an inscribed scroll written upon me. I delight to do your will"[4]. So God definitely wants us to know his will for our salvation and that of the world.

But what does "on earth as it is in heaven" mean? It does not mean 'in any way'. Jesus does not want the will of the Father to be done in any way or by force, as it would not be 'his will' which is ever a loving gift. He is not a despot; indeed his kingdom is the kingdom of truth, freedom and love. God absolutely does not want us just to do his will. In actual fact, the Word of God reminds us: "Each must do as already determined, without sadness or compulsion, for God loves a cheerful giver"[5].

God knows how to answer our heart and our generosity: as my mother used to say, "God is never outdone in generosity". God wants

---

[1] *Magisterium.* Benedict XVI, *Jesus of Nazareth*, Doubleday, New York 2007, pp. 147-149.
[2] *Bible.* Gospel of John 4:34.
[3] *Bible.* Cfr. Gospel of John 10:30.
[4] *Bible.* Book of Psalms 40:7-8.
[5] *Bible.* Second Letter to the Corinthians 9:7.

us to do his will "as in heaven". We note here that there is an *'as'* that we absolutely cannot ignore or remove from the Gospel: it is the 'as of God'. That 'as' tells us the heart of God, tells us 'as' He wants us to do his will. Only in this way, by doing the will of God day by day, can we build the family of the children of God and therefore his kingdom. This is the way; there is no other way.

Even if we believe in God, how can we accept the will of God according to his heart when the 'as' is not really what we want, for example the illness of a child or the death of a loved one? On earth the 'as' closes: evil, suffering and the various situations in life are 'as' we live them, trying to overcome them yet coming up against all our limitations. We need to ask ourselves: "How is God near us in our situations and how is He in communion with our suffering?". Certainly, we cannot think that God wants our suffering, that we have to endure it, and that's all there is to it! There is the 'as of God'; it is an 'as' that resolves, an 'as' that, while recognising sins, evil, suffering and death, sees everything as surmountable and as surmounted in the victory of Good that Jesus has shown us in the Resurrection. This "as in heaven" opens up to another way of life, the way of the children of God. Jesus gives it to us in the *Our Father*, so that we do not stop at the 'as' on earth, often loaded with injustice and evil. This is why Christians, with critical awareness, contribute so that history proceeds well, and things are done well, according to the heart of God "on earth as it is in heaven".

## Scandals

There are, however, also 'unfavourable winds', many 'unfavourable winds', and people often find themselves adrift and confused. Many, though baptized, give rise to scandal for their lack of adherence to the will of God, or even for a way of life at odds with that advocated in the Gospel. On the one hand, this fact fills us with sorrow, and on the other it prompts us to pray both for those affected and those who are the serious cause.

When scandals occur with all the ensuing uproar, hearts are hardened and turn away from the truth, and so evil acts. The *enemy*, as Jesus warns us[6], first causes us to fall into sin, and then makes use of the evil produced, including that of scandals. This is why Jesus warned 'everyone' not to make use of them because they are a tool of evil. "He said to his disciples, 'Things that cause sin will inevitably occur, but woe to the person through whom they occur. It would be better for him if a

---

[6] *Bible.* Cfr. Gospel of Matthew 13:36-43.

120

millstone were put around his neck and he be thrown into the sea than for him to cause one of these little ones to sin. Be on your guard!'"[7]. Even those who divulge scandal are the mouthpiece of evil. Thus, not always do those who make evil public distance others from evil! The 'breadth of evil', in fact, is the effect produced by 'scandal' that extends evil in the world, and can be confusing for the weak and young causing them to fall into error. This is the sowing that the devil does and which Jesus speaks of in the Gospel. It needs to be asked: are those who divulge scandals truly opposed to evil or do they seek its diffusion? Do those who expose evil and make it generally known want to say that everything is bad? This is one of the disguises of satanic work. When evil is spoken about, this does not always mean it is being fought against or indeed that good is being sought. Underneath there might be the instigation for further evil, destruction and hatred, a kind of explosive fuse. The Word of God recalls that those who "sow the wind, (...) will reap the whirlwind"[8].

Certainly information and the right to information through the mass media are very important: they are achievements of the modern democratic world. However, the power of the media has a great responsibility for the effect of good or evil that it can operate. In his Message for the XLII World Day of Social Communications, Benedict XVI stressed the importance of truth and responsibility on the part of the producers of information[9], all the more necessary given the increased power of the media: "When communication loses its ethical underpinning and eludes society's control, it ends up no longer taking into account the centrality and inviolable dignity of the human person. As a result it risks exercising a negative influence on people's consciences and choices and definitively conditioning their freedom and their very lives. (...) The media must avoid becoming spokesmen for economic materialism and ethical relativism, true scourges of our time"[10].

Through frequenting evil and the works of the Evil One many people become *malignant* themselves smearing everything and everyone. Conversely, Jesus reminds us to always put forward the good: "Do not be conquered by evil but conquer evil with good"[11]. Evil intrigues, but it is the good that builds: "Finally, brothers, whatever is true, whatever is honorable, whatever is just, whatever is pure, whatever is lovely, whatever

---

[7] *Bible*. Gospel of Luke 17:1-3.

[8] *Bible*. Book of the Prophet Hosea 8:7.

[9] *Magisterium*. Cfr. Benedict XVI, *Message for XLII World Communications Day* (24 January 2008) (text no. 42 in Appendix).

[10] *Magisterium*. Benedict XVI, *Message for XLII World Communications Day* (24 January 2008).

[11] *Bible*. Letter to the Romans 12:21.

is gracious, if there is any excellence and if there is anything worthy of praise, think about these things"[12]. In fact, throughout the Bible, God who is our Father never stops when faced with evil, however terrible, but always goes beyond, teaching us to take a look at his good that wins.

Isn't it perhaps so that the man of today, having lost sight of God, no longer knows where to gather the hopeful signs of good, and just denounces the evil that threatens him? This is why much news about crime invades the world of information in a way that is totally out of proportion to good news, thus burdening the hearts of so many people! Many have evil within them and throw it out through bitter and violent reports in the erroneous belief they will thereby become better people and make others better too. Conversely, this only increases the evil that perhaps they would like to fight.

However, the more the Church is struck by evil the more it recognises its humanity, even in its children that err, and through the presence and help of the Lord is made capable of purification so as to better serve God and man. Thus renewed by the light and grace of the Lord Jesus Christ it is better able to reflect his light.

On the occasion of the Jubilee in 2000, in his Apostolic Letter *Tertio millennio adveniente*, John Paul II expressed the needs of the whole Church to "purify themselves, through repentance, of past errors and instances of infidelity, inconsistency, and slowness to act"[13]. He repeated his regret for the painful memories that mark the history of divisions among Christians, as already expressed by Paul VI and Vatican Council II, and on 12 March 2000, on behalf of all Christendom made a *request for forgiveness*[14] for the many historical events in which the Church or individual groups of Christians had been implicated in various capacities. Under persecution the Church strengthens and grows ever closer to the Lord that, purifying it, enriches it with gifts. The problem is for those who are 'less mature in their faith' and those who are 'weaker by reason of their defects' because evil blocks them even more! In these cases, the charity of everyone is needed to help each one; here there is needed the love that Jesus recommended to us in order to overcome evil and the 'unfavourable winds' that go against the construction of a new humanity.

Many are content to be Christians in a superficial way –modified to suit their convenience and give them comfort – without delving into the

---

[12] *Bible*. Letter to the Philippians 4:8.

[13] *Magisterium*. John Paul II, Apostolic Letter *Tertio millennio adveniente* (1994) no. 33 (text no. 43 in Appendix).

[14] *Magisterium*. Cfr. John Paul II, *Universal Prayer with Confession of sins and request for forgiveness during Eucharistic Celebration for the First Sunday of Lent, Day of Pardon* (12 March 2000) (text no. 44 in Appendix).

'as' of being a Christian according to the will of God. There is an 'as' of God that Jesus revealed to us, that is done 'as' in heaven, where it is the delight of all. God does not lack trust in us, considering us too little and incapable. God is Father and wants us to live well as responsible adults. He does not want weak and fragile people. He sees us as precious. "On earth as it is in heaven" expresses the way in which we can be well and happy before God in a communion of love, within which instead of being less of ourselves we are evermore ourselves; finding God more and not less. Bringing about the kingdom of God requires our renewed love for the will of God, so that it grows within us, since his will is truth, freedom, and love.

## The relationship between heaven and earth

It is the infinite love of Jesus which conquers sin through his death on the cross; this re-establishes the communion between man and God: "Jesus gave a loud cry and breathed his last. The veil of the sanctuary was torn in two from top to bottom"[15]. There is no longer a separation between heaven and earth. The temple of his body, offered on the Cross for us, is open: "one soldier thrust his lance into his side, and immediately blood and water flowed out"[16] that bathe the land of our humanity. For this we pray "Thy will be done on earth as it is in heaven". We can, thus, want it, ask for it, and love it thanks to the great and extraordinary communion with God the Father brought about through Jesus Christ!

If it were not for Jesus, true God and true man, who made the 'bridge' with his body and his will to love, and made this 'as' possible, we could not pray like this! Now there is openness and communion in Jesus Christ, between heaven and earth. While the world often wants to separate earth from heaven, Jesus, in the prayer of the *Our Father*, and by offering up his life, has united them. He made the relationship between earth and heaven possible in a manner so deep and complete that his will, perfectly fulfilled in harmony and joy in heaven, was thus done also on earth!

## The two gifts to bring about the 'as' of his will

Now the question arises: how can what God wants be done on earth which is done perfectly in heaven? Where does one begin? God's response is wonderful: in giving us Jesus, the new Temple[17], He has also

---

[15] *Bible*. Gospel of Mark 15:37-38.
[16] *Bible*. Gospel of John 19:34.
[17] *Bible*. Cfr. Gospel of John 2:18-22.

given us his Spirit, the *Holy Spirit* to do on earth what is done in heaven; it is his gift, the gift of the Father and the Son, the gift of the Holy Spirit, the gift of Pentecost[18].

Through his passion and death, and his resurrection and ascension into glory Jesus has given us a new relationship with God and with the world. Precisely because the veil of the temple was ripped, the new Temple, his Glorious Body, is open for us in his pierced heart, and open too is the new relationship between heaven and earth: the Risen Jesus has given us his way, his heart, his love, and the grace of the Holy Spirit. "The love of God has been poured out into our hearts through the holy Spirit that has been given to us"[19]. It is the very gift of the Holy Spirit bringing to fulfilment, for the kingdom, 'the image of God' that is in every man, so that by becoming more like Christ, we show our 'likeness' to God, and can live 'as children'. Of course, only Jesus is the Son, He has always been so and is eternally in relationship with God the Father, He is the Word of the Father, One with the Father, only He can say 'my Father'. Whereas we are children by the grace of having received the gift of his Holy Spirit, and because of this we can say, 'Our Father'. "You received a spirit of adoption, through which we cry, 'Abba, Father!' The Spirit itself bears witness with our spirit that we are children of God"[20]. Created in Jesus Christ 'in the image and likeness of God', redeemed by him who 'restored' our wounded image deformed by sin, it is by the gift of the Holy Spirit in Baptism that we have become 'children in the Son', able to live with him the three functions, i.e. priestly, prophetic and kingly[21].

This deep bond is not a theoretical conviction, but a profound experience: first in regard to God because we have his love in our hearts to build the family of the children of God and his kingdom. Secondly, we have an experiential form of understanding which makes us realise that the Holy Spirit tells our human spirit that we are 'children of God'. It is Jesus Christ that gives us this ability through the Paschal gift of the Holy Spirit.

We can then begin to understand that the *Our Father* is not just any prayer. It is extraordinarily unique: in it there is the *'heart'* of God, there is the explanation of the new heaven-earth relationship brought about by the Easter of Jesus, and there is also the revelation of our identity, and how we can exist on earth in such a way as to renew people and civilization. We can say that the *Our Father*, the Lord's Prayer, is the *new prayer* of the new life.

---

[18] *Bible*. Cfr. Acts of Apostles 2:1-36.
[19] *Bible*. Letter to the Romans 5:5.
[20] *Bible*. Letter to the Romans 8:15-16.
[21] *Magisterium*. Cfr. *Catechism of the Catholic Church*, nos. 783-786; 871-873.

As "the love of God has been poured out into our hearts"[22] *we can* love not only with our human love – however partial, weak, confused or enthusiastic it may be – but also with the very gift of the Holy Spirit received in baptism. This is a great opportunity for which we are responsible. "As proof that you are children, God sent the spirit of his Son into our hearts, crying out, 'Abba, Father!'"[23]. Our relationship with God is not a fanciful claim, a feeling, an opinion or a solely human desire! It is not an aspiration, a need, a projection of ourselves, a human faith of ours. We have the reality, i.e. the real possibility of having this relationship with God, not with the idea of God, but with God himself through the power of the Holy Spirit, so that we may "give all men and women a desire for God the Father, the joy of his creative presence in the world"[24]. This is extraordinary. This is the beautiful new gift.

Until we 'see' the gift of God we cannot call ourselves Christians. So why have our children baptized? Why be baptized as adults? To accept and live this gift. Why be a Christian? For this reason, namely to live the communion of love with God the Father in Jesus Christ, which is the only good and right way to be capable of building a new civilization, in cooperation with God. As my father showed me by his life "God is truly the greatest reality of our lives".

God is so supreme and fascinating that, if He were not so, He would not have created us for eternity! In fact, only love can live forever. Love is at the very heart of the Christian revolution. This is why life is, in any case, no matter what, unsuspectedly wonderful!

A Christian is one who knows how to pray and act under the powerful action of the love and light of the Holy Spirit[25].

One can thus understand that the reality of wanting to pray to know God's will is not theoretical since it matures through the action of the Holy Spirit within us, especially in intimate personal prayer. This is why we pray: Jesus teaches us to ask that his will be done, since it is He who brings it about within us, but also through us and our work. This is the first gift: *finding us again with God* through the Word of God and the faith.

There is then a second gift, that of the *sacraments* by which God creates the 'as' of God in our lives to build his kingdom. The *Catechism of the Catholic Church* reminds us of this in the following way: "Seated at the right hand of the Father and pouring out the Holy Spirit on his body which is the Church, Christ now acts through the sacraments he

---

[22] *Bible*. Cfr. Letter to the Romans 5:5.
[23] *Bible*. Letter to the Galatians 4:6.
[24] *Magisterium*. Benedict XVI, Apostolic Exhortation *Africae munus* (2011) no. 176.
[25] *Bible*. Cfr. Letter to the Ephesians 4:29-32.

instituted to communicate his grace"[26]. They are the gift of his presence and his love and are to be rediscovered and lived in our lives[27].

Every sacrament has a powerful saving action which enlightens our lives and bestows upon us the special grace to accomplish God's will "on earth as it is in heaven". However, we must make sure, when receiving the sacraments, that we allow the power of God and his grace to act in our souls, and that we really do want to do the will of God and establish his kingdom.

Conversely, if through 'hardness of heart' we take the sacraments superficially and not with the proper disposition, then we will not succeed in doing the will of God, let alone doing his will "on earth as it is in heaven". Nor will we succeed in building his kingdom, since cooperation with God always involves the gift of our free will. Indeed, God's will is not automatically applied once and for all, because it must pass through the human heart from which it was distanced by sin. It is in the human heart that it must be sought and loved again. The sacraments have to find a ready heart to bear the fruit of love and brotherhood.

The two sacraments, "Holy Orders and Matrimony, are directed towards the salvation of others; if they contribute as well to personal salvation, it is through service to others that they do so. They confer a particular mission in the Church and serve to build up the People of God"[28]. This is something I would like to emphasize. As the sacrament of Holy Orders is not given for the priest but for others, so also that of Marriage is given for the salvation of spouses and children, but also of others. The family is naturally open to life and to the 'gift' for others: in this it shows its true love. It is always a question of not 'taking' the sacraments selfishly but receiving them with the gratitude and love with which one accepts a 'gift'. The words used by Benedict XVI in addressing priests and couples at the XXV National Eucharistic Congress in Ancona are indeed most significant[29].

There are people who would like to 'take' the sacraments to suit their own needs, as they do with the Gospel when they select 'something' that may be more attractive or of greater interest. That which is subjective gives greater pleasure and interest, and seems to give

---

[26] *Magisterium. Catechism of the Catholic Church*, no. 1084.

[27] *Magisterium.* Cfr. Benedict XVI, *Message for XXIV World Youth Day* (22 February 2009) (text no. 45 in Appendix).

[28] *Magisterium. Catechism of the Catholic Church*, no. 1534.

[29] *Magisterium.* Cfr. Benedict XVI, *Address at Meeting with Families and Priest, Cathedral of Saint Cyriac for Conclusion of XXV Italian National Eucharistic Congress in Ancona* (11 September 2011) (text no. 46 in Appendix).

greater reassurance: it is today's *subjectivism* which undermines also the Christian faith, as it implies the tendency to take a part, 'one's own part'.

Here, we are seeking reliable, fundamental and *objective* answers. To find our Christian roots we have to carry out research on reliable texts, those of the Bible and the Magisterium of the Church, whose value is certain and does not change over time, and precisely because of this deepens, thereby increasing our understanding. This is why we can find and even rediscover our Christian roots!

Many today would like to take from Christianity not the salvation of Jesus Christ in its entirety, but those ideas that can satisfy them: picking out what appears to be more useful. Here, too, there emerges a human heart that is more prone to utilitarianism than to the loving service of God; more prone to theft than to true love towards brothers to whom to deliver the whole truth; more prone to keeping up the appearance of declaring themselves as Christians than belonging in essence to Jesus Christ.

In addition, some have also been lost following bad pastors[30] as Saint Augustine reminds us in his *Discourses*. In not serving God well, you do not serve man well. Basically this is the yardstick by which to assess good or bad pastors. Saint Gregory the Great speaks of this in his *Pastoral Rule*[31]. Not seeking the glory of God, but one's own, speaking for one's own glory, or remaining silent so as not to lose it, is the big temptation, a serious evil for everyone, whether clergy or laity. It is this search 'for self' that prevents faith, as Jesus reprimands in the Gospel when He says: "I came in the name of my Father, but you do not accept me; yet if another comes in his own name, you will accept him. How can you believe, when you accept praise from one another and do not seek the praise that comes from the only God?"[32]. This is the main reason why many in the world do not have faith: for they seek the fleeting glory that the world can give.

---

[30] *Tradition.* Cfr. Saint Augustine (354-430), *Augustine's Sermon "On Pastors"* – *excerpts as found in the Liturgy of the Hours, Office of Reading*, Volume IV, Catholic Book Publishing Corp., New York. 1975 (http://fathergilles.net/parishministry/ On_Pastors_by_St_Augustine.pdf, accessed in July 2014. Text no. 47 in Appendix).
[31] *Tradition.* Cfr. St. Gregory the Great (540-604), *The Book of Pastoral Rule*, translation with introduction by G. Demacopoulos, St. Vladimir's Seminary Press, New York 2007 (text no. 48 in Appendix).
[32] *Bible.* Gospel of John 5:43-44.

## The reductive process and de-Christianization

Not to get lost in *useful reductionism* and idolatry, humanity desperately needs that 'whole Jesus Christ' the Church brings. "Do not go without anything. Take everything", says the world. This is the idolatry[33] of the world which believes in instant gratification, in the 'grab and run'. Man has become ever more a fugitive! He has become an idol to himself: what he thinks is all and everything. This is what Benedict XVI denounced about the modern world while on his Apostolic Journey to France[34]. The idol is only pleased with himself, taken up with his own thought and freedom as separated from the rest. Many, as Jesus warns us, are deceived in their own thoughts: "You are misled because you do not know the scriptures or the power of God"[35]. Together with the use of worldly goods that 'mammon' offers, this attitude of free thought and freedom, elevated to the status of idols, is the fundamental creed of secularism against which Jesus puts us on our guard[36]. These attitudes have been instilled in the younger generations to move them away from the Church and from true Christianity.

Through the 'useful reductionism' approach everything is degraded and fragmented for use. Thus, without the Church that Jesus wanted, the Christ person becomes a written Gospel and the Gospel a moral ideology that can be interpreted according to the culture of the time. We need to have the courage to accept the totality and depth of all revelation, for unless we do so 'wolves' descend, devouring and tearing 'apart' everything they come across[37]. They take parts of Christianity and the Gospel to then 'use' or 'sell' when it may be useful for them to do so. Many of our children and young people have been misled in this way and have either a very vague or totally incorrect idea of Jesus and Christianity.

This reductive process, which is at the basis of de-Christianization, has its own false centre: *idolatry of self.* In the wake of the fascinating discovery of the 'I' in the last century, many have followed the seduction of their own 'mirror', as, too, have various cultures and art, forgetting that the image man has received is of God. Cultures have been placed at the service of the 'I' which has grown to such an extent as to feed,

---

[33] *Bible.* Cfr. Letter to the Colossians 3:5.

[34] *Magisterium.* Cfr. Benedict XVI, *Homily at Eucharistic Celebration on the Esplanade des Invalides, Paris.* Apostolic Journey to France on occasion of 150th Anniversary of Apparitions at Lourdes (13 September 2008) (text no. 49 in Appendix).

[35] *Bible.* Gospel of Matthew 22:29.

[36] *Magisterium.* Cfr. Benedict XVI, *Jesus of Nazareth*, Doubleday, New York 2007, p. 98 (text no. 50 in Appendix).

[37] *Bible.* Cfr. Gospel of John 10:10-12.

also abnormally, the forms of narcissism and individualism to the point of stating that there is no limit to its rights. This cultural transformation does not use the weapons of violence but rather those of revolution which, starting with 'free thought', have gone as far as 'free pleasure'. The technique of argumentation is not one of fighting what is contrary to this idolatry, but one of not listening, or listening with indifference or conceit, so as to have the 'truth' fall into oblivion. Force is provided by the psychological pressure of the mass media which, even through a few operators, impose this *cultural dictatorship* on many. This does not assert itself in men from the outside, but from within, in a peaceful and seemingly painless manner. Man is considered a 'big animal' to be satisfied, this supposedly being the common factor of all men. Here, too, the trick has been to divide and separate rather than unite and see the entire man, 'the whole man'.

**The 'return'**

The principle of 'return' to the Christian faith is that which is inclusive of all values. I believe that this new *inclusive capacity* in fidelity will have to be the hallmark of the *new evangelization*, which is necessary today for a service encompassing all the new knowledge. This is what is being done at the Centre 'Family – Little Church' (*Famiglia Piccola Chiesa*) of the Movement of Family Love which continues to extend its activities for a new culture and for the mission.

Jesus Christ brings the journey of humanity to completion through the world and through the Church. He does so through the Church which, vivified by the Holy Spirit, is confronted with the world, with its pressures for progress or regression, with its multiplicity and diversity, with the various sciences and its human and scientific achievements, so as to purify and direct them to the 'good of the whole man and of all men'. This is why the 'announcement of Christ' is the first and principal factor for the development of human society[38], as is the need to mature the Word of God.

For the 'return', the sacraments also help to do the will of God, the 'as of God'. Indeed, every sacrament is a way of experiencing something of Jesus, something of heaven on earth. Sacraments communicate the love of Jesus that motivates us to do as He did, to do good for others, *'caritas urget nos'*[39], building the kingdom of God in truth and charity with brothers and for brothers. "None of us lives for oneself, and no one

---

[38] *Magisterium*. Cfr. Benedict XVI, Encyclical Letter *Caritas in Veritate* (2009) no. 8 (text no. 51 in Appendix).
[39] *Bible*. Cfr. Second Letter to the Colossians 5:14.

dies for oneself. For if we live, we live for the Lord, and if we die, we die for the Lord; so then, whether we live or die, we are the Lord's. For this is why Christ died and came to life, that he might be Lord of both the dead and the living."[40]. In whatever situation we find ourselves, whether of life or death, we, in our entirety, belong to him.

Every aspect of our reality is important to God, we are precious in his eyes, everything is important, beautiful, great, and of immense value, because God really loves us and loves us entirely. The joy, suffering and difficulties we experience during our lives fulfil the will of God, that of sanctification through the gift of the Holy Spirit received in the sacraments. The sacraments accompany us in this way, so that our human reality 'returns' to be for God the Father and for our brothers, overcoming conditioning[41] and worldly pressures.

When faith grows and becomes mature, with the warmth of God's love and fraternal help, we are able to love and help the poor and the poorest in a practical and tangible way. Parishes and Christian communities also become ever more communities of faith, charity and hope for society. It is the love for our neighbour which makes us better, and opens up our horizons for this service. It is always true, as confirmed by the Pope, that: "Only if I serve my neighbour can my eyes be opened to what God does for me and how much he loves me. (...) Love grows through love. Love is 'divine' because it comes from God and unites us to God; through this unifying process it makes us a 'we' which transcends our divisions and makes us one, until in the end God is 'all in all' (*1 Cor* 15:28)"[42].

But to get into this relationship, which is the love and light of God, we have to act in a way that our will breathes again in unison with God's will, so that it is done "on earth as it is in heaven", with love for the Word of God through the action of the Holy Spirit and the gift of the sacraments. "I urge you therefore, brothers, by the mercies of God, to offer your bodies as a living sacrifice, holy and pleasing to God, your spiritual worship. Do not conform yourselves to this age but be transformed by the renewal of your mind, that you may discern what is the will of God, what is good and pleasing and perfect."[43].

No one is born from himself and for himself; so the new life of a child is not only expressed in the human celebration, but is also shown as a celebration of God the Father. This is the reason for the choice of

---

[40] *Bible*. Letter to the Romans 14:7-9.
[41] *Magisterium*. Cfr. John Paul II, Encyclical Letter *Dominum et vivificantem*, (1986) n. 60 (text no. 52 in Appendix).
[42] *Magisterium*. Benedict XVI, Encyclical Letter *Deus caritas est* (2005) no. 18.
[43] *Bible*. Letter to the Romans 12:1-2.

Baptism: a child is not only 'our child' but a 'child of God in Jesus Christ by the work of the Holy Spirit', called to build the city of men and also the kingdom of God. In short, a human life *for God*, like Jesus who belongs to the Father.

'For God': this is why a Christian will love, give light and love to others "in the name of the Father, the Son and the Holy Spirit", and be able to say "Thy will be done Father here on earth as it is in heaven", precisely because he has something of heaven, he has the 'image', which has become more and more similar to Christ through the action within him of the grace of the Holy Spirit. This is what is conferred by the sacrament of Baptism. We see Baptism, but what God wants is that we profoundly understand and love what He does. We must understand that as it is on earth so it is in heaven, we must have our eyes on earth, but our hearts in heaven. The profound reality is that of the spirit captured with the eyes of faith welcoming the things of heaven on earth.

Thus the sacrament of *Confirmation* is the very sacrament that reinforces and gives direction to the life of a child or young person. God has called each one into existence on earth through love for a mission that cannot be reduced to emotions, the satisfactions of the body, friendships, school, money, the motor bike, and work. These are the means to relate to others, but there is something greater than all of this, that we should be able to say to each of them: "There is a greater reality than the one you see: God is beside you, He sustains you, He opens up your mind and heart to reveal to you the meaning of your existence and love for others, the mystery of your being. This mystery is revealed through Christ and your future is God: He is eternal life, He is the love with which you were thought of, planned and loved before us. He is your fundamental vocation". Indeed, one thing is what a young person wants to be, with his ability and talents, while another is his fundamental vocation by which God entrusted him with his plan and the meaning of his life. But if Christians hide these gifts of God, who will help the new generations? "But how can they call on him in whom they have not believed? And how can they believe in him of whom they have not heard? And how can they hear without someone to preach?"[44].

Who will reveal to children and young people their mystery and their fundamental vocation? Why hide it and deceive them, leaving them easy prey to their instincts or interest and thirst for the deceptions of 'mammon'?

It is true that they should be free, this is their good. But are they really free, or has a trick been used to 'buy' them pulling them far from

---

[44] *Bible*. Letter to the Romans 10:14.

their fundamental vocation? To construct what project? Are they free when they are confused and weak, with no roots or destination? Too many adult Christians allow themselves to be intimidated and do not bring about the kingdom, and... they do not even allow the others to enter it!

As we shall see in the next chapter, freedom seeks to implement a project of life and love.

# 9

# On earth as it is in heaven (II)
## *On earth as in heaven*

Following on from the previous chapter, we shall now consider the development of human life with the help of the grace of the Holy Spirit which enables us to bring about the kingdom of God through his *'as'*. This is what Jesus has taught us to ask for in the *Our Father*. Human life matures in the gift, which implies the exercise of human freedom. So when two young people feel they are called together by love, they are able not only to stay together, but to bring about something that does not exist as yet: the family, created by two hearts that love each other and give themselves to each other to be "one body"[1], thereby encountering and embracing the mystery of life, love and God. God desired to express something of himself in the love of man and woman, created in his image[2].

Is it really conceivable that human love does not belong to God? That it is something that just belongs to the couple? That it is simply the expression of natural eros, aimed at ensuring the survival of the human species on earth, a biological and perhaps also an emotional need so as not to remain alone? Or vice versa, in the love of a couple is there a larger project that opens up to the Other? In fact, for those that mature it in the truth, human love is revealed as something much greater than 'their' thoughts and 'their' projects, something 'greater than the two of them'! How can one think that God, the Source of Love, does not care for the two of them? Or that Jesus does not have something that is specifically his to give the bride and groom? The Sacrament of *Matrimony* is God's answer: the gift of Jesus to create the family of God's children and the kingdom of God. It thereby follows that human love is not given for use. Love is from God, and has already been bestowed on

---

[1] *Bible.* Book of Genesis 2:24.
[2] *Bible.* Cfr. Gospel of John 10:30.

humans in their 'image', so that the mystery of God shines forth from them. This love is enhanced through the sacrament of Matrimony so that their love is 'the one for the other' and 'for the others'. However, this human and spiritual reality can be understood by praying to God the Father "Thy will be done, on earth as it is in heaven". It is then that the sacrament of Matrimony can be lived. This means being 'Christian spouses', i.e. 'of Christ': in this way the couple does not belong only to itself but to Christ. This is the reason why engaged couples ask that their life and their love be blessed and directed, purified and supported by the sacrament of Matrimony. But for human love to be capable of welcoming and manifesting the sacrament of marriage, the couple must also have a 'Christian way of love and eros'[3].

Let us explore this aspect. Benedict XVI in his first encyclical letter *Deus caritas est*, dealing with 'eros' and 'agape', and the distinction between them and their unity, emphasised: "Man is truly himself when his body and soul are intimately united; the challenge of *eros* can be said to be truly overcome when this unification is achieved. Should he aspire to be pure spirit and to reject the flesh as pertaining to his animal nature alone, then spirit and body would both lose their dignity. On the other hand, should he deny the spirit and consider matter, the body, as the only reality, he would likewise lose his greatness. (...) *Eros*, reduced to pure "sex", has become a commodity, a mere "thing" to be bought and sold, or rather, man himself becomes a commodity"[4]. The problem of man is that, like his thought which can become insane through deception, his love can similarly become perverted.

**The action of the Holy Spirit and eros**

It is the sanctification produced in us by the Holy Spirit that makes us resemble Christ more and more, and enables the maturation of the whole person: *from "erotic" love to "agapic" love*, whereby the energies of eros, i.e. the psycho-sexual ones, are integrated with the inner energies of man, i.e. the psycho-spiritual ones. It should not be forgotten that it was precisely the testimony of an integrated, healthy and untainted human love, a love capable of overcoming 'passions', combined with a love and generosity for the poor and the sick, that convinced the pagans of the human and spiritual superiority of Christianity.

'Mammon' is rife, not only in the drive towards luxury, but also in the field of eros, seeking to paganise eros as much as possible. The sexual revolution has brought about the liberalization and the exaltation of sex

---

[3] Cfr. Chapter 5.
[4] *Magisterium.* Benedict XVI, Encyclical Letter *Deus caritas est* (2005) no. 5.

turning it into use, but in doing so has also led to the loss of its meaning and value resulting in its very idolatry. Humanity needs to regain the human value of sexuality, tearing it away from the instinctual and bestial meaning it has been given in the commercial and advertising spheres of the sexy at all costs. In this context, the laity and married couples have a great new opportunity to Christianize neo-paganising society with the resources that the spirit and new humanisation bring to the life of the body and sexuality.

Therefore, through God's love, i.e., the work of the Holy Spirit, *eros*, the human love of man and woman, becomes more and more one of love as a gift, *agape*, which seeks the good of the other: it is then that the two find their common mystery in God Love[5]. This love too is part of God's kingdom that we ask for in the prayer of the *Our Father*.

Eros and agape are two necessary expressions of love: need and gratuitousness, bonding and freedom. Love is circular, in giving it receives, in receiving it gives: it cannot only be expressed through giving[6], it must also receive, nor can it only ever receive, it must also be able to give. This is the law of love. In order to grow, love needs God's Love. Benedict XVI, during his Apostolic Journey to France, speaking to young people and their need for love declared: "The Spirit gives us a deep relationship with God, who is the source of all authentic human good. All of you desire to love and to be loved! It is to God that you must turn, if you want to learn how to love, and to find the strength to love. The Spirit, who is Love, can open your hearts to accept the gift of genuine love"[7]. Love searches for love until everything becomes love and God, that is Love, "may be all in all"[8].

## God accompanies man

There are, however, countless situations in life in which we also experience selfishness, weakness and sin, the 'no' said to God. This does not leave God the Father indifferent. Instead, through his Son Jesus He tells man: "Let's start again! I'll bring you my mercy, my forgiveness, and my strength". This is the mercy of God that we receive in the sacrament

---

[5] This is the testimony of many couples in the Movement of Family Love who experience this in practice.

[6] *Magisterium*. Cfr. Benedict XVI, Encyclical Letter *Deus caritas est* (2005) no. 7.

[7] *Magisterium*. Benedict XVI, *Address at prayer vigil with the young in front of Notre-Dame Cathedral, Paris*. Apostolic Journey to France on the occasion of the 150th Anniversary of the Apparitions of the Blessed Virgin Mary at Lourdes (12 September 2008).

[8] *Bible*. First Letter to the Corinthians 15:28.

of *Reconciliation.* It is one and the same with the love of God, because He has paid for us, making up for that love that was lacking in the fall of sin. God wants to be close to man and wants man to be close to him.

He gives the force of love, mercy and hope so that Christians may continue that plan that is in Baptism, is strengthened in Confirmation, and is directed and sanctified in Matrimony. This is extraordinary! There, where love is imperfect, where man is weak and falls, God comes to pick him up, "Come on, come on, it's me... I have carried your sins, I have carried the cross, I have paid in person, come on, receive my grace, resume your journey". God embraces man and says, "Let's start again!". Only God is capable of so much love and of giving it through Jesus in a perceptive human manner. Only Jesus Christ could bring God so close to man and man so close to God. Only He, the Son of the Father.

Without Jesus and without the Church which continues his presence and his work, the world would be infinitely poorer! The sacraments are also human and have to pass through the humanity of the priest. Since God was made man for us, He communicates his grace in a human way. This is true of all the sacraments, including marriage, where grace passes through the bride and groom as they themselves are the ministers of the sacrament.

Only God, the Emmanuel, could accompany us in this way throughout our lives. God accompanies every human reality, including the suffering of old age and disease to take it in his hands. Here, medicine is not enough. This is the function of the sacrament of the *Anointing of the Sick*! It is a great reality! But we have to understand that God's will is to be done on earth, as it is in heaven, according to the heart of God. And this is what we ask for in the *Our Father.*

We do not die and that's it, we do not become elderly by mistake, we do not burn out like a candle, and then everything is over! Saint John Paul II in his Pastoral Visit to Paris and Lisieux, recalled that "man is in the heart of the mystery of Christ, man is in the heart of the Father and of the Son and of the Holy Spirit. And this from the beginning. Was he not perhaps created in the image and likeness of God? Otherwise man has no sense. Man has no meaning in the world other than as the image and likeness of God; otherwise, as some say, man would be a 'useless passion'"[9]. There is God who sustains us, who loves us, who gives full meaning to our lives and, more importantly, welcomes us in union with Christ crucified. God gathers the tears and sufferings of man for the resurrection: let's remember this, God the Father does not want death, and through Christ promises us the resurrection. God the Father

---

[9] *Magisterium.* John Paul II, *Homily Holy Mass at Le Bourget.* Pastoral visit to Paris and Lisieux (1 June 1980).

is merciful and powerful, He is the "Ruler and Lover of souls"[10]. In this sacrament which is for the living who are experiencing suffering, God gives strength, forgiveness and comfort in life.

Here the question arises: "Have the lives of older people developed only by and in view of the means of 'mammon'?". Has there not also been a growth in their faith enabling them to see that their lives are supported and directed also by the Lord in view of him and his kingdom? And if so why not show it? With what love and hope do many older people die? Should we not die, amidst so many medical treatments, also with the comfort of our loved ones' affection and the help of God's love? Have we made death the final inhumanity? Perhaps as older people we will regret having created such a barren world... and having done too little for the faith in the resurrection that awaits us!

God has given seven sacraments to support our humanity, and give meaning and direction to our lives so that we may not be alone, as God is with us. The veil of the temple is broken and torn, and there is now communion between heaven and earth in the Body of Christ that is the new Temple: it is in him that men now meet God who gives himself[11] through him, the temple of his glorious Body but also the divine presence made accessible to us in the *Eucharist*. In Christ, heaven and earth are united, and the kingdom of God is already on earth in his Presence through the Church and its works in the world[12]. The Word of God, the humanity of Jesus Christ and his Church are the three greatest manifestations given by God to man and to the world for salvation.

The great communion with God is built through the sacraments that accompany us in the development of our lives. This is why Jesus has become food for us in the sacrament of the Eucharist, a gift and grace of new life that sustains us weekly: this is extraordinary! He renews us, purifies us, and immerses us in the absolute of his power, in his saving Cross, in the Glory of his resurrection. "*The Eucharist is also the sacrifice of the Church.* The Church which is the Body of Christ participates in the offering of her Head. With him, she herself is offered whole and entire. She unites herself to his intercession with the Father for all men. In the Eucharist the sacrifice of Christ becomes also the sacrifice of the members of his Body. The lives of the faithful, their praise, sufferings, prayer, and work, are united with those of Christ and with his total

---

[10] *Bible*. Book of Wisdom 11:26.

[11] *Bible*. Cfr. Letter to the Ephesians 2:19-22.

[12] *Magisterium*. Cfr. Benedict XVI, *Homily at Holy Mass with dedication of the Church of the Sagrada Familia and of the Altar*. Apostolic Journey to Santiago de Compostela and Barcelona (7 November 2010) (text no. 53 in Appendix).

offering, and so acquire a new value"[13]. That is why the Eucharist is the everyday Sacrament, but above all the Sacrament of Sundays and Feast Days, it is "the source and the summit of evangelization and of the world's transformation"[14].

We can now understand that God has given us 'his heart', his Love with the gift of the Holy Spirit, whose grace can work – if we let him – also through the sacraments and transform the 'as' of our hearts and lives. Yet, this is something we have forgotten.

We have also forgotten the pedagogy of 'sacrifice *for love*'. The sense of *sacrifice for the Lord*, which was once taught to children, so that they were driven to acts of love towards their neighbour and to self-giving in marriage, has been replaced by *the sense of sacrifice of parents* only for their children without asking anything of them. Besides, what could parents ask of their children? Love without God has thus become secularized. In this way, in the impossibility of asking for themselves and having eliminated from the hearts of children the rightful offer to God, parents have created conceited and selfish children, so turned in on themselves as to be unable to 'give' not only to their parents, but in their turn not even to their children and to others.

God is Father and Jesus taught us 'sacrifice for God the Father' so that we would find love, that love which is self-giving and is vital to the life of the world. God does not need our sacrifices, but through his own example of giving his Son Jesus and giving him for us, He wanted to teach us what love is. Jesus is the only one who, in the heart of each of us, opens up the road that leads to rediscovering the love for God the Father and for all humanity. And this is the meaning of the Eucharist which is communion, sacrifice and thanksgiving. The sacrifice is born of love, and therefore needs God's Love so that it is good and does not degenerate and become perverted.

When love is genuine and invests the deep energies of the whole person it is capable of self-giving, becoming an offer and a sacrifice for the good that it builds. This is the love that builds, and that is quite different from the sort of frivolous, light-hearted and inept love easy subculture has accustomed us to. We have forgotten the beauty of Christianity and the grace to understand the will of God the Father! All of which we are reminded of in the *Our Father* and the love of Jesus.

---

[13] *Magisterium. Catechism of the Catholic Church*, no. 1368.

[14] *Magisterium*. Pontifical Committee for International Eucharistic Congresses, *The Eucharist: God's gift for the life of the world. Foundational theological document for the 49th International Eucharistic Congress of Quebec* (2008) no. 5-A (text no. 54 in Appendix).

Who is it that really does the will of God? The angels and the Saints in heaven. They certainly love the will of God. To do the will of God also on earth, it is necessary to love the will of God; only then will we be able to do it. To love it, one must also understand it. We have to love it to understand it, and we have to understand it to love it. This is why Jesus has us ask for it, with love, in the prayer of the *Our Father*, so that we may be able to do it as He does it, with confidence and love. Only in this way can we build day by day the family of God's children and his kingdom.

## The 'as' of God and the 'as' of the world

The Christians then build the city of men together with other men but with the 'as' that is of God and builds the kingdom of God. This Christian 'as' is the expression of communion between God and man; God gives his presence and action through his grace, and man restores to God – with his contribution of something new – that which is of God and that God has entrusted to him: nature and its possibilities, the universe and its energies. The Creator has placed man at the apex of creation to praise God for the gift of life and for all creatures. This is well expressed by Saint Francis of Assisi in his *Canticle of Creatures*[15]. But today man thinks it is 'mother nature' that has put him in this state of *superior consciousness*. Therefore, it is easy for children and young people, driven by the fashions of the New Age and yoga, to end up praying, almost unconsciously, to the sun and praising creatures rather than, as Saint Francis reminded us, the Creator *for* the creatures.

By denying or ignoring God the Creator, nature also falls to the mercy of man who wants to make another reality, a different creation, his own creation. This is why religion is seen as restrictive and intrusive, and understood as something mythical and transitory, coming from a pre-scientific era incapable of revealing anything to 'builder and technological' man. Religion and Christian morality would seem to belong to a bygone era, while today science and technology are the new religions to rely upon! In this way you can be happy, free at last in an adult world, without restrictions of a moral or religious nature, a modern and secular world with new civil rights, where rules are dictated only by one's own freedom. However, we may well ask ourselves whether, in these new principles, there is perhaps not an echo

---

[15] *Tradition.* Cfr. Saint Francis of Assisi (1182 ca.-1226), *The Writings of Saint Francis of Assisi. Translated from the Critical Latin Edition,* edited by Fr. Kajetan Esser, O.F.M., Franciscan Archive, 2000 (http://www.franciscan-archive.org/patriarcha/opera/preces.html, accessed in July 2014).

of the ideologies that have marked history and lacerated humanity as in the last century. Is it not instead the task of Christians too to purify history so that there might be true good progress for everyone?

Also the application of new technologies – such as biotechnology, genetic engineering and neuropharmacology – to the human body distorts the concept of human nature by going beyond its natural limits. For this reason, a review of the complexity of the reality of human nature and its true roots, which cannot be reduced to pure materiality, becomes increasingly urgent. Indeed, the reality of human nature is more extensive and richer than the matter that composes it.

Isn't it so that, today more than ever, the new scientific frontiers require pathways of truth, goodness and wisdom for the good of humanity? Have not balance and responsibility been needed in the difficult task of managing nuclear energy? It is a great gift that Christians and the Church are in the world. Are there not signs of a greater wisdom to be seen? The Church is a gift of Jesus to the world.

Ultimately, isn't the environmental problem too, like every social problem, a matter of conscience and humanity for which the Church has much to offer?

Is it not perhaps the case that the world needs the 'as' to know how to proceed and make life viable on this planet? Wouldn't the world do better, if it were in good faith, to open itself up with more courage and without prejudice to the gifts of God and his wisdom? Saint John Paul II during his pastoral visit to Paris touched upon the important theme of modern development that needs to get back on track[16].

## The 'as' of God's gift to humanity

In the precious words of the *Our Father*, "on earth as it is in heaven", Jesus gives us the 'as' that He himself lives and came to bring us. In these words, He expresses a heart, harmony, peace, depth, and great security because He shows the way; not in any way, as the world would, in the way of earthly tyrants, but "on earth as it is in heaven": in the way of God! Christianity does not only bring the truth of God, but his presence, and with it also the 'as' of God, his wisdom. It is the Holy Spirit that accomplishes this communion of Covenant: it is the New Covenant fulfilled by Jesus Christ through the gift of his life to open us up to the gift of the love of God and of his Holy Spirit. "This cup is the new covenant in my blood, which will be shed for you"[17].

---

[16] *Magisterium*. Cfr. John Paul II, *Homily Holy Mass at Le Bourget*. Pastoral visit to Paris and Lisieux (1 June 1980) (text no. 55 in Appendix).
[17] *Bible*. Gospel of Luke 22:20.

With his Holy Sacrifice Jesus achieves purification, a new heart and a new spirit as promised through the prophet Ezekiel: "I will sprinkle clean water over you to make you clean; from all your impurities and from all your idols I will cleanse you. I will give you a new heart, and a new spirit I will put within you. I will remove the heart of stone from your flesh and give you a heart of flesh. I will put my spirit within you so that you walk in my statutes, observe my ordinances, and keep them."[18].

So the author of the Letter to the Hebrews, in describing the New Covenant, cites the Word of God according to the prophet Jeremiah: "For if that first covenant had been faultless, no place would have been sought for a second one. But he finds fault with them and says:

> 'Behold, the days are coming, says the Lord,
> when I will conclude a new covenant
> with the house of Israel and the house of Judah. (...)
> But this is the covenant I will establish with the house of Israel
> after those days, says the Lord:
> I will put my laws in their minds
> and I will write them upon their hearts.
> I will be their God,
> and they shall be my people'"[19].

This is the New Covenant promised[20] and brought about by Jesus Christ who, through the Paschal gift of the Holy Spirit, accomplishes salvation by creating an intimate relationship with God[21] and beginning the kingdom of God on earth.

Ultimately, it is the Holy Spirit who is building the kingdom of God in Christians and men of good will, and it is He who helps us to give effect to the 'as' of God in our lives. It is with him that the *image of God* in man becomes more and more a *likeness* to Jesus Christ. Created and redeemed in Jesus Christ, through his love and the work of his grace in us by the Holy Spirit, we become more and more 'like' him, we more and more resemble Christ. The Holy Spirit works this (Christification) deification in man by increasingly bringing about the divine 'image' in 'likeness' to Christ. "For by the Hands of the Father, i.e., by the Son

---

[18] *Bible.* Book of the Prophet Ezekiel 36:25-27.
[19] *Bible.* Letter to the Hebrews 8:7-10.
[20] *Bible.* Cfr. Book of the Prophet Jeremiah 31:31-34.
[21] *Magisterium.* Cfr. John Paul II, Encyclical Letter *Dominum et vivificantem,* (1986) n. 59 (text no. 56 in Appendix).

and the Spirit, Man is made after the Image of God: man, not a part of man"[22].

It is by the loving and sanctifying action of the Holy Spirit that the creation of man and woman, as well as history, goes back to God: from image to likeness, this is the work of the Holy Spirit in the conversion of the person; from human love to the sacrament of marriage for Christian spouses to return to the heart of God; and from the city of men to the kingdom of God for the history of mankind.

With his irruption in the history of Israel, God has revealed his existence, his power and his promise of salvation to the world. God the Father with Jesus Christ has revealed to us his 'as' and has given it to man. The 'as' of God is not an external regulation or a series of laws, but a way of life in truth, freedom and love.

Christianity implies not only believing that God exists, but believing in his love[23]: it means welcoming God who gives himself to mankind with Christ in the Holy Spirit. Above all Christianity is about receiving the 'as' of God that is the Trinitarian Communion of Father, Son and Holy Spirit. In this way, Christians as children of God live the 'as' of God. The 'as' of Jesus shows us 'how' to live and 'how' to die, and this is our salvation brought to us by Jesus. The 'as' of Jesus becomes the 'salvation' for each person, for love and human life, the 'salvation' for the whole of mankind.

This is why Jesus left the New Commandment; it is 'his': "This is my commandment: love one another as I love you"[24].

Love was already on earth but it did not save: the 'as' of God was needed to save mankind. The 'as' of God is power and light, it is his kingdom on earth. The Church makes the 'as' of Jesus hers, and conjugates it in life, in opposition to the 'as' of the spirit of the world that is without God. This is why Jesus reminds us: "Do not think that I have come to bring peace upon the earth. I have come to bring not peace but the sword"[25]. It is the strength of love that shapes and prepares the 'as' of God's children that make up the people of God.

There is the 'as' of God's children in the human love between man and woman and in the formation of the couple and the family.

There is the 'as' of God's children in the conception of human life, which is instead lacking in all other possible conceptions.

---

[22] *Tradition*. St. Irenaeus bishop of Lyons (130-202), *Against Heresies*, translated by J. Keble, James Parker and Co., London, Oxford and Cambridge 1872, p. 460.
[23] *Bible*. Cfr. First Letter of John 4:16.
[24] *Bible*. Gospel of John 15:12.
[25] *Bible*. Gospel of Matthew 10:34.

There is the "as" of God's children in avoiding conception using natural methods and not contraceptives[26].

There is the 'as' of God's children in the world of work and in contributing to development and human progress.

There is the 'as' of God's children in having fun. The 'as' in the entertainment of the world disintegrates man rather than restoring him to his best capacities.

There is the 'as' of God's children in fighting evil.

There is the 'as' of God's children in building the city of men.

There is the 'as' of God's children in the use of science and technology.

There is the 'as' of God's children in bringing the peace of Jesus: "not as the world gives do I give it to you"[27].

There is the 'as' of God's children in living and dying.

Only by living in communion with Christ, who tells us "Remain in my love"[28], is it possible to draw on this 'as' of God. This is what the Church says. This is what the Church announces in proclaiming the Kerygma[29], the Gospel, the Good News, and in going from loving the faith in the dead and risen Christ to incarnating the Gospel in everyday life.

This is the task of all Christians and the whole Church: living Christ in the love of the Father and brothers, embodying the 'as' of God in history. The more the 'as' is according to God, the more the salvation for humanity is made manifest. Like Jesus, the Church courageously proposes the 'as' of God for love: "'Master, [then] what happened that you will reveal yourself to us and not to the world?' Jesus answered and said to him, 'Whoever loves me will keep my word, and my Father will love him, and we will come to him and make our dwelling with him'"[30].

At the same time, however, the Church denounces the 'as' of the world in history when it presumptuously deviates from truth, goodness and righteousness: it does so by urging the conscience of believers and non-believers not to be carried away by historical appearances; hers is a prophetic call in history for individuals, families and the world. The Church loves and wants good; it loves life and progress, and it is for man and with man and history. Faithful to Jesus Christ who said: "I am the way and the truth and the life. No one comes to the Father except

---

[26] International Documentation by FIAMC (World Federation of the Catholic Medical Association), Forty Years of HUMANAE VITAE from a medical perspective (http://www.fiamc.org/bioethics/humanae-vitae, accessed in July 2014).

[27] *Bible*. Gospel of John 14:27; Cfr. Letter to the Ephesians 2:17-18.

[28] *Bible*. Gospel of John 15:9.

[29] *Bible*. Cfr. Acts of Apostles 2:14-39; 3:12-26; 4:9-12; 5:29-32; 10:34-43; 13:16-41.

[30] *Bible*. Gospel of John 14:22-23.

through me"[31], the Church of God points the way for those who want to listen.

The road to God is with Christ, "the way and the truth and the life", and with the gift of the Holy Spirit, the Spirit of Love and Truth. God is the Only One, there is no other, God is the Most High, there is only one God! In himself how can He be Father? Only Jesus showed us the secret of God, which is the revealed mystery. God is a communion of Love: Father, Son and Holy Spirit. God has revealed to us his 'as', the Trinitarian 'as' of his Being.

In this secret of God there is also ours, which we increasingly need to know not only to survive but to live well. Machines become more and more perfect, but man is still very small. It is not enough to make some small discovery, a few steps more: we need to know the whole, the 'heart' of the system. It is through the Church that Christ gives us the key. But why would God have chosen the Church? Precisely because it is human and, like all humanity, it is made up of saints and sinners, but it has one thing in particular: it is humble, it cannot boast, it leaves room for God, it will never take his place. With the Church, his Bride, Christ is comfortable, at ease. In the same way He chose straw to be laid in the midst of men, so too He chose his Church. The Church must be loved; loved and understood: to the humble of heart, whether shepherds or magi, it opens up the treasures of Christ who is the 'heart' of the system.

## The humanity of the Church

The humanity of the Church is a good road and one that God has chosen for every man and woman to move closer to him. He has not chosen the hosts of angels, He has not chosen extraordinary human ability, the energies of the cosmos or the opposition and hatred of rebellious spirits, He has not chosen the power of miracles that solve the impossible, He has not chosen the glory that men seek so much. Instead, He has chosen[32] the Church, her humanity with all her limitations, but where Christ is present because the heart of the human being, loving and listening to her, certainly meets God. If, on the other hand, the human being rejected and despised her, he would express that contempt for himself, that lack of love for his own humanity, for himself, that we commonly refer to as 'hardness of heart': this is the atrium of hatred and hell.

Also the demand for a perfect Church recalls the anger of the 'lost paradise': this demand does not look for love to find it again. Anger,

---

[31] *Bible*. Gospel of John 14:6.
[32] *Bible*. Cfr. First Letter to the Corinthians 1:26-31.

controversy, contempt, strife or cunning, class or power struggles are all methods that are not in line with the spirit of the Gospel. Some simply consider the Church as a human organization, and therefore lose the benefit of what the Church really is. This was recalled by Pope Emeritus Benedict XVI on his Apostolic Journey to Germany[33].

God is deliberately present in the human reality of the Church. In this sense, God hides himself in order to give himself to us! Is He not also present in children, the poor, the sick and the marginalized? He hides so that man is not frightened and it is easier for him to come back to love the greatness of God. Is this not also the meaning of the Christmas of Jesus?

The Church, faithful to God, brings and shows God's 'way' in history, pointing the way to God[34], 'the way' of Jesus. It is the "as" of God given to men who love the truth and love. Though within the limits of a human existence, evangelical fidelity is fundamentally the interest and love of the Church. For this reason the Church, though recognising that it is made up of saints and sinners, is faithful to Christ and announces the truth and salvation for all mankind and for the world. In each diocese, the Christian community led by its pastor, the Bishop, increasingly develops this mission and work of salvation[35].

In its mission, in its pastors as in the faithful, the Church shows that the 'as' of God it brings to humanity does not come from the 'world'. In this way, it manifests its prophecy in the world. You "are in the world" but "do not belong to the world"[36], Jesus says to us in the Gospel. "If you belonged to the world, the world would love its own; but because you do not belong to the world, and I have chosen you out of the world, the world hates you"[37]. It is the spirit of the world that is bitterly opposed to and fights the Church, and it is the Church that fights the spirit of the world[38] denouncing and showing its falsity and deception when it wants to set itself up without God, in spite of God, against God, or foolishly above God.

In the midst of new discoveries, scientific applications, and new 'rights', Christians must seek the 'as' of God so as to live in the world as

---

[33] *Magisterium.* Cfr. Benedict XVI, *Homily at Holy Mass in the Olympic Stadium, Berlin.* Apostolic Journey to Germany (22 September 2011) (text no. 57 in Appendix).
[34] *Bible.* Cfr. Gospel of Matthew 7:13-14.
[35] *Magisterium.* Cfr. Benedict XVI, *Address at Meeting with the Bishops of Cameroon at Christ-Roi Church in Tsinga, Yaounde.* Apostolic Journey to Cameroon and Angola (18 March 2009) (text no. 58 in Appendix).
[36] *Bible.* Cfr. Gospel of John 17:11-16.
[37] *Bible.* Gospel of John 15:19.
[38] *Bible.* Cfr. Gospel of Matthew 10:34.

God's children and give living witness of their faith in their daily lives. "But when the Son of Man comes, will he find faith on earth?"[39].

Faith manifests itself in life, in the 'as' you live life, especially where there are more possibilities of choice: so today being a Christian is more 'luminous' even if it is not easy. The 'as' of Christians in the world is for the good of the world: it is not a 'creed' that is closed within itself; instead, it must be able to show that Christians and Christian choices favour 'more good', 'more freedom', 'more love' and 'more justice' in the fields of sexuality, the family, technology, medicine, politics, economics, education, as well as in every other field.

In this respect, the Christian faithful, who are faithful to Christ, are not only faithful to the past but also faithful 'for the future': they act as proponents when, in the synthesis between science and faith, they know how to revive this 'extra good' for the future, without allowing themselves to be overcome by compromise or isolation, by blackmail or despair! It is important today to have a proper missionary attitude[40], also with regard to the new migratory situation[41]. The Lord urges us to see his presence in every man, and his project of love and salvation throughout history. This is the reason why the prayer of the *Our Father* resonates as the prayer *par excellence* for every man and for all mankind; more than any other prayer it expresses the heart of God, his love for the good of everyone.

For this reason, we are also called upon to join all our efforts in *common ecumenical action* aimed at the recognition of the religious dimension and its freedom, as pointed out by Pope Emeritus Benedict XVI during his Apostolic Journey to the United Kingdom in 2010, when he stated that 2010 marked "the 100th anniversary of the World Missionary Conference in Edinburgh, which is widely acknowledged to mark the birth of the modern ecumenical movement. Let us give thanks to God for the promise which ecumenical understanding and cooperation represents for a united witness to the saving truth of God's word in today's rapidly changing society"[42]. On that same trip, the Pope recalled that the ecumenical dimension needs dialogue and peaceful,

---

[39] *Bible*. Gospel of Luke 18:8.

[40] *Magisterium*. Cfr. John Paul II, Encyclical Letter *Redemptor hominis* (1979) nos. 12-14 (text no. 59 in Appendix).

[41] *Magisterium*. Cfr. Benedict XVI, *Message for the 98th World Day of Migrants and Refugees* (21 September 2011) (text no. 60 in Appendix).

[42] *Magisterium*. Benedict XVI, *Homily at Holy Mass in Bellahouston Park, Glasgow*. Apostolic Journey to the United Kingdom (16 September 2010).

free and respectful cooperation[43]. The world has an increasingly greater need to rediscover the religious and Christian vision of life.

## The New Evangelization

Benedict XVI has often recalled the urgent need for a new evangelization, for example, in the Pastoral Letter to the Catholics of Ireland[44], the Address to the Bishops of the Episcopal Congregation of Canada[45], and at the General Audience in February 2010: "Christ, in fact, is the most precious good that the men and women of every time and every place have the right to know and love! And it is comforting to see that in the Church today too there are many pastors and lay faithful alike, members of ancient religious orders and new ecclesial movements who spend their lives joyfully for this supreme ideal, proclaiming and witnessing to the Gospel!"[46].

In the field of evangelization the *world of art and beauty* is equally important. As Benedict XVI reminded us during his Apostolic Journey to Santiago de Compostela and Barcelona, this is also a privileged field of the human 'spirit' and can open our hearts and minds to the mystery of God and of man[47]. Again on the same journey to Barcelona, Benedict XVI emphasised: "Indeed, beauty is one of mankind's greatest needs; it is the root from which the branches of our peace and the fruits of our hope come forth. Beauty also reveals God because, like him, a work of beauty is pure gratuity; it calls us to freedom and draws us away from selfishness"[48].

In every field it comes down to travelling the road of men and human development showing, in communion with God, his 'as', the best choice for humanity, without stopping at apparent 'human conquests'.

---

[43] *Magisterium*. Cfr. Benedict XVI, *Address at Meeting with Clerical and Lay Representatives of other Religions in the Waldegrave Drawing Room of St Mary's University College in Twickenham, London*. Apostolic Journey to the United Kingdom (17 September 2010) (text no. 61 in Appendix no. 61).

[44] *Magisterium*. Cfr. Benedict XVI, *Pastoral Letter to the Catholics of Ireland* no. 12 (19 March 2010) (text no. 62 in Appendix).

[45] *Magisterium*. Cfr. Benedict XVI, *Address to Bishops of the Episcopal Conference of Atlantic Canada on their Ad Limina Visit* (20 May 2006) (text no. 63 in Appendix).

[46] *Magisterium*. Benedict XVI, *General Audience* (3 February 2010).

[47] *Magisterium*. Cfr. Benedict XVI, *Interview with journalists during the flight to Spain*. Apostolic Journey to Santiago de Compostela and Barcelona (6 November 2010) (text no. 64 in Appendix).

[48] *Magisterium*. Benedict XVI, *Homily at Holy Mass with Dedication of the Church of the Sagrada Familia and of the Altar.* Apostolic Journey to Santiago de Compostela and Barcelona (7 November 2010).

We need to go beyond appearances to grasp the truths of good and of the heart. As Sacred Scripture teaches: "God does not see as a mortal, who sees the appearance. The LORD looks into the heart"[49]. In this way, Christians are not only the critical consciousness of history but also the *proactive consciousness*: they work for the good and the best of humanity. This is what the Church does through 'faithful' Christians.

For this reason the 'new evangelization' that the Church implements will not be 'exclusive' but 'inclusive' of the various realities which arise, capable as it is to bring about a new synthesis, for the 'as' of God is embodied in human history with all its novelty but with faithfulness to God and his kingdom. This process of renewal and acquisition in the truth and in dialogue requires true and deep roots that we can and must find.

As Benedict XVI reminded us, the task of a new evangelization[50] lies before us. It is far from over and awaits the new generations. The world still needs it to be able to know and welcome the Gospel of salvation and the new life of Jesus.

Having so far commented on the first part of the *Our Father*, in the next chapter we will start the second part, in which Jesus indicates the necessary gifts and conditions that must be known in order to carry out his loving plan for each and every one of us, and for all humanity.

---

[49] *Bible*. First Book of Samuel 16:7.
[50] *Magisterium*. Benedict XVI, *Homily at First Vespers of the Solemnity of the Holy Apostles Peter and Paul in Basilica of Saint Paul Outside the Walls* (28 June 2010) (text no. 65 in Appendix).

# 10

# Give us this day our daily bread

## *Give us today our daily bread*

In the second part of the Our Father, Jesus tells us the four conditions which are necessary to bring about God's Kingdom and do his will "on earth as it is in heaven".

While in the first part of the *Our Father* Jesus has taught us three prayer petitions that are more concerned with 'heaven', in the second part Jesus teaches us four petitions to be addressed to the Father that mainly concern our humanity, the 'earth'. These are the four necessary conditions on earth to bring about the Kingdom of God and his will that is our salvation.

Worthy of note is that the two parts of the *Our Father* 'recall' the two Tablets of the Decalogue[1]. In the Prayer of the *Our Father*, Jesus takes up the Ten Commandments bringing them back to our relationship with God the Father, which is essential for understanding their meaning and value. Without the love of God these moral teachings are misrepresented. To 're-establish' the new human life on its roots Jesus leads us back to our relationship with the Father.

The *Our Father* shows us the beauty and the greatness of life. To achieve them, without deluding ourselves and without falling into the deceptions which derive partly by our human limitations and partly by 'adverse headwinds', there is no path other than the one which Jesus teaches us. In the *Our Father*, the Lord points out the conditions so that we may have fullness of life.

**Why bread**

Considering in particular our human earthly life, we know that food is necessary for our existence. Bread is a sign of survival and

---

[1] *Bible.* Cfr. Book of Deuteronomy 5:1-22.

growth. Jesus teaches us to ask the Father for bread, "Give us this day our daily bread", which we need on a daily basis. This request, which seems obvious to us, may encourage us to move on to the rest of the text. This would be a mistake. Instead, we should look at it closely to understand it well. Why does Jesus have us express this request in the *Our Father*? And then, isn't there work to give us the requested 'bread'? Is it perhaps a prayer for children and not for adults who earn it by hard work 'every day'? Couldn't this request entice someone to disengagement and sloth?

Certainly, asking God the Father for 'bread' in prayer does not mean lying back and not working or working badly without any sense of commitment. In short, it does not offer us an escape route from our daily work and responsibilities.

On this point it is useful to read what John Paul II wrote on the significance and dignity of labour in the Encyclical Letter *Laborem exercens* (Through work): "Work is a good thing for man – a good thing for his humanity – because through work man *not only transforms nature,* adapting it to his own needs, but he also *achieves fulfilment* as a human being and indeed, in a sense, becomes "more a human being". (...) This fact in no way alters our justifiable anxiety that in work, whereby *matter* gains in *nobility, man* himself should not experience a *lowering* of his own dignity"[2].

For man, the personal objective of work is to sustain and fulfil his life. Clearly, when we speak of man, we refer to the human being, man and woman. Work is important, but nowadays what is becoming ever more necessary, for work to be 'humane', for it to be for and not against man, is to restore the dignity of work. Benedict XVI also stressed the importance of reconciling work and family. He stated: "In our day, unfortunately, the organization of work, conceived of and implemented in terms of market competition and the greatest profit, and the conception of a holiday as an opportunity to escape and to consume commodities, contribute to dispersing the family and the community and spreading an individualistic lifestyle. It is therefore necessary to promote reflection and commitment which aim at reconciling the needs and schedule of work with those of the family. They must also aim at recovering the true meaning of celebration, especially on Sunday, the weekly Easter, the day of the Lord and the day of man, the day of the family, of the community and of solidarity"[3]. Work, like life, is an achievement for us, but also a gift from God, to achieve self, family and

---

[2] *Magisterium.* John Paul II, Encyclical Letter *Laborem exercens* (1981) no. 9.
[3] *Magisterium.* Benedict XVI, *Letter to the President of the Pontifical Council for the Family on the occasion of the Seventh World Meeting of Families* (23 August 2010).

society[4]. For this, we need to be brought back to our roots through the prayer of the *Our Father* so as to find the reasons for life, work and family.

Within the family we are educated for work; namely we learn to open up to responsibility, sharing, overcoming our own selfishness, initiative, industriousness, and creativity: individuals and society are founded on a basis which is the family. Moreover, work has an extraordinary dimension of unity also among human beings, and of good for humanity, over and above that of personal and family subsistence. Work involves an extremely important dynamic for personal, family and social life affecting every layer of our lives. It would appear that work is more the result of our initiative, our intelligence, and our creativity rather than the result of a gift received from above.

But then, if for all these reasons work is so important to earn bread why does Jesus teach us to ask God for bread in the *Our Father*? The answer is that He wants to put us on our guard for two essential reasons that concern the first condition needed to live the *Our Father*, and bring about his kingdom and his will "on earth as it is in heaven".

The first reason is that bread must be requested and 'given', and not stolen! Jesus has us ask for it, and this awakens us to our responsibility. The second reason is that the request "give us" in the prayer addressed to God expresses recognition that bread must always remain his gift, to remain good. This is why Jesus teaches us to ask for it from God the Father. Let's see why in more detail.

This is something we easily forget and goes unnoticed: we must not lose sight of the fact that the bread we take every day assimilates us to the world. Indeed, when we earn 'bread', we make it 'ours', and while we use bread and food as resources to survive, we are actually assimilating to what the world gives us. In other words, we become what makes us grow and gives us life, what enables us to survive: this is 'the power of bread'!

**Corrupted Bread**

It is we who earn it, touch it, make it, feed on it, and use it to stave our hunger, but we forget that in this necessary relationship, we gradually assimilate it and become what we eat, what makes us live. Consequently, without realising it we become 'addicted' to the power of bread: dealing with it from morning to night, and having our hands tied up in work, we are constantly in danger of becoming like that

---

[4] *Magisterium*. Cfr. John Paul II, Encyclical Letter *Laborem exercens* (1981) no. 10 (text no. 66 in Appendix).

which nurtures us and allows us to live. Somehow the bread becomes an 'idol', making people slaves without their noticing it. Work, evermore industrialized and technological, tends to transform human beings and human relationships so that they begin to function like machines.

There is a page in the Gospel, which sheds light on this point, and never fails to impress, where we are told of a day when the disciples had forgotten to take bread. "They had forgotten to bring bread, and they had only one loaf with them in the boat. He enjoined them, 'Watch out, guard against the leaven of the Pharisees and the leaven of Herod'"[5]. One needs to ask oneself: who is behind the bread?

In fact, we are not bound only to the bread, but also to he who gives it to us! Therefore it is not only the bread that is important but also from whom we take it. And it is here that there comes the dependency that enters the human soul. "Guard against the leaven", says Jesus! The *leaven* makes the bread rise, but the bread, along with the availability of means, gives security for survival and allows people to grow. In the end, you wonder: who made us grow? Here we have a dual dependency: on bread but also on those who obtain it for us. There is an ever closer tie to those who are secure in producing it, and one becomes more and more dependent on those who promise it, on those who give it, and on those who sell it. This mechanism makes its way into our hearts, our minds, and our way of life. Beware, therefore, Jesus says, of the leaven that comes from the Pharisees or Herod, because by eating this bread, there also grows a dependency. You do not see the dependency because you see only the bread!

You see the consumption good, but you do not notice that you are entering a dynamic of dependency and progressive slavery. The child who does not have a particular item of clothing or shoes of a particular brand nags persistently at his/her parents. Even classmates and friends have become dependent on so many things that are superfluous but have come to characterize their lives: it is an economic mechanism that creates ephemeral, false security, made up of many 'useless' things for both children and adults.

The Pharisees have their security in the Law, and Herod in political and economic power. Jesus indicates his security in the will of God the Father. The 'leaven of the Pharisees' indicates when religion becomes ideology, and the 'leaven of Herod' when economic and political power become an idol.

To stay free, Jesus recalls the need to ask God, the Father, for bread so as not to assimilate that which comes from the world, because it would raise man in the world creating a dependency, and the world

---

[5] *Bible.* Gospel of Mark 8:14-15.

within man creating the idol! No doubt the disciples did eat loaves with the leaven of the Pharisees and that of Herod, but Jesus calls upon humanity to be careful and watch out for 'leaven' which might also come from a dimension, albeit religious, that is self-sufficient without the heart of God, or one that might come from political power or economic wealth flaunting autonomy from God. Beware – Jesus says – of that which tranquillizes but comes from 'mammon'.

Secondly He recommends us to be careful not to distance ourselves from that one bread that the Father gives us and which is Christ himself: "So Jesus said to them, 'Amen, amen, I say to you, it was not Moses who gave the bread from heaven; my Father gives you the true bread from heaven. For the bread of God is that which comes down from heaven and gives life to the world'"[6]. On the boat that day there was just one bread... it was Jesus![7] He wants the children of God to have a conscience that is alert and capable of distinguishing the true from the false good, the good from the bad bread.

The prayer "Give us this day our daily bread" is the first condition to do the will of God and have the kingdom grow within us. It is an indispensable prayer. Only by praying like this can we purify the barrier of human mediation to have the necessary food.

The kingdom cannot grow if we allow 'another yeast' to grow within us. In fact, it progressively grows within us, and we go from honesty to covetousness, from sobriety to greed, from well-being to brutishness; witness the rude and ill-mannered behaviours and the sadness on people's faces! We must remember that smiling is not a characteristic of animals but of human beings created in the image of God. When we no longer smile, the soul is in darkness. This is the process of *consumerism*: use and throw away. One always wants the new object because it is better, but the new one serves to throw out the old one. We could say that consumerism takes hold when consumption becomes destiny.

This is demonstrated by expressions such as "earn more, consume and die" because this is what is needed. But who needs it? Thus, the economic system and its development, together with technological progress, have to take account, for every man and for all men, not only of the economic dimension and the problems of consumption and the market, but also of the spiritual dimension, and the values of the spirit that are in man.

The *Our Father* has been taught and many have received the sacraments, but the question arises: have many Christians experienced the Word of God that gives life? Have they experienced Jesus, the bread

---

[6] *Bible*. Gospel of John 6: 32-33.
[7] *Bible*. Cfr. Gospel of Mark 8:14-15.

of God for eternal life? We have to ask ourselves: in the end, who makes love live? Only the bread of men? Soon their love and their family will end, if men have fed only on the bread of men. Since the bread of men is often also made of betrayal... we shall see this in the final chapter. It is necessary to know how to eat it, being careful about the 'leaven'. But who can teach this if we are all human beings? Only God can give us his Bread, Jesus. Without him, sooner or later we grow addicted to the bread of men, being increasingly enslaved to it, finishing up well-inside the mechanism of self-interest to the point of losing our bearings and becoming prisoners of our own selfishness and pleasure. Dealing with this issue has become all the more urgent in our society given the collapse of conscience on the one hand, and ethical relativism on the other.

And so, rendered unjust by one's own way of thinking and acting, one easily becomes greedy, while still wanting the good of life. Wealth takes over and leads to coarsening: things become more important than everything else. Work and the maximum economic profit become the 'essential' things of life, doing becomes more important than being, putting the earth to rights more important than building heaven together with God! Nowadays, we are witnessing a serious and dangerous shift towards material growth, which puts 'work' at the centre of life, sacrificing the 'Feast Day' and the Festive Mass that for us Christians are the social basis of communion with God and with our brothers. In this way, along with consumerism, first an ever more widespread materialism and then an ever more rampant hedonism have developed: 'the search for food' has thus become 'the pursuit of pleasure'. Subsequently, from hedonism there has been a slippery descent towards eroticism and the transformation of sexual relations into 'things', considered as a pleasure necessary to nature. Hence awareness has been lost of the progressive impoverishment of human feelings, moral values, and individual and collective responsibility. 'Use' has downgraded 'honesty', and *corruption*, big and small, has invaded life!

### Time for reconstruction

Thus, while the outside world becomes increasingly beautiful and better organized, the inner life of those without God, as Saint Paul reminds us in his Letter to the Romans[8], becomes increasingly ugly and wicked: more and more squalid. There are those who truly believe

---

[8] *Bible*. Cfr. Letter to the Romans 1:18-32.

that this is progress and freedom, but is this the good and the future that we want to hand down to the next generations? Is this the greatest expression of our humanity? It is time to rebuild. It is they, the younger generations that are asking us to do so. The signs of the malaise are apathy and the view that does not consider life as precious. Life is worthless, or worth less and less. We need to rediscover the value and preciousness of life and the family. For this reason God wants us to feed on his Bread, beauty and greatness of God, gratuitousness and goodness that feed the greatest reality: his image and likeness in us which makes us more fully men and women. Yes, we need Jesus, but this 'need' is not the dependency produced by the bread of the world. This dependency is a bond of love and of Covenant, the New Covenant; it is love and gratuitousness for us. So human life and the bread of life meet each other in the gift of love. The Eucharistic gift is beautiful and sublime!

God is providence and gratuitousness: this gratuity is not like the free offers advertised in shops with the intention of attracting more people so as to sell more. It is not the deception of interest. It is the gratuitousness of God, of the love with which God wants to support our life, make us mature and grow by giving Himself to us. Yet, it is not true that, given the gratuitousness of his love, God expects nothing of us. God expects our faith and our love that is capable of receiving God. He does not need us, while we humans need God: this bond of love is the truth of our lives and is different from a dependency. Only this belonging which is gratuitous love – whereby God wants us to be gratuitously existing, living in him, in his glory and eternal happiness – is the condition of our lives, otherwise we would not exist!

Pope Emeritus Benedict XVI made countless appeals to families and parents who are particularly vulnerable in today's world. He addressed them on a number of occasions; on one such occasion he urged as follows: "Dear parents, commit yourselves always to teach your children to pray, and pray with them; draw them close to the Sacraments, especially to the Eucharist, (...) and introduce them to the life of the Church; in the intimacy of the home do not be afraid to read the sacred Scriptures, illuminating family life with the light of faith and praising God as Father. Be like a little Upper Room, like that of Mary and the disciples, in which to live unity, communion and prayer!

By the grace of God, many Christian families today are acquiring an ever deeper awareness of their missionary vocation, and are devoting themselves seriously to bearing witness to Christ the Lord. Blessed John Paul II once said: 'An authentic family, founded on marriage, is in itself 'good news' for the world'. And he added: 'In our time the families that collaborate actively in evangelization are ever more numerous (...) the hour of the family has arrived in the Church, which is also the hour of the missionary family' (Angelus, 21 October 2001). (...) Dear families, be courageous! Do not give in to that secularized mentality which proposes living together as a preparation, or even a substitute for marriage! Show by the witness of your lives that it is possible, like Christ, to love without reserve, and do not be afraid to make a commitment to another person! Dear families, rejoice in fatherhood and motherhood! Openness to life is a sign of openness to the future, confidence in the future, just as respect for the natural moral law frees people, rather than demeaning them! The good of the family is also the good of the Church"[9].

The historical process we are going through is also characterized, in particular, by the speed of telecommunications via the internet and that form of contact, that is so radical, so deep, and that binds us to one another, which is *globalisation*. It is not only the laws of the market that guide history and its development, but also the choices we make with regard to the way in which we want the world to progress. The use of globalization itself depends on us, i.e. on us all, as stated by the Pope in the Encyclical *Caritas in veritate*[10].

It has to be asked: who will take hold of globalization? For a more humane world, who will do it, God or 'mammon'? The values of goodness, truth and justice or the interest of power and unlimited economic profit? As Jesus reminds us in the Gospel: "You cannot serve God and mammon"[11]. Which path is the world taking? Where is humanity heading? There resounds the warning call of Jesus: "Watch out"[12].

The Christian spirit involves a critical and constructive vision of man's relationship with *the financial world*, aimed at building the kingdom and helping the human development of the whole man and of all men. For this, the destination of profit is important: it contributes to progress when it can be transformed into responsible productive investment and the development of human resources. Conversely, when the search for maximum profit is allocated to financial speculation and, in general, to activities that undermine the just interest of all parties involved (*stakeholders*), it shows its inconsistency both as to the 'method' of

---

[9] *Magisterium*. Benedict XVI, *Homily at Holy Mass on the occasion of the National Day of Croatian Catholic Families in Zagreb Hippodrome*. Apostolic Journey to Croatia (5 June 2011).

[10] *Magisterium*. Cfr. Benedict XVI, Encyclical Letter *Caritas in veritate* (2009) no. 42 (text no. 67 in Appendix).

[11] *Bible*. Gospel of Luke 16:13.

[12] *Bible*. Gospel of Mark 8:15.

hoarding, because this eventually ends in collapse, and as to the 'end', because it shows wickedness, by ceasing to be at the service of all men and of the whole man.

To avoid falling into greed, the *Our Father* teaches us the 'daily life'.

The adjective *daily* expresses the demand for what is sufficient for each day. In fact, there is also the temptation to accumulate, entering the deception of greed where things are no longer enough; from a state of serenity one thus turns to distress and arrogance, thinking that the accumulation of wealth may bring peace, serenity and happiness. This is the great deception that feeds the temptation that is in the world. It has taken its grip on many people: many families have educated their children in this way believing in the idol of human bread. There then comes the humiliation when they discover that all this is false, an idol, and they find themselves without anything: false peace, a happiness that fades, a security that does not exist! It is an ugly big trap from which the Lord seeks to free us by having us pray, "Give us today our daily bread".

"Give us today", every day: it implies the recognition that everything comes from God who provides for his children on a daily basis. It implies believing in God's providence since everything is in his hands[13]. Jesus reminds us: "So do not worry and say, 'What are we to eat?' or 'What are we to drink?' or 'What are we to wear?' All these things the pagans seek. Your heavenly Father knows that you need them all. But seek first the kingdom [of God] and his righteousness, and all these things will be given you besides. Do not worry about tomorrow; tomorrow will take care of itself. Sufficient for a day is its own evil"[14].

*Providence* is learned as a child seeing the signs of God the good Father that follows and accompanies our existence, and abundantly gives us help and resources: these signs come through the world even if the 'world' is not always aware. The world of wealth and technology cannot imagine these realities. The truth is that we depend in any case on God: the beatitudes[15] start from here; they are the measure, so to say, of our being Christians. Many are forgetting providence, as if God were an idea, did not exist, were not Father, or did not listen. They have forgotten to understand our Father. Many have drawn close to 'mammon' and become slaves of wealth, forgetting God, our Heavenly Father.

---

[13] *Bible*. Cfr. Book of Psalms 9:13.
[14] *Bible*. Gospel of Matthew 6:31-34.
[15] *Bible*. Cfr. Gospel of Matthew 5:1-12.

**With what bread?**

If we want to build the kingdom of God we must also feed in a certain way, with *another food*. Basically, we need to ask ourselves: to sustain ourselves, what other bread should we feed on if not human bread? This is why Jesus has come and taught us to ask for this food from God in the *Our Father* so that we may not be satisfied by human bread, so that we may not deceive ourselves and be misled by it!

God wants man, his creature, to be free from any bondage. Jesus reminds us in the Gospel that "It is written: 'One does not live by bread alone, but by every word that comes forth from the mouth of God'"[16]. Jesus points out the need to feed on the Word of God and, therefore, his will. It is the Word of God that reveals and matures personal identity and the plan of salvation for humanity. The Word of God applies to everything[17]. While many, going after 'false science', have got lost[18]. *Pride* in believing they know and *greed* in the enjoyment of wealth are the two evils that have always afflicted man – the result of deception and lies. We are reminded of this in the Word of God: "Those who want to be rich are falling into temptation and into a trap and into many foolish and harmful desires, which plunge them into ruin and destruction. For the love of money is the root of all evils, and some people in their desire for it have strayed from the faith and have pierced themselves with many pains"[19].

The Word of God has a particular effect of light and wisdom for the faith that it arouses as we are reminded by a prayer of the Sunday liturgy: "O God, who teach us that you abide in hearts that are just and true, grant that we may be so fashioned by your grace as to become a dwelling pleasing to you"[20]. The new generations have to see within their families that the Word of God is never missing in the same way as bread is never missing! No day should go by without feeding on the Word of God! The Word of God builds us up and brings us into an honest dialogue with him.

Benedict XVI in his Apostolic Exhortation *Verbum Domini* (The Word of the Lord) says: "The word of God in fact is not inimical to us; it does not stifle our authentic desires, but rather illuminates them, purifies them and brings them to fulfilment. How important it is for

---

[16] *Bible*. Gospel of Matthew 4:4.

[17] *Bible*. Cfr. Second Letter of Saint Paul to Timothy 3:16-17.

[18] *Bible*. Cfr. First Letter of Saint Paul to Timothy 6:20-21.

[19] *Bible*. First Letter of Saint Paul to Timothy 6:9-10.

[20] *Tradition*. Cfr. Liturgy of the Holy Mass, Collect – Sixth Sunday in Ordinary Time (http://www.liturgies.net/Liturgies/Catholic/ roman_missal/ordinarymass. htm#week6, accessed in July 2014).

our time to discover that *God alone responds to the yearning present in the heart of every man and woman!* Sad to say, in our days, and in the West, there is a widespread notion that God is extraneous to people's lives and problems, and that his very presence can be a threat to human autonomy. Yet the entire economy of salvation demonstrates that God speaks and acts in history for our good and our integral salvation. Thus it is decisive, from the pastoral standpoint, to present the word of God in its capacity to enter into dialogue with the everyday problems which people face. Jesus himself says that he came that we might have life in abundance (cfr. Jn 10:10). (...) As Saint Bonaventure says in the *Breviloquium*: 'The fruit of sacred Scripture is not any fruit whatsoever, but the very fullness of eternal happiness. Sacred Scripture is the book containing the words of eternal life, so that we may not only believe in, but also possess eternal life, in which we will see and love, and all our desires will be fulfilled'"[21].

Also on the occasion of XXVI World Youth Day when addressing young people, Pope Emeritus Benedict XVI stressed the importance of the Word of God in building their lives[22].

While the bread of men is a means, the Bread of God is the gift that God the Father gives us: Jesus, his Word, even up to the giving of himself that is the Eucharist, the Bread of Eternal Life. Without the heart that trusts in God the Father, it must be recognised that the battle for survival, social climbing, and the craving instilled by 'mammon' take over. In the end, the soul is sad: it is not just tired because of hard work, a hectic life, the stressful traffic of our cities, or the concerns and worries that dominate us. The truth is that we lack this 'other bread', the bread for our spiritual soul, because we are also made of spirit. This is why Jesus reminds us: "One does not live by bread alone, but by every word that comes forth from the mouth of God"[23].

This involves asking it of God, waiting for it as a gift from his hands or, in an even more pregnant sense, as a gift that "comes forth from the mouth of God". He has given us his Word. The Word of God, in the full and complete sense, is the *Verbum*, Jesus, who becomes food for us. The Word of God was made man by the power of the Holy Spirit in the womb of the Virgin Mary[24]: it is the man, Jesus of Nazareth, true God and true man. He makes a gift of himself to humanity in the Eucharist:

---

[21] *Magisterium*. Benedict XVI, Apostolic Exhortation *Verbum Domini* (2010) no. 23.
[22] *Magisterium*. Benedict XVI, *Address at Welcome Ceremony with young people on the occasion of the XXVI World Youth Day*. Apostolic Journey to Madrid (18 August 2011) (text no. 68 in Appendix).
[23] *Bible*. Gospel of Matthew 4:4.
[24] *Magisterium*. Cfr. John Paul II, Encyclical Letter *Redemptoris mater* (1987) no. 30.

"I am the living bread that came down from heaven; whoever eats this bread will live forever"[25]. Jesus, the only bread of life[26] for our life: it is He the Bread that our Father gives us every day.

God does not want us to forget the greatness and the goodness of who we really are in his sight: God our Father wanted us as his children forever and for eternity. He does not want us to stop at human bread. "Jesus said to them, 'Amen, amen, I say to you, unless you eat the flesh of the Son of Man and drink his blood, you do not have life within you. Whoever eats my flesh and drinks my blood has eternal life, and I will raise him on the last day'"[27]. For this reason the Father gives us his Son, the Word and the Bread of eternal life, so that we may remain and grow as children of God, able to do his will and collaborate in the building of his kingdom.

Of course, to earn the bread of men that is necessary for personal, family and social life, there is the weight of work, the difficulty of finding it, the specific circumstances and the effort of those who work every day with the worry of an uncertain future. But we know that this is a temporary situation.

So for us to live we need two types of bread: human bread which is a means to survive, but then we die; and the bread of God that is a gift for the future, for something else, it is above and beyond, it is the beyond. The Eucharist, the gift of Jesus to us, is the beyond; it is something more that brings us closer to God, and that brings us closer to ourselves and to all men, because it feeds the mystery of personal, family and social life, introducing us into the future of eternity and happiness of God. It is for this that God became man and... food for us with his own self-giving, thereby conquering sin and death. A wonderful and sublime gift! A unique and unimaginable gift compared with all the other religions. An invention of God for us. God is truly our 'heavenly' Father.

Our life does not end with us, with our earthly life. The earthly bread nourishes and sustains our life in good health but the bread of Jesus, the Eucharist, enables us to achieve the purpose for which we exist, it gives us the meaning of life, and has us return with Jesus to the Father and to eternal life. And this food which is Holy Communion becomes for us the strength and love of fraternal sharing.

This is the gift we ask for when we say "Give us today our daily bread". Let us be grateful for what we have, content with what is necessary so as not to become slaves of the world and of the masters

---

[25] *Bible*. Gospel of John 6:51.
[26] *Bible*. Cfr. Gospel of John 6:35.
[27] *Bible*. Gospel of John 6:53-54.

of the world; and let us purify ourselves constantly of the present and future deception of 'mammon'. It is in this way that we become more human, better, wiser and holier people, receiving from God not only the necessary human bread but also the bread of God, Jesus, for our eternal joy, "for the bread of God is that which comes down from heaven and gives life to the world"[28]. We all need Jesus!

"Give us this day our daily bread", is the first condition that Jesus teaches us in the *Our Father* in order to become truly human and to bring about the family of God's children and the kingdom of God.

In the *Our Father* there is the whole of God's plan that Jesus came to bring us and to entrust us with. Christians know the prayer of the *Our Father*, but not everyone knows so deeply the scope, the light and power of this prayer with all its consequences on life, family and society. It is a precious reality that opens up horizons for our good and that of our families but also for the whole world, because Jesus is the light[29] come into the world and for the world. He is the light for all men who want the light, and love the profound truth, so that the world does not fall into the hands of fools and into the hearts of those who have the darkness within them.

---

[28] *Bible*. Gospel of John 6:33.
[29] *Bible*. Cfr. Gospel of John 8:12.

# 11

# And forgive us our trespasses
## *And forgive us our debts*

We have seen that the first condition Jesus indicates in the *Our Father* to fulfil the will of God, his Kingdom and the family of God's children is to ask God for our 'daily bread'. We have noted the importance of this prayer, the fourth of the seven petitions that we make in the *Our Father*. The Lord has us pray to the Father for our daily bread so that we remain free and authentic, and discover the gratuitousness and Providence of God the Father. In this way, He has us stay human without falling slaves in the mechanisms of 'mammon' or of those who fly the 'no God' banner and live as though God did not exist.

The fifth petition: "Forgive us our trespasses as we forgive those who trespass against us" refers to the second *sine qua non* condition for our human life to fulfil the will of God and bring about his kingdom. The first condition concerns things; 'bread'. Instead, this second condition concerns the 'heart'. Let's see why it is so essential to our lives.

This petition gives us the awareness and the ability to remain human if we live the dimension of gratuitousness in our hearts that is essential for us and for the world. God's gratuitousness concerning things has led us to consider his providence. The gratuitousness of God in our hearts shows us his mercy; indeed, He has love and compassion for us. The Word of God reveals his heart! "But you have mercy on all, because you can do all things; and you overlook sins for the sake of repentance. For you love all things that are and loathe nothing that you have made; for you would not fashion what you hate. How could a thing remain, unless you willed it; or be preserved, had it not been called forth by you? But you spare all things, because they are yours, O Ruler and Lover of souls"[1]. Each man needs God's heart for his heart!

---

[1] *Bible.* Book of Wisdom 11:23-26.

That God continues to love us, to speak to us and take care of us is also an expression of his mercy.

After the *Our Father*, which is the most beautiful prayer we can say, the prayer which is the most authentic, the nearest to our human reality, and which Jesus shows us to appreciate in the Gospel is[2]: "O God, be merciful to me a sinner". Indeed, as Saint Bernard says by looking at our mistakes and our sins: "The whole of the spiritual life consists of these two elements. When we think of ourselves, we are perturbed and filled with a salutary sadness. And when we think of the Lord, we are revived to find consolation in the joy of the Holy Spirit. From the first we derive fear and humility, from the second hope and love"[3].

What is mercy? Mercy consists of the truth and gratuitousness of God towards us: this attitude is fundamental for us, it is like 'bread' for the soul. It is directed by God to our 'hearts' where our debts accumulate. By 'heart' what is meant is the seat of consciousness, of the will, of feelings and of our spirit. It concerns the great mystery that is within every man and woman, the reality of 'the image and likeness of God'[4]: in fact, to live and survive we need this dimension of ours, the heart, to be acknowledged and visited by someone who, with love, knows how to understand, accept and heal. This is mercy. But where can we find it? Only in God, only God can give it!

In other words to be persons, to build families and society on a human scale, we need to perceive and experience the dimension of God's mercy. In teaching us in the *Our Father* to ask for the forgiveness of sins, Jesus helps us to rediscover and live the dimension of mercy in people, in families, in society, in the whole world. In the same way that life becomes brutalized without the bread of God – the theme we have dealt with in the previous chapter – without the mercy of God people become brutalized in their hearts, to the extent of becoming 'hard of heart'.

Also for the Jews God is merciful, and Allah is called 'The Merciful One' by the Muslims. What does Jesus Christ add?

Already in the Old Testament we read: "The LORD is gracious and merciful, slow to anger and abounding in mercy. The LORD is good to all, compassionate toward all your works. All your works give you thanks, LORD and your faithful bless you. They speak of the glory of your reign

---

[2] *Bible*. Cfr. Gospel of Luke 18:9-14.
[3] *Tradition*. Saint Bernard of Clairvaux (1090-1153), *From a Sermon by Saint Bernard, Liturgy of the Hours, Office of Readings, Wednesday, 23rd week, Ordinary Time* (http://www.liturgies.net/Liturgies/Catholic/loh/week23wednesdayor.htm, accessed in July 2014).
[4] *Bible*. Cfr. Book of Genesis 1:26.

and tell of your mighty works, Making known to the sons of men your mighty acts, the majestic glory of your rule. Your reign is a reign for all ages, your dominion for all generations. The LORD is trustworthy in all his words, and loving in all his works. The LORD supports all who are falling and raises up all who are bowed down"[5]. And this is the beauty and greatness of the mercy that God the Father has shown and abundantly bestowed, as attested to by the Holy Scriptures, and that He has given us maximally and permanently in Jesus Christ his Son for the salvation of humanity.

In this chapter we reflect on the first part of the petition addressed to God, "Forgive us our trespasses". In the next we shall consider the second part of the petition, "as we forgive those who trespass against us".

### Is mercy out of fashion?

Why does it seem hard to talk about? Does the world need it? And why does Jesus put it in the *Our Father*? Have we perhaps forgotten about it, or do we try to live as if we did not need it?

The Encyclical Letter *Dives in misericordia* (God who is rich in mercy) by John Paul II helps us in this quest. He writes in the encyclical: "The word and the concept of 'mercy' seem to cause uneasiness in man, who, thanks to the enormous development of science and technology, never before known in history, has become the master of the earth and has subdued and dominated it. This dominion over the earth, sometimes understood in a one-sided and superficial way, seems to have no room for mercy. (...) At times (...) we see in mercy above all a relationship of inequality between the one offering it and the one receiving it. And, in consequence, we are quick to deduce that mercy belittles the receiver, that it offends the dignity of man. The parable of the prodigal son shows that the reality is different: the relationship of mercy is based on the common experience of that good which is man, on the common experience of the dignity that is proper to him. (...) The genuine face of mercy has to be ever revealed anew. In spite of many prejudices, mercy seems particularly necessary for our times"[6].

Today man prefers law and justice to mercy because with justice he feels more confident in building what belongs to him, the 'his'; instead with mercy he is afraid of losing it. In this sense he has less or no interest in mercy. But mercy is not a loss, it is the achievement of love and the value of the dignity of the human person; it does not oppress

---

[5] *Bible*. Book of Psalms 145:8-14.
[6] *Magisterium*. John Paul II, Encyclical Letter *Dives in misericordia* (1980) no. 2; no. 6.

or humble, because it recognises the preciousness of each and every human being and the deepest human reality, that mystery of humanity that is within us, the 'image of God', which can err in freedom. Being merciful one to the other means recognising ourselves as human and good.

Mercy is indispensable to the human being. Redemption is not only that which stems from justice[7]; it is also brought about through mercy that allows man to find his reality, his preciousness, that of a being a child of God.

Speaking of mercy reminds us of the terms: error and sin. Sometimes people are heard to say, "What sin have I committed that this should happen to me?" As if to say: "I do not deserve this suffering". In this prayer, Jesus reminds us that we are sinners, that every day we must ask the mercy of God the Father. This makes us more human in recognising what we are: sinners, loved and saved by God if we so choose. If sins are not recognised, if reality and human errors are not seen, we become superficial to the extent of figuring ourselves as super-men and super-women. Basically, we do not realise that we are becoming inhuman with a 'hardness of heart' which the world has already begun to boast about.

If we want the freedom to be rightly free, we must also recognise and accept the possibility of error and forgiveness; if we want to be free to choose, we must then also accept the dimension of mercy, and that means also acknowledging ourselves as sinners, in need of mercy from each other and in need of God's salvation. Being in need of mercy gives the awareness of who we really are, because sin is destructive of the person, the family and society. I would say that mercy is realistic because it has to reckon with our humanity and that of the others.

Mercy should not be confused with weakness or with indifference. People are sometimes heard to say, "God is good, he forgives everyone, he excuses everything. Sin?! But it does not exist! Hell? It does not exist! Nothing exists! God is good, He understands everyone, He excuses everyone. We should not worry at all about anything!". This is another heresy of our world, and of today's secularism: believing we can build a good future even with sins, even without God! We cannot build the future without mercy. With their consciousnesses sometimes confused and sleepy, many Christians too do not heed the extent to which this request in the *Our Father* is covered over and set aside. They have put aside the heavy reality of sin which today has become 'nothing'. But then why does Jesus teach us to ask God in the Our Father: "Forgive us our trespasses"?! This means that we have debts with God! Why

---

[7] *Magisterium*. Cfr. John Paul II, Encyclical Letter *Dives in misericordia* (1980) no. 7 (text no. 69 in Appendix).

would Jesus teach us to ask for forgiveness in the *Our Father*, making us acknowledge our sins and our shortcomings, if this were not our truth and our own good?

## Trespasses and sins

What are "our trespasses" and what is meant by the term *sin*? Saint John Paul II's Apostolic Exhortation *Reconciliatio et paenitentia* (Reconciliation and Penance) helps us to understand this important point. It is easy to lose awareness of our sins and distance ourselves ever further away from the Lord by slipping into the false presumption of being self-sufficient.

"In the words of St. John the apostle, 'If we say we have no sin, we deceive ourselves, and the truth is not in us. If we confess our sins, he is faithful and just and will forgive our sins' (...). To acknowledge one's sin, indeed – penetrating still more deeply into the consideration of one's own personhood – to recognize oneself as being a sinner, capable of sin and inclined to commit sin, is the essential first step in returning to God. (...) In order to carry out this penitential ministry adequately, we shall have to evaluate the consequences of sin with 'eyes enlightened' by faith. These consequences of sin are the reasons for division and rupture not only within each person, but also within the various circles of a person's life: in relation to the family, to the professional and social environment, as can often be seen from experience; it is confirmed by the passage in the Bible about the city of Babel and its tower"[8].

The biblical account of Genesis tells us that men at some point arrogantly agreed to build a tower that rose towards the sky; in this project there is great pride. In his Apostolic Exhortation, John Paul II continues his analysis: "Intent on building what was to be at once a symbol and a source of unity, those people found themselves more scattered than before, divided in speech, divided among themselves, incapable of consensus and agreement.

Why did the ambitious project fail? Why did 'the builders labour in vain'? They failed because they had set up as a sign and guarantee of the unity they desired a work of their own hands alone and had forgotten the action of the Lord. They had attended only to the horizontal dimension of work and social life, forgetting the vertical dimension by which they would have been rooted in God, their creator and Lord, and would have been directed toward him as the ultimate goal of their progress.

---

[8] *Magisterium*. John Paul II, Apostolic Exhortation *Reconciliatio et paenitentia* (1984) no. 13.

Now it can be said that the tragedy of humanity today, as indeed of every period in history, consists precisely in its similarity to the experience of Babel. (...) As a rupture with God, sin is an act of disobedience by a creature who rejects, at least implicitly, the very one from whom he came and who sustains him in life. It is therefore a suicidal act. Since by sinning man refuses to submit to God, his internal balance is also destroyed and it is precisely within himself that contradictions and conflicts arise. Wounded in this way, man almost inevitably causes damage to the fabric of his relationship with others and with the created world. (...) Therefore one can speak of personal and social sin: From one point of view, every sin is personal; from another point of view, every sin is social insofar as and because it also has social repercussions"[9]. At this point the Apostolic Exhortation indicates three meanings of sin.

*First meaning.* "To speak of *social sin* means in the first place to recognize that, by virtue of human solidarity which is as mysterious and intangible as it is real and concrete, each individual's sin in some way affects others. This is the other aspect of that solidarity which on the religious level is developed in the profound and magnificent mystery of the *communion of saints*, thanks to which it has been possible to say that 'every soul that rises above itself, raises up the world'. (...) Consequently one can speak of a *communion of sin*, whereby a soul that lowers itself through sin drags down with itself the church and, in some way, the whole world. In other words, there is no sin, not even the most intimate and secret one, the most strictly individual one, that exclusively concerns the person committing it. With greater or lesser violence, with greater or lesser harm, every sin has repercussions on the entire ecclesial body and the whole human family. According to this first meaning of the term, every sin can undoubtedly be considered as *social* sin"[10].

*Second meaning.* "Some sins, however, by their very matter constitute a direct attack on one's neighbour (...) They are an offense against God because they are offenses against one's neighbour. These sins are usually called *social* sins, and this is the second meaning of the term. In this sense social sin is sin against love of neighbour, and in the law of Christ it is all the more serious in that it involves the Second Commandment, which is 'like unto the first'. Likewise, the term social applies to every sin against justice in interpersonal relationships, committed either by the individual against the community or by the

---

[9] *Magisterium.* John Paul II, Apostolic Exhortation *Reconciliatio et paenitentia* (1984) no. 13; no. 15.
[10] *Magisterium.* John Paul II, Apostolic Exhortation *Reconciliatio et paenitentia* (1984) no. 16.

community against the individual. Also *social* is every sin against the rights of the human person, beginning with the right to and including the life of the unborn or against a person's physical integrity. Likewise social is every sin against others' freedom, especially against the supreme freedom to believe in God and adore him; social is every sin against the dignity and honour of one's neighbour. Also *social* is every sin against the common good and its exigencies in relation to the whole broad spectrum of the rights and duties of citizens. The term social can be applied to sins of commission or omission – on the part of political, economic or trade union leaders, who though in a position to do so, do not work diligently and wisely for the improvement and transformation of society according to the requirements and potential of the given historic moment; as also on the part of workers who through absenteeism or non-cooperation fail to ensure that their industries can *continue to advance the well-being of the workers themselves, of their families and of the whole of society"*[11].

From the viewpoint of justice we must never forget obligations as well as rights, as Benedict XVI reminded us in Apostolic Exhortation *Africae munus* (Africa's commitment): "Today, many decision makers, both political and economic, assume that they owe nothing to anyone other than themselves. 'They are concerned only with their rights, and they often have great difficulty in taking responsibility for their own and other people's integral development. Hence it is important to call for a renewed reflection on how rights presuppose duties, if they are not to become mere licence'"[12].

*Third meaning.* "The third meaning of *social sin* refers to the relationships between the various human communities. These re-lationships are not always in accordance with the plan of God, who intends that there be justice in the world and freedom and peace between individuals, groups and peoples. Thus the class struggle, whoever the person who leads it or on occasion seeks to give it a theoretical justification, is a *social evil*. Likewise obstinate confrontation between blocs of nations, between one nation and another, between different groups within the same nation all this too is a social evil. (...) the church (...) knows and she proclaims that such cases of social sin are the result of the accumulation and concentration of many *personal sins*. It is a case of the very personal sins of those who cause or support evil or who exploit it; of those who are in a position to avoid, eliminate or at least limit certain social evils but who fail to do so out of laziness, fear

---

[11] *Magisterium*. John Paul II, Apostolic Exhortation *Reconciliatio et paenitentia* (1984) no. 16.
[12] *Magisterium*. Benedict XVI, Apostolic Exhortation *Africae munus* (2011) no. 82.

or the conspiracy of silence, through secret complicity or indifference; of those who take refuge in the supposed impossibility of changing the world and also of those who sidestep the effort and sacrifice required, producing specious reasons of higher order"[13].

This broad analysis that the Exhortation has outlined for us makes it possible to understand the magnitude of "our debts", human debts to God the Father and to his children, our brothers and sisters. Sin is always damage that calls for recognition.

## Loss of the sense of sin

It has to be asked: what are the causes of the loss of the sense of sin in the world today? Apostolic Exhortation *Reconciliatio et paenitentia* by Saint John Paul II at nos. 17 and 18 illustrates a number of important reasons:

– "'Secularism' is by nature and definition a movement of ideas and behaviour which advocates a humanism totally without God, completely centred upon the cult of action and production and caught up in the heady enthusiasm of consumerism and pleasure seeking, unconcerned with the danger of 'losing one's soul'. This secularism cannot but undermine the sense of sin. At the very most, sin will be reduced to what offends man". It can be seen here that the presence of God is not only eclipsed in the world but also in the human conscience and the human being.

"In fact, God is the origin and the supreme end of man, and man carries in himself a divine seed. Hence it is the reality of God that reveals and illustrates the mystery of man". The Vatican Council II document *Gaudium et spes*[14] refers to this "divine seed" as does the Bible[15]. This concerns the dimension of the spiritual soul and the human spirit which we have already dealt with[16].

– "Another reason for the disappearance of the sense of sin in contemporary society is to be found in the errors made in evaluating certain findings of the human sciences. Thus on the basis of certain affirmations of psychology, concern to avoid creating feelings of guilt or to place limits on freedom leads to a refusal ever to admit any shortcoming. Through an undue extrapolation of the criteria of the science of sociology, it finally happens – as I have already

---

[13] *Magisterium*. John Paul II, Apostolic Exhortation *Reconciliatio et paenitentia* (1984) no. 16.
[14] *Magisterium*. Cfr. Vatican Council II, Pastoral Constitution *Gaudium et spes* no. 3.
[15] *Bible*. Cfr. First Letter of John 3:9.
[16] Cfr. Chapter 3.

said – that all failings are blamed upon society, and the individual is declared innocent of them". This takes place through a sadly well-known mechanism: putting always the blame on others! In this way, one becomes so immature and superficial as to no longer even realise one's own responsibilities! In this way human coexistence becomes highly complex.

– "Again, a certain cultural anthropology so emphasizes the undeniable environmental and historical conditioning and influences which act upon man, that it reduces his responsibility to the point of not acknowledging his ability to perform truly human acts and therefore his ability to sin". Social influence, the media, the continuous examples of others... Is it not strange that in the midst of so much individualism, the individual disappears?

– "The sense of sin also easily declines as a result of a system of ethics deriving from a certain historical relativism. This may take the form of an ethical system which relativizes the moral norm, denying its absolute and unconditional value, and as a consequence denying that there can be intrinsically illicit acts independent of the circumstances in which they are performed by the subject. Herein lies a real 'overthrowing and downfall of moral values', and 'the problem is not so much one of ignorance of Christian ethics', but ignorance 'rather of the meaning, foundations and criteria of the moral attitude'".

– "Finally the sense of sin disappears when – as can happen in the education of youth, in the mass media and even in education within the family – it is wrongly identified with a morbid feeling of guilt or with the mere transgression of legal norms and precepts".

Let us consider how deeply these thoughts are part of today's way of thinking! In this way, the sense of sin in people has been shaken and awareness weakened. The argumentation goes as follows: if there is nothing absolute then there is no absolute rule; it then follows precisely that everything is relative. In the end, there is no sin.

– "The loss of the sense of sin is thus a form or consequence of the *denial of God*: not only in the form of atheism but also in the form of secularism. If sin is the breaking off of one's filial relationship to God in order to situate one's life outside of obedience to him, then to sin is not merely to deny God. To sin is also to live as if he did not exist, to eliminate him from one's daily life". This has resulted in a general situation of "obscuring or weakening the sense of sin" and the need for forgiveness[17].

---

[17] *Magisterium*. Cfr. John Paul II, Apostolic Exhortation *Reconciliatio et paenitentia* (1984) no. 18 (text no. 70 in Appendix).

Most of the time the world arrogantly states that self-fulfilment is achieved by disobeying rules and unscrupulously carrying out one's will as much as possible, beyond any established boundary lines. Conversely, for us Christians the fulfilment of man is to be found in the return of human capacity to the will of God the Father, where God and man *meet*. Jesus shows this to us by his whole life. The return to God in truth, in freedom and love, is presented by Jesus as humility and obedience whereby man finds himself more human and humanity more real and fraternal. In disobedience to God and in the pursuit of his own pride and vanity, man has lost the root of his own good and true humanity, of which we are constantly reminded in the prayer of the *Our Father*.

One thus realises where the mindset and spirit of the world attack to undermine the Christian roots of life, the family and society, and why they want to relegate religion to a corner, away from life. This is the starting point for the attack on Christianity and the consciences of Christians. The analysis of Saint John Paul II is very useful to understand also our society and how it has evolved to one of religious indifference! The transition has largely taken place through forgetting the paternity of God. This is why it is very important to start again by getting to know the *Our Father* better. This is something we have to acknowledge! Today there is a need and urgency for the faithful to take up, with greater awareness, the preciousness of Christianity! This should be done in the search of its roots of truth, with serenity, objectivity and in dialogue with the world, in the light of the faith and the Magisterium of the Church. For this, as Benedict XVI reminded us in Apostolic Exhortation *Verbum Domini*[18], a new evangelisation is essential.

**The work of mercy**

Sin is a real fact and its significance is not to be identified with the feeling that can be experienced. In the world, in the midst of a lot of really good and splendid realities, the mystery of evil is present; *the mystery of iniquity*. But there is a greater, more powerful mystery; that of the mercy of God, his love for humanity, for all men, for each and every man. Divine mercy "is a love more powerful than sin, stronger than death. When we realize that God's love for us does not cease in the face of our sin or recoil before our offenses, but becomes even more attentive and generous; when we realize that this love went so far as to cause the passion and death of the Word made flesh who consented to

---

[18] *Magisterium.* Cfr. Benedict XVI, Apostolic Exhortation *Verbum Domini* (2010) no. 96 (text no. 71 in Appendix).

redeem us at the price of his own blood, then we exclaim in gratitude: 'Yes, the Lord is rich in mercy', and even: 'The Lord is mercy'"[19].

Really great is the work that God accomplishes through his mercy, to welcome man, to meet him, embrace him and give him forgiveness and 'the true life'. Forgiveness passes through the offer of the life of Jesus, and then pours into the world through the ministers of mercy, as Saint John Paul II reminds us in his book *Gift and Mystery*[20]. Forgiveness, as precious as 'daily' bread, passes into the world and the soul of people through the sacrament of Reconciliation, commonly known as Confession, instituted by Jesus as his Paschal gift, the gift of his Spirit of love, mercy and salvation "Receive the Holy Spirit. Whose sins you forgive are forgiven them, and whose sins you retain are retained"[21]. The new life of the resurrection begins with the mercy of Jesus received in us through his Church. Between the Church and Christ there exists a communion and an extraordinary unity of life and mission. This is what the Church lives by announcing Jesus, the Bridegroom[22].

The priest must be a man of God, a man of mercy and peace: his heart and his life must be intimately united with Christ so as to reproduce in himself the spiritual traits of Jesus the Good Shepherd, as we were reminded by Saint John Paul II in his Apostolic Exhortation *Pastores dabo Vobis* (I will give you shepherds)[23].

For this reason the priest only acquires light and strength for his ministry in the intimacy of prayer with God. Pope Emeritus Benedict XVI reminded every priest of this and of the preciousness of each personal call from God to his service: "he is called to rediscover in prayer the ever new face of his Lord and the most authentic content of his mission. Only those who have a profound relationship with the Lord are grasped by him, can take him to others, can be sent out. 'Abiding with him' must always accompany the exercise of the priestly ministry. It must be its

---

[19] *Magisterium*. John Paul II, Apostolic Exhortation *Reconciliatio et paenitentia* (1984) no. 22.
[20] *Magisterium*. Cfr. John Paul II, *Gift and Mystery*, Doubleday, New York 1996, pp. 86-87 (text no. 72 in Appendix).
[21] *Bible*. Gospel of John 20:22-23.
[22] *Tradition*. Cfr. Blessed Isaac of Stella, Abbot (1100 ca.-1169), *Sermon 11, Liturgy of the Hours, Office of Readings, Friday, 23rd week, Ordinary Time* (http://www.liturgies.net/Liturgies/Catholic/loh/week23fridayor.htm, accessed in July 2014. Text no. 73 in Appendix).
[23] *Magisterium*. John Paul II, Apostolic Exhortation *Pastores dabo vobis* (1992) no. 22 (text no. 74 in Appendix). In the Movement of Family Love, "Amici dello Sposo" are a group of priests available to help those who seek to live in the light of Apostolic Exhortation *Pastores dabo vobis* (22) of Saint John Paul II, i.e., the spirituality of the "great mystery" of Love to be poured in any apostolate, especially in those for families and Christian spouses.

central part, even and above all in difficult moments when it seems that the 'things that need doing' should have priority, wherever we are, whatever we are doing, we must always 'abide with him'"[24].

Just as God blesses a family with the 'gift' of children[25] for every natural or adoptive motherhood and fatherhood, so God blesses a community through the 'sign' of the special call of men and women to his service[26] for them and for the world. We must also not forget that good vocations and good priests come from good families. These men and women also have their human dimension which is an instrument of grace, since God works through them. There is a twofold need for mercy: in human relations but also in the relationship with God, to draw from him mercy and reconciliation, and to live these out in the world. It is important to live mercy also among people and in our cities.

The whole of humanity, families, individuals, and society itself have to recognise their need for mercy! Indeed, without mercy, people soon wither, closing themselves within a claim for formal justice that is poor in substance, since it is not inhabited by God's love for his creatures.

In his Apostolic Exhortation *Sacramentum Caritatis* (Sacrament of Charity), Benedict XVI called again for generosity, commitment and competence in administering the sacrament of Reconciliation[27]. The Church is caring so that no one may lack the gift of mercy! Because it feels that mercy is needed for the souls, for people in the family and society. Because it understands how important mercy is for personal equilibrium, for the ability to love, to see the light, to build relationships in a healthy way, to heal the inner distortion of the spirit, especially given the loss of consciousness of sin. In this regard, Benedict XVI in his Apostolic Exhortation recalled the connection between the sacrament of the Eucharist and Reconciliation[28].

Someone, without due reflection, may unworthily approach Holy Communion listening only to his own desire. It is actually an act to be done 'in communion', and 'in communion' to be lived with Christ and with the Church.

Superficiality in approaching Holy Communion is often due to not reflecting on what the Lord thinks of our lives, what "our debts", our

---

[24] *Magisterium*. Benedict XVI, *Homily at Holy Mass for the Priestly Ordination of the Deacons of the Diocese of Rome* (20 June 2010).
[25] *Bible*. Cfr. Book of Psalms 127:3-5.
[26] *Magisterium*. Cfr. Benedict XVI, *Address to the Bishops of the Episcopal Conference of Romania on their Ad Limina Visit* (12 February 2010) (text no. 75 in Appendix).
[27] *Magisterium*. Cfr. Benedict XVI, Apostolic Exhortation *Sacramentum caritatis* (2007) no. 21 (text no. 76 in Appendix).
[28] *Magisterium*. Cfr. Benedict XVI, Apostolic Exhortation *Sacramentum caritatis* (2007) no. 20 (text no. 77 in Appendix).

sins, are and how long we have neglected the life of purity of spirit by not living the sacrament of Reconciliation.

In actual fact, we cannot be up to our human tasks of responsibility and love without the experience of forgiveness: forgiveness is part of our ability to live; removing the ability to be forgiven by God means leaving the world to its evil, an evil which grows in the minds and lives of men, and is revealed in work and human relations. The forgiveness that God gives is not formal; it is restoration of man in the truth, in the life and joy that is lost through sin. Not receiving God's forgiveness means destroying man, destroying families and couples, and destroying society: a *do-ut-des* society cannot exist! There cannot simply exist commercial barter! There can be no functional exchange in the relationship between man and woman! There can be no barter, no functional exchange in the relationship between parents and children! If we do not live mercy towards ourselves and towards others, life does not hold together and sooner or later collapses and sinks into betrayal or the evil of blackmail!

Mercy is made of truth! And it is also made of justice! But it also consists in an overcoming of the application of justice, because it recognises a greater value, beyond historical, occasional and temporary limitations: this is the mercy that carries within it forgiveness and reconciliation. The world cannot grow in justice and peace without mercy since the world itself cannot be simply the result of economy, mathematical knowledge, and a legalistic justice. Justice, though human and imperfect, is necessary to combat lawlessness and systems of illegality, because *legislation and law* defend the dignity of the person and the common good. It is for this that legality must be promoted and defended together with justice, imperfect as this is. But justice and legality, although necessary for a good and orderly human society, must also take into consideration human and divine mercy. Indeed there is something greater in the human world that we must always bear in mind. Our human world comes from God: this is why Jesus teaches us to make this request to God in the *Our Father*: "Forgive us our trespasses": we can pray in this way and our better life will come to the light.

We need to go to the roots of our existence and understand what is most right also for the world and what the world needs most. For this reason Saint Paul urges us that "supplications, prayers, petitions, and thanksgivings be offered for everyone, for kings and for all in authority, that we may lead a quiet and tranquil life in all devotion and dignity. This is good and pleasing to God our savior, who wills everyone to be saved and to come to knowledge of the truth. For there is one God.

There is also one mediator between God and the human race, Christ Jesus, himself human, who gave himself as ransom for all"[29].

With his mercy, we will understand even better why Jesus is the Saviour of all mankind and what He has brought which is unique and immensely great, and should not be hidden from the world. This is expressed and explained in the second part of this wonderful petition in the *Our Father*: "as we forgive those who trespass against us", which we shall now see.

---

[29] *Bible*. First Letter to Timothy 2:1-6.

# 12

# As we forgive those who trespass against us
## As we forgive our debtors

In the petition "Forgive us our trespasses" addressed to God in the *Our Father*, Jesus adds a second part: "as we forgive those who trespass against us". So that our prayer may not be formal and may be active in our personal, family and social life, here too Jesus teaches us God's 'as'. In fact, we cannot automatically receive from God his mercy and forgiveness: He has placed a particular condition that is the fundamental respect of 'as' we act. As we shall see, this second part is an important specification; irreplaceable and most enlightening.

We have already noted that the ability to be free also involves our acknowledgement of the seriousness of our errors, omissions and sins, and the need to ask for forgiveness in recognising ourselves as sinners, and therefore in need of mercy. The merciful love of God, who so loved the world[1] as to give himself with his forgiveness of mercy, helps us to understand that this is the only way for us, who are fallible and sinners, not to lose our human reality as God's children, and to regain energies of goodness and truth. Only in this way can we find ourselves and fulfil the need of our hearts to remain 'human' and to build together a world that is not of 'stone'.

We have seen how necessary mercy is for the truth of life, people, the family and society: indeed everyone in our human kingdom needs mercy, from the lowest to the greatest. The reality of sin weighs upon us and we would like to escape from it. We would like not to see, to forget and not to have all these trespasses... For this there is the great love of God the Father who has us draw close to him through the good humanity of Jesus. In order to save us, He took all our sins upon

---

[1] *Bible*. Cfr. Gospel of John 3:16.

himself[2], and brings us redemption with divine mercy, reintroducing goodness and truth in human relationships.

## Sin and corruption

Sin is a disordered love of oneself which we call egoism, excessive love of self that rebels against God and turns its back on him. Basically, it is a closing within the self in a self-referential and self-justifying existence. This erroneous love of self destroys life, family and society. This is why, in living along with our sins and using those of others, we do not manage to live as God's children, do his will, and build his kingdom! The world of sin extends to vice and to personal and social corruption. Failures to open up to God the Father from whom we come, and failures to open up to other people, even if we do not wish to see them, remain in us and spread evil: they contaminate the family and all that surround us with the evil that we and other people carry within... Mortal sin and negative consequences spread around us, and often form the backdrop to custom and a common mentality, a way of life that carries within those minor corruptions which in turn prepare the way for major ones.

At first, corruption takes a superficial but constant form that digs into the conscience destroying justice and love, religious faith and human values to then bring about major social corruption. Indeed, 'mammon' initially consists of lies and intrigues, slyness and deception with which it acts to the detriment of others, in a war where everything seems to be legitimate to prevail at any cost on one's opponent. Careerism and social climbing, deceits, false appearances, fraud, injustice, violence and intrigue: this is what makes up the daily corruption of life, increasingly uncivilized, but cloaked in civility and false legality. And this is what the ordinary man has to face every day thereby becoming more and more injured. If he is not healed from this evil in its many forms, sooner or later he too ends up – like the drug dealer – sowing a life of minor and major corruption.

In this regard, the *Catechism of the Catholic Church* reminds us that: "Sin creates a proclivity to sin; it engenders vice by repetition of the same acts. This results in perverse inclinations which cloud conscience and corrupt the concrete judgment of good and evil. Thus sin tends to reproduce itself and reinforce itself, but it cannot destroy the moral sense at its root"[3]. "Vices can be classified according to the virtues they oppose, or also be linked to the *capital sins* which Christian experience has distinguished, following St. John Cassian and St. Gregory the Great.

---

[2] *Bible*. Cfr. Book of the Prophet Isaiah 52:13; 53:12.
[3] *Magisterium. Catechism of the Catholic Church* no. 1865.

They are called 'capital' because they engender other sins, other vices. They are pride, avarice, envy, wrath, lust, gluttony, and sloth or acedia"[4].

Our spiritual dimension, with which God has willed every human being created in freedom and love, has the ability to do good or evil, lifting itself in God or corrupting itself. For man's return 'to self', it is essential that there be the light, the return to God and the truth, the tenderness of love, and the power of grace. Saint Paul reminds us: "For God delivered all to disobedience, that he might have mercy upon all"[5].

And this is the extraordinary divine mercy toward us: it is an incredibly powerful force which the world needs. It passes from the redemptive sacrifice of Jesus to the Church, and from the Church to Christians who live and give witness to it in the world, not as a private matter to be ashamed of for the sins confessed, but as a proclamation of salvation. In fact, by 'confessing' his mercy we bear witness to the greatest gift that God has given us to restore our truest and most beautiful image, the one which belongs to us the most, to restore in us the joy of existence, the gratitude and beauty of living a renewed life and being able to start afresh with God... for He has confidence in us.

### 'As' Jesus

Now since God's mercy is unconditional love, the question is: "Why does Jesus teach us in the *Our Father* to ask his forgiveness linking it to the condition of an 'as' on our part?". It should be noted that He does not say "as we too should forgive" but "as we forgive". This means we receive God's forgiveness to the extent that we too 'are able' to live mercy towards "those who trespass against us". In fact, if we live mercy our hearts are open to receive it. If, on the other hand, our hearts are closed, then life does not germinate within us, and we do not accept the grace of the forgiveness of God, and of Reconciliation, and we do not reinvest it in our neighbour.

"As we". That 'as' is revealing, it is the 'as' that Jesus reminds us of many times and is crucial because it opens us up to the deepest dimension of our ability. Again it concerns the 'as' that we have previously seen[6]. *The Catechism of the Catholic Church* states: "This 'as' is not unique in Jesus' teaching: 'You, therefore, must be perfect, as your heavenly Father is perfect' (Mt 5:48); 'Be merciful, even as your Father is merciful' (Lk 6:36); 'A new commandment I give to you, that you love one another, even as I have loved you, that you also love one

---

[4] *Magisterium. Catechism of the Catholic Church* no. 1866.
[5] *Bible.* Letter to the Romans 11:32.
[6] Cfr. Chapters 8 and 9.

another' (Jn 13:34). It is impossible to keep the Lord's commandment by imitating the divine model from outside; there has to be a vital participation, coming from the depths of the heart, in the holiness and the mercy and the love of our God. Only the Spirit by whom we live (Gal 5:25) can make 'ours' the same mind that was in Christ Jesus (Ph 2:15). Then the unity of forgiveness becomes possible and we find ourselves 'forgiving one another, as God in Christ forgave' us (Eph 4:32)"[7].

This human ability does not have its roots in thought, corporeality, sexuality, affectivity, character, or the psyche. Instead, it is rooted principally in the specificity of being created "in the image and likeness of God", that is, in the human spirit. It is here that the mercy of God enters to be then spread to others.

"As we" therefore "forgive those who trespass against us": it is an opportunity that we have. Because we are animated by our spirit we too can do it following the example of God the Father. This is a greatness we can live so as to receive and accept God's mercy, his merciful love for us and for others. Either a person lives in the mercy of God, and is then capable of accepting and offering it, or is closed, not living it with anyone, and thinks he will receive it from God, but as he receives it, so to speak, it does not enter his heart, his spirit and his life, because his heart and his will are closed. In short, in ourselves and in others we have to 'overcome evil with good', as Saint Paul reminds us: "Do not be conquered by evil but conquer evil with good"[8]. The evil that is in each one of us is to be defeated with the good.

We cannot take possession of the good or even of the forgiveness asked of God and received from him, thinking that in this way we have calmed God or our conscience. Conversely, we are called to live in the love of the gift: in the same way we receive it from God our Father, so too must it reach our brothers.

When Jesus speaks in the Gospel of the kingdom of heaven and the mercy of God, He tells the parable of the heartless servant[9], and shows that the 'trespasses' we have with our brothers are always much smaller than the ones we have with God! What God wants from us is that we forgive our brothers with all our hearts cancelling those 'small debts' they owe us for the wrongs or offences they have caused us.

---

[7] *Magisterium. Catechism of the Catholic Church* no. 2842.
[8] *Bible.* Letter to the Romans 12:21.
[9] *Bible.* Cfr. Gospel of Matthew 18:23-35.

**More than Justice**

Of course, 'justice' entails establishing the truth of the evils committed. This is not a process that can be evaded, as some instead would, because the evil done to one person today, might very well be repeated to another tomorrow. Justice, in fact, is to be built in regard both to the self and to the others; yet, the spiral of evil cannot be broken just with the exercise of 'law'. What is needed is the practice of that love that is typically Christian, and which takes to heart even those who make mistakes, by giving them too the chance to rebuild themselves in the good they lacked. To 'for-give' is to serve one's brother: it is 'a gift for', so that those who have done wrong may pick themselves up in good: that same good that they were perhaps unable to get in their own life, but can now see and find in those who forgive them. To forgive is not the same as saying, "not to worry, no harm done". It does not mean suffering evil either by accepting it or by taking no notice. It means instead facing it with strength to circulate the good, dedicating oneself to serving brothers even when they do evil and cause suffering. It is necessary 'to oppose' evil with good: it is necessary to stop it, purify it and heal the man so that, healed, he will shine in the light.

This is the way that Jesus taught us to overcome evil: take it upon us as He did and heal with the good of mercy! Mercy is power, it is not weakness, and does not even stop at an equal justice: it is that 'extra' which the world needs to be a human world, the family of God's children. Jesus calls upon us: "Love your enemies"[10]. Benedict XVI commented on this important exhortation by Jesus as follows: "But what do his words mean? Why does Jesus ask us to love precisely our enemies, that is, a love which exceeds human capacities? Actually, Christ's proposal is realistic because it takes into account that in the world there is *too much* violence, *too much* injustice, and therefore that this situation cannot be overcome except by countering it with *more* love, with *more* goodness. This *'more'* comes from God: it is his mercy which was made flesh in Jesus and which alone can 'tip the balance' of the world from evil to good, starting with that small and decisive 'world' which is the human heart. (...) Love of one's enemy constitutes the nucleus of the 'Christian revolution', a revolution not based on strategies of economic, political or media power: the revolution of love, a love that does not rely ultimately on human resources but is a gift of God which is obtained by trusting solely and unreservedly in his merciful goodness. Here is the newness of the Gospel which silently changes the world! Here is the

---

[10] *Bible*. Gospel of Luke 6:27.

heroism of the 'lowly' who believe in God's love and spread it, even at the cost of their lives"[11].

Only this gift of Jesus – mercy – '*more* than love, *more* than goodness' can truly renew history introducing a novelty. Christianity has made the world aware of forgiveness by delivering new sources of good to humanity. So let us not allow ourselves to be confused by defects, or by the serious scandals of the world or those involving some Christians and even some clergymen. The enemy has infiltrated everywhere to confuse people and to separate them from God and the Church. Only a true 'faith' lived in charity alienates operators of iniquity and Satan. Let us not allow ourselves to be blocked by evil and despair! The sins and scandals of a few cannot cover the immense good carried out over twenty centuries by legions of countless Christians who have conquered evil with good.

In short, we can say that merciful love is a way of living, the most important, the most necessary one, just like bread. After material bread – "Give us this day our daily bread" – the deepest need of human beings is to be loved and forgiven, learning from God the Father to give, in our turn, forgiveness. "Give us this day our daily bread and forgive us our trespasses, as we forgive": this is also our good, because if we do not cancel the evil we have received, it remains within and deforms us creating a 'heart of stone'. If the evil is addressed by bringing about another evil, similar to the offence received, the evil will continue to exist turning into revenge, rancour, and envy, manifesting itself in closure and contempt, spreading as hate or the wish for further evil that continues to circulate, expand and come back multiplied! It is then that a man, so wounded by the evil of his brothers, is in his turn no longer a man who brings justice and peace, but, on the contrary, sows the seeds of revenge and destruction. Even if he feels he wants to restore right, nevertheless, very often, because he is wounded, he mistakes the 'as' of the good he wants to do, and does evil. We often get sick because of this. Many diseases stem also from a lack of love that has not been received, or from an evil suffered, or even from a lack of love that has not been given through forgiveness.

In the same way that God our Father overcomes evil with good, we too can and must live this way; otherwise each day we will die a little as people, as families and as a society. That is why, after having clarified and sought truth and justice, it is so important to be able to forgive. We must fundamentally live mercy for our life and our true well-being; a spiritual well-being that reverberates throughout life.

---

[11] *Magisterium.* Benedict XVI, *Angelus* (18 February 2007).

To be able to appreciate and receive mercy, the human being must be able to give it, as Jesus tells us: "For as you judge, so will you be judged, and the measure with which you measure will be measured out to you"[12]. We will gather what we have sown. "Blessed are the merciful, for they will be shown mercy"[13]: in the measure we live it, we are capable of breathing and enjoying it, accepting and giving it. A free heart is capable of forgiveness as the Letter of James reminds us: "So speak and so act as people who will be judged by the law of freedom. For the judgment is merciless to one who has not shown mercy; mercy triumphs over judgment"[14].

**The two thieves**

The image of Jesus on the cross next to the two thieves can help us to understand: "Now one of the criminals hanging there reviled Jesus, saying, 'Are you not the Messiah? Save yourself and us'"[15]. He reproached insulting the envoy, the Christ of God, Jesus and, by not accepting him, remained locked within his sin and the disorder of his life. "The other, however, rebuking him, said in reply, 'Have you no fear of God, for you are subject to the same condemnation? And indeed, we have been condemned justly, for the sentence we received corresponds to our crimes, but this man has done nothing criminal'"[16].

The good thief, as we call him, defends Jesus; here his mercy is revealed, which makes him able to oppose the evil and injustice he perceives in another, and to tell the truth about their sentence: "And indeed, we have been condemned justly, for the sentence we received corresponds to our crimes, but this man has done nothing criminal". He is merciful and defends the righteous struck unjustly, Jesus on the cross. Worthy of note are his love and trust: "Then he said, 'Jesus, remember me when you come into your kingdom'"[17]. This is his prayer. First, through truth, the good thief halted the expansion of evil propagated by the other thief who was angry against God and man. Then, he defended Jesus. Subsequently, he prays entrusting himself to the mercy of Jesus: "remember me when you come into your kingdom". Jesus replies with that wonderful phrase: "today you will be with me in

---

[12] *Bible*. Gospel of Matthew 7:2.
[13] *Bible*. Gospel of Matthew 5:7.
[14] *Bible*. Letter of James 2:12-13.
[15] *Bible*. Gospel of Luke 23:39.
[16] *Bible*. Gospel of Luke 23:40-41.
[17] *Bible*. Gospel of Luke 23:42.

Paradise"[18]. He had faith, entrusting himself to the mercy of Jesus, but first he had shown mercy towards Jesus. To the extent that our hearts are open and act with mercy they are ready to receive the mercy of God a thousand times more!

It is crucial to overcome evil with good. As Saint John Paul II once said: "as we ask forgiveness, let us also forgive"[19]. It concerns the removal of evil in the world: and this is the power of mercy. Humanly, we would not know where to take strength for good when we are wounded, humiliated, or trampled by injustice and evil. But with the help of Jesus and the power of the Holy Spirit it is possible to take from him new energies for the good; indeed this is necessary to break the *spiral of evil*. The *Catechism of the Catholic Church* says in this regard: "It is not in our power not to feel or to forget an offense; but the heart that offers itself to the Holy Spirit turns injury into compassion and purifies the memory in transforming the hurt into intercession"[20].

"Now – and this is daunting – this outpouring of mercy cannot penetrate our hearts as long as we have not forgiven those who have trespassed against us. Love, like the Body of Christ, is indivisible; we cannot love the God we cannot see if we do not love the brother or sister we do see (Cfr.1 Jn 4:20). In refusing to forgive our brothers and sisters, our hearts are closed and their hardness makes them impervious to the Father's merciful love; but in confessing our sins, our hearts are opened to his grace"[21].

The ability to forgive implies healing. On this point, Benedict XVI in his book *Jesus of Nazareth* writes: "Forgiveness exacts a price – first of all from the person who forgives. He must overcome within himself the evil done to him: he must, as it were, burn it interiorly and in so doing renew himself. As a result, he also involves the other, the trespasser, in this process of transformation, of inner purification, and both parties, suffering all the way through and overcoming evil, are made new"[22].

The purification process is necessary every time evil is experienced and therefore God's help is needed. We cannot do it on our own. It is not possible if we are isolated and weak.

---

[18] *Bible*. Gospel of Luke 23:43.
[19] *Magisterium*. Cfr. John Paul II, *Angelus* (12 March 2000) (text no. 78 in Appendix).
[20] *Magisterium*. Catechism of the Catholic Church no. 2843.
[21] *Magisterium*. Catechism of the Catholic Church no. 2840.
[22] *Magisterium*. Benedict XVI, *Jesus of Nazareth*, Doubleday, New York 2007, p. 158-159.

## Why justice is not enough

But the question is: what to do with injustice? What happens to trampled justice? The injustice of evil must in some way be burned, purified, not only in those affected, but also in the culprits. For this reason injustice must be identified in truth and dealt with, as we are reminded in the Encyclical Letter *Dives in Misericordia*: "Christ emphasizes so insistently the need to forgive others that when Peter asked Him how many times he should forgive his neighbour He answered with the symbolic number of 'seventy times seven', meaning that he must be able to forgive everyone every time. It is obvious that such a generous requirement of forgiveness does not cancel out the objective requirements of justice. Properly understood, justice constitutes, so to speak, the goal of forgiveness. In no passage of the Gospel message does forgiveness, or mercy as its source, mean indulgence towards evil, towards scandals, towards injury or insult. In any case, reparation for evil and scandal, compensation for injury, and satisfaction for insult are conditions for forgiveness"[23]. It must be made clear that forgiveness and mercy are not a 'laissez-passer' for further evil, an 'indulgence towards evil or the wrong done', as forgiveness implies repair of the harm caused.

Forgiveness has to come to terms with justice and cannot ignore responsibility, since the other has to repair the damage caused and renew his life. You cannot leave the other in sin, error, deception, and in the danger that he continues to harm both himself and others creating new victims. Man, however, to recognise his evil, needs justice, but also forgiveness.

But the world asks itself: "At the end of the day what is the point of mercy? Isn't justice sufficient? Isn't this the only remedy for social ill?". This I would say is a solution that is not only materialistic, naive and blind, but also one that takes no heed of history as Saint John Paul II reminds us in the Encyclical *Dives in misericordia*, where he states: "The experience of the past and of our own time demonstrates that justice alone is not enough, that it can even lead to the negation and destruction of itself, if that deeper power, which is love, is not allowed to shape human life in its various dimensions. It has been precisely historical experience that, among other things, has led to the formulation of the saying: *summum ius, summa iniuria*. This statement does not detract from the value of justice and does not minimize the significance of the order that is based upon it; it only indicates, under another aspect, the need to draw from the powers of the spirit

---

[23] *Magisterium*. John Paul II, Encyclical Letter *Dives in misericordia* (1980) no. 14.

which condition the very order of justice, powers which are still more profound"[24].

"True mercy is, so to speak, the most profound source of justice. If justice is in itself suitable for 'arbitration' between people concerning the reciprocal distribution of objective goods in an equitable manner, love and only love (including that kindly love that we call 'mercy') is capable of restoring man to Himself. (...) However, the equality brought by justice is limited to the realm of objective and extrinsic goods, while love and mercy bring it about that people meet one another in that value which is man himself, with the dignity that is proper to him"[25]. Thus, 'equal justice', "an eye for eye, a tooth for a tooth", is too limited a justice compared to the man that is 'bigger' than the laws he makes and whose rights are far beyond what we can measure. In the end 'equal justice' increasingly reveals itself as a utopia compared to the dilation of relationships caused by globalization. Today, more than ever before the need is felt for a more extensive justice: that of love. So love and mercy dilate the hearts and conscience in anticipation of a greater justice.

**For greater justice**

In short, justice is necessary, but it is not only human justice that is needed, since man is made in the 'image and likeness' of God. If this truth is forgotten or ignored, individuals, families, children, and society are harmed. Conversely, to build a humanity that is intact, good, true, and supportive it is essential to consider the need not only for justice but also for mercy. As John Paul II said during the XXXV World Day of Peace: "No Peace without Justice, No Justice without Forgiveness"[26]. "Society can become ever more human only if we introduce into the many-sided setting of interpersonal and social relationships, not merely justice, but also that 'merciful love' which constitutes the messianic message of the Gospel"[27].

This is the Gospel for the world, the Gospel that must touch life[28]. The world needs it, and it is up to us Christians to bear witness to and bring mercy. The prayer of the *Our Father* therefore makes us more

---

[24] *Magisterium.* John Paul II, Encyclical Letter *Dives in misericordia* (1980) no. 12.

[25] *Magisterium.* John Paul II, Encyclical Letter *Dives in misericordia* (1980) no. 14.

[26] *Magisterium.* John Paul II, *Message for the Celebration of the XXXV World Day of Peace* (8 December 2001).

[27] *Magisterium.* John Paul II, Encyclical Letter *Dives in misericordia* (1980) no. 14 (text no. 79 in Appendix).

[28] *Magisterium.* Cfr. John Paul II, Encyclical Letter *Evangelium vitae* (1995) no. 2 (text no. 80 in Appendix).

human and closer to each and every man. This prayer of Jesus, given to the heart and conscience of all, helps the path of history and humanity, and makes us grow as brothers, capable of a truer and greater justice; for a hope that grows.

Both alongside and inside justice there is also the need for merciful love. The world needs mercy[29] to be saved. These aspects, that are easily forgotten, are recalled in the *Our Father*: "Forgive us our trespasses, as we forgive those who also trespass against us". Now we are beginning to understand more and more the scope of the *Our Father* that Jesus entrusted and delivered to mankind. Mercy, which is so necessary to the person, to family life and the construction of a human society, is a mandate for the Church[30]; this is why this call is often found in the Documents of the Church.

At this point the reader, noting the abundant citations of the Magisterium, may wonder: what is the value of these Documents which attest to a past and also a future?

The Encyclicals and other Documents of the Magisterium of the Church guide us in our research, because they are words to be seriously taken into account and ones that really commit us in the review of our life towards finding the depth of our Christian roots. These Acts of the Magisterium are ever valid. All these Acts refer to the Holy Bible, the Scripture that is the Word of God, and also to the Tradition of the Church: they constitute for us a continuous deepening and confirmation, the confirmation that Jesus asked Peter to carry out: "you must strengthen your brothers"[31]. They accompany the Church and humanity through history[32]. This is why we refer to the Documents of the Magisterium of the Pope. The "Pope, as the Bishop of Rome, who bears the highest responsibility for Catholic Christianity"[33] is a great gift of Jesus to the Church and to mankind. Ever since the very beginning, Christians have been aware of the importance of fidelity to the truth revealed by Jesus, as Saint Paul reminds us: "you should know how to behave in the household of God, which is the church of the living God, the pillar and foundation of truth"[34].

---

[29] *Magisterium.* Cfr. John Paul II, *Memory and Identity*, Rizzoli International Publications, Inc., New York 2005, pp. 54-55 (text no. 81 in Appendix).

[30] *Magisterium.* Cfr. John Paul II, Encyclical Letter *Dives in misericordia* (1980) no. 15 (text no. 82 in Appendix).

[31] *Bible.* Gospel of Luke 22:32.

[32] *Magisterium.* Cfr. *Catechism of the Catholic Church* no. 95.

[33] *Magisterium.* Benedict XVI, *Address to the Federal Parliament, Reichstag Building, Berlin.* Apostolic Journey to Germany (22 September 2011).

[34] *Bible.* First Letter to Timothy 3:15.

The prayer of the *Our Father* is a great beacon of light that crosses past and future history, and accompanies us in our personal and social life opening it up to the greatest hope.

This prayer has always been particularly loved by the Magisterium of the Church and by all believers because it helps us to understand and love God, rich in forgiveness, and to live the faith and love our neighbour. The world, in fact, needs our prayer along with the power of mercy that, together with justice, turns into the capacity for love and light towards a better world. Woe to us if we guiltily fail to bring mercy into the world so that the world derails towards a justice closed in on itself. It is necessary to illuminate humanity, to warm hearts, and to guide relationships too, purifying them with evangelical mercy.

And this is also the task of bearing witness: to forgive ourselves and to forgive others, also calling for reparation from those that have erred. This is why the powerful and very human image of the *crucifix* is the sign of mercy, but also of justice because Jesus the Redeemer took upon himself our sins – he "bore the sins of many"[35] – and our trespasses. Jesus gave the example that shows the need for reparation and therefore for justice. Being men of peace and love also means being men of mercy, capable of spreading goodness in the world. We will be judged by love, and by mercy, in a word: by goodness. Only goodness will enter Heaven, only goodness will stand up before the fire of God's love, only goodness will be with God: "Come, you who are blessed by my Father. Inherit the kingdom prepared for you from the foundation of the world. For I was hungry and you gave me food, I was thirsty and you gave me drink, a stranger and you welcomed me, naked and you clothed me, ill and you cared for me, in prison and you visited me"[36]. This is why we need the world of God and his Spirit of Holiness and Love, the 'bread of forgiveness', because without it we will die within, love within us will die: every friendship will be extinguished, every love shattered, every life will fall into oblivion.

---

[35] *Bible*. Cfr. Book of the Prophet Isaiah 53:1-12.
[36] *Bible*. Gospel of Matthew 25:34-36.

# 13

# And lead us not into temptation (I)
## *And do not subject us to the final test*

In the second part of the *Our Father* the two requests for bread are to be found: one for the bread of the body and one for the bread of the spirit and heart; their being necessary for 'human' life.

It ought to be borne in mind that if the *Our Father* had been invented by man and was solely human, it might very well end here. In order to develop our lives and build the city of men, wouldn't perhaps 'bread' and the love of goodness and mercy be sufficient for us to live and live together in peace? Why does Jesus put a further two conditions before us to establish his kingdom and do his will? Jesus, true God and true man, entrusts us with the sixth petition in the *Our Father*: "And lead us not into temptation", which in the Gospel of Matthew of the *New American Bible, revised edition* (2010) reads "And do not subject us to the final test".

God is Father and calls all people to co-operate together with him in building 'his kingdom' and 'the good of life on earth'. In this way Jesus brings us back to the Father and his kingdom with a fundamental passage: "Lead us not into temptation!" which means 'do not let us go wrong!', 'do not abandon us to temptation', do not let us be deceived by false security, by appearances that can seduce us, do not let us wander in the dark, do not allow us to be distorted, confused and overwhelmed by temptation, since we could then make mistakes throughout our lives and lose everything; human life and eternal life!

This petition that Jesus has given us makes us recognise our condition, a condition we often forget or wish to forget, namely that we are tempted. This is a real fact, and the love of Jesus for us is such that he wants us to remember this so as to return with love to the love for God. Following original sin, in the freedom we have, the relationship of love and confidence was ruined: temptation took over. To return to the initial condition it is necessary to recognise temptation and freely reject it, asking for help from God the Father.

Jesus in the *Our Father* shows us *the way back*, a path to be taken consciously and freely, placing our trust in God the Father! After having reopened our hearts with mercy and forgiveness, there comes the time to rise up, the time for renewal. The Prayer of the *Our Father* leads everything back to Love and Communion with God the Father, in the truth of both God and man. It is a prayer in which we confide in God entrusting ourselves to him so that He may help us not only to live and survive but to cooperate with him, He who calls us to be happy with him. He, Our Father, has consideration for us, his children, and wants us to rejoice with him in his kingdom that is already growing on earth. The kingdom of God, his Lordship, is a kingdom that will only establish itself in the light of truth, so as to grow in freedom and love.

Man, 'seduced' by evil, realises he could also build something else, something not only different but opposed to that kingdom. In fact every passion that becomes an idol for man drives him towards building a 'principality' and losing the kingdom of God. As children of God we have the capacity to bring about this horrendous possibility. This is the temptation against God. However, man can also bring about a magnificent, wonderful and good project by freely and faithfully working with his God! This is fidelity to God, and for which man will never have cause to repent.

## Tested for growth or tempted for destruction?

How does this 'temptation' present itself, that stands in the way to the bringing about of the kingdom of God, to his will and, thereby, to our truest happiness as well as to the future of the world? This requires closer examination. In what sense can the human being be 'seduced' and become lost?

This is a concern for those who love. Back in 1977, at a General Audience, Pope Paul VI said that Christian life is a dramatic and incessant confrontation between good and evil, and this lends the world its character of permanent battle. Our Lord, he continued, included this in the official formula of our prayer to God the Father, thus having us always invoke his help to be defended from a menace that constantly looms on our path through time: temptation. In its gradual move towards a fake moral maturity, towards indifference and insensitivity to the distinction between good and evil, it is no wonder that society has departed from authentic humanity. Recalling the warning in the Scriptures that "the whole world is in the power of the Evil One (1 John 5:19)", Paul VI urged not to be seduced by the world, which is not from God, lest it instil into us an illusory conception of life deprived of true values. The Pope's exhortation is to stand by Christ to partake of the victory he has announced and promised: "be courageous: I have conquered the world (John 16:33)"[1].

It is through the Pope and the faithful Church that the Lord addresses his appeals and accompanies us throughout history.

We can thus understand that the Lord leads history towards finding again, in the *Our Father*, the most profound Christian roots of life, family and society. This is also part of the love of God who calls each person to the revelation of not only who he is but what his future is.

Let's again consider that temptation is part of our lives. *The Catechism of the Catholic Church* reminds us: "we therefore ask our Father not to 'lead' us into temptation. It is difficult to translate the Greek verb used by a single English word: the Greek means both 'do not allow us to enter into temptation' and 'do not let us yield to temptation'. 'God cannot be tempted by evil and he himself tempts no one' (Jam 1:13); on the contrary, he wants to set us free from evil. We ask him not to allow us to take the way that leads to sin"[2].

"The Holy Spirit makes us *discern* between trials, which are necessary for the growth of the inner man, and temptation, which leads to sin and death. We must also discern between 'being tempted' and 'consenting' to temptation"[3]. Only our free consent to temptation generates sin in us.

The Gospel tells us that Jesus, by virtue of being man was, like every human, tempted in the desert. Pope Emeritus Benedict XVI in his book *Jesus of Nazareth* points out: "God certainly does not lead us into temptation. In fact, as Saint James tells us: 'Let no one say when he is tempted, - I am tempted by God -; for God cannot be tempted with evil and he himself tempts no one' (Jas 1:13). (...) Temptation comes from the devil, but part of Jesus' messianic task is to withstand the great temptations that have led man away from God and continue to do so. (...) In order to mature, in order to make real progress on the path leading from a superficial piety into profound oneness with God's will, man needs to be tried, (...) man needs purifications and transformations; they are dangerous for him, because they present an opportunity for him to fall, and yet they are indispensable as paths on which he comes to himself and to God. Love is always a process involving purifications, renunciations, and painful transformations of ourselves – and that is how it is a journey to maturity. (...) Saint Cyprian interpreted the sixth

---

[1] *Magisterium.* Cfr. Paul VI, *General Audience* (23 February 1977).
[2] *Magisterium. Catechism of the Catholic Church* no. 2846.
[3] *Magisterium. Catechism of the Catholic Church* no. 2847

petition. He says that when we pray, 'And let us not into temptation', we are expressing our awareness 'that the enemy can do nothing against us unless God has allowed it beforehand, so that our fear, our devotion and our worship may be directed to God – because the Evil One is not permitted to do anything unless he is given authorization' (*De dominica oratione* 25; CSLE III, 25, p. 285f.)"[4].

Man can overcome temptation and evil with the help of the grace of God[5], as the Apostle John reminds us: "I write to you, young men, because you are strong and the word of God remains in you, and you have conquered the evil one"[6]. It is true that all temptation comes from the Evil One but it is not always directly from him as the Apostle James states: "Rather, each person is tempted when he is lured and enticed by his own desire. Then desire conceives and brings forth sin, and when sin reaches maturity it gives birth to death"[7].

## How temptation proceeds

How does this process come about in the human heart? How is it possible that man, with his intelligence, freedom, and dignity resulting from the 'image of God', allows himself to be so easily confused and diverted by evil? What is the mechanism by which man is progressively corrupted in making his choices? The Word of God reveals the process of the human heart. It is Jesus who reveals it in the Gospel: "For God so loved the world that he gave his only Son, so that everyone who believes in him might not perish but might have eternal life"[8]. This is the love of God for us: He wants us to have eternal life, the life of God. But man, though so much loved by God, has ambiguity in himself: "And this is the verdict, that the light came into the world, but people preferred darkness to light, because their works were evil. For everyone who does wicked things hates the light and does not come toward the light, so that his works might not be exposed. But whoever lives the truth comes to the light, so that his works may be clearly seen as done in God"[9]. Man is tempted to love the darkness more than the light of the truth! One may very well ask why.

---

[4] *Magisterium.* Benedict XVI, *Jesus of Nazareth*, Doubleday, New York 2007, p. 160-163.
[5] *Bible.* Cfr. First Letter to the Corinthians 10:13.
[6] *Bible.* First Letter of John 2: 14.
[7] *Bible.* Letter of James 1:14-15.
[8] *Bible.* Gospel of John 3:16.
[9] *Bible.* Gospel of John 3:19-21.

The text of the Word of God tells us: "because their works were evil"! When man begins to build unjust and iniquitous structures, and adopts evil behaviour to defend the result of his system, he ends up by loving the darkness covering the lies and the evil he has done, so that this remains hidden and is not lost. Through evil, man steals and keeps the theft and possession obtained.

In Chapter 3 of the Book of Genesis, particular images and language are used to describe the wickedness of the initial fall of Adam and Eve: they wanted something of God, going against God, without God and, therefore, stealing from him. There is theft, "sensual lust, enticement for the eyes, and a pretentious life"[10] referred to in the First Letter of Saint John the Apostle: "Yet the world and its enticement are passing away. But whoever does the will of God remains forever"[11]. "Passing away", because the world destroys itself, and "the world and its enticements are passing away", because "the world in its present form is passing away"[12]. It is necessary to look ahead to a new world that God the Father prepares for his children where egoism no longer reigns.

To maintain possession of his 'small principality', man prefers darkness and concealment, avoiding the light since he cannot use it. As ever, this is the temptation of today, i.e. that of making 'principalities', and not building the kingdom of God. This is because man wants something that belongs to himself, to the individual self, to his 'own' family or society. This is why the Gospel of Light and Truth is not accepted, and this is where opposition to religion stems from. The wicked say: "I cannot achieve my interests with religion!".

As long as God speaks to us of love, gives us his Son, and with him all the other gifts, man is willing to listen and receive from God. However, the man corrupted by sin and selfishness no longer thinks of the kingdom of God, but rather of his 'little principality', which he wants to snatch from the kingdom: "For everyone who does wicked things hates the light and does not come toward the light, so that his works might not be exposed". This expression means that the corrupt man will take any steps to avoid his deeds being exposed, and himself being reprimanded, and hence losing what he has 'taken' and 'stolen'. This is why he avoids the light. Conversely, "whoever lives the truth comes to the light". He "lives the truth," not because it is his; he lives it because he sees it: man sees what is true and what is right, and brings it about, without appropriating it, because the truth and the good existed before him! He then builds not his principality but the truth of the kingdom,

---

[10] *Bible*. First Letter of John 2:16.
[11] *Bible*. First Letter of John 2:17.
[12] Bible. First Letter to the Corinthians 7:31.

which is goodness, justice, and light. He builds it because he receives it as a gift from God, and he is in communion with God.

The man who is in the light fulfils his life to the extent that he captures its mystery and truth. He does not create life in the laboratory, saying that it is his, but brings to fulfilment what already exists as a 'gift' received from God.

He who does the truth comes to the light, because he clearly sees that his works are "done in God"[13]. They have not been made by man and for man, but 'have been done in God': they already exist in God and belong to him. Things, truth, goodness, justice, fundamental values exist in God: man discovers them and then has no trouble in showing everyone that his life, his family, his work, his contribution to the construction of society are made in God: this means building the kingdom of God. This is the big difference between those who receive life as a gift, discovering the truth of life and giving glory to God in living their lives, and those instead who secretly take possession of life and manage it with impunity as 'their very own', keeping it as a theft. This is the inner temptation hidden in man.

For this reason, Jesus in the *Our Father* teaches us to detect it, to realise that we are tempted, to entrust ourselves to God, and to ask to be held safely in his hands. We must, indeed, be aware of what we are building and what kind of future awaits us. At this juncture, it is of interest to examine seven temptations that have arisen in our time.

## Seven Temptations

*The first temptation* is fundamental, and is the one we have already come across in Chapter 7 when commenting on Genesis 3. Being made in the 'image and likeness'[14] of God, the first temptation for man is wanting to take the place of God. Under the pressure of original sin, this temptation presents itself as the temptation to live as if God did not exist so as to build our own lives, families, and society, i.e. everything, while ignoring religion and our relationship with God.

This dynamic involves three degrees. The first is *indifference*, hence God is not important! The question of the relationship with God has become a matter of indifference for our world and for people. It is of no interest, and many do not think about it. Indifference is terrible! The second degree is *irreligiousness*. Any relation with God is considered 'useless', with the result that religion begins to be challenged and opposed by arguing that economic and human resources must be

[13] *Bible*. Gospel of John 3:21.
[14] *Bible*. Cfr. Book of Genesis 1:26.

used in more constructive and more useful activities. The third degree is *atheism*: God does not exist and we close ourselves up in opposition. This is the greatest temptation: not to take God seriously.

*The second temptation* of the contemporary world can be described through the image of the 'barrel' of wine. Wanting to be full of himself and fulfilled, man seeks every satisfaction that may fill life. Man remains alone with his 'I', and there is a kind of self-aggrandizement, a form of self-obsession, so typical of the narcissist.

Today, there seem to be many people who are narcissistic, and it is very difficult even to reason with them because they are so 'full of themselves', but in actual fact they are 'empty of spirit'. These people seek to satisfy themselves with a hedonistic way of life, characterized by those deadly sins which we have already discussed in the previous chapter. They have passed from temptation to their choice of life, that of vice. Yet, this type of life, far from being defined as 'depraved', is considered by them as 'natural'!

The question then arises as to how the first and second temptations have developed in today's world. How have they been assimilated by the new generation? Why is it that many adults, including Christians, fail to notice them, and when faced by such temptations remain so passive? Here lies the focal point of the third temptation.

*The third temptation* is the very strong one of *relativism*[15], above all for the lack of the essential bond between Truth, the Good and Freedom, of which the Magisterium of the Church speaks with concern in the Encyclical Letter *Veritatis Splendor* (The Splendour of Truth), where Saint John Paul II states: "Indeed, something more serious has happened: man is no longer convinced that only in the truth can he find salvation. The saving power of the truth is contested, and freedom alone, uprooted from any objectivity, is left to decide by itself what is good and what is evil. This relativism becomes, in the field of theology, a lack of trust in the wisdom of God, who guides man with the moral law. Concrete situations are unfavourably contrasted with the precepts of the moral law, nor is it any longer maintained that, when all is said and done, the law of God is always the one true good of man"[16].

When man thinks that truth no longer exists and that he therefore has no need to discover it, it is then that he wants to create it by establishing what is good and what is evil: man far from God and without God thus becomes 'creator and arbiter of good and evil'. This is his mad claim. Basically, this is the result of original sin and

---

[15] *Magisterium*. Cfr. John Paul II, Encyclical Letter *Veritatis Splendor* (1993) no. 84 (text no. 83 in Appendix).

[16] *Magisterium*. John Paul II, Encyclical Letter *Veritatis Splendor* (1993) no. 84.

satanic temptation[17]. Concern for such relativism is very present in the Magisterium and the conscience of Christians. Pope Emeritus Benedict XVI addressed this theme during his Apostolic Journey to Cameroon and Angola, stating: "Indeed, as a corrective to a widespread relativism which acknowledges nothing as definitive and, even more, tends to make its ultimate measure the individual and his personal caprice, we hold out another measure: the Son of God, who is also true man. Christ is the measure of true humanism. The Christian marked by an adult and mature faith is not one who is borne along by the waves of fashion and the latest novelties, but one who lives deeply rooted in the friendship of Christ. This friendship opens us up to all that is good, and it provides us with the criterion for discerning between error and truth"[18].

God is the Absolute Good, only He is the Source, the foundation of good; it is in him that man has his deepest root, the root of life. Man cannot take possession of it to live 'outside', uprooted from God, because, at that point, he would die. The temptation of satanic deception, in which humanity has fallen, has been the claim to decide, far from God, what is good and what is bad.

Once God is put aside, there is no longer objectivity in truth, what is truly good and truly bad. Without God, man is at the mercy of this terrible temptation to manage everything himself, to invent himself the truth and good, for himself and for the world. The creative capacity of man is pushed to such an extent that, under this great illusion, he makes two enormous errors. The first is that man thinks he can decide on the absolute, when he is not even willing to recognise what he is himself, a relative being. The second, vice versa, is that man thinks he is so relative as to deny the possibility of recognising the existence of God, the Absolute!

It is true that man is made in the 'image and likeness' of God, who is Absolute, but his ability to understand him cannot be decoupled from communion with him, otherwise he falls into the trap of these two big errors. Only by recognising the absolute dimension of God, and the relative dimension of man, created in his image, can man affirm in a logical manner both God and himself. Vice versa, by denying the Absolute of God, man falls into the void of nihilistic self-destruction: 'nothing has value and nothing is true and safe'; or into mad exaltation: 'what has value, meaning and power is only that which man does who creates what he wants'.

---

[17] *Bible*. Cfr. Book of Genesis 3.

[18] *Magisterium*. Benedict XVI, *Address at Meeting with the Bishops of Angola and Sao Tome*. Apostolic Journey to Cameroon and Angola (20 March 2009).

The third temptation is one that causes us to fall into pride and the greatest errors, leading us away from God and his wisdom. Instead this is the only way to get to know and love him without getting lost. We are 'small' but 'powerful', because in our smallness there is an extraordinary greatness which needs the relationship with God in order to be made manifest for the good of man and society. This is why Jesus taught us to pray in the *Our Father*: "lead us not into temptation", "do not subject us to the final test", do not let go of us.

*The fourth temptation* concerns the man who will not listen to the Word of God and does not believe in *eternal life*, but only in life on earth and, therefore, does not believe in the Final Judgment! Yet, God continues to speak, but as for 'the fool' it is as though he does not hear! Scripture reminds us: "How great are your works, Lord! How profound your designs! A senseless person cannot know this; a fool cannot comprehend"[19]. While "The Lord knows the plans of man; they are like a fleeting breath"[20].

Yet God has spoken to us and speaks to us constantly with his Word: "Do not court death by your erring way of life, nor draw to yourselves destruction by the works of your hands. Because God did not make death, nor does he rejoice in the destruction of the living. For he fashioned all things that they might have being, and the creatures of the world are wholesome; There is not a destructive drug among them nor any domain of Hades on earth, For righteousness is undying. It was the wicked who with hands and words invited death, considered it a friend, and pined for it, and made a covenant with it, Because they deserve to be allied with it"[21]. Furthermore, "not thinking rightly, they said among themselves: 'Brief and troubled is our lifetime; there is no remedy for our dying, nor is anyone known to have come back from Hades. For by mere chance were we born, and hereafter we shall be as though we had not been'"[22].

The judgment of God upon them is that they do not reason, they "do not think rightly"; it is like a folly of the mind and heart which is then followed by their evil works: "Let us oppress the righteous poor; let us neither spare the widow nor revere the aged for hair grown white with time. But let our strength be our norm of righteousness; for weakness proves itself useless"[23]. Having become blind and having lost their hearts and minds they go against Christ: "He professes to have knowledge of

---

[19] *Bible*. Book of Psalms 92:6-7.
[20] *Bible*. Book of Psalms 94:11.
[21] *Bible*. Book of Wisdom 1:12-16.
[22] *Bible*. Book of Wisdom 2:1-2.
[23] *Bible*. Book of Wisdom 2:10-11.

God and styles himself a child of the LORD"[24]. "He calls blest the destiny of the righteous and boasts that God is his Father. Let us see whether his words be true; let us find out what will happen to him in the end. For if the righteous one is the son of God, God will help him and deliver him from the hand of his foes. With violence and torture let us put him to the test that we may have proof of his gentleness and try his patience. Let us condemn him to a shameful death; for according to his own words, God will take care of him"[25]. This is one of the prophetic passages concerning Jesus.

This is the answer of the Word of God recorded in the Book of Wisdom: "These were their thoughts, but they erred; for their wickedness blinded them, And they did not know the hidden counsels of God neither did they count on a recompense for holiness nor discern the innocent souls' reward. For God formed us to be imperishable; the image of his own nature he made us. But by the envy of the devil, death entered the world and they who are allied with him experience it."[26]. God has allowed death but he does not want it: for this reason the Risen Jesus has brought and promised resurrection. God does not desire the death of the sinners, the wicked, "but rather that they turn from their ways and live"[27], and "He never commands anyone to sin, nor shows leniency toward deceivers"[28]. After the resurrection, in the Acts of the Apostles it is written: "God has overlooked the times of ignorance, but now he demands that all people everywhere repent because he has established a day on which he will 'judge the world with justice' through a man he has appointed, and he has provided confirmation for all by raising him from the dead"[29].

Too often, we forget eternal life and the Last Judgment which awaits us all with the return of Jesus Glorious. There is a widespread temptation of thinking that our life is only on this earth. There are many who fall into this temptation inducing others to follow their lead. It is also forgotten that there is always something missing in life here on earth, at least a part of justice... Will this aspiration have to remain unheard? Certainly not. But let us first look at the other temptations.

---

[24] *Bible*. Book of Wisdom 2:13.
[25] *Bible*. Book of Wisdom 2:16-20.
[26] *Bible*. Book of Wisdom 2:21-24.
[27] *Bible*. Book of the Prophet Ezekiel 33:11.
[28] *Bible*. Book of Sirach 15:20.
[29] *Bible*. Acts of Apostles 17:30-31.

# 14

# And lead us not into temptation (II)
## And do not subject us to the final test

In today's succession of events, conflicts, ideas and interests, a *fifth temptation* is making its way forward, and seems to pass unnoticed: it is the *superficiality* of those who say, "But what do I care about delving in depth and understanding? What is important is to live". "Live life! Don't think about it, it is too complicated to understand: everybody has their own opinion. Everybody is right. Everybody is wrong. What's the use of knowing!". At this point, people give primacy to doing and to a merely factual knowledge. In this way, by never going in depth people take a bad shortcut; in the end, they are incapable to choose and truly build a solid life. Superficiality is nurtured by *laziness* or *lack of confidence* to reach the truth. People may well be ready to cultivate interpersonal relationships and exchange opinions and ideas. Yet, also to enter into dialogue with other cultures and religions, what is required first and foremost is to have a good knowledge of one's own, and this involves examining our Christian roots. To the contrary, the easier and less demanding path is chosen. The First Letter of Saint Peter reminds Christians: "Do not be afraid or terrified with fear of them, but sanctify Christ as Lord in your hearts. Always be ready to give an explanation to anyone who asks you for a reason for your hope"[1].

In the superficiality of today's world we do not fight, we do not use a pickaxe to reach the rock, mentioned by Jesus, on which to build a sound home[2]. We are content to build our house precariously on the sand. It therefore follows that every initiative is then just an attempt... even life itself, since this too has become mediocre[3].

---

[1] *Bible*. First Letter of Peter 3:14-15.
[2] *Bible*. Cfr. Gospel of Matthew 7:24-27.
[3] *Bible*. Cfr. Book of Genesis 25:29-34.

Superficiality also affects the relationship with God and his word: what God says is not taken seriously nor examined in depth. In the end, faith becomes an opinion! This is the superficiality of today's world. It is also a manifestation of the cover up, i.e. of the will never to reach the light, 'not to come into the light', not to believe in the light, and not to love the light because there is no love for the truth. Instead it is comfortable to simply lapse into laziness and sloth.

*The sixth temptation* of the world is that of *false prophets*, people that attract and inspire appreciation: bigheads, to a greater or lesser extent, with some idea in various fields. They are the false rumours that deviate from the truth of God and lead into temptation. Jesus in the Gospel warns us: "Many false prophets will arise and deceive many; and because of the increase of evildoing, the love of many will grow cold. But the one who perseveres to the end will be saved"[4]. "Beware of false prophets, who come to you in sheep's clothing, but underneath are ravenous wolves. By their fruits you will know them"[5].

False prophets exist and still others will appear in the future. History is filled with them! The result is the spread of *distrust,* and the good that could be done is not done. This too is a serious temptation because 'through fear' the good that could be done and the justice that must be done are impeded, and one becomes sterile, without fruit to bring God, like the 'lazy' servant in the Gospel parable of the talents[6], or the dishonest judge[7] who did not want to be bothered. Christian faith is required precisely to have greater strength, momentum and magnanimity of soul and heart, so as not to slip into a state of *lukewarmness* and suffer the reproach of God[8]. Trust in God must support Christians in being an active and proactive presence in the world, so as to set true examples and inject life into temporal realities. In his Apostolic Journey to the United Kingdom, Benedict XVI pointed out the need in today's society for Christians to act as beacons of light and clarity in the work of evangelization[9].

*The seventh temptation* arises from the observation that *evil prospers* and grows strong. Scripture says that the wicked man "lives with the delusion: his guilt will not be known and hated. Empty and false are the words of his mouth; he has ceased to be wise and do good. On his

---

[4] *Bible.* Gospel of Matthew 24:11-13.

[5] *Bible.* Gospel of Matthew 7:15-16a.

[6] *Bible.* Cfr. Gospel of Matthew 25:14-30.

[7] *Bible.* Cfr. Gospel of Luke 18:1-8.

[8] *Bible.* Cfr. Book of Revelation 2:4-5; 3:16.

[9] *Magisterium.* Cfr. Benedict XVI, *Homily at Holy Mass in Bellahouston Park, Glasgow.* Apostolic Journey to the United Kingdom (16 September 2010) (text no. 84 in Appendix).

bed he hatches plots; he sets out on a wicked way; he does not reject evil"[10]. The person sees that evil grows with the wicked and unjust, and this allows despair and perplexity to take over. God seems to be absent, and sometimes one loses hope as it is the wicked that prosper and evil appears to be more powerful than good. As a result many lose faith in God and, without Christian hope, are invaded by evil and become brutalized. Some adapt and succumb to the common evil.

Man needs the Word of God in the same way that he needs bread, otherwise he dies inside. God has the answer to the evil which is in the world and so harasses it. This response is required for the heart of each one of us before we succumb adapting ourselves to evil. A first such response of God is to be found in one of the Psalms of the Bible that I am quoting here which tells of a person who is very upset by the presence of evil in the world. At the mercy of many negative examples that surround him, disconsolate, he turns to God who responds by providing him with spiritual enlightenment: "How good God is to the upright, to those who are pure of heart! But, as for me, my feet had almost stumbled; my steps had nearly slipped, Because I was envious of the arrogant when I saw the prosperity of the wicked. For they suffer no pain; their bodies are healthy and sleek. They are free of the burdens of life; they are not afflicted like others. Thus pride adorns them as a necklace; violence clothes them as a robe. Out of such blindness comes sin; evil thoughts flood their hearts. They scoff and spout their malice; from on high they utter threats. They set their mouths against the heavens, their tongues roam the earth"[11].

Strong language that shows how much the wicked rant and rave, asserting themselves through arrogance and violence. "They say, 'Does God really know?' 'Does the Most High have any knowledge?' Such, then, are the wicked, always carefree, increasing their wealth. Is it in vain that I have kept my heart pure, washed my hands in innocence? For I am afflicted day after day, chastised every morning. Had I thought, 'I will speak as they do,' I would have betrayed this generation of your children. Though I tried to understand all this, it was too difficult for me, Till I entered the sanctuary of God and came to understand their end. You set them, indeed, on a slippery road; you hurl them down to ruin. How suddenly they are devastated; utterly undone by disaster! They are like a dream after waking, Lord, dismissed like shadows when you arise. Since my heart was embittered and my soul deeply wounded, I was stupid and could not understand; I was like a brute beast in your

---

[10] *Bible*. Book of Psalms 36:2-4.
[11] *Bible*. Book of Psalms 73:1-9.

presence. Yet I am always with you; you take hold of my right hand. With your counsel you guide me, and at the end receive me with honor"[12].

God responds to man so that he does not succumb to temptation. It is a moving response. He gives and keeps his promise, exhorts man and comforts him. Moreover, we must also remember that man has an enemy, the devil, who tempts him through the presence of evil in the world. For man this is a great temptation, one that confuses and attracts him. However, God's most comprehensive answer to the evil in the world is ever that of the life of Jesus. On our behalf Jesus addressed every manifestation of evil present in human life, and showed us how to suppress and overcome it. In the Gospel, Jesus, as man, faces Satan's three temptations. In fact, the problem concerning the presence of evil is central to human life; it is here that human temptation and the 'provocation' of Satan are mainly focused since temptation is *disguised* as good, often in the form of challenges.

**The three satanic temptations**

But how does the devil tempt? Jesus had to face 'the enemy' of man, the devil, to show us the fundamental temptations and how to reject them. In this regard what Pope Emeritus Benedict XVI provides us with in his book *Jesus of Nazareth* is most enlightening: "At the heart of all temptations, as we see here, is the act of pushing God aside because we perceive him as secondary, if not actually superfluous and annoying, in comparison with all the apparently far more urgent matters that fill our lives. Constructing a world by our own lights, without reference to God, building on our own foundation; refusing to acknowledge the reality of anything beyond the political and material, while setting God aside as an illusion – that is the temptation that threatens us in many varied forms. (...) It pretends to show us a better way, where we finally abandon our illusions and throw ourselves into the work of actually making the world a better place. (...) what's real is what is right there in front of us – power and bread. By comparison, the things of God fade into unreality, into a secondary world that no one really needs.

God is the issue: Is he real, reality itself, or isn't he? Is he good, or do we have to invent the good ourselves? The God question is the fundamental question, and it sets us down right at the crossroads of human existence"[13].

---

[12] *Bible*. Book of Psalms 73:11-24.
[13] *Magisterium*. Benedict XVI, *Jesus of Nazareth*, Doubleday, New York 2007, p. 28-29.

In the quoted text of Benedict XVI, there follows a comment on the three temptations described in Saint Matthew's Gospel, which we shall now consider.

## Attack on the faith

Let us dwell on the *first temptation of Jesus*. "'If you are the Son of God, command these stones to become loaves of bread' (Mt 4:3) – so the first temptation goes. 'If you are the Son of God' – we will hear these words again in the mouths of the mocking bystanders at the foot of the Cross – 'If you are the Son of God, come down from the Cross' (Mt 27:40). (...) Mockery and temptation blend into each other here: Christ is being challenged to establish his credibility by offering evidence for his claims. (...)

And we make this same demand of God and Christ and his Church throughout the whole of history. 'If you exist, God', we say, 'then you'll just have to show yourself. You'll have to part the clouds that conceal you and give us the clarity that we deserve. If you, Christ, are really the Son of God, and not just another one of the enlightened individuals who keep appearing in the course of history, then you'll just have to prove it more clearly than you are doing now. And if the Church is really supposed to be yours, you'll have to make that much more obvious than it is at present'"[14].

Benedict XVI continues his analysis of the Gospel text by saying: "Is there anything more tragic, is there anything more opposed to belief in the existence of a good God and a Redeemer of mankind, than world hunger? Shouldn't it be the first test of the Redeemer, before the world's gaze and on the world's behalf, to give it bread and to end all hunger? (...) Isn't the problem of feeding the world and, more generally, are not social problems – the primary, true yardstick by which redemption has to be measured? (...) Marxism quite understandably – made this very point the core of its promise of salvation: It would see to it that no one went hungry anymore and that the 'desert would become bread'. 'If you are the Son of God' – what a challenge! And should we not say the same thing to the Church? If you claim to be the Church of God, then start by making sure the world has bread – the rest comes later. (...) Jesus is not indifferent toward men's hunger, their bodily needs, but he places these things in the proper context and the proper order"[15].

The reply of Jesus to the tempter, and also to all those who can tempt on this delicate point on which the world often launches its

---

[14] *Magisterium.* Benedict XVI, *Jesus of Nazareth,* Doubleday, New York 2007, 30-31.
[15] *Magisterium.* Benedict XVI, *Jesus of Nazareth,* Doubleday, New York 2007, 31-32.

challenge is this: "One does not live by bread alone, but by every word that comes forth from the mouth of God"[16]. In his book *Jesus of Nazareth*, Benedict XVI refers to this point as he writes: "When this ordering of goods is no longer respected, but turned on its head, the result is not justice or concern for human suffering. The result is rather ruin and destruction even of material goods themselves. When God is regarded as a secondary matter that can be set aside temporarily or permanently on account of more important things, it is precisely these supposedly more important things that come to nothing. It is not just the negative outcome of the Marxist experiment that proves this.

The aid offered by the West to developing countries has been purely technically and materially based, and not only has left God out of the picture, but has driven men away from God. And this aid, proudly claiming to 'know better', is itself what first turned the 'third world' into what we mean today by that term. It has thrust aside indigenous religious, ethical, and social structures and filled the resulting vacuum with its technocratic mind-set. The idea was that we could turn stones into bread; instead, our 'aid' has only given stones in place of bread. (...) History cannot be detached from God and then run smoothly on purely material lines. If man's heart is not good, then nothing else can turn out good, either. And the goodness of the human heart can ultimately come only from the One who is goodness, who is the Good itself. (...) It is in this world that we are obliged to resist the delusions of false philosophies and to recognize that we do not live by bread alone, but first and foremost by obedience to God's word. Only when this obedience is put into practice does the attitude develop that is also capable of providing bread for all"[17].

It can therefore be understood that the response given by Jesus to the tempter is much more powerful and profound than one might think, touching the heart of every man so that hunger may be overcome in the world. It is only by growing with the Word of God[18] that man can mature in fraternal and universal love to aid, in justice, all peoples and each and every person. By 'pursuing' only material bread with all its human means, mankind will never come to the 'kingdom' of God, but just to 'principalities' fighting with one another; conversely, as we feed in obedience on the Word of God 'those sentiments arise and develop that enable us to provide bread for all'.

---

[16] *Bible*. Gospel of Matthew 4:4.
[17] *Magisterium*. Benedict XVI, *Jesus of Nazareth*, Doubleday, New York 2007, p. 33-34.
[18] *Magisterium*. Cfr. Benedict XVI, *Jesus of Nazareth*, Doubleday, New York 2007, p. 35-36 (text no. 85 in Appendix).

Again Benedict XVI reminds us that "man often succumbs to the illusion that he can 'make stones become bread'. After setting God aside, or after having tolerated him as a private choice that must not interfere with public life, some ideologies have aimed to organize society with the force of power and of the economy. History shows us, dramatically, that the objective of guaranteeing everyone development, material well-being and peace, by leaving out God and his revelation, has been resolved by giving people stones instead of bread. Bread, dear brothers and sisters, is 'a fruit of the work of human hands', and this truth contains the full responsibility entrusted to our hands and to our ingenuity; but bread is also and before that: 'a fruit of the earth', which receives the sun and the rain from on high: it is a gift to ask for that takes away all our pride and enables us to invoke with the trust of the humble: 'Our Father... give us this day our daily bread' (Mt 6:11). The human being is incapable of giving life to himself, he understands himself only by starting from God: it is the relationship with him that gives our humanity consistence and makes our life good and just. In the 'Our Father' we ask that *his* name be hallowed, that *his* kingdom come, that *his* will be done. It is first and foremost God's primacy that we must recover in our world and in our life, because it is this primacy that enables us to discover the truth of what we are, and it is in knowing and following God's will that we find our own good; giving time and space to God, so that he may be the vital centre of our existence"[19].

**The attack on the Church**

We shall now take a closer look at the *second temptation of Jesus* drawing again on the text of *Jesus of Nazareth* by Benedict XVI. He writes: "The devil cites Holy Scripture in order to lure Jesus into his trap. He quotes Psalm 91:11f. (...) 'For he will give his angels charge of you to guard you in all your ways. On their hands they will bear you up, lest you dash your foot against a stone'. (...) The devil proves to be a Bible expert who can quote the Psalm exactly. (...) Remarking on this passage, Joachim Gnilka says that the devil presents himself here as a theologian. The Russian writer Vladimir Soloviev took up this motif in his short story 'The Antichrist'. The Antichrist receives an honorary doctorate in theology from the University of Tübingen and is a great Scripture scholar. (...) The fact is that scriptural exegesis can become a tool of the Antichrist. Soloviev is not the first person to tell us that; it is the deeper point of the temptation story itself. The alleged findings of

---

[19] *Magisterium.* Benedict XVI, *Homily Holy Mass at conclusion of XXV Italian National Eucharistic Congress* in Ancona (11 September 2011).

scholarly exegesis have been used to put together the most dreadful books that destroy the figure of Jesus and dismantle the faith"[20].

The Lord reminds us of the presence and action of the *Antichrist* in some passages of Holy Scripture such as in the First Letter of John the Apostle: "Children, it is the last hour; and just as you heard that the antichrist was coming, so now many antichrists have appeared. Thus we know this is the last hour. They went out from us, but they were not really of our number; if they had been, they would have remained with us. Their desertion shows that none of them was of our number"[21].

As regards the "alleged results of exegesis" mentioned above and badly used to "dismantle" the faith, we understand the circumstances of those who, without the necessary competence and without a deep rooted Christian faith, have ventured, almost without noticing it, into a false scientific culture of biblical interpretation, in the end believing more in themselves and their dominant thought than in the living God and the divine promises that have already been fulfilled in history, or are yet to be fulfilled. Thus, while declaring themselves to be 'believers', they have left the firm faith of the Church and have enriched themselves with theological hypotheses 'in step with the (dark) times' and with hypothetical considerations; so sure are they of their scholarly knowledge that they have become 'wise men' and have ceased to be true shepherds, or have become pastors in their own name and of their own reasoning instead of that of the true Master[22], who is Christ.

Many among the faithful and the clergy have fallen into this *ideological maze*, meandering within it, serving mainly their flair for research and creativity, and their own ideas, of which they boast, without realising that they are prisoners of a transitory culture and are distancing themselves from the certain faith and the faithful Church. At times, also the lack or loss of the relationship with God the Father has an influence on these positions. Maybe faith and prayer have been lost, especially the prayer of the *Our Father*. Indeed, the absence of the value of paternity is also reflected in the Church. That which should mature more in the Church and in the life of the Church is the dimension of *spiritual paternity*. As always, halting only at 'fraternity' leads, in the long run, to careerism, individualistic or partisan positions, and simplistic contrasts. Our structures should never neglect but rather assume the fundamental structures created by God in human nature. This has been made clear since the very beginning of the Church, as attested to in the

---

[20] *Magisterium*. Benedict XVI, *Jesus of Nazareth*, Doubleday, New York 2007, p. 34-35.
[21] *Bible*. First Letter of John 2:18-19.
[22] *Bible*. Cfr. Gospel of Matthew 23:9-10.

letters of Saint Ignatius[23]. The fundamental anthropological structures of the human person are those of being children, spouses, parents, siblings and friends.

The attack on the Church and her work is not only external but also *internal*. There are workers who 'dismantle the faith of the faithful', thinking, out of presumption and *spiritual pride*, and at other times out of *ignorance*, that they can build, and build better than others, in a space which to them seems to be free. Yet, they fail to see that this space is occupied, as they do not have eyes to see God and hearts to hear what the Church says.

Today there is also talk of a 'relativism' in the theological field, as well as a 'secularist' vision that seeks to reinterpret the Holy Scriptures: it is 'the world' that wants to invade and sophisticate Christian faith and only the 'Christian' one! All this produces a sense of insecurity and scepticism among the faithful, which is then followed up by indifference towards the certainties of faith. By following these *false doctrines* and these false prophets with their outlandish ideas, the faithful often find themselves mentally engulfed as if in arid pasture land, without a road. In this way, so many spiritual resources have been blocked, so as to prevent them from bringing fruit to the Church and the world.

Today, as in the past, there are those who prefer to set up ideological alliances to the point of betraying the Christian faith and the Gospel, by introducing a new transforming vision of Christianity to "enable people to reappropriate Jesus' supposed message", as pointed out by Benedict XVI in his book *Jesus of Nazareth*[24]. In the face of these modern and worrying attempts, he states: "But the main thing that leaps out is that God has disappeared; man is the only actor left on the stage. The respect for religious 'traditions' claimed by this way of thinking is only apparent. The truth is that they are regarded as so many sets of customs, which people should be allowed to keep, even though they ultimately count for nothing. Faith and religions are now directed toward political goals. Only the organization of the world counts. Religion matters only insofar as it can serve that objective. This post-Christian vision of faith and religion is disturbingly close to Jesus' third temptation"[25].

[23] *Tradition.* Cfr. St. Ignatius of Antioch (...-107), *Epistles of St. Ignatius of Antioch*, (http:// www.catholicculture.org/culture/library/view.cfm? recnum=3836, accessed in July 2014).
[24] *Magisterium.* Cfr. Benedict XVI, *Jesus of Nazareth*, Doubleday, New York 2007, p. 53.
[25] *Magisterium.* Benedict XVI, *Jesus of Nazareth*, Doubleday, New York 2007, p. 54-55.

**The 'criterion of the whole'**

To get out of the ideological maze, and equally not to fall inside it, the *criterion of the whole* is ever applicable: both in Holy Scripture, the Bible, considered as the full compendium of its books, and in the doctrine of Christian faith, that implies the need to hold together three cornerstones, namely Holy Scripture, the Magisterium of the Church, and the Tradition of the Church. In fact, they are all interconnected, each needing the other[26]. In the course of two thousand years of history, these three cornerstones have not been built by the wisdom of human thought – as this would not have been possible given the passage of such a long time – but instead by "a demonstration of spirit and power"[27]. They are a sign for those who love the truth, a sign of the presence of God in history; God who never abandons his Church, the Church of Jesus and with it all of mankind.

*Holy Scripture* is the base, *Tradition* is its fulfilled expression, but it is the *Magisterium* which unites and allows Holy Scripture and the Tradition of the faith to persist and be embodied in history.

Indeed, the total loss of human tradition compromises freedom and good for humanity: to build 'after' presupposes that there is a 'before'. In fact, man has to deal with his historicity and mortality, and if he wants to build and develop he must recognise the need to make use of the knowledge, experience and skills acquired by others. *Development and tradition* should be part of human progress.

The Tradition of the Church is not just a list of things to believe, but expresses the sense of the reality of God, the interpretation of the texts of biblical revelation: "[Holy] *Tradition* transmits in its entirety the Word of God which has been entrusted to the apostles by Christ the Lord and the Holy Spirit. It transmits it to the successors of the apostles (...)"[28]. Although a distinction must be drawn between apostolic tradition and other "theological, disciplinary, liturgical or devotional 'traditions' born over time in local churches"[29], Tradition rests on a profound sense that the Church has, and which has given birth to the 'Christian Tradition' of the various 'traditions', an intimate sense that is in the life of the faithful, in Christian gestures and customs, in rites and in the liturgy[30].

To understand and faithfully live the fullness of Christianity, it is necessary to combine Sacred Scripture and Tradition as two

---

[26] *Magisterium.* Cfr. Vatican Council II, Dogmatic Constitution *Dei Verbum* nos. 8-10.
[27] *Bible.* First Letter to the Corinthians 2:4.
[28] *Magisterium. Catechism of the Catholic Church* no. 81.
[29] *Magisterium. Catechism of the Catholic Church* no. 83.
[30] *Magisterium.* Cfr. *Catechism of the Catholic Church* no. 83.

complementary tools which are both required to receive it. This is the task of the Magisterium of the Church.

Jesus, in particular, has given the gift of the Holy Spirit to the Church for its faithful mission with the promise: "when he comes, the Spirit of truth, he will guide you to all truth"[31]. But in a specific way to Peter and his successors, Jesus says: "I have prayed that your own faith may not fail; and once you have turned back, you must strengthen your brothers"[32]. For this reason, what the Pope says and writes is decisive.

Theological research, which is imperative, must be free and courageous as well as scholarly. As happens also in the scientific field, its results cannot, however, be immediately adopted. The doctrine of the faith matures also through studies and research: for this we must thank the Lord. For us Christian Catholics fidelity to the Magisterium of the Church is indispensable precisely because of this: until they are recognised and accepted by the Magisterium of the Church, theological hypotheses must neither replace nor tarnish what is believed and lived in the Church in the unity of doctrine, sentiment and life[33]. Unity in love has been recommended and entrusted to us by Jesus so that the world might believe[34].

### Serving God and not using God to serve oneself

Quite rightly, the Church is most attentive at safeguarding the 'purity' of faith and the faithfulness to the mandate received from Jesus Christ. Truth and charity are the pillars of Christian life. In fact, faith and love are joined. Thus Holy Scripture warns: "Whoever teaches something different and does not agree with the sound words of our Lord Jesus Christ and the religious teaching is conceited, understanding nothing, and has a morbid disposition for arguments and verbal disputes. From these come envy, rivalry, insults, evil suspicions, and mutual friction among people with corrupted minds, who are deprived of the truth, supposing religion to be a means of gain"[35]. All too often 'distorted religious ideas' have disturbed pastors and faithful.

Only fidelity to the three sources – Scripture, Tradition and Magisterium – allows each individual to remain firmly adherent to his Christian roots. Only by accepting these sources 'all together' can we grasp the partial truth that is always true in a whole. Benedict XVI refers to this most important principle when speaking about interpretative

---

[31] *Bible*. Gospel of John 16:13.
[32] *Bible*. Gospel of Luke 22:32.
[33] *Bible*. Cfr. Letter to the Ephesians 4:1-4.
[34] *Bible*. Cfr. Gospel of John 17:21.
[35] *Bible*. First Letter to Timothy 6:3-5.

cuts[36]. In the final analysis, to repel and overcome the second temptation what is required is love for the Word of God and for the faithfulness of the Church which can guarantee the completeness and veracity of the faith.

If we want to know how to respond to temptations and overcome them we must listen to God. In order to listen to God we must welcome and consider the Word of God in 'all' its entirety, and not allow ourselves to be deceived by those who 'use' just a part, a piece of it. Those who really 'listen' to God, do not exploit any one part, any one sentence of the Word of God in the Bible, as do instead those who 'use' God to serve their own interests.

## Satan instead of God

Finally, let us consider *the third temptation of Jesus*. Commenting on this latter temptation Benedict XVI writes: "The devil takes the Lord in a vision onto a high mountain. He shows him all the kingdoms of the earth and their splendour and offers him kingship over the world. Isn't that precisely the mission of the Messiah? Isn't he supposed to be the king of the world who unifies the whole earth in one great kingdom of peace and well-being? We saw that the temptation to turn stones into bread has two remarkable counterparts later on in Jesus' story: the multiplication of the loaves and the Last Supper. The same thing is true here"[37].

In his book, Benedict XVI points out that over the course of human history, this temptation constantly takes on new forms[38]. "Jesus, however, repeats to us what he said in reply to Satan, what he said to Peter, and what he explained further to the disciples of Emmaus: No kingdom of this world is the Kingdom of God, the total condition of mankind's salvation. Earthly kingdoms remain earthly human kingdoms, and anyone who claims to be able to establish the perfect world is the willing dupe of Satan and plays the world right into his hands.

Now, it is true that this leads to the great question that will be with us throughout this entire book: What did Jesus actually bring, if not world peace, universal prosperity, and a better world? What has he brought?

The answer is very simple: God. He has brought God. (...) Jesus has brought God and with God the truth about our origin and destiny: faith, hope and love. It is only because of our hardness of heart that we think

---

[36] *Magisterium*. Cfr. Benedict XVI, *Jesus of Nazareth*, Doubleday, New York 2007, p. 59 (text no. 86 in Appendix).
[37] *Magisterium*. Benedict XVI, *Jesus of Nazareth*, Doubleday, New York 2007, p. 38.
[38] *Magisterium*. Cfr. Benedict XVI, *Jesus of Nazareth*, Doubleday, New York 2007, p. 39-44 (text no. 87 in Appendix).

this is too little. Yes indeed, God's power works quietly in this world, but it is the true and lasting power. Again and again, God's cause seems to be in its death throes. Yet over and over again it proves to be the thing that truly endures and saves. The earthly kingdoms that Satan was able to put before the Lord at that time have all passed away. Their glory, their *doxa*, has proven to be a mere semblance. But the glory of Christ, the humble, self-sacrificing glory of his love, has not passed away, nor will it ever do so.

Jesus has emerged victorious from his battle with Satan. To the tempter's lying divinization of power and prosperity, to his lying promise of a future that offers all things to all men through power and through wealth – he responds with the fact that God is God, that God is man's true Good. To the invitation to worship power, the Lord answers with a passage from Deuteronomy, the same book that the devil himself had cited: 'You shall worship the Lord your God and him only shall you serve" (Mt 4:10; cfr. Deut 6:13)'"[39]. In the words of Benedict XVI we can grasp a great truth about Jesus, indeed the most important: "He has brought God, and now we know his face, now we can call upon him. Now we know the path that we human beings have to take in this world"[40]. And this is the response that the world needs to choose the good and the truth. This is the reality that constitutes the Church and her mission in the world.

Jesus, tempted in the wilderness, always fights the devil on our behalf with the Word of God. This is what Jesus has taught us and we have to continue to do this in our own lives. It is the Word of God, not the human one, that overcomes Satan. But to do so we must be aware that every man, and all mankind, is tempted by the Evil One and his works. With the Word of God we can overcome temptations which are present in the world and have been made increasingly more widespread through the media, affecting individuals, families and society, especially children and young people. Only enlightened and sustained by the Word of God and the work that Christ, by his grace, has done and is doing in the world, opening our eyes to the faith and our hearts to the love of the *Our Father*, can we build a new world, snatching it from its absurd claim to save itself by itself.

But to be fully reinstated in God's plan, in communion and eternal happiness with him, it is not enough to be saved from temptations; we need the seventh and last prayer, which is fundamental: "Deliver us from evil". It is not only the last petition that Jesus teaches us in the *Our Father* to ask of God the Father but also the most needed.

---

[39] *Magisterium*. Benedict XVI, *Jesus of Nazareth*, Doubleday, New York 2007, p. 43-45.
[40] *Magisterium*. Benedict XVI, *Jesus of Nazareth*, Doubleday, New York 2007, p. 44.

# 15

# But deliver us from evil (I)

## *But deliver us from the evil one*

We have noted that there are limitations not only to achieving all the good we seek but also to eliminating all the evil that threatens us. These limitations form part of our humanity, and we must have the courage to truthfully acknowledge them. In the prayer of the *Our Father,* the seventh and final petition has us ask with historical and anthropological realism to 'deliver us from evil'. In fact, it is only God that frees us and will free us from any and all forms of evil.

By the term 'evil' we clearly mean anything that disrupts our lives causing us to suffer; however, it is not only this. 'Evil' may be the disruption of nature and the universe; for us it is any bodily pain, suffering, disease and death itself. Yet, in today's naturalistic vision, all these aspects are considered as part of natural evolution.

'Evil' is also the inner one, of the psyche, which manifests itself in the expression of sentiments and suffering caused by affective conflicts or brought about by disorders that are not visible externally but disrupt within. Today, however, these situations too can be 'read' as stages in a useful and necessary process of maturation, the development of which is left to personal responsibility.

**Spiritual illness**

'Evil' can also be understood as the disease of the spirit: moral and indeed spiritual ill-being. This is the most profound, the most radical and difficult to identify, and is the first to which man adapts as it is something he neither sees nor initially senses. Only later does it reveal itself, and like cancer it spreads and grows, and can lead to 'death'. It is the expression of a 'disorderly life', one not lived in the truth since man adapts to everything, even to being blind... as Jesus says: "they are blind

211

guides [of the blind]"[1]. It is true that one always sees what one is, 'one sees according to one's heart'. The wicked man "lives with the delusion: his guilt will not be known and hated"[2]. Ultimately, he does not see his guilt because he is in the dark! The same applies to dust: it is only visible in sunlight. We can see evil only in as much as we have the light of God, in the presence of the boundless love of God Creator and Father.

Evil is the absence of good; therefore, to see evil, the light and the truth of the Good are needed. Conversely, to see the good there is no need for evil, as some instead theorize to justify the presence of evil in the world, as if wishing to preserve it by assigning it a slot. Man would greatly enjoy the good if there were no evil, since he comes from the Good, namely God, and is made for the good and eternal happiness. People who are healthy in their inner life have no need for evil to appreciate that they are well.

Only God can deliver us from evil, because man adapts even if he suffers within; this is why he becomes accustomed to not listening to the good and luminous part that God has put within him with 'his image', his spirit. Sometimes, he senses the call and also nostalgia, like the son in the Gospel parable[3] who begins to find himself again when he lifts himself 'up' from the withdrawal within himself. It is necessary to 'raise' one's sights, and elevate one's life to God the Father, to his face imprinted on the Son Jesus Christ.

Human history, albeit in the midst of errors and atrocities, has maintained its charm and grandeur: in it there is God who acts so that the human beings may achieve the *fullness of life and sense*. God communicates this sense and the value of life to believers in the faith, and helps them to live with love and intelligence, with hope and lucidity. The sense and meaning of life cannot be solely determined by economics or technology. Sometimes, when a person suffers too intensely or for too long, it may happen that he or she is weighed down with such a depersonalizing heaviness that human life is perceived as worthless and hopeless. Through personal effort on one hand and the necessary assistance providing enlightenment and strength on the other, each and every person is able to overcome and recover from his spiritual illness. But how to explain the presence of evil? We shall take a closer look.

First of all, we can state a fundamental truth: there is no absolute evil, there is no god of evil. There is only one God, Creator of all things

---

[1] *Bible*. Gospel of Matthew 15:14.
[2] *Bible*. Book of Psalms 36:3.
[3] *Bible*. Cfr. Gospel of Luke 15:11-32.

and Creator of human creatures, made 'in his image and likeness'[4]. So, why are we weighed down with evil in personal, family and social history? What are these upheavals and these disorders in the world which has come from the good hands of God? Where was the need for a world like this?

As there is no absolute evil, evil is good which became perverted following rebellion against God. In fact, the good of man without communion with the Source, that is God, becomes rebellion, pride, disobedience and, ultimately, madness and death. Therefore, evil is disordered good that is decoupled from both its source and its purpose: to exist it appeals to good but deforms it, perverting it for its own use. It is difficult to fight against because it is often disguised as good, with its perversion successfully concealed.

Why pray to be delivered from evil? Why wait for God to deliver us? Is this not encouraging passivity? Are we not able to deliver ourselves using our own strength, progress, intelligence, rationality, will, and all the means that God and progress have put into our hands?

## Only God can deliver us from evil

God wants progress, improvement and freedom from that which harms us. He also wants this through our contribution in the form of intelligence, will, science and technology, and all the other means which are his gifts. Nevertheless, it is only God who can deliver us from *evil* without bringing harm to us. We can free ourselves of *ills*, various forms of suffering and disease thanks to increasingly advanced scientific and technological progress, such as for instance in the fields of neuroscience, cybernetics and informatics. What results and what achievements are to be seen in every field! But from 'evil' and 'the Evil One' only God can deliver us: for this we pray, "Deliver us from evil".

There is a human limit to liberation. Only God can deliver us from evil without causing us harm, and He does so by solely operating through good. The prayer of the *Our Father* confirms this fact which was shown by Jesus in the Gospel when recounting the parable of the wheat and the weeds: "He proposed another parable to them. 'The kingdom of heaven may be likened to a man who sowed good seed in his field. While everyone was asleep his enemy came and sowed weeds all through the wheat, and then went off. When the crop grew and bore fruit, the weeds appeared as well. The slaves of the householder came to him and said, 'Master, did you not sow good seed in your field?

---

[4] *Bible*. Cfr. Book of Genesis 1:26.

Where have the weeds come from?' He answered, 'An enemy has done this.' His slaves said to him, 'Do you want us to go and pull them up?' He replied, 'No, if you pull up the weeds you might uproot the wheat along with them. Let them grow together until harvest; then at harvest time I will say to the harvesters, 'First collect the weeds and tie them in bundles for burning; but gather the wheat into my barn'"[5].

The reality of the world comes from the hands and heart of God who created it good and varied. But as Jesus explains, the enemy, the Evil One, 'came and sowed weeds' that, growing, create such disorder as to endanger the life of the grain. We men would like to go into the field and in some way rip out the weeds; Jesus warns us that this is a task that can only be done by God at the end of time, because to do so now would also destroy the grain. We are this grain. Here is the delicacy and power of God who wants good to triumph, but does not want it to be partly eliminated with the destruction of evil. As the saying goes "the good end does not justify the use of bad means".

How many choices are made today in this very way: by invoking and adhering to a value such as the right to health, we find ourselves destroying the human embryo and trampling on the very beginnings of human life! Or, in defending a certain right we find ourselves lacking in charity, offending and extinguishing a little goodness, the flickering flame[6] in a weak person! In this life, good and evil are intertwined and confused, and it is not always easy to tell them apart. It is from the fruits that we can understand the difference: the grain is the fruit of the seed that sprouts and grows with the power that God has given it, thus doing his will. It supports man and therefore serves in the development of life. Weeds too grow, creating division, arrogantly making space for themselves, but although they are resplendent in wealth and glory, they deceive, since they are not needed for the life of man. Likewise, evil, represented by the weeds, grows, occupies space, manifests itself with power, wealth and glory, as Psalm 74 (verse 23) reminds us: "Do not forget the clamor of your foes, the unceasing uproar of your enemies".

Hence, evil spreads and can increase in strength during the course of history, also because the enemy often uses it disguised as freedom and well-being in order to come to power. We ask for the intervention of God: "But deliver us from evil". This 'but' indicates that simply fleeing from temptation is not enough, we must also ask God to free us from evil itself.

Indeed, there is also a corrupting, destructive power, that opposes the good of man, it is from this 'evil' we ask God to free us. We know

---

[5] *Bible*. Gospel of Matthew 13:24-30; cfr. 13:36-43.
[6] *Bible*. Cfr. Book of the Prophet Isaiah 42:3; Gospel of Matthew 12:20-21.

that God will liberate us. So we express faith in the salvation of Jesus Christ: "There is no salvation through anyone else"[7]. "He delivered us from the power of darkness and transferred us to the kingdom of his beloved Son, in whom we have redemption, the forgiveness of sins"[8].

All are called to salvation: there is always the possibility of salvation for each and every person in Jesus Christ. Every person, precisely because he has within him the 'image and likeness' even if cloaked in sin, aspires to total salvation and seeks justice. Those who, through no fault of their own, do not know Jesus Christ, may achieve salvation when they truly seek God, and with the help of grace endeavour to do his will as recognised by their conscience[9].

In his Encyclical Letter *Spe salvi*, Benedict XVI states: "there is a God, and God can create justice in a way that we cannot conceive, yet we can begin to grasp it through faith. Yes, there is a resurrection of the flesh. There is justice. There is an 'undoing' of past suffering, a reparation that sets things alright. For this reason, faith in the Last Judgement is first and foremost hope – the need for which was made abundantly clear in the upheavals of recent centuries. I am convinced that the question of justice constitutes the essential argument, or in any case the strongest argument, in favour of faith in eternal life. (...) but only in connection with the impossibility that the injustice of history should be the final word does the necessity for Christ's return and for new life become fully convincing. (...) Only God can create justice. And faith gives us the certainty that he does so. The image of the Last Judgement is not primarily an image of terror, but an image of hope; for us it may even be the decisive image of hope"[10].

Jesus came for all men, so that "they might have life and have it more abundantly"[11]: we must give God the space needed for the liberation of our lives and history, and detect the evil of the weeds.

We need eight deliverances.

## The first deliverance: from deception

Jesus, who says of himself "I am the way and the truth and the life"[12], comes to free us from deception because man, unlike animals, needs

---

[7] *Bible*. Acts of Apostles 4:12.
[8] *Bible*. Letter to the Colossians 1:13-14.
[9] *Magisterium*. Cfr. Paul VI, *Homily Holy Mass for the conclusion of the Year of Faith* (30 June 1968).
[10] *Magisterium*. Benedict XVI, Encyclical Letter *Spe Salvi* (2007) nos. 43-44.
[11] *Bible*. Gospel of John 10:10.
[12] *Bible*. Gospel of John 14:6.

the revelation of the truth to live, precisely as Jesus said: "the truth will set you free"[13].

This gives cause for reflection. After giving birth to their offspring, animals do not need anything else; whereas, a human being, in addition to maintaining life, also needs the revelation: who am I? Who are you? Why is there life? Where do I come from? What kind of future is there? Right from a very young age children start to ask who their mothers and fathers' parents are, and also who their parents' grandparents are. And then they ask: "Who made God?" Although small, the child wants to get straight to the mystery of life: "No-one made God. God has always existed!" In fact, God not only 'has' life, but God 'is' the life.

Man needs the revelation, as well as life, and this shows that he has something special: the human spirit. For this reason throughout history, God has sent prophets and then He sent his Word, the Word who was made man for all mankind. History allows us to see that his is an inner Presence, discreet[14] and not sensational, one that does not impose itself with overwhelming evidence!

God manifests himself with love and humility, offering himself to the freedom and intelligence of man. If He did not work in this way, man would be overwhelmed! God does not need to impose himself in order to convince man, as He does not seek to curb him. What use would be a humanity curbed and forced by his Absolute Power? The heart of man that God the Father seeks is an attentive watchful love which is open to him, since it is only this love towards God that can help man grow and make him able to meet and receive God "as he is"[15].

If there had been a better way for us and for all humanity, God would have certainly used it: if He shows himself as a 'hidden' God it is not only because He remains Other than us, the mysterious God, but because He loves man. The good of man, in fact, is to be able to seek God and receive him in love, expanding his capabilities day by day, until "God may be all in all"[16]! To the apostles who asked him: "Master, [then] what happened that you will reveal yourself to us and not to the world?", Jesus replied: "Whoever loves me will keep my word, and my Father will love him, and we will come to him and make our dwelling with him"[17]. Jesus came to reopen the hearts of men to the gift of Transcendence, the gift of God the Father: "Go into the whole world and proclaim the

---

[13] *Bible*. Gospel of John 8:32.
[14] *Bible*. Cfr. Book of Revelation 3:20.
[15] *Bible*. First Letter of John 3:2.
[16] *Bible*. First Letter to the Corinthians 15:28.
[17] *Bible*. Gospel of John 14:22-23.

gospel to every creature"[18]. Christian faith can only be proposed in freedom and love, not imposed. To live, we need *love of the truth*, of which we are made.

Man must also defend himself from violence and intrigue that manipulate and hide the truth, create lies and oppress with violence: just think of the torture in the world, and the oppressive or coercive means used against the freedom of conscience and respect of the person. Think of the need felt by some to obscure, through envy, that which shines of good and goodness in others: malignant or evil people cannot tolerate the light and goodness, they seek to cover and obscure it with envy, gossip and falsehood! Think of the media system, when for economic or partisan interests it is ready to manipulate the truth by responding with 'targeted information' to satisfy the lowest passions. Isn't it a cowardly deception when assisted fertilization for the birth of a human being is encouraged through the mass media, while at the same time hiding from public opinion the fact that fertilized eggs, i.e. human embryos that have not been implanted, are killed or used in the lab? In this way, many innocent embryonic human lives are destroyed! Many people slip into the nets of evil without realising it, and become accustomed to such evil. 'Targeted information' creates mass opinion, a mindset and, inadvertently, an addiction to evil and injustice with consequences for the victims. This is an evil technique for which we ask the Lord "Deliver us from evil".

As John Paul II recalled in the Encyclical *Dives in misericordia*: "Man rightly fears falling victim to an oppression that will deprive him of his interior freedom, of the possibility of expressing the truth of which he is convinced, of the faith that he professes, of the ability to obey the voice of conscience that tells him the right path to follow. The technical means at the disposal of modern society conceal within themselves not only the possibility of selfdestruction through military conflict, but also the possibility of a 'peaceful' subjugation of individuals, of environments, of entire societies and of nations"[19].

We must therefore find a way to defend ourselves from the growing manipulation of information, which is becoming increasingly limited and distorted for utilitarian purposes. It would be positive if there were greater love for the Church which strives incessantly for peace. In this regard, the media could also express greater respect and appreciation for the work of love and peace that the Church brings to the world. In fact, respect for one another, reconciliation and love are the only paths to peace on earth.

---

[18] *Bible*. Gospel of Mark 16:15.
[19] *Magisterium*. John Paul II, Encyclical Letter *Dives in misericordia* (1980) no 11.

Jesus came to free us from adaptation and manipulation so as to renew our love for the truth which God knows in its entirety, and to which He has destined us, his children.

So the first deliverance brought about by Jesus is from every deception and from the power of Satan, the "father of lies"[20], as Jesus defines him.

## The second deliverance: from injustice

Injustice consists in the surfacing of that very evil which is most pervasive in society and everyday life. John Paul II, in the Encyclical *Dives in misericordia*, denounced the difficulty we have in our world of breaking away from situations of injustice: "a defective machinery is at the root of contemporary economics and materialistic civilization, which does not allow the human family to break free from such radically unjust situations"[21]. Ongoing injustice pushes people towards seeking refuge in 'mammon', in money and power, but experience shows that this leads to greater injustice and corruption. Conversely, God loves justice and wants us too to love and practise it.

Disorder, social malaise, dishonesty, fraud and theft, as well as violence in any form make life increasingly inhuman to the point that people isolate themselves in their selfishness, shutting out values and ideals. Courage is required to put an end to injustice in the world: this can be accomplished through the implementation and enforcement of law, the spreading of good around us, and prayer which matures our hearts.

We must endeavour to make this a more just world. This is a priority, also of politics as pointed out by Benedict XVI on his visit to the Federal Parliament during his Apostolic Journey to Germany: "Politics must be a striving for justice, and hence it has to establish the fundamental preconditions for peace. Naturally a politician will seek success, without which he would have no opportunity for effective political action at all. Yet success is subordinated to the criterion of justice, to the will to do what is right, and to the understanding of what is right. (...) 'Without justice – what else is the State but a great band of robbers?', as Saint Augustine once said. (...) To serve right and to fight against the dominion of wrong is and remains the fundamental task of the politician. At a moment in history when man has acquired previously inconceivable power, this task takes on a particular urgency. Man can destroy the world. He can manipulate himself. He can, so to speak,

---

[20] *Bible*. Gospel of John 8:44.

[21] *Magisterium*. John Paul II, Encyclical Letter *Dives in misericordia* (1980) no. 11.

make human beings and he can deny them their humanity. (...) For most of the matters that need to be regulated by law, the support of the majority can serve as a sufficient criterion. Yet it is evident that for the fundamental issues of law, in which the dignity of man and of humanity is at stake, the majority principle is not enough"[22].

A healthy relationship with God and His wisdom develops the love for justice and honesty... Praying "deliver us from evil" also expresses that love and, at the same time, commits us to working together to build a more just world inasmuch as this may depend on us. So we ask the Lord to deliver us from evil and teach us to desire what is good for all: without God everyone is eventually trapped in their own self-interest, thereby becoming conceited and arrogant. A society is undermined from within as long as it accepts dishonesty and deviousness in evading the law; in turn, this fuels organised crime and irreligiousness. Similarly, a religiosity that is not authentic or that is two-faced ends up being hypocritical and benefiting people who profess religion while acting dishonestly! For this reason, coherence in Christian life is not tolerated by hypocrites and the abject. The plague of inconsistency as well as duplicity must give way to a genuine living faith, as Saint James the Apostle reminds us: "faith of itself, if it does not have works, is dead. (...) You believe that God is one. You do well. Even the demons believe that and tremble. Do you want proof, you ignoramus, that faith without works is useless?"[23].

## The third deliverance: from abuse and crime

More often than not, abuse and crime are hidden in the behaviour of man and quietly feed on the passions of resentment and hatred, oppression and revenge. We need God. The Encyclical *Evangelium vitae* of Saint John Paul II makes us reflect on their weighty actuality, when he states: "There is an even more profound aspect which needs to be emphasized: freedom negates and destroys itself, and becomes a factor leading to the destruction of others, when it no longer recognizes and respects its *essential link with the truth*"[24].

Furthermore: "If the promotion of the self is understood in terms of absolute autonomy, people inevitably reach the point of rejecting one another. Everyone else is considered an enemy from whom one has to defend oneself. Thus society becomes a mass of individuals placed

---

[22] *Magisterium*. Benedict XVI, *Address to the Federal Parliament, in the Reichstag Building, Berlin*. Apostolic Journey to Germany (22 September 2011).
[23] *Bible*. Letter of James 2:17-20.
[24] *Magisterium*. John Paul II, Encyclical Letter *Evangelium vitae* (1995) no. 19.

side by side, but without any mutual bonds. Each one wishes to assert himself independently of the other and in fact intends to make his own interests prevail. Still, in the face of other people's analogous interests, some kind of compromise must be found, if one wants a society in which the maximum possible freedom is guaranteed to each individual. In this way, any reference to common values and to a truth absolutely binding on everyone is lost, and social life ventures on to the shifting sands of complete relativism. At that point, *everything is negotiable, everything is open to bargaining*: even the first of the fundamental rights, the right to life"[25].

As men and as Christians we need to reflect. Life is distorted by the same tyrant who, without people realising it, resurfaces in different guises with 'mammon'. At some point, life becomes sick, and from deception we find ourselves sliding on a downwards slope towards ever increasing injustice and ultimately abuse of power and crime. The prayer of the *Our Father* shelters and protects us in truth and love; when we pray to God the Father "deliver us from evil", this is also 'from these evils' that society and the current way of thinking may conceal.

## 'Non-negotiable' principles

What are these 'non-negotiable' principles? Since everything has become negotiable, everything can be established by convention, everything has become relative, an opinion... In this way abuses and crimes have multiplied. As a result, the Church, in order to robustly oppose this attempt to render negotiable those very values that refer to the 'intrinsic good of the person' has, for the first time, established clear limits, showing the need for 'boundary posts'. These are the markers of our humanity, our truth, our respect for life, the person, 'human dignity', the family, and also of the human family which must build the value of peace on earth through justice. These points are not open to compromise: the future of the earth depends on them. The prayer of the *Our Father*, when we pray "deliver us from evil", makes us attentive to these values but also to these evils, so that we might not only avoid them but also help others to do the same.

In November 2002, the 'Congregation for the Doctrine of the Faith' emanated the *Doctrinal Note on some questions regarding the commitment and participation of Catholics in political life*. This document was then approved by Pope John Paul II, while the then Prefect of the Congregation was Cardinal Joseph Ratzinger. This Doctrinal Note does

---

[25] *Magisterium*. John Paul II, Encyclical Letter *Evangelium vitae* (1995) no. 20.

not set forth theoretical considerations but norms that illuminate and bind the conscience, constituting a moral duty for all Christians, even those who consider themselves to be 'adult Catholics': we must not take part in works of evil, the Lord wants us to be free of evil! Love for the truth and freedom of conscience must therefore go hand in hand.

The reader will find in the Appendix the important Doctrinal Note[26] which at point 4 goes into the details we are dealing with here.

Again John Paul II's Encyclical *Evangelium vitae*, when dealing with the value of human life that is being called into question by the mentality of the world, states: "This is what is happening also at the level of politics and government: the original and inalienable right to life is questioned or denied on the basis of a parliamentary vote or the will of one part of the people – even if it is the majority. This is the sinister result of a relativism which reigns unopposed: the 'right' ceases to be such, because it is no longer firmly founded on the inviolable dignity of the person, but is made subject to the will of the stronger part. In this way democracy, contradicting its own principles, effectively moves towards a form of totalitarianism. The State is no longer the 'common home' where all can live together on the basis of principles of fundamental equality, but is transformed into a *tyrant State*, which arrogates to itself the right to dispose of the life of the weakest and most defenceless members, from the unborn child to the elderly, in the name of a public interest which is really nothing but the interest of one part"[27]. This is what is happening in the world today through major plans for economic power – as denounced by the same John Paul II[28] – also with the help of false Christians or people who misinterpret rights and the Gospel itself, or just make use of the parts that suit them. Only God can deliver us from the presumption of this evil.

## The three dimensions of life

This is why Jesus says in the Gospel: "without me you can do nothing"[29] and "whoever does not gather with me scatters"[30]. We must recognise that like every other reality, identifiable in the three

---

[26] *Magisterium.* Cfr. Congregation for the Doctrine of the Faith, *Doctrinal Note on some questions regarding the commitment and participation of Catholics in political life* no. 4 (24 November 2002) (text no. 88 in Appendix).

[27] *Magisterium.* John Paul II, Encyclical Letter *Evangelium vitae* (1995) no. 20.

[28] *Magisterium.* Cfr. John Paul II, *Memory and Identity,* Rizzoli International Publications, Inc., New York 2005, p. 48 (text no. 89 in Appendix).

[29] *Bible.* Gospel of John 15:5.

[30] *Bible.* Gospel of Luke 11:23.

dimensions of space and one of time, life too, over and above the fourth dimension of time, has its three dimensions that express its value. Life has its own *fullness* which is its extension, its own *meaning* made manifest by the body as well as by the whole of nature with its roots, and has its own *sense* that indicates its development. These are the three *value dimensions* of fullness of life, meaning, and sense, which show the need to unearth the roots to human life. Only then can we talk seriously about life and of what we really are, rather than speaking in a superficial, abstract or seductive manner.

Those who love life do not tolerate the *reductionism* of life which runs counter to its *fullness*. The 'world' and 'mammon' attempt to extend and impose reductionism because a 'fragmented' reality is 'more marketable', while a precious and unique reality is not marketable, and this is true precisely for each human life, in its preciousness and uniqueness.

Those who love life do not go against the *meaning* that nature gives us. The manipulation of nature represents the desire to assign new meanings to life. In this case, there would be no more true meaning to be discovered in human nature or in corporeality and human sexuality, and no 'word' of God the Creator in this for us.

Those who love life do not hide the transcendent dimension and the reality of the spirit, since they do not hide the deepest *sense* of life; otherwise, what sense would there be to 'life and death'?

God wants to free us from oppression and crime, for the love of life that is entrusted by him to man, the family and the human community. Already back in 1976 Joseph Ratzinger wrote: "When he despises his body, man quarrels on a radical level with Being itself, which he understands, no longer as God's creation, but as 'the existing order', which must be destroyed. (...) When the existence of the family and thereby the human reality of fatherhood and motherhood, is defamed as an alleged hindrance to freedom; when honesty obedience, fidelity, patience, kindness, and trust are portrayed as inventions of the ruling classes, and our children are taught hatred, mistrust, and disobedience (since these are the true virtues of the man who liberates himself) – then the Creator himself and his creation are at stake (...). Where reality as a whole is slandered and the Creator is scorned, man cuts off the roots of his own self. We are beginning to recognize this in a very palpable manner on a much lower level, in the environmental question"[31]. This is a matter of unearthing the law that comes from nature, "that is

---

[31] *Magisterium*. Joseph Cardinal Ratzinger, *The God of Jesus Christ. Meditations on the triune God*, Ignatius Press, San Francisco, 2008, pp. 22-23.

'naturally' right"[32]. This concerns an essential question that touches upon many aspects of today's culture. Its importance was highlighted by Benedict XVI in his address to the Federal Parliament on the occasion of his Apostolic Visit to Germany[33].

## Nature too speaks to us

Man has lost sight of the fact that nature is a source of law, and it shows us limitations which we cannot overcome through rejection, but which love for human life compels us to accept if we are not to lose and destroy life itself by becoming 'inhuman'.

In his speech to the UN in 2008, Pope Emeritus Benedict XVI, referring to the Universal Declaration of Human Rights, wished to recall that: "This document was the outcome of a convergence of different religious and cultural traditions, all of them motivated by the common desire to place the human person at the heart of institutions, laws and the workings of society, and to consider the human person essential for the world of culture, religion and science. (...) They are based on the natural law inscribed on human hearts and present in different cultures and civilizations. Removing human rights from this context would mean restricting their range and yielding to a relativistic conception, according to which the meaning and interpretation of rights could vary and their universality would be denied in the name of different cultural, political, social and even religious outlooks. This great variety of viewpoints must not be allowed to obscure the fact that not only rights are universal, but so too is the human person, the subject of those rights"[34].

## Destruction of man

The Church, which is prophetic and in the forefront, wants to avoid further disasters! The petition "deliver us from evil" in the prayer of the *Our Father* accompanies us all along our lives and in our efforts to overcome, through God, all evils, also modern ones by which the devil brings about death through pride. In this regard, Joseph Ratzinger

---

[32] *Magisterium.* Joseph Cardinal Ratzinger, *The God of Jesus Christ. Meditations on the triune God,* Ignatius Press, San Francisco, 2008, p. 23 (text no. 90 in Appendix).
[33] *Magisterium.* Cfr. Benedict XVI, *Address to the Federal Parliament, in the Reichstag Building, Berlin.* Apostolic Journey to Germany (22 September 2011) (text no. 91 in Appendix).
[34] *Magisterium.* Benedict XVI, *Address at Meeting with the Members of the General Assembly of the United Nations Organization, New York.* Apostolic Journey to the United States of America (18 April 2008).

wrote in his book *The God of Jesus Christ*: "We cannot separate man's becoming man and his knowledge of God precisely because he is 'the image' of God. When his humanity is destroyed, something happens to the image of God. The dissolution of fatherhood and motherhood, which some would prefer to relocate in a laboratory or at least reduce to a biological moment that does not concern man *qua* man, is linked to the dissolution of childhood, which must give way to a total equality from the very beginning. This is a program of hubris, which at one and the same time wants to remove man from the biological sphere and enslaves him completely within it; this hubris reaches into the very roots of human existence and into the roots of the ability to think of God, for where he can no longer be depicted in an image, it is no longer possible to think of him"[35].

This is precisely the path that is being taken in today's so-called civilizations, and which goes from the manipulation of man to atheism. Isn't this too part of the *satanic plan* to make use of human *pride* and *insolence*, in order to lay hands on human life, subtracting it more and more from the 'image and likeness' of God in view of the Antichrist?[36] The 'enemy' is increasingly directing his forces at the beginnings of life and the little ones: it is only the love for Jesus Christ and the Virgin Mary that is going to save them. The Lord tells us to resist! "Be sober and vigilant. Your opponent the devil is prowling around like a roaring lion looking for [someone] to devour"[37].

**The 'man of iniquity'**

The '*Antichrist*' serves Satan, the devil. In fact, as Scripture tells us, this is "the lawless one (...) the one doomed to perdition, who opposes and exalts himself above every so-called god and object of worship, so as to seat himself in the temple of God, claiming that he is a god (...). And then the lawless one will be revealed, whom the Lord [Jesus] will kill with the breath of his mouth and render powerless by the manifestation of his coming, the one whose coming springs from the power of Satan in every mighty deed and in signs and wonders that lie, and in every wicked deceit for those who are perishing because they have not accepted the love of truth so that they may be saved. Therefore, God is sending them a deceiving power so that they may believe the lie, that

---

[35] *Magisterium.* Joseph Cardinal Ratzinger, *The God of Jesus Christ. Meditations on the triune God*, Ignatius Press, San Francisco, 2008, p. 17.
[36] *Bible.* Cfr. Second Letter to Thessalonians 2:3-12; First Letter of John 2:18-23.
[37] *Bible.* First Letter of Peter 5:8-9.

all who have not believed the truth but have approved wrongdoing may be condemned"[38]. This will mark the end of the satanic plan.

## The beast

As Joseph Ratzinger wrote in his book *The God of Jesus Christ*: "The Revelation of John speaks of the adversary of God, the 'beast'. This beast, the power opposed to God has no name, but a number. The seer tells us: 'Its number is six hundred and sixty-six' (13:18). It is a number, and it makes men numbers. We who lived through the world of the concentration camps know what this means. The terror of that world is rooted in the fact that it obliterates men's faces. It obliterates their history. It makes man a number, an exchangeable cog in one big machine. He is his function – nothing more. Today, we must fear that the concentration camp was only a prelude and that the universal law of the machine may impose the structure of the concentration camp on the world as a whole. For when functions are all that exist, man, too, is nothing more than a function. The machines that he himself has constructed now impose their own law on him: he must be made readable for the computer, and this can be achieved only when he is translated into numbers. Everything else in man becomes irrelevant. Whatever is not a function is – nothing. The beast is a number, and it makes men numbers. But God has a name, and God calls us by our name. He is a Person, and he seeks the person. He has a face, and he seeks our face. He has a heart, and he seeks our heart. For him, we are not some function in a 'world machinery'. On the contrary, it is precisely those who have no function that are his own. A name allows me to be addressed. A name denotes community"[39].

All this evokes the conscience, the instrument with which we can approve good and reject evil with its "structures of sin"[40]. In particular, these are rooted around the trade in arms and drugs and the like which exploit man, and are of special interest to the mafia and the underworld. The evil 'of abuse and crime' is consolidated in some "structures of sin" and grows through them! It grows in the 'darkness'. One thing is confidentiality and privacy, another is to love 'the darkness', as in the case of sects and any kind of mafia. This is the place where Satan finds bait: lies, theft, death are part of him since he has chosen to stay in the darkness, i.e. the opposite of light, love and life.

---

[38] *Bible.* Second Letter to the Thessalonians 2:3-4, 8-12.
[39] *Magisterium.* Joseph Cardinal Ratzinger, *The God of Jesus Christ. Meditations on the triune God*, Ignatius Press, San Francisco, 2008, p. 13.
[40] *Magisterium. Catechism of the Catholic Church* no. 1869.

With the abuses and crime that the wicked spread and implement, tyranny takes hold in the world and weeds grow alongside good grain. The Church, in seeking to faithfully accomplish the will of God and His kingdom, accompanies humanity throughout history, proclaiming true freedom and true love for every man. A renewed commitment is thus needed so that the conscience of each individual awakens to goodness and justice. The petition "Deliver us from evil" in the prayer of the *Our Father* helps us to love what is good and reject evil so that, as John Paul II reminded us, we do not lose ourselves in evil, in the confusion that lies today in consciences and in society[41].

In the world, we must have a conscience which is faithful to the primary values to be defended and maintained through the light we receive from Jesus Christ and his Spirit. Future generations will have many means; yet good and bad will be even more confused. Christians must do their part for the good of man, the family and society.

**The fourth deliverance: from eternal damnation**

To find a life of love and justice, fraternity and humanity, an awakening is therefore needed: a *new consciousness* on the part of men of good will, men who believe in true good and the truth of good. A greater presence on the part of Christians is also called for in society, together with a greater and more powerful prayer such as the one Jesus entrusted to us in the *Our Father* in that "Deliver us from evil...". By reason of our freedom and our conscience we all have, in some measure, our responsibility as entrusted to us by God. There is a divine court. Secularization and atheism have led people to believe it does not exist; while in actual fact no one will escape judgment. The court is truth itself calling us, it is the greatest and fairest truth there is: the Supreme love of God. The Word of God reminds us: "For we must all appear before the judgment seat of Christ, so that each one may receive recompense, according to what he did in the body, whether good or evil"[42].

We were created in the love of God in Jesus Christ, to love and be loved in eternal happiness. Jesus reminds us in the Gospel that we will be judged by true love[43]. "The resurrection of all the dead, 'of both the just and the unjust' (Ac 24:15), will precede the Last Judgment. This will be 'the hour when all who are in the tombs will hear [the Son of man's]

---

[41] *Magisterium.* Cfr. John Paul II, Encyclical Letter *Evangelium vitae* (1995) no. 24 (text no. 92 in Appendix).

[42] *Bible.* Second Letter to the Corinthians 5:10.

[43] *Bible.* Cfr. Gospel of Matthew 25:31-46; 5:25-26.

voice and come forth, those who have done good, to the resurrection of life, and those who have done evil, to the resurrection of judgment' (Jn 5:28-29). Then Christ will come 'in his glory, and all the angels with him... Before him will be gathered all the nations, and he will separate them one from another as a shepherd separates the sheep from the goats, and he will place the sheep at his right hand, but the goats at the left... And they will go away into eternal punishment, but the righteous into eternal life' (Mt 25: 31-33:46)"[44]. Scripture tells us of the Last Judgement: "we shall all stand before the judgment seat of God; (...) each of us shall give an account of himself [to God]"[45].

Thus Saint Polycarp exhorted Christians to lead an exemplary life: "Let us serve Him in fear and with all reverence, even as He Himself has commanded us and as the apostles who preached the Gospel onto us, and the prophets who proclaimed beforehand the coming of the Lord [have alike taught us]. Let us be zealous in the pursuit of that which is good, keeping ourselves from causes of offence, from false brethren, and from those who in hypocrisy bear the name of the Lord, and draw away vain men into error. For whoever does not confess that Jesus Christ has come in the flesh, is antichrist; and whoever does not confess the testimony of the cross, is of the devil; and whoever perverts the oracles of the Lord to his own lusts, and says that there is neither a resurrection nor a judgement, he is the first-born of Satan. Wherefore, forsaking the vanity of many, and their false doctrines, let us return to the word which has been handed down to us from the beginning"[46].

**The love that enters heaven**

That is why God has us grow in love: with love solely of the senses we will not enter heaven, because the body dies; a somewhat more elevated love is needed, as is the one coming from a heart that is capable of doing good. Jesus reminds us of this in the Gospel by urging us to do works of goodness and mercy[47].

We are beings who have freedom, but who also have a great responsibility. The prayer of the *Our Father*, that has us ask God the Father "Deliver us from evil," prepares us to share with God his judgment of salvation, because in life we have sought to distance all evil. And yet,

---

[44] *Magisterium. Catechism of the Catholic Church* no. 1038.
[45] *Bible*. Letter to the Romans 14:10,12.
[46] *Tradition*. Saint Polycarp (69-155), *The Epistle of Polycarp to the Philippians. The Greek and Latin Text of the Epistle, verse by verse,* compiled by D. R. Palmer (www.bibletranslation.ws, accessed in July 2014).
[47] *Bible*. Cfr. Gospel of Matthew 25:34-46.

people forget or let the Last Judgment slip their mind, while instead they should ward off evil...

There comes the time of judgment and reckoning: "Our Lord warns us that we shall be separated from him if we fail to meet the serious needs of the poor and the little ones who are his brethren [Cfr. Mt 25:31-46]. To die in mortal sin without repenting and accepting God's merciful love means remaining separated from him forever by our own free choice. This state of definitive self-exclusion from communion with God and the blessed is called 'hell'"[48].

"Jesus often speaks of 'Gehenna' of 'the unquenchable fire' (Mt 5:22; Mt 5:29; Mt 13:42; Mt 13:50; Mc 9:43-48), reserved for those who to the end of their lives refuse to believe and be converted, where both soul and body can be lost (Mt 10:28). Jesus solemnly proclaims that he 'will send his angels, and they will gather... all evil doers, and throw them into the furnace of fire' (Mt 13: 41-42), and that he will pronounce the condemnation: 'Depart from me, you cursed, into the eternal fire!' (Mt 25:41)"[49]. Benedict XVI also reminded us of this with pastoral love and apprehension: "Jesus came to tell us that he wants us all in Paradise and that hell, about which little is said in our time, exists and is eternal for those who close their hearts to his love. (...) our real enemy is attachment to sin, which can lead us to failure in our lives"[50].

## How can one speak of hell?

But how is it possible to speak of hell when God is Goodness and Love? How can hell exist if God wants everyone to be saved and uses infinite mercy towards everyone? Many people are stumped by these questions: the presence of evil on earth blocks them, but so does the thought of heaven. This calls for closer examination.

Love itself is a flame of love; human love already is a flame, and much more so is God that is infinite Love and Truth, and therefore also Supreme Good and Justice. He thus becomes a barrier for those who have not loved and do not want to love, insuperable for those who neither want to love nor forgive or be forgiven by the Love of mercy. This is why Jesus says in the Gospel: "Amen, I say to you, all sins and all blasphemies that people utter will be forgiven them. But whoever blasphemes against the holy Spirit will never have forgiveness, but is

---

[48] *Magisterium. Catechism of the Catholic Church* no. 1033.
[49] *Magisterium. Catechism of the Catholic Church* no. 1034.
[50] *Magisterium.* Benedict XVI, *Homily during Pastoral Visit to the Roman Parish Church of "Santa Felicita e Figli Martiri"* (25 March 2007).

guilty of an everlasting sin"[51]. All sins will be forgiven apart from one, that against the Holy Spirit, namely against love, the mercy with which God wants to give himself to humanity and to each person. The sin against the Holy Spirit is the refusal of the Merciful Love of God, as affirmed in John Paul II's Encyclical Letter *Dominum et Vivificantem* (The Lord who gives life)[52].

## A key to understanding

But where to go when there will be solely the Absolute Love of God "so that God may be all in all"?[53]. Conversely, what is love, pleasure and eternal happiness for those who have loved and love God, thus becomes hell, that is, 'hate', impossibility of love itself! This is the hell that 'burns'. "What would be happiness to clear minds would be a torment to those that are defiled", said Saint Leo the Great[54].

The salvation that Jesus has revealed and brought us is also *salvation from the fires of hell*. Jesus speaks clearly about this in the Gospel giving a number of examples on several occasions: "The Son of Man will send his angels, and they will collect out of his kingdom all who cause others to sin and all evildoers. They will throw them into the fiery furnace, where there will be wailing and grinding of teeth. Then the righteous will shine like the sun in the kingdom of their Father. Whoever has ears ought to hear."[55].

Jesus made every attempt to warn us[56]. The Bible reminds us: "God looks out from the heavens upon the children of Adam, To see if there is a discerning person who is seeking God"[57]. The possibility of eternal damnation should be seriously considered in its own logic.

Saint Paul spoke of this with deep emotion and apprehension: "For many, as I have often told you and now tell you even in tears, conduct themselves as enemies of the cross of Christ. Their end is destruction. Their God is their stomach; their glory is in their 'shame.' Their minds

---

[51] *Bible*. Gospel of Mark 3:28-29.

[52] *Magisterium*. Cfr. John Paul II, Encyclical Letter *Dominum et vivificantem*, (1986) no. 46 (text no. 93 in Appendix).

[53] *Bible*. First Letter to the Corinthians 15:28.

[54] *Tradition*. Saint Leo the Great (400 ca.-461), *From a Sermon on the beatitudes, Liturgy of the Hours, Office of Readings, Monday, 23rd week, Ordinary Time* (http://www.liturgies.net/Liturgies/Catholic/loh/week23mondayor.htm, accessed in July 2014).

[55] *Bible*. Gospel of Matthew 13:41-43.

[56] *Bible*. Cfr. Gospel of Matthew 11:23; 13:49-50; Gospel of Luke 13:28; 16:27-31; Gospel of Mark 9:43-48.

[57] *Bible*. Book of Psalms 53:3.

are occupied with earthly things"[58]. In his Letter to the Romans he wrote: "The wrath of God is indeed being revealed from heaven against every impiety and wickedness of those who suppress the truth by their wickedness. For what can be known about God is evident to them, because God made it evident to them. (...) As a result, they have no excuse; for although they knew God they did not accord him glory as God or give him thanks. Instead, they became vain in their reasoning, and their senseless minds were darkened. While claiming to be wise, they became fools (...) Therefore, God handed them over to impurity through the lusts of their hearts for the mutual degradation of their bodies. They exchanged the truth of God for a lie and revered and worshiped the creature rather than the creator, who is blessed forever. Amen. Therefore, God handed them over to degrading passions. Their females exchanged natural relations for unnatural, and the males likewise gave up natural relations with females and burned with lust for one another. Males did shameful things with males and thus received in their own persons the due penalty for their perversity. And since they did not see fit to acknowledge God, God handed them over to their undiscerning mind to do what is improper. They are filled with every form of wickedness, evil, greed, and malice; full of envy, murder, rivalry, treachery, and spite. They are gossips and scandalmongers and they hate God. They are insolent, haughty, boastful, ingenious in their wickedness, and rebellious toward their parents. They are senseless, faithless, heartless, ruthless. Although they know the just decree of God that all who practice such things deserve death, they not only do them but give approval to those who practice them"[59] . Powerful pages that give us cause to reflect on modern day events!

These are the words of Holy Scripture, the Word of God which addresses the heart and mind of man. God respects the freedom and responsibility of man, but man does not respect his mystery, his roots, when he does not "see fit to acknowledge God"!

Saint Paul in his Second Letter to Timothy says: "But understand this: there will be terrifying times in the last days. People will be self-centered and lovers of money, proud, haughty, abusive, disobedient to their parents, ungrateful, irreligious, callous, implacable, slanderous, licentious, brutal, hating what is good, traitors, reckless, conceited, lovers of pleasure rather than lovers of God, as they make a pretense of religion but deny its power. Reject them"[60]. Corrupt men deceive each

---

[58] *Bible*. Letter to the Philippians 3:18-19.
[59] *Bible*. Letter to the Romans 1:18-19, 20-22, 24-32.
[60] *Bible*. Second Letter to Timothy 3:1-5.

other, and fall into the traps of the very same disease they love, because, as the Bible says, the evil-doer "falls into the pit he has made"[61].

It is necessary to pray that "we may be delivered from perverse and wicked people, for not all have faith. But the Lord is faithful; he will strengthen you and guard you from the evil one"[62]. It is necessary to guard against evil in all its forms, with respect to people who are not good, and who do not love God. We thus need to pray to God: "Do not drag me off with the wicked, with those who do wrong, Who speak peace to their neighbors though evil is in their hearts"[63]. This, too, Jesus wants to teach us in the "Deliver us from evil" petition in the *Our Father*.

## The possibility of eternal damnation

The greatest false illusion, that of a corrupt heart which does not want God, is capable of bringing about the most serious tragedy, i.e. *eternal damnation*, as attested to by Sacred Scripture: "Do you not know that the unjust will not inherit the kingdom of God? Do not be deceived; neither fornicators nor idolaters nor adulterers nor boy prostitutes nor sodomites nor thieves nor the greedy nor drunkards nor slanderers nor robbers will inherit the kingdom of God"[64]. Each and every deception and act of selfishness will remain outside heaven: "Outside are the dogs, the sorcerers, the unchaste, the murderers, the idol-worshipers, and all who love and practice deceit"[65]. "But as for cowards, the unfaithful, the depraved, murderers, the unchaste, sorcerers, idol-worshipers, and deceivers of every sort, their lot is in the burning pool of fire and sulfur, which is the second death"[66].

You may now well ask: why should hell be eternal? And why should damnation be forever? Why is it not possible for God to 'take us out'? What we do know is that, at that point, man would hate salvation. Looking at the situation from a human point of view, you could say that 'the damned' would continue to hate salvation and mercy as they have done for years and years on earth by doing nothing about their soul! Looking at the situation from the point of view of God, that is Love, you might say, 'precisely because God is Love'. Love burns and does likewise to itself like two flames that come together in a single flame. When God

---

[61] *Bible*. Book of Psalms 7:16.
[62] *Bible*. Second Letter to the Thessalonians 3:2-3.
[63] *Bible*. Book of Psalms 28:3.
[64] *Bible*. First Letter to the Corinthians 6:9-10.
[65] *Bible*. Book of Revelation 22:15.
[66] *Bible*. Book of Revelation 21:8.

is "all in all"[67] there will be only the Love of God in each one, and each one in God, in a communion of eternal life since the spirit is immortal. Who knows human love also knows that one of its characteristics is that it has no end, as God himself has revealed to us in the Holy Scripture: "Its arrows are arrows of fire, flames of the divine. Deep waters cannot quench love, nor rivers sweep it away"[68].

If the love of the soul rebelled and became *hatred*, rejecting God and his love, like satanic hatred, what would the soul do that does not love God but is in such close contact with the light of Love, that is God Absolute? What would it do, but burn from the love it hates? It would burn from an everlasting hatred. If it had chosen not to love God and to reject him, where would it go far from him if God is "all in all"[69]. It would not burn of love, but of atrocious suffering: the same flame of love, joining all spiritual souls in the joy of God, would be, by the will of those who 'do not want to love or be loved', an eternally devouring fire. Hence, death, like suicide, is never the solution to life. Love is the only solution.

If hate is the opposite of love and God is love, wherever could one go that is far from God when He manifests himself as God Love? At this point, hell has its own terrible logic. Some could argue that since there is goodness and love it would be unbearable to see and know of anyone in hell... Of course. Unless it is the same immense love, loved by saints but hated by the damned who do not want it, 'each having what he wants, what he loves, what he hates'. The glory of God will be the full manifestation of his Love in everyone, and as the Bible says: "Surely the wrath of man will give you thanks; the remnant of your furor will keep your feast"[70]. As the Psalmist says: "You, terrible are you; who can stand before you and your great anger? From the heavens you pronounced sentence; the earth was terrified and reduced to silence, When you arose, O God, for judgment to save the afflicted of the land"[71].

In short, there is heaven, because God that is Love lives eternal happiness, but, since He is respectful of the freedom of the human being and does not wish to force anyone to truly love him, there is the terrible possibility of being in the contrary situation, that of hell. It is a choice of 'no return' that may occur on earth or in eternity. This is why Jesus has openly and persistently revealed the existence and the real possibility of hell on several occasions. But more often still, and in every

---

[67] *Bible*. Cfr. First Letter to the Corinthians 15:28.
[68] *Bible*. Song of Songs 8:6-7.
[69] *Bible*. Cfr. First Letter to the Corinthians 15:28.
[70] *Bible*. Book of Psalms 76:11.
[71] *Bible*. Book of Psalms 76:8-10.

way possible with words and gestures He has invited and urged us to return to *love God* and *love our neighbour.*

God does not 'banish' anyone to hell: it is the person himself who chooses a definitive state of self-exclusion. It is true that in the Gospel as in the parable of the wedding[72] feast and the Last Judgement[73], Jesus uses images in which it is God that banishes from the kingdom, as happened in earthly heaven[74]; but with these images, Jesus wants us to understand the gravity, and to remember the "wrath"[75] of God that is immense love. It would be this said same Love felt as Love that, when 'hated' by man, creates a 'separation'. Therefore, as the Catechism of the Catholic Church reminds us: "To die in mortal sin without repenting and accepting God's merciful love means remaining separated from him forever by our own free choice"[76].

It is possible to be in hell for not wanting and not accepting mercy, for rejecting it and hating it: in the end, this leads to not loving God that is Love, and 'burning' of hatred, in opposition to him. What in fact are we left with, without Jesus and his mercy? We give thanks to God because by delivering us from sin, death and hell, He has reopened the doors to life and the love of heaven for us, towards that 'happiness' for which we have been created! The petition "But deliver us from evil" helps us grow day by day so that our heart may love what is pleasing to God, and reject that which He hates, the evil that hurts us.

In the next chapter we will take a look at the other four deliverances, vital to human life, promised by God and requested in the rich profound prayer of the *Our Father.*

---

[72] *Bible.* Cfr. Gospel of Matthew 22:11-13.
[73] *Bible.* Cfr. Gospel of Matthew 25:41.
[74] *Bible.* Cfr. Book of Genesis 3:23-24.
[75] *Bible.* Cfr. Letter to the Romans 1:18.
[76] *Magisterium. Catechism of the Catholic Church* no. 1033.

# 16

# But deliver us from evil (II)
## But deliver us from the evil one

We have seen the first four deliverances from evil. Let us now examine the other four which deal with the most obscure aspect of evil; sin.

## The fifth deliverance: from sin

Sin is spiritual, but no less real than injustice, abuse and crime which, as we have previously seen, are more easily verifiable, while the gravity and the extent of sin need to be examined in greater depth.

God wants our fulfilment and our own good, but always in the light of the truth. When man, to live in freedom, disregards God's presence in his daily life, reality is distorted and the truth of life betrayed. Sin is when man no longer recognises who he is and who God is. Sin is a *break-up* in the relationship between man and God. It entails 'turning away' from God and rebelling against him. And this results in man losing everything. This is the gravity and also the absurdity of sin. For this reason, the more man comes closer to God and recognises him as such, the more he recognises 'his sin' and the extent to which he has fallen into darkness.

Sin is not an idea or a sentiment, but a fact that can be grasped and understood in the light of God, who came to remove the human being from the darkness of sin, and bring him into the light, the truth and total love. Deliverance from sin gives greater freedom to life making it more human.

The reality of sin seeps into the human conscience to the point of leaving people disturbed: often angry, closed within themselves, and sad. As it progresses, the evil of sin closes and corrupts the heart, removing love and joy and thereby bringing sadness. In the end the person is left without hope, preferring the darkness. This is because evil, by its own nature, always covers a part of truth and goodness, thus diminishing joy and hope. The more sin advances the more it burns the land of our true life, it being always a lack of love, a 'no' said to God, hence an evil for everyone.

As recalled by John Paul II: "Refusal of God's fatherly love and of his loving gifts is always at the root of humanity's divisions"[1]. "God is faithful to his eternal plan even when man, under the impulse of the evil one and carried away by his own pride, abuses the freedom given to him in order to love and generously seek what is good, and refuses to obey his Lord and Father. God is faithful even when man, instead of responding with love to God's love, opposes him and treats him like a rival, deluding himself and relying on his own power, with the resulting break of relationship with the one who created him. In spite of this transgression on man's part, God remains faithful in love"[2].

How mighty is God! He is always a good and merciful Father, forgiving everything and everyone. While we are still in time we should not ignore his appeal. God – as John Paul II affirmed – "does not close his heart to any of his children. He waits for them, looks for them, goes to meet them at the place where the refusal of communion imprisons them in isolation and division. He calls them to gather about his table in the joy of the feast of forgiveness and reconciliation. This initiative on God's part is made concrete and manifest in the redemptive act of Christ, which radiates through the world by means of the ministry of the church"[3]. In fact the Risen Jesus delivers his Spirit of mercy and forgiveness to the whole world through the Church[4].

Mercy is not a feel-good sensation that justifies the running away from responsibility but, as we have previously seen, a reconstruction that is solely brought about by God[5]. Jesus, as the Apostle Paul reminds us, has entrusted his mercy to the Church and her ministers: "And all this is from God, who has reconciled us to himself through Christ and given us the ministry of reconciliation, namely, God was reconciling the world to himself in Christ, not counting their trespasses against them and entrusting to us the message of reconciliation. So we are ambassadors for Christ, as if God were appealing through us. We implore you on behalf of Christ, be reconciled to God"[6].

---

[1] *Magisterium*. John Paul II, Apostolic Exhortation *Reconciliatio et paenitentia* (1984) no. 10.
[2] *Magisterium*. John Paul II, Apostolic Exhortation *Reconciliatio et paenitentia* (1984) no. 10.
[3] *Magisterium*. John Paul II, Apostolic Exhortation *Reconciliatio et paenitentia* (1984) no. 10.
[4] *Bible*. Cfr. Gospel of John 20:20-23.
[5] Cfr. chapters 11 and 12.
[6] *Bible*. Second Letter to the Corinthians 5:18-20.

Among the works that the enemy, as Jesus calls him[7], evokes is the external attack, i.e. the sins against the Church, her works and the faith. However, there is also an attack which comes from within the Church through the sins of her children, and this is why the Church must battle against sin both externally and internally. The Church is made up of saints and sinners, so love, conversion and the reparation of sins are all equally and actively present within it. There are people who, rather than being upset, appear to be pleased about the sins committed by some members of the Church. This is disconcerting since it shows that the Evil One dwells in their hearts. Does this not mean they are aiding Satan in his works? Surely, they should be sad not only about brothers falling into deep sin and error but also for the many who have suffered the consequences! Perhaps, they do not see themselves as brothers, even though they are.

Asking "Deliver us from evil" in the *Our Father* makes us more aware and attentive to the evils that are present in the world, without us consenting to them, and also prompts us to repair the harm done to our brothers and sisters! Jesus reminds us: "Settle with your opponent quickly while on the way to court with him. Otherwise your opponent will hand you over to the judge, and the judge will hand you over to the guard, and you will be thrown into prison"[8]. The less we feel like brothers and sisters, the more evil increases and with it also sins. Already here on earth, we should be especially careful not to deny forgiveness and mercy.

**The sixth deliverance: from the Evil One**

The word 'evil' can also be translated as 'Evil One'. In his book *Jesus of Nazareth*, Benedict XVI commenting on the prayer of the *Our Father* states: "The new German translation of the Our Father says 'vom Bösen', thus leaving it open whether 'evil' or 'the Evil One' is meant. The two are ultimately inseparable. (...) It is only when you have lost God that that you have lost yourself; then you are nothing more than a random product of evolution. (...) Evils (plural) can be necessary for our purification, but evil (singular) destroys. This, then, is why we pray from the depths of our soul not to be robbed of our faith, which enables us to see God, which binds us with Christ. This is why we pray that, in our concern for goods, we may not lose the Good itself; that even faced with the loss of goods, we may not also lose the Good, which is God; that we ourselves may not be lost: Deliver us from evil!"[9].

---

[7] *Bible*. Cfr. Gospel of Matthew 13:39.
[8] *Bible*. Gospel of Matthew 5:25.
[9] *Magisterium*. Benedict XVI, *Jesus of Nazareth*, Doubleday, New York 2007, p. 165-166.

Closeness to God distances the Evil One. Conversely, the more man turns away from God, closing within himself and in the use of life, without understanding God and loving him as such, to the point of forgetting the profound mystery of his soul, created and willed by God "in his image and likeness", the more man exposes himself to the mercy of Satan's forces that tend to isolate him. Here it must be said that the forces of evil tend to transform the relationship that Christians have with God into something to be despised and isolated. The devil does exist, and is a being. It is not an 'evil' in the philosophical or psychological sense of the word. However, some have preferred to consider it as such in their imagination, and teach so in order to obtain respect and human consensus while distancing themselves, although not openly saying so, from the faith of the Church. When in the name of respect and tolerance, the truth is renounced and hidden, it is then that manipulation seeps in. This leaves space to the deceiver and those who deceive. It is here that liberty, law, and rights start to disappear.

Jesus was made man to deliver us from the Evil One: "Indeed, the Son of God was revealed to destroy the works of the devil"[10]. Thus, there are the works of the devil with all his machinations: disease, temptations, harassment, possession, and death itself, but all are destroyed by Jesus with his word and his miracles. Jesus, whose name means 'God saves', came to save us from the devil and his evil works that are against God, against our life, and against love, truth and freedom. With freedom we can love; yet Satan does not want love, indeed he hates it, and also hates freedom that makes us 'similar' to God. This is the reason why evil and the Evil One use coercion, threats, oppression, fear and blackmail.

Jesus also warns us against the mad claim of another father... The *Our Father* begins precisely with the invocation to God, Our Father whom we must find again, and at the end has us pray to be freed from the falsehood of another father, the "father of lies"[11], the one that is determined to take God's place and build a kingdom of darkness, hatred and death.

**The work of the Evil One**

In the Gospel Jesus says of the devil: "He was a murderer from the beginning and does not stand in truth, because there is no truth in him. When he tells a lie, he speaks in character, because he is a liar and the father of lies"[12]. Satan wants to bring about a kingdom of deceit,

---

[10] *Bible*. First Letter of John 3:8.
[11] *Bible*. Cfr. Gospel of John 8:44.
[12] *Bible*. Gospel of John 8:44.

a camouflaged kingdom. However, he lacks the power to accomplish this plan. His action is a futile opposition, a 'mimicking' of that which in God is absolutely true.

In fact, anyone who desires to live cannot break away from God the Source of all created existence, even that of Satan who has chosen to live 'in opposition', in hatred of God that is Love. The Evil One wants to hide in the darkness and in the 'non-life' and, since he offends and hates life, spreads death and rebellion against God.

Although the Evil One opposes and hates God, he unwillingly affirms God as God, and hence, contrary to his wishes, he is actually forced to give him glory. Therefore, evil cannot touch, diminish or tarnish the good in heaven but can 'only recognise' it.

Jesus calls Satan "the father of lies" because he generates them. Lies are opposition to the Truth, that is God. Those who go against the truth and the pursuit of truth do not want to belong to God. Conversely, those who 'love the truth' embark upon a true relationship with God. Those who love truth find God. The problem for humanity has always been that of loving the truth. When there is no love for the truth, lies, deception, abuse, and in the end also crime are preferred. These are stages that mark the increasing gravity of man's sins. This escalation of sin is in full accordance with the plan and work of Satan.

Jesus also calls Satan "a murderer from the beginning"[13]; this is because he seeks the destruction of life, death in any form, but even more so where there is the 'image of God', through murder and suicide. The fear, as we were warned by Saint John Paul II, that the 'culture of death' is gaining ground is well-founded. Indeed, some countries have accepted the 'culture of death' as a sign of tolerance, while in reality it is the result of the abuse present in the subculture of a minority, a 'tentacle' of the satanic plan. Is it not in fact one of his triumphs when so many elderly are 'democratically' pushed to terminate their lives, perhaps lived with much effort, in the end denying them any value with the suicide 'solution'? Or, when the lives of so many human embryos and foetuses are destroyed with impunity, or again when these defenceless beings are secretly used as 'inhuman' guinea pigs in experiments or, indeed, are 'sacrificed' in satanic rituals in total contempt and hatred for human life? Why this terrible ungodliness in satanic rituals, unless it were not an outrage to human life, i.e. the 'image of God' present from the very moment of conception and therefore precious in the eyes of God? Folly and wickedness strike in a twofold manner: first atheistic materialism ignores the value of these little human beings, and then satanism uses them!

---

[13] *Bible*. Gospel of John 8:44.

Isn't this massacre of so many human beings sufficient to see the work of the devil, the "enemy"[14] of God and of man? Hasn't the culture of war in previous centuries been enough to denounce satanic works and to draw everyone to the *Our Father* without having the culture of death fuelled in our day by terrorism and the evil occult?

Our Father, good Father "Deliver us from evil"! But we have to ask ourselves: do we really want God to deliver us from evil? It is up to us to understand and want this. Good or bad grows within us, in the soul, since within us there is the spiritual reality that should decide for God.

Being 'children' we seek our roots, we look for a father. This is why Jesus warns us not to allow ourselves to be deceived by the "father of lies" and hate, who is disguised with the appearance of freedom and democracy. At first, it seems that there is goodness and freedom, and it is only later that the seeds of perversion and death are revealed.

**Deliverance through exorcism**

Only God the Father frees us from the Evil One, i.e. the one we call the devil, Satan, or the enemy. Jesus gave his Church the power to free of the devil; therefore, those who cannot speak of the devil, cannot speak of true human reality or even of the Gospel... Many non-believing Christians or 'weak Christians' evade this reality believing it to be mythical. But is it not enough just to take a look at all the evil in the world to understand that Satan exists and operates? Can't we see this just by looking at history? And most of all, is it not enough to have Jesus who, with his work of liberation, has taught the Church how to fight? The Church fights Satan and his works with the prayer of exorcism as Jesus gave her the power and task to do so.

The devil wants to enter and disturb man when he does not find love for the truth and for God. The devil is to be cast out in the name of Jesus and as Jesus commanded: "drive out demons"[15]. Therefore, it is the power of Jesus that through our faith frees us from the Evil One.

On being interviewed about the devil, a friend of mine, an exorcist Father, expressed himself in these words: "The devil is a living and spiritual being, he is not an invention of religion to keep men 'good'. He pushes man to sin and away from God, sowing hatred, division, confusion and discord. Those who deny the existence of the devil fall outside biblical and Church teaching. He is a real, living, spiritual, highly intelligent being, without body because he is a pure spirit. The devil tries to worm his way into the patterns of existence to bring division,

---

[14] *Bible.* Cfr. Gospel of Matthew 13:39.
[15] *Bible.* Gospel of Matthew 10:8.

confusion, rebellion, suffering and to turn us away from God. He needs concealment and anonymity in order to act effectively; most of the time his work is not flashy, but subtle and constant. Where selfishness, hatred, violence, immorality, division, corruption reign... the devil is not absent. His power is limited, his work is always subordinate to divine permission and never exceeds our strength. The devil is a loser and only strong with the weak. A good relationship with the Lord, a life of constant and faithful prayer, the sacraments, the Eucharist and Confession, the Word of God and the recitation of the Rosary, are powerful and certain means to defend us from evil and the Evil One".

## The victory of Peace and Love

The future, which above all the believer must look to, is not marked so much by victory over the Evil One, but rather by love, peace and the joy of God's heart, which is our true and ultimate future[16]: heaven is our future, the future of humanity. The strength of the Christian is to be found in the love and peace that God has and gives. It is in Good that we find the strength to fight evil, and not in opposition. It is not hatred that drives us in the fight but love, the love of the Lord, the love with which we are loved by him!

In fact, Christianity is not the religion of resentment but of love and of the peace that is in God. This is why Mary Most Holy, the Mother of Jesus, begins the Magnificat[17] with words of joy and peace:

"And Mary said:
'My soul proclaims the greatness of the Lord;
my spirit rejoices in God my savior'"[18].

*The Compendium of the Catechism of the Catholic Church* reminds us: "Why do we conclude by asking: 'But deliver us from evil'? Evil indicates the person of Satan who opposes God and is 'the deceiver of the whole world' (Revelation 12:9). Victory over the devil has already been won by Christ. We pray, however, that the human family be freed from Satan and his works. We also ask for the precious gift of peace and the grace of perseverance as we wait for the coming of Christ who will free us definitively from the Evil One"[19].

---

[16] *Bible*. Cfr. Gospel of Luke 10:17-20.
[17] *Magisterium*. Cfr. John Paul II, Encyclical Letter *Redemptoris mater* (1987) nos. 36-37.
[18] *Bible*. Gospel of Luke 1:46-47.
[19] *Magisterium*. *The Compendium of the Catechism of the Catholic Church* no. 597.

**Satanic plan**

The First Letter of John the Apostle speaks of the children of God and the children of the devil[20]. The children of the devil are those who serve him, not loving the truth but the lie, they are those whose father is concealed, and it is only in the end that he shows himself in his 'principality', that of 'mammon', made up of wealth, pleasure, occult power and darkness. It is only when he has finally imposed himself as master in an attempt to replace God, that he will reveal himself in his identity as the "father of lies", the 'perverter', whom they will have served by failing "to act in righteousness" and by "hating"[21] their brothers and sisters.

Let's reflect on this. The widespread belief among many people that we should not search for 'neither father nor master' because each one of us is self-sufficient, is a great illusion. There is always someone behind holding the strings, wanting to steer our real life away from the truth. Because of this constant temptation, Jesus shows us our real roots, which are in the life of God the Father: a house does not rest on sand, foundations are needed[22]. A life without 'Our Father' without a cause and without an end, is a nonsense, a folly. And madness leads to self-destruction. It is from here that the *satanic plan* takes its cue.

Saying "no father nor master is needed: everyone is free and relies on himself..." is also a falsehood, because at first everything possible is done to remove God the Father from the perspectives of life and man's heart, and then there are those who put themselves in his place directing weak people with occult power, whether economic (the hidden interests of multinationals and financial lobbies), political, ideological, cultural (cultural dictatorship), or scientistic-technological, or that of other sects or powers that will come into being.

This too is part of the satanic plan: denying the spiritual reality in man, encouraging an atheist anthropology so that man turns away from God, and introducing, in his place, a generic spiritual dimension of peace and well-being, tolerance and serenity such as, for example, the New Age, in which neither the reality of God, nor God the Father, nor Jesus Christ are named, but where there appears a kind of *atheist religiosity*. Thus, what has been taken away from the Christian vision of life is subsequently taken up and adapted, and, by excluding God, used in a perverse way, in view first of *spiritism* and then *satanism*. The

---

[20] *Bible*. Cfr. Gospel of Luke 16:8; First Letter of John 3:10.
[21] *Bible*. Cfr. First Letter of John 2:11.
[22] *Bible*. Cfr. Gospel of Matthew 7:21-27.

Word of God reminds us, "The fool says in his heart, 'There is no God.' Their deeds are loathsome and corrupt; not one does what is good"[23].

The devil has a plan and the foolish man, who does not listen to God, is deceived, sometimes thinking he is more cunning than the devil! Only God frees us from the devil. According to Scripture: "Indeed, the Son of God was revealed to destroy the works of the devil"[24].

## The victory of Jesus Christ

We know of the victory of Christ over Satan. It is a spiritual war. It is not a war directed at man nor of man, it is not anything human, but a fight against evil spirits that are rebellious to God.

We too are involved, because although Jesus has won the war, it is our task to win battles in the daily struggle against evil and all its powers and machinations, until the final showdown that Christ will have against the devil, as the Word of God in the Bible reminds us. "For our struggle is not with flesh and blood but with the principalities, with the powers, with the world rulers of this present darkness, with the evil spirits in the heavens"[25].

With Jesus we can and must conquer the Evil One: "Therefore, put on the armor of God, that you may be able to resist on the evil day and, having done everything, to hold your ground. So stand fast with your loins girded in truth, clothed with righteousness as a breastplate, and your feet shod in readiness for the gospel of peace. In all circumstances, hold faith as a shield, to quench all [the] flaming arrows of the evil one. And take the helmet of salvation and the sword of the Spirit, which is the word of God"[26].

## The fight against evil and darkness

This is therefore the fight against evil and darkness of which Jesus speaks in the Gospel of Matthew when he says: "Do not think that I have come to bring peace upon the earth. I have come to bring not peace but the sword"[27]. Here Jesus refers to the fight against evil, Satan, to free man and all humanity. This is the service that the Church faithfully continues to perform, united with Jesus in doing his works.

Here it may be useful to recall some passages of the Magisterium of the Church. Paul VI recalled that "Evil is not merely an absence

---

23 *Bible*. Book of Psalms 14:1.
24 *Bible*. First Letter of John 3:8.
25 *Bible*. Letter to the Ephesians 6:12.
26 *Bible*. Letter to the Ephesians 6:13-17.
27 *Bible*. Gospel of Matthew 10:34.

of something but an active force, a living, spiritual being that is perverted and that perverts others. It is a terrible reality, mysterious and frightening. (...) The Devil is the number one enemy, the preeminent tempter. So we know that this dark disturbing being exists, (...) he is the hidden enemy who sows errors and misfortunes in human history. (...) He is 'a murderer from the beginning, ... and the father of lies' as Christ defines him (cfr. Jn 8:44-45). (...) Some think a sufficient compensation can be found in psychoanalytic and psychiatric studies or in spiritualistic experiences, which are unfortunately so widespread in some countries today. (...) 'We know', writes St. John the Evangelist, 'that we are of God, and the whole world is in the power of the evil one' (1 John 5: 19)"[28].

Saint John Paul II also similarly expressed himself at a General Audience: "the devil (or Satan) and the other demons 'were created good by God but have become evil by their own will'. (...) When, by an act of his own free will, he rejected the truth that he knew about God, Satan became the cosmic 'liar and the father of lies' (Jn 8:44). For this reason he lives in radical and irreversible denial of God, and seeks to impose on creation 'on the other beings created in the image of God, and in particular on people' his own tragic 'lie about the good' that is God. (...) As the result of the sin of our first parents, this fallen angel has acquired dominion over man to a certain extent. (...) The action of Satan consists primarily in tempting people to evil, by influencing their imaginations and higher faculties, to turn them away from the law of God. (...) Satan has the skill in the world to induce people to deny his existence in the name of rationalism and of every other system of thought which seeks all possible means to avoid recognizing his activity"[29].

Likewise, Benedict XVI warned us about the work of the devil when he recalled that "the Church is also not only a gift of God and divine, but also very human: 'fierce wolves will come' (Acts 20:29). The Church is constantly threatened, there is always danger, the opposition of the devil who does not accept the presence of this new People of God in humanity, or that God should be present in a living community. Thus we should not be surprised that there are always difficulties, that there are always tares in the Church's field. It has always been so, and always will be. But we must be conscious, with joy, that truth is stronger than falsehood, love is stronger than hatred, God is stronger than all the forces in opposition to him"[30].

---

[28] *Magisterium*. Paul VI, *General Audience* (15 November 1972).

[29] *Magisterium*. John Paul II, *General Audience* (13 August 1986).

[30] *Magisterium*. Benedict XVI, *Lectio Divina at Meeting with the Parish Priests of the Rome Diocese* (10 March 2011).

We should not be afraid of Satan because Jesus has won and we are victors with Jesus. As Saint John the Apostle wrote: "I am writing to you, young men, because you have conquered the evil one"[31]. The devil, as we have previously seen, is vanquished by Jesus. Rather than fearing God, Saint John tells us to treat God as God[32], since in the end it is with him and with his love that we have to relate.

## The seventh deliverance: from death

God not only 'has' but 'is the Life'. God does not want death, He did not create death[33]: He is the God of Life[34], and will therefore free us from death. Before bringing his friend Lazarus back to life after being dead for four days, Jesus shows us all his pain in the tears he sheds before the drama of human death[35]. Following the first radical sin, original sin, God has left 'the consequence' in humanity, the sign of death being the external manifestation of the gravity of sin that has damaged our life[36] and that, because it is internal, is not visible.

God the Father gave his Son Jesus to mankind[37] to enable us to pass from death to eternal life, to the life of the resurrection. To this end, Jesus, by living our human reality up to his death on the cross and overcoming death by his resurrection, gives us his life as Risen Lord: he wants our total deliverance, our 'resurrection' in Christ. We know that "the one who raised the Lord Jesus will raise us also with Jesus and place us with you in his presence. (...) For we know that if our earthly dwelling, a tent, should be destroyed, we have a building from God, a dwelling not made with hands, eternal in heaven"[38].

The death of Jesus, albeit a human one, is unique[39] and was not just any death. His death, as well as his resurrection, was "in accordance with the Scriptures", it was according to what God over the centuries had announced in the Holy Scriptures. Also his resurrection is a historical but unique fact that transcends human space and time. The study of the prophecies concerning his birth, death and resurrection is impressive and has brought about the conversion of countless people.

---

[31] *Bible*. First Letter of John 2:13.
[32] *Bible*. Cfr. Gospel of Matthew 10:28.
[33] *Bible*. Cfr. Book of Wisdom 1:13.
[34] *Bible*. Cfr. Book of Wisdom 11:26.
[35] *Bible*. Cfr. Gospel of John 11:1-44.
[36] *Bible*. Cfr. Book of Genesis 3:3.
[37] *Bible*. Cfr. Gospel of John 3:16.
[38] *Bible*. Second Letter to the Corinthians 4:14; 5:1.
[39] *Magisterium*. Cfr. Joseph Cardinal Ratzinger, *The God of Jesus Christ. Meditations on the triune God*, Ignatius Press, San Francisco, 2008 (text no. 94 in Appendix).

Jesus regretfully denounced the hardness of the human heart when it closes before the divine event of the resurrection: "If they will not listen to Moses and the prophets, neither will they be persuaded if someone should rise from the dead"[40]. It is precisely the resurrection which marks the passage of history as coming before or after Christ! This is something we should not forget.

But what do we mean when we speak of the resurrection? It is certainly not an 'awakening' from a particular state, such as that of hibernation. Nor is it the revival of the body in the sense of simply bringing it back to life. Benedict XVI wrote on this aspect in the second volume of *Jesus of Nazareth*: "Now it must be acknowledged that if in Jesus' Resurrection we were dealing simply with the miracle of a resuscitated corpse, it would ultimately be of no concern to us. For it would be no more important than the resuscitation of a clinically dead person through the art of doctors. For the world as such and for our human existence, nothing would have changed. The miracle of a resuscitated corpse would indicate that Jesus' Resurrection was equivalent to the raising of the son of the widow of Nain (Lu 7:11-17), the daughter of Jairus (Mk 5:22-24, 45-43 and parallel passages), and Lazarus (Jn 11:1-44). After a more or less short period, these individuals returned to their former lives, and then at a later point they died definitively. (...) In Jesus' Resurrection a new possibility of human existence is attained that affects everyone and that opens up a future, a new kind of future, for mankind"[41].

At this point it is possible to talk about *metahistory*, a history that is different from our way of living and which is mentioned in the Bible[42]. While human history is the passage of existence in the four known dimensions of time and space, metahistory is living beyond history, in other dimensions that are unattainable for us, those of the Absolute of God. This makes it possible for human history to find its meaning and for the life of each one to get out of the 'deception of the end'. The mythology of former times is a failed attempt showing man's aspiration towards these dreamt and imagined frontiers. Today, the possibility of other 'worlds and ways' that are different from the human one has appeared in the collective imagination, as well as in scientific research. The error of today's world is its failure to take seriously and with gratitude the gift brought by Jesus Christ, i.e. introducing us – through the Christian faith and the grace that operates in the sacraments – in the *metahistory*

---

[40] *Bible*. Gospel of Luke 16:31.

[41] *Magisterium*. Benedict XVI, *Jesus of Nazareth. Holy week: from the Entrance into Jerusalem to the Resurrection*, Part two, Ignatius Press, San Francisco 2011, pp. 243-244.

[42] *Bible*. Cfr. Letter to the Romans 8:18-25; Book of Revelation 21:1.

by the gift of *his* resurrection offered to humanity. This is the reason that no one faith is the same as another, and the *Christian faith* is unique. The resurrection is the overcoming of sin and death in order to live in another way, in God's way. No other prophet of any religion has ever resurrected from the dead: Jesus Christ is the Risen One, the only one and the first of the new humanity[43]. With the coming of Christ, 'believing in God' means believing that God, for our good, is able to raise the dead in this unknown way[44]. "We have come to know and to believe in the love God has for us"[45]. Nowadays, the widespread subculture, having obscured faith in God, seeks to play down death and therefore also *suicide*, seeing and pursuing it as a right, only to then fumble for a disappointing hope in *reincarnation*[46], an idea that stems from pre-Christian human culture. The gift of Jesus Christ has nothing to do with the vision of the so-called *buddhahood, cosmic energy,* or even *Christ energy*[47]. With the loss of faith in Jesus, culture is bound to regress in its development: to avoid believing in the resurrection of Jesus Christ and in the power of God to resurrect from the dead, man is even willing to imagine a soul that wanders here and there to then reincarnate in another body or animal for the purposes of purification! Instead, it is only God who purifies the life of man who is made 'in his image'. Reincarnation does not purify anyone because it is not the suffering, which you would experience passing from one body to another, that liberates life itself from sins. It is the love we experience, which comes from God, that purifies life and suffering. We need the Crucified Jesus, to lovingly live suffering and death itself, so as to experience and overcome it together with him.

## Two pitfalls

Unless we accept Jesus Christ, the only one to have defeated and overcome death, we find ourselves facing two great temptations.

The reality of death can give rise to fanciful and illusory ideas, such as reincarnation which characterizes Eastern philosophy, is present in yoga techniques, and is supported by the New Age and spiritism. Reassurance is thereby provided through the deception that the life of the spirit grows in a 'natural', 'naturally divine' way, without any real need for either the Person of God or Jesus the Redeemer, 'not wanting

---

[43] *Bible*. Cfr. Letter to the Colossians 1:18; Letter to the Philippians 3:20-21.
[44] *Bible*. Cfr. Gospel of Mark 9:10.
[45] *Bible*. First Letter of John 4:16.
[46] *Magisterium*. Cfr. *Catechism of the Catholic Church* no. 1013.
[47] *Magisterium*. Cfr. Pontifical Council for Culture, *Jesus Christ the Bearer of the Water of Life. A Christian reflection on the "New Age"* (2003) nos. 2.3.4; 3.3; 7.2.

to pass with him from death to resurrection' and to the Kingdom of God the Father. This first temptation leads man to deviate towards pre-Christian philosophical thought that fails to address the problem of 'death', by constantly putting it off.

Conversely, the other temptation is to live by 'clinging on to life', ignoring death, as if it did not exist and were not part of human life. Along this path, two other extreme pitfalls await man:

– the exasperation of well-being to the extent of getting so 'drunk' with it as to forget the human reality of death, with the result of becoming inhuman;

– the despair of those approaching death without the hope and consolation of finding the face of God the Father.

In the first case, there is a growing fear of death and a clinging on to life, consuming it and, all the while, becoming ever more victims of this fear. Instead of living in goodness, love and light, life is lived in fear of suffering, being ill and dying. This is a satanic technique[48] because it pushes man to adapt to 'mammon', circumventing difficulties and suffering, replacing love with money, in the belief that wealth can solve any problem. Man becomes inhuman, unjust, brash, violent, aggressive, and heavily materialistic, losing sight of our truest and most profound reality. In this way, we enter the terrible trap of 'mammon' from which Jesus came to deliver us.

In the second case, there is a widespread sense of emptiness and despair for a world which would appear to have no meaning. This, too, is a terrible satanic trap. Indeed, the light of the intellect, truth, and the goodness of life seem to fade. Life appears to be without meaning, without love, and without God, driving people into the tunnel of depression and pushing them to bring forward their deaths through suicide.

In both cases, it is a life from which one flees, as from God, to live in fear and terror.

For this reason God makes himself manifest in history and with his Word, so as to give man hope[49] to be able to heal and find again the mystery and the meaning to human life.

Creature comforts and riches will be lost on death, and death will only be defeated with Jesus Christ because, as the Word of God says, "the last enemy to be destroyed is death"[50]. One day there will be no more death. Then, believers will be truly comforted by God himself as He has promised; He in fact "will wipe every tear from their eyes, and

---

[48] *Bible*. Cfr. Letter to the Hebrews 2:14-15.
[49] *Bible*. Cfr. Gospel of Matthew 11:28.
[50] *Bible*. First Letter to the Corinthians 15:26.

there shall be no more death or mourning, wailing or pain, [for] the old order has passed away"[51].

This is the fullness of life and the way of being that the Risen Jesus has shown the nascent Church[52]: this is the deliverance from death. So Jesus responds to Martha for her brother's death: "Jesus told her, 'I am the resurrection and the life; whoever believes in me, even if he dies, will live, and everyone who lives and believes in me will never die. Do you believe this?' She said to him, 'Yes, Lord. I have come to believe that you are the Messiah, the Son of God, the one who is coming into the world.'"[53]. Of itself this certainty would already be enough to love Jesus. He is the Lord of life and eternal life. No prophet has ever said: "I am going to prepare a place for you"[54].

## The eighth deliverance: from cosmic upheavals

God reminds us: "the world in its present form is passing away"[55]. This concerns the 'end of the world', of this world. As with all the books in the Bible, written under the inspiration of the Holy Spirit, the Book of Revelation, aimed in particular to console Christians who suffer in the world, tells us: "Then I saw a new heaven and a new earth. The former heaven and the former earth had passed away, and the sea was no more"[56]. God is preparing "a new heaven and a new earth".

## The end of evil

Already in the Old Testament God announces an "appointed time" when evil will end, consoling the prophet Habakkuk, who prays to him full of anguish: "Your eyes are too pure to look upon wickedness, and the sight of evil you cannot endure. Why, then, do you gaze on the faithless in silence while the wicked devour those more just than themselves? (...) I will stand at my guard post, and station myself upon the rampart; I will keep watch to see what he will say to me, and what answer he will give to my complaint. Then the LORD answered me and said: Write down the vision; Make it plain upon tablets, so that the one who reads it may run. For the vision is a witness for the appointed time, a testimony to the end; it will not disappoint. If it delays, wait for it, it

---

[51] *Bible*. Book of Revelation 21:4.
[52] *Bible*. Cfr. First Letter to the Corinthians 15:1-34.
[53] *Bible*. Gospel of John 11:25-27.
[54] *Bible*. Gospel of John 14:2.
[55] *Bible*. First Letter to the Corinthians 7:31.
[56] *Bible*. Book of Revelation 21:1.

will surely come, it will not be late. See, the rash have no integrity; but the just one who is righteous because of faith shall live"[57]. Here God promises the end of evil in a meaningful way.

But with Jesus "we await new heavens and a new earth in which righteousness dwells"[58]. Humanity is in the hands of God: He is our future and will free us from the upheaval that sooner or later will take place. Thus, one can understand the importance of having good and deep roots and knowing how to find them. There will be deliverance from the scene of this world for a new world. We read this promise in the Bible, that Creation itself will "be set free from slavery to corruption and share in the glorious freedom of the children of God. We know that all creation is groaning in labor pains even until now"[59]. All nature, then, will be led back to God. Indeed, the will of God is "to sum up all things in Christ, in heaven and on earth"[60]. With the work of Christ the Messiah the same dangers posed by nature and animals will be no more[61].

We must recognise that God has set *an end to evil* and every time we pray "Deliver us from evil" we take courage and strength to actively participate as children of God in Jesus' victorious deliverance from all evils. At the same time, we entrust ourselves to God the Father, knowing that, in the end, with the return of Jesus on earth, He will intervene freeing us and putting 'an end' to the work of evil and of 'all evils'.

**The true great hope**

The same 'end' to the work of evil was announced by the Most Blessed Mary, the Virgin Mary, the mother of Jesus, in the Magnificat, seeing prophetically accomplished the final work of the Saviour when she exclaimed with joy:

> "He has shown might with his arm,
> dispersed the arrogant of mind and heart.
> He has thrown down the rulers from their thrones
> but lifted up the lowly.
> The hungry he has filled with good things;
> the rich he has sent away empty"[62].

---

[57] *Bible*. Book of the Prophet Habakkuk 1:13; 2:1-4.
[58] *Bible*. Second Letter of Peter 3:13.
[59] *Bible*. Letter to the Romans 8:21-22.
[60] *Bible*. Letter to the Ephesians 1:10.
[61] *Bible*. Cfr. Book of the Prophet Isaiah 11:1-9.
[62] *Bible*. Gospel of Luke 1:51-53.

Faith fuels this *final hope* that Christians offer the world together with their collaboration for construction. In the *Our Father*, as we pray that God the Father delivers us from evil trusting in his return, our hearts open up also to constructive commitment so that, upon his return, the Lord may find us actively working for his Kingdom. "But when the Son of Man comes, will he find faith on earth?"[63]. The hope, the real one, does not disappoint and the petition "Deliver us from evil" must make us remember that the world needs hope, real hope, absolute hope that only God can give.

In the Encyclical *Spe salvi*, Benedict XVI has us reflect on the serious attempt to replace the hope of the Kingdom of God with that of the "kingdom of man", when he says: "Thus Biblical hope in the Kingdom of God has been displaced by hope in the kingdom of man, the hope of a better world which would be the real 'Kingdom of God'. This seemed at last to be the great and realistic hope that man needs. (...) In the course of time, however, it has become clear that this hope is constantly receding. Above all it has become apparent that this may be a hope for a future generation, but not for me. (...) It has also become clear that this hope is opposed to freedom, since human affairs depend in each generation on the free decisions of those concerned. If this freedom were to be taken away, as a result of certain conditions or structures, then ultimately this world would not be good, since a world without freedom can by no means be a good world. Hence, while we must always be committed to the improvement of the world, tomorrow's better world cannot be the proper and sufficient content of our hope"[64].

To live well, man does not need only the human kingdom but the Kingdom of God! This profound need is not to be denied and hidden from younger generations. Man looks for a Future in the same way he looks for a Father. In the same way that he seeks his Source he also seeks his future.

And here is the importance of finding God, our Father, and the prayer of the *Our Father*. The world as a whole seeks hope. The disillusioned younger generations do not know what to expect for the future. It is the crisis of hope affecting many young people that puts them in the heart of the Pope and the Church[65]. Who on the world stage is able to propose solutions or new ways? What economic and political model can guarantee the common good for everyone? The world of economics and multinational companies, industry and finance, should also open

---

[63] *Bible*. Gospel of Luke 18:8.

[64] *Magisterium*. Benedict XVI, Encyclical Letter *Spe salvi* (2007) no. 30.

[65] *Magisterium*. Cfr. Benedict XVI, *Message on the occasion of the XXIV World Youth Day* (22 February 2009) (text no. 95 in Appendix).

up to God, serving the genuine needs of man and of humanity, without making use of and multiplying faults or defects.

What then should be the contribution of Christians to the construction of a global sustainable future on earth? Many people have been attracted by the ideologies of Marxism and communism. On this point, in the Encyclical *Spe salvi*, Benedict XVI says: "Marx not only omitted to work out how this new world would be organized – which should, of course, have been unnecessary. (...) He forgot that freedom always remains also freedom for evil. He thought that once the economy had been put right, everything would automatically be put right. His real error is materialism: man, in fact, is not merely the product of economic conditions, and it is not possible to redeem him purely from the outside by creating a favourable economic environment. (...) We have all witnessed the way in which progress, in the wrong hands, can become and has indeed become a terrifying progress in evil. If technical progress is not matched by corresponding progress in man's ethical formation, in man's inner growth (cfr. Eph 3:16; 2 Co 4:16), then it is not progress at all, but a threat for man and for the world"[66].

These are the important and forceful issues which the Church tackles, not in a political way, but by entering social and political debate and getting close to every man and every human situation, all the while purifying every human kingdom, religious or civil, bringing the goodness of the Gospel and the charity of Christ present in the world, both for the needs of this earth in the present time, and for the "new heavens and new earth"[67] of eternity.

In fact, nothing and no one can fill the great hope that man needs, and as Benedict XVI reminded us: "Experience shows that personal qualities and material goods are not enough to guarantee the hope which the human spirit is constantly seeking. As I wrote in the Encyclical *Spe Salvi*, politics, science, technology, economics and all other material resources are not of themselves sufficient to provide the *great hope* to which we all aspire. This hope 'can only be God, who encompasses the whole of reality and who can bestow upon us what we, by ourselves, cannot attain' (no. 31). This is why one of the main consequences of ignoring God is the evident loss of direction that marks our societies, resulting in loneliness and violence, discontent and loss of confidence that can often lead to despair. The word of God issues a warning that is loud and clear: 'Cursed are those who trust in mere mortals and make mere flesh their strength, whose hearts turn away from the Lord. They shall be like a shrub in the desert, and shall not see when relief comes'

---

[66] *Magisterium*. Benedict XVI, Encyclical Letter *Spe salvi* (2007) nos. 21-22.
[67] *Bible*. Second Letter of Peter 3:13.

(Je 17:5-6)"[68]. We shall never regret listening to God, placing our trust in him.

The "Deliver us from evil" becomes a tangible commitment for social liberation and evangelization of brothers, as stated by Saint John Paul II in 1999 speaking to the Bishops of Canada[69]. To be authentic, social liberation and evangelization need the proclamation of the "great, true hope", as recalled by Benedict XVI in the Encyclical *Spe salvi*[70].

God, our Father, the Father of light, beauty, goodness, truth, love, is before all. He is God, the Father of Life, Truth and Love, the Lord of history who calls all to him. This is the sense of Liturgical Celebrations in the Catholic Church, which are public, open, under the eyes of all. This too is a sign of light and love, for those who can see it; this is also an appeal to the mercy of God for humanity. For us Christians, our encounter with God is before the whole world because it is 'for all the world'. We must not forget the preciousness of what Jesus has given us and wants to continuously give to all mankind.

In the petition "Deliver us from evil" there is not only the desire to be free from every evil, but also the yearning hope for a full and happy life, for a certain and complete future, a new world, the Kingdom of God for us! And this is the beauty and grandeur of the prayer of the *Our Father*. The richness of Christian roots should be found again and made known to future generations.

We Christians are particularly involved in giving witness to the life and the glorious Gospel of Christ[71], indispensable to each and everyone and to the world to rediscover the reality of God and to build a good world. To remain steadfast in the good that is present in the world and to overcome evil that is also present, we need the presence of Jesus Christ and his Holy Spirit, who brings history to fulfilment in truth and goodness. Jesus reminds us: "In the world you will have trouble, but take courage, I have conquered the world"[72].

---

[68] *Magisterium*. Benedict XVI, *Message on the occasion of the XXIV World Youth Day* (22 February 2009).
[69] *Magisterium*. Cfr. John Paul II, *Address to the Bishops of the Episcopal Conference of Ontario (Canada) on their "ad Limina" Visit"* (4 May 1999) (text no. 96 in Appendix).
[70] *Magisterium*. Cfr. Benedict XVI, Encyclical Letter *Spe salvi* (2007) no. 27; no. 31 (text no. 97 in Appendix).
[71] *Bible*. Cfr. Second Letter to the Corinthians 4:4.
[72] *Bible*. Gospel of John 16:33.

# 17

# Betrayal

Betrayal is a theme that fascinates because on one hand it shocks and scares, and on the other it intrigues. Why does this subject cause such a reaction? What does the word 'betrayal' bring to mind? Perhaps the thought that we would not like someone to betray us and our trust. The idea and possibility of being betrayed give way to insecurity because relationships cannot be built unless they are based on credible trust. This tells us that many aspects in life are entrusted to freedom and, therefore, necessarily to a relationship of trust. The word 'betrayal' brings to mind a situation of insecurity and instability. Underneath, there is not just something sought and desired, but also something that is feared and that undermines a serene and trusting relationship.

All human relationships whether between friends, colleagues, lovers, engaged couples, married couples, parents and children, brothers and sisters, imply a relationship of trust and freedom. We cannot truly build our whole life on economics and self-interest; trust and freedom are needed: this is true because in man there dwells the great mystery of being in the 'image and likeness'[1] of God. Indeed, it is only in this way that the human being can experience the beauty of love, freedom, friendship and solidarity.

The drama and laceration of treason lie at the core of our inner life, expanding afterwards to our external one; hence our sensitivity to this word. We are basically made of love and trust, but we are also made of something that can betray love and trust, i.e. freedom. It is through the very gift of freedom, which makes us persons, that it is possible to betray!

The prayer of the *Our Father* is an extraordinary prayer which shows us the way back to our identity, our relationship with God, and our human fraternity. In the *Our Father*, Jesus teaches us how to return to what is essential and true, and therefore how to get out of 'fundamental

---

[1] *Bible.* Cfr. Book of Genesis 1:26.

betrayal' so that humanity, man and woman, cease betraying and fuelling that spiral of disintegration and destruction which brings about betrayal.

Sin has entered human life befogging trust, love and freedom. It takes courage to admit it.

Who is it that actually believes in love and the love of God?

With sin there is belief not so much in love as in self-interest,

not so much in trust as in fear,

not so much in reward as in cunning,

not so much in goodness as in gain,

not so much in innocence as in malice,

not so much in justice as in arrogance.

This is the corruption in the soul which is manifested in the body: this is the death of love which is manifested in the death of the body. This is sin that dwells in the human being and distances him from God, lurking within man, who is more intrigued by evil than goodness.

But man tires of evil and turns in search of the light and goodness, he hungers for goodness and hope, he sees that love, day by day, can defeat the threat of evil that drives him to betray life. Without realising it, he 'hopes in God'!

**The need for revelation**

We come from God and we are always in need of the truth that makes us 'persons'. Interestingly, while animals live tranquilly and have in their lives all that is necessary, this is not so in the lives of human beings. Beyond life and in the course of life, from a very early age, human beings want to know... the truth and seek the 'revelation'. Humans do not only have external models that attract them but they have within them a force that moves them, not only to grow physically and culturally, but towards something that they do not know: it is the search for the sense and meaning of life and what to make of life. The existential questions: why live, why die, why marry, why love require, in life and beyond life, the response of a 'revelation'. We want to know history, not only our own but also that of others because it is essential; we are made of history, and we seek its meaning. This fact is due to the spiritual dimension of human beings. For an animal, just to survive, mate, and have offspring is sufficient. However, in addition to recognising the needs of biological life, we humans have the need to acquire the history of our life and of our being together, and to plan for our future. Revelation and truth are an essential part of the need to live life in a human and dignified way.

We are sensitive to the truth, having been created in the 'image and likeness' of the one living and true God. For example, if one looks at an engaged or married couple, one can see how sensitive they are to the truth between them to build their relationship and future. If a child is lied to by his parents, this may result in a breakdown of the trust in the relationship he has with them, and may disturb his normal growth and development. The lie snaps human bonds, affecting our mind, our psyche, our heart, and our freedom.

Underlying the dynamics of betrayal is precisely the lie with its immediate evidence: "it is not true what you told me". Then, the relationship breaks down. Human life does not go forward by instinct, as in relationships between animals, but in the freedom to love, according to which we are fundamentally subject to the truth or the lie. In the end, what is greater than love? True love. What does love basically want? The truth. Without truth, there is no true love. Without truth it is not possible to be 'human'. On this typically anthropological basis of freedom, trust and truth there creeps the experience of 'betrayal'. In the Bible, God has shown us the path of betrayal taken by human beings.

## The first betrayal

Betrayal starts from afar and within man through sin.

In fact, as Holy Scripture tells us in the Book of Genesis chapter 3, the experience of betrayal is to be found in the roots of human history. Here we are told of the betrayal of our progenitors. Since then, unless man has a vigilant conscience, he can incur betrayal almost without realising it. This is because his faculties have been somewhat disrupted by original sin, i.e. the first sin committed by man and woman.

## The first effect

In choosing to sin for the first time, Eve absorbs the lie, the proposal of betrayal and rebellion. In this way, she decides to distance herself from God that is Holy. The first effect of sin is to lose God and the sanctity of human life. By distancing herself from the Creator, the woman decides to take what belongs to God, instead of living with love for God in his kingdom where He has placed her with Adam. Satan led her to act against God, without God, in spite of God. Rebellion and disobedience to the fundamental relationship with God form original sin: not wanting to belong; living outside the relationship with God, despite having been created by God in his 'image and likeness' in love; fleeing the relationship with God to create an alternative reality outside God. Also Adam takes part in this terrible break with God that is Love.

In this way, instead of being free in the relationship of love, they want to be free outside this relationship; this is the betrayal.

Indeed, having believed in Satan's lie, their trust in God is broken: Adam and Eve no longer feel the love and truth of his reality, but hide themselves from him! Which – come to think of it – is a foolish thing to do. Sin is a crossing over into the absurd, when the logic of thought is turned upside down, i.e. 'reversed'. It is logical to hide through fear[2] but Adam and Eve hide without logic, because they hide from God... and this is impossible! Thus was born in humans the fear that is much more extensive than that experienced by animals. They ask the earth to cover them, and they will die in this way, 'covered' by earth... unless they decide to renew their trust in God so as to be brought back by him to the Light, the Beautiful, the Good, the Holy, the Just. It was to take all the goodness of God, who sends his Son and gives him even unto death, to show man his love, with which He wants to save him.

## The second effect

The second effect of sin and betrayal is the inner fracture of the human being: his life has become disordered. He has lost the integrity of his basic energies: sexual, psychical, emotional, mental, all the energies of heart and spirit are no longer integrated but broken apart and in disarray. For this reason, death entered human life, the death of man that God would not have wanted for him. God, as the Scripture tells us, "did not make death"[3]. Through original sin, cellular, psychical, emotional, and spiritual disruption came about. Man, who was created as an intact being, has lost his unity and so too has woman. The human being has many dimensions but they are disjointed. Thus, there are those who take refuge only in the spiritual dimension; there are those who succumb to sexual addiction; there are those who find fulfilment in the satisfaction of the body and material well-being; there are those who hide in the affective dimension alone, and attempt to build their own world within it; while there are still others who seek security in the possession of houses, goods, and property, or in the security of thought and imagination.

In short, there are a thousand manifestations of a life that betrays since man, in betraying the mystery of the relationship with God, has betrayed himself, his own mystery, and finds himself split 'into many fragments' of which he tries to satisfy at least one. In this one 'fragment' he remains a 'prisoner' because he can no longer easily get out of it

---

[2] *Bible*. Cfr. Book of Genesis 3:8-10.
[3] *Bible*. Book of Wisdom 1:13.

to open up to the light. Each and every human being has within him the desire for life and integrity, while living a situation that is quite the opposite[4].

Inner and external fractures and conflicts, suffering, absurdities, sins and betrayals are part of human existence. We have lost that unity which is our peace, our joy. Peace, to which we all aspire, is happiness; it is the ability to bring together in harmony all the faculties, all the dimensions with which God created us. For this, we need to find God in faith and in the love of Jesus Christ.

Some, locked inside their 'fragment', make no effort to be freed by God and to enter by the narrow gate[5] so as to 'belong' to the full and complete life offered by God. They do not ask to be freed from the prison in which they find themselves and for which they even claim recognition as a free choice of theirs, whatever it may be, with all rights – including religious ones. They then unfairly blame the Church for not surrendering these rights, as if such rights belonged to her. Indeed, the Church, faithful to Jesus Christ, cannot change or invent rights that do not exist. These people would seem to treat the Church as if it were a mere Organization they were addressing rather than the Family of God's children.

The *Our Father* leads us back[6] in stages to recover our profound reality with God, our holiness and our human reality, made of love and brotherhood. The *Our Father* enables us to find our way back home; it is 'the prayer of return' to the Father's house. We are important to him; He is the Truth that saves us from lies, rebellion, sin, betrayal and death.

The Holy Spirit, the gift of God and of Jesus, was needed to sanctify us and enable us to gradually regain our holiness and also our integrity.

It required Jesus to take upon himself all our sins and pay for us in person. Only by seeing his thorns, seeing how we reduced him, 'how we have reduced man' – "Behold, the man!"[7] – can everyone open their eyes and realise that they are looking at the image of their own evil; because Jesus crucified is the photo of humanity, of the atrocities which humanity is capable of doing to the Beautiful, the Good, the True, the Holy, the Just. The Crucifix speaks to us of God's immense love for us and of that terrible evil which, through sin, can manifest itself in men and women. We have things that are not good inside us; we hit out at the poor, the little, the humble, and those who love. We hit and we hurt; it is not true that we only do good. Jesus is like a photo of our humanity,

---

[4] *Bible*. Cfr. Letter to the Romans 7:18-23.
[5] *Bible*. Cfr. Gospel of Matthew 7:14.
[6] *Bible*. Cfr. Gospel of John 10:14-18.
[7] *Bible*. Gospel of John 19:5.

he took upon himself our humanity, our sins, our sense of destruction, and betrayal to the very point of showing it to us.

This is the love of Jesus for us. He redeems us and makes us see that He, in mercy, is stronger than sin and the piercing evil that humanity has within and is capable of doing. This is what emerged in a dramatic fashion with Judas.

## Judas

Before betrayal is translated into external action, it is consumed within and directed against the truth and the good that dwell within each one of us. Let us consider the betrayal by Judas. He had heard the preaching and witnessed the many miracles performed by Jesus: how then is it possible that he betrayed Jesus? And why did Jesus choose someone like Judas to be one of the twelve apostles? Jesus had no 'need' for the betrayal of Judas, He does not need our sins, God does not use us. Therefore, if it had not been for sin and the need to redeem humanity, Jesus would have always shown his love for us! But since our human reality 'is' in sin, Jesus faced it and chose to redeem it: that is why he chose Judas 'too' as one of the apostles. Hence, Judas represents the human reality of all of us.

Each of us is attracted by Judas, because in one way or another we all have something of Judas within us. It is the 'poison' of sin, as symbolised by the serpent, which is in our humanity, although it is not something that is properly 'ours' through and through; it is something we would like to eradicate from society, families, children, and friends. But how can this be done? Let us now look at the path taken by Judas.

What is particular about Judas? Why does he never improve and sinks instead lower and lower? Events worsen rather than improve him. What happened to Judas? A comparison with Peter can help us to understand. Peter, with so much enthusiasm, had taken Jesus to his heart and loved him, but at a certain point when he too was going to be accused of being one of the apostles, through fear he began to deny him: "I am not"[8] one of his disciples, once, twice, three times. He denied him out of fear, a fear that contradicted his love. However, he repented for the love he had for Jesus, and Jesus later asked him: "do you love me more than these?"[9]. Jesus asked him his love three times, like the three times Peter failed Jesus through weakness and fear. He wanted to follow Jesus, but in his own way, for fear of having to follow

---

[8] *Bible.* Cfr. Gospel of John 18:15-27.
[9] *Bible.* Gospel of John 21:15.

him perhaps into prison. But Peter repents and continues to love Jesus, and for this he receives the strength to follow Jesus.

Instead Judas did not love Jesus and although he remained close to him, he loved something else. He took from Jesus what he wanted. Jesus had called him close to him, just like the other apostles, and had entrusted him with 'his love for the poor', and hence the common fund for the poor[10], from which instead Judas 'stole': "because he was a thief and held the money bag and used to steal the contributions"[11]. He used the love of Jesus for the poor for his own purposes, he made himself seen collecting 'for the poor' but he did not love them. Therefore, betrayal always passes first in the lie, and then in theft. At the end of the evening, Judas was peaceful, 'satisfied' like so many people who serenely go to bed with sins on their conscience.

Was stealing for Judas just a vice or did he use the things belonging to others for his own 'plan'? We do not know. But what happened with Judas is emblematic for all of us. Judas was a 'thief' first within, and then externally. He had no respect for Jesus, instead he used Jesus. He did not love Jesus but loved what Jesus did, not because Jesus did it, but because, when approaching the crowds, his 'collection bag' was filled. Jesus kept Judas close to him, giving us the example, because in view of redemption he wants to stay close to man even when he sins. When Judas asked Jesus the identity of the one who was to betray him, instead of denouncing him in front of all the other apostles, Jesus showed him once again his compassion, and his love, offering as a sign of friendship a piece of bread he had dipped in the dish[12]. Jesus is our true life companion! Anytime, anywhere, until the very last... Unfortunately it was Judas who 'put an end to it': perhaps he thought Jesus would not have forgiven him as he had with Peter?

Why didn't Judas convert? When Jesus spoke, Judas did not listen but, given the many people who would come, he simply calculated how much he could steal from the common fund. Judas did not want to follow God's plan but 'his own' plan: he loved himself more than he loved God. This is the betrayal. Judas agreed to deliver Jesus to the Jews[13] for thirty silver coins, "The man I shall kiss is the one; arrest him"[14]. Judas used a gesture of affection for money, for ambition, for his own plan. Jesus appealed to his conscience: "Friend, do what you

---

[10] *Bible.* Cfr. Gospel of John 12:6.
[11] *Bible.* Gospel of John 12:6.
[12] *Bible.* Cfr. Gospel of Matthew 26:25; Gospel of John 13:26.
[13] *Bible.* Cfr. Gospel of Luke 22:47-48.
[14] *Bible.* Gospel of Matthew 26:48.

have come for"[15], showing him that he was using love and affection to betray his trust! Judas, convinced he was doing the right thing, once again failed to listen.

This is the folly that has entered the human being with sin: thinking he can do many right things through betrayal! It is here that psychology, physics, chemistry, and even neuroscience come to a dead end, they are not able to explain the profound reasons for the human spirit and human liberty.

Jesus tells Judas the truth, but he will not hear the truth. Why not? Because in his life he had no love for the truth, he had stifled love for the truth, he was not interested in it, he simply wanted to pursue his own ends. What does he show himself to be sensitive to? The loss of what he wanted. When Jesus is arrested, Judas realises, contrary to what he may have hoped, that Jesus is not going to perform any miracle or do anything to overcome his captors, because what he had not seen in Jesus' miracles was his love for every man. He had seen in the miracles what he wanted to see: the power and ability to raise cash from which he stole. He does not know the love of God, he does not know the truth of God's plan, for years he had not wanted to know the Word of God and the 'as' of God. Judas wanted to use Jesus, he wanted to bring his plan to fruition also through Jesus, but things did not go as he had thought. It was at this point that his plan of betrayal falls apart. Once again, the thoughts of the man who does not follow God are deceived, as the Bible says: "they are like a fleeting breath"[16]. So also: "It is better to listen to the rebuke of the wise than to listen to the song of fools"[17].

This is the downward path leading to self-destruction, as shown by the 'excellent' suicides in history! Here Satan appears once again, and pushes Judas towards self-destruction and suicide. The satanic plan advances by degrees: deceit, betrayal, theft, despair, self-destruction, killing, and death. The satanic process concludes with murder or suicide.

It is also possible to attain repentance and reject one's own perverse history, but Jesus and his mercy are in any case needed for salvation! Judas "deeply regretted what he had done. He returned the thirty pieces of silver"[18], money that was to serve his self-love, and not the love of God and his neighbour. When his plan falls apart, that self-love also becomes rejection of self and of what he has done. So with disordered love, his life also collapses. Incapable of achieving its

---

[15] *Bible*. Cfr. Gospel of Matthew 26:49-50.
[16] *Bible*. Book of Psalms 94:11.
[17] *Bible*. Book of Ecclesiastes 7:5.
[18] *Bible*. Gospel of Matthew 27:3.

fulfilment and in the absence of other strong values, his life ends in self-destruction, through suicide[19].

There is a wrong self-love that goes as far as self-betrayal. One betrays because life is betrayed. Betrayal manifests itself at three levels: the first is defined as 'disintegration', i.e. man is no longer whole and continues to make disintegrated choices.

The first betrayal is overcome in finding the authenticity of the person. Healing is brought about by taking in hand the person's whole life, namely the spiritual, emotional, physical and sexual, cultural, mental, historical, and environmental dimensions, reviewing and harmonizing them, removing falsehood and ambiguities. It is a process of authenticity to find the roots and unity of the human being. Today, vice versa, what is being proposed is the fulfilment of only one part of the self – travel, career, work, etc., that is, fragments which can enable a person to become dominant and satisfied. This exaggeration of human fulfilment is the betrayal that appeals to the economy, because in this way the market can sell many useful 'products' so that each may fulfil a part of self. That idolized part of self becomes the whole. This is the dehumanizing betrayal which is organized and proposed in society.

### Betrayal in the couple

The second level of betrayal is the break-up of the couple and the family: betrayal of the given word, the word of belonging 'in the sincere and faithful gift from person to person'.

Unless personal authenticity is first found, this gift of the marital unity, as a unity of persons, cannot be offered. Today, the majority of people are educated to possess, exploit, and profit. So, man and woman do not easily manage to put their lives together without using each other in a relationship that interlocks them: if they have to give their life they do not know from what fragment to give it.

This is the problem today: what do man and woman give to each other? Common interests? And to what extent and for how long can these hold the couple together? This is the fear of getting married, the fear of love and having children. Life is blocked. "Financially, will I be able to satisfy my child's wishes?". "How long will we manage to stay together?". The couple goes into crisis because the first betrayal is to be found at its roots. Human life cannot be cheated, otherwise it will not function. If life is betrayed, life betrays you. We have sought to use life without respecting it. Man has betrayed the mission that God has

---

[19] *Bible*. Cfr. Gospel of Matthew 27:5.

entrusted him to govern nature in the name of God[20]: he exploits and manipulates nature, consequently at a certain point, nature no longer functions as it should.

If we do not love ourselves, respecting the way God has made us, we cannot love others; we cannot love the family unless we function in harmony with the profound truth. Relationships, too, will be tainted by utilitarianism; there will be no mutual donation of life in communion, one to another, not even life to other children in the name of true love. Unless of course they are children to be used for personal ambition! This is why the future of children is in danger! In fact, people will want children on a made to measure basis. In the same way we choose a car, an apartment, and clothes according to our personal taste, this too can be done with children – yet another fundamental betrayal, not only of the person's own life but also the lives of children: the modern day slaves.

The couple with its roots firmly planted in the 'rock' experiences, in walking with God, the beauty and grandeur of life, i.e. the ability – which we derive from being "in the image of God" – to love and give, for the benefit of the lives of other human beings capable of loving. This mystery of life as 'gift', which is not limited to the mere life 'of the two', is entrusted to their love.

The betrayal of personal reality, when this reality is ignored and trampled over, leads to a betrayal of the reality, gift and mystery to which the couple has been called. By trampling over the sacrament of marriage of which they are ministers, they trample the gift and commitment of love and of faith. This is adultery[21]. It would be better to ascertain the authenticity of the bond and sacrament before making any further choices. But to do this we need to feel we belong to something larger than our own 'fragment' which has been won or lost in life, it is necessary to feel part of a Christian community; the 'Church'.

The economy, too, has been developed to meeting a need, the individual's own 'fragment' of life, and this is how we are educating children, to choose a fragment. And it does not matter if this fragment goes against others; if you want it, that is all that matters. Also within the family, everyone in the end chooses their 'own' fragment, thus using the family without discovering its true mission.

This is the betrayal of the family because, when the mystery is hidden, manipulated or broken, each one steals life to grab what is of interest, to obtain what is desired, what each has decided to 'have' so that life might become that very dream or accomplishment one has in

---

[20] *Bible*. Cfr. Book of Genesis 1:28 ss.
[21] *Bible*. Cfr. Gospel of Matthew 19:3-9; Gospel of Mark 10:11-12.

mind – and not the mystery of life, the mystery of the couple and the family. Here is the betrayal of the family. In the same way that there is a 'culture of death' there is a also a 'culture of betrayal', and this is something which people do not often realise. Therefore, unearthing the Christian roots of the person, the family and society is essential in order to find out who we are and what future God wants for us.

## Betrayal in society

Finally we can see betrayal in society. Failure to achieve maturity and authenticity in personal life as in married life and its social mission entails a perversion in society. This can be seen at a personal level where rather than seeking to bring something good to share in social life, there is instead an attempt to use others in order to exploit any opportunity that may arise. Personal selfishness becomes social egoism; selfishness of the strongest, the most cunning, those with the greatest possibilities and 'useful' friendships.

Selfishness in the family becomes the selfishness of families in social life, and the situation worsens even further when society becomes the place and the means for crime, the proliferation of various forms of racket and the mafia: prostitution, drugs, arms trafficking and the exploitation and trading of human lives. As a result, also law and the love for justice sooner or later disappear... The law becomes the right of a few. As we have seen the well-being of each and every individual, 'of the whole of man and of all men', is not sought.

On the contrary, we get together in large economic aggregations in order to support one another in our selfish interests. In large shopping malls, everything can be found: well-being is made easily available both in summer and winter; here people meet, are free, and do anything they wish. Malls are like small towns on a human scale where the needs and desires of everyone can be satisfied, but where you only perceive what you see and is profitable to business.

Everyone uses everything but without knowing who they are and where they are heading: the world is being organized without spirituality, without God the Father, without knowing who we are and where we are going. We aggregate and mate: a bit like a humanized animal world, or a human world made of 'respectable animals'... If people, young as well as adults, then commit suicide and anyone can go to the pharmacy to ask for death, as is the case in some countries, doesn't this stir anybody's conscience? Social life, instead of serving the mystery of the person and the mystery of the couple, serves self-interest, a life and culture of speculation and the tyranny of profit.

But what is missing in this plan for the human well-being of all, with the countless resources and possibilities available for its realisation? There lacks that dimension, i.e. the true spiritual dimension, which humanity is systematically forgetting, in the same way that the plan and ideal of the common good have also disappeared. Development has become ambition and economic power that exploits and is to be exploited: this life and everyone's resources are used to the full, and people are given what they want to eat. The important thing is that they are content, like well-fed piglets... because this is their use, that everyone is satisfied in a selfish way, or even better within a 'mass egoism'.

It is no longer love and goodness that keep things moving but love of self, interested love, one that is built on self-interest – *do ut des* – and not on goodness and truth. In other words, I'll give something to you if you give something to me. This is the reason why our society and the world are becoming more and more arid, without love, without spirituality, and without God. It is no longer a humanity, a society that reveals the truth to man and helps him. It is a society that causes him to regress because it uses him. Mutual and democratic exploitation! Globalisation, world financial networks and 'virtual' economic development are putting the social model of development into deep crisis.

Who has taken over the common plan? As you might well guess the 'Fire-eater' who, just as in the symbolic story of Pinocchio, remains out of sight behind the scenes, all the while pulling the strings of his puppets! We know there is, as Jesus calls him, the enemy[22] who wants to take the place of God, and for this he needs 'minions', spirits but also men, the various 'Fire-eaters' who play with fire, or the various tyrants that come and go. They have removed God so as to take his place in society.

The third level of betrayal is seen in society when it fails to serve the common good and all the citizens: it is then that society betrays itself! In the end, social life no longer serves all citizens, but only those who 'succeed' in the system. It is not for the whole man, but for that 'fragment' of man that is useful to the economic, political and social mechanism. It is basically a purely ambitious and greedy society, in which the individual project, or that of the few, becomes the highest aspiration. So in the end, for convenience and as a compromise, evil becomes acceptable. The task of Christians in this society is to foreground once again, through respect, freedom and solidarity, the meaning and importance of values. We are called upon to overcome

---

[22] *Bible*. Cfr. Gospel of Matthew 13:39.

betrayal by injecting new energy and hope for the benefit of the city of men and the Kingdom of God.

Where are we heading? This depends on us. The downward road leads to self-destruction. The betrayal of life brings to a life that betrays: in the person, this is shown in suicide; in the couple, adultery and 'new experiences' are suggested as a means to render life more enjoyable. In this way, we have mutual betrayal and the breaking up of families with serious consequences for children. Of these children, who will continue to believe in a stable and faithful family? There then follows the disintegration; and the destruction of society, as history has shown us, becomes the destruction of human beings by death and murder. The meaning and sense of life are being destroyed today. This process is already underway.

For example, this is already happening in the life of human embryos: we are talking about millions and millions of lives being destroyed every year! There is already advertising which encourages abortion. Is there not mass abortion when people are democratically induced to eliminate 40 million lives each year? "If the life of the other gets in your way, get rid of it". It is the story of ethnic cleansing, though of another kind. It is reminiscent of Hitler... a plan of destruction to become the best. So tomorrow we will kill for a better world future. What future? If this is earth, if there is no other solution, if there is no heaven, then let us make a super earth. Not a super race as Hitler said, but a super society... Why give birth to sick children who will not be able to live long? And what about an old person who can no longer produce? Do we want to take money away from the construction of a nice park for children so that they can grow up decently, and give it to decrepit old people instead?! *Life* will increasingly become the problem, in its initial and final phases: from conception to the end. It is for this reason that the Church has made an impassioned appeal in recent years to start anew in true love and true service to life. This is something we are constantly reminded of throughout and at every stage of the prayer of the *Our Father*.

Betrayal, in itself, leads to the destruction of life in the very same society that defends, proposes and implements it with the consent and economic resources of its citizens. The word 'betrayal' truly makes a plea to the conscience so that humans may stop and redeem themselves by accepting Jesus' invitation to follow him.

"Judas, are you betraying the Son of Man with a kiss?"[23]. This is what happens! They cover and camouflage betrayal with affection and goodness, as Judas did. The enemy, Satan, the author of every 'betrayal of life' uses good to bring evil. And so Judas betrays with a kiss! It is

---

[23] *Bible*. Gospel of Luke 22:48.

with the money of your husband or wife that you betray your spouse! It is through 'short-sighted' dedication to their children that parents betray their mission. It is through selfish affection that parents betray their children, and children betray themselves and their parents. So, with a nicely coloured gag and various laws, their source unknown, society betrays citizens and human beings with something beautiful and pleasant that attracts, fascinates and strikes; since betrayal always pounces on you. This is why it is so lethal: it enters the home, the heart, the body, the economy, and politics. Betrayal is always a breakdown; against social life, against God and against oneself.

But the very word 'betrayal' may also be used in the new evangelization, since it awakens our understanding and conscience. It is the same appeal Jesus made to Judas, that before death and destruction strike we halt and see how we might intervene and stop evil. It is a great appeal that we can respond to and, as Christians, put before our hearts, minds and consciences not only at a purely personal level, but also in the couple and in society.

In fact, we can love and help one another as we are all in the same situation, in one big global village. We would all do better to listen more to one another without shirking our responsibilities, instead of believing ourselves to be more intelligent, as Judas did by not listening to the call of Jesus.

Jesus, with his love, comes back to look for us, standing and knocking at our door[24], insisting repeatedly with his invitation: "But when the Son of Man comes, will he find faith on earth?"[25]. God rebukes us to call us to himself: "When you do these things should I be silent? Do you think that I am like you? I accuse you, I lay out the matter before your eyes. 'Now understand this, you who forget God'"[26]. "Do not court death by your erring way of life"[27]. "Those whom I love, I reprove and chastise"[28].

The teaching of the *Our Father* helps us get back on top again, and out of personal, family and global betrayal. "The counsel of the LORD belongs to those who fear him; and his covenant instructs them"[29]. At the beginning of wisdom, as God reminds us in the Bible, there is the holy 'fear of the Lord'[30]: for us it is a good dimension, it does us good because "The fear of the Lord rejoices the heart, giving gladness, joy, and

---

[24] *Bible*. Cfr. Book of Revelation 3:20.
[25] *Bible*. Gospel of Luke 18:8.
[26] *Bible*. Book of Psalms 50:21-22.
[27] *Bible*. Book of Wisdom 1:12.
[28] *Bible*. Book of Revelation 3:19.
[29] *Bible*. Book of Psalms 25:14.
[30] *Bible*. Cfr. Book of Sirach 1:14.

long life"[31]. The 'holy fear of the Lord' is not the fear of something above us that we do not know: it means – because we know God – considering that God is truly God our Father, that we can return to him and to all his Good, to his power of love with Jesus Christ, our Lord and Saviour. We already see this and rejoice when someone returns and recovers from betrayal.

How many couples and how many families are saved! How many social actions have been purified from 'betrayal' by returning once again to be of genuine service and help for the true welfare of citizens. How much wonderful solidarity has been taught to many by true humanity! As John Paul II reminds us in his Encyclical Letter *Dominum et Vivificantem*: "Man lives in God and by God: he lives 'according to the Spirit,' and 'sets his mind on the things of the Spirit'"[32].

To break away from betrayal, a return of heart to true wisdom is needed. And this is brought about through the prayer of the *Our Father*.

---

[31] *Bible*. Book of Sirach 1:12.
[32] *Magisterium*. John Paul II, Encyclical Letter *Dominum et vivificantem*, (1986) no. 58 (text no. 98 in Appendix).

# Conclusion

God waits for us in prayer, God waits for us among men. We come from the Supreme Good and the Supreme Love of God, and this is also our deepest root and true destination. Only within this perspective can we stay human by remaining well-grafted in our reality and not getting lost.

With evil the meaning of life is lost and consciences become brutalized. There is not only the withering away of any ideal and of the boundary between good and evil, but also dullness of thought and ineptitude of freedom; in a word, adaptation to what is wild, first to the taste of pleasure and then of destruction.

In distancing ourselves from God, the root and sap of life for every human being, we cannot expect anything good for the whole of humanity! Conversely, by returning to the love of God, humanity can only benefit.

So, before nations and the entire planet are scattered with the fruits of death in thoughts, feelings, actions and programmes, it is up to all men of good will, especially Christians standing on 'solid' roots, to roll up their sleeves to restore the sap of life to the plant.

It is up to Christians living in communion with God the Father and our Lord Jesus Christ to join with people of good will in the service of life, family and society and to do so with that love for the truth which is Jesus Christ, before it becomes too late, as God reminds us in the Bible:

> "Before the silver cord is snapped
> and the golden bowl is broken,
> And the pitcher is shattered at the spring,
> and the pulley is broken at the well"[1].

It is love that propels the Church, the same love she receives from the Lord and which she is capable of spreading: "This is love for people – it desires every true good for each individual and for every

---

[1] *Bible*. Book of Ecclesiastes 12:6.

human community, every family, every nation, every social group, for young people, adults, parents, the elderly – a love for everyone, without exception. This is love, or rather an anxious solicitude to ensure for each individual every true good and to remove and drive away every sort of evil. (...) No matter how strong the resistance of human history may be, no matter how marked the diversity of contemporary civilization, no matter how great the denial of God in the human world, so much the greater must be the Church's closeness to that mystery which, hidden for centuries in God, was then truly shared with man, in time, through Jesus Christ"[2].

The shepherd always stays close to his flock even when, not listening to him, it errs and wanders off the path. Nonetheless, the shepherd's voice continues to be close to bewildered humanity. This is "the lost sheep" mentioned by Jesus in the Gospel[3], as are the individual, human love, the family and society that, in straying off the way of God, have become lost.

Jesus Christ goes out to every person and the whole person, to the whole of humanity: "But as it is written:

'What eye has not seen, and ear has not heard,
and what has not entered the human heart,
what God has prepared for those who love him,'

this God has revealed to us through the Spirit. For the Spirit scrutinizes everything, even the depths of God. Among human beings, who knows what pertains to a person except the spirit of the person that is within? Similarly, no one knows what pertains to God except the Spirit of God. We have not received the spirit of the world but the Spirit that is from God, so that we may understand the things freely given us by God"[4].

It is in a sincere relationship with God that there grows a sense of good and the true meaning of life. Jesus has taught us this in the supreme prayer of the *Our Father* that we address to God. It is in prayer that our love for God and humanity grows. When we pray, things change. "Prayer is the gift of the Spirit that makes us men and women of hope, and our prayer keeps the world open to God (cfr. *Spe Salvi*, 34). (...) Following in the footsteps of the people of hope – composed of prophets and saints of every age – we continue to advance towards the fulfilment of the Kingdom, and on this spiritual path we are accompanied

---

[2] *Magisterium*. John Paul II, Encyclical Letter *Dives in misericordia* (1980) no. 15.
[3] *Bible*. Cfr. Gospel of Luke 15:1-7.
[4] *Bible*. First Letter to the Corinthians 2:9-12.

by the Virgin Mary, Mother of Hope. She who incarnated the hope of Israel, who gave the world its Saviour, and who remained at the foot of the Cross with steadfast hope, is our model and our support. Most of all, Mary intercedes for us and leads us through the darkness of our trials to the radiant dawn of an encounter with the Risen Christ"[5]. This is the meaning of her apparitions and messages so full of love: that the world might be saved.

On earth, in addition to the signs of the presence of Jesus[6] and his Kingdom – for those who wish to see them by purifying their hearts – there is also the gift of the Word of God. God comforts and encourages us through his Word, the Bible, where He shows us, as fulfilled in love, what He promises and will be fully lived in paradise: the unity of humanity with God in *eternal marriage.*

> "'Alleluia!
> The Lord has established his reign,
> [our] God, the almighty.
> Let us rejoice and be glad
> and give him glory.
> For the wedding day of the Lamb has come,
> his bride has made herself ready.
> She was allowed to wear
> a bright, clean linen garment.'
> (The linen represents the righteous deeds of the holy ones.)
> Then the angel said to me, 'Write this: Blessed are those
> who have been called to the wedding feast of the Lamb.'
> And he said to me, 'These words are true; they come from God'"[7].

Each person, like all humanity, is therefore travelling towards the Love that is light and life.

After having understood, prayed and lived the prayer of the *Our Father,* the prayer of Jesus for us and for all humanity, our last words addressed to God in prayer can only be the same as those used by the early Christians, and found at the end of the Bible in the Book of Revelation: "Come, Lord Jesus!"[8].

---

[5] *Magisterium.* Benedict XVI, *Message for XXIV World Youth Day* (22 February 2009).
[6] *Bible.* Cfr. Gospel of Matthew 28:20.
[7] *Bible.* Book of Revelation 19: 6-9.
[8] *Bible.* Book of Revelation 22: 20.

# Appendix

# MAGISTERIUM TEXTS

## Introduction

**(1)** "One can say that in the answer to the Pharisees, Christ laid out before his interlocutors also this 'integral vision of man', without which no adequate answer can be given to the questions connected with marriage and procreation. Precisely this integral vision of man must be built from the 'beginning'.

This point is valid for the contemporary mentality just as it was, though in a different way, for Christ's interlocutors. We are, in fact, the children of an age in which, due to the development of various disciplines, this integral vision of man can easily be rejected and replaced by many *partial conceptions* that dwell on one or another aspect of the *compositum humanum* but do not reach man's *integrum* or leave it outside their field of vision". [John Paul II, *Man and Woman He Created Them. A Theology of the Body*, Pauline Books & Media, Boston, MA 2006, p. 220]

## 1 – Father

**(2)** "Without Jesus, we do not know what 'Father' truly is. This becomes visible in his prayer, which is the foundation of his being. A Jesus who was not continuously absorbed in the Father and was not in continuous intimate communication with him would be a completely different being from the Jesus of the Bible, the real Jesus of history. Prayer was the center out of which he lived, and it was prayer that showed him how to understand God, the world, and men. To follow Jesus means looking at the world with the eyes of God and living accordingly". [Joseph Ratzinger, *The God of Jesus Christ. Meditations on the triune God*, Ignatius Press, San Francisco 2008, p. 18]

**(3)** "But, beyond these sayings, let us look at the very tradition, teaching and faith of the Catholic Church from the beginning, which the

273

Lord gave, the Apostles preached, and the Fathers kept. Upon this the Church is founded, and he who should fall away from it would not be a Christian, and should no longer be so called. There is, then, a Triad, holy and complete, confessed to be God in Father, Son and Holy Spirit, having nothing foreign or external mixed with it, not composed of one that creates and one that is originated, but all creative; and it is consistent and in nature indivisible, and its activity is one. The Father does all things through the Word in the Holy Spirit. Thus the unity of the holy Triad is preserved". [Saint Athanasius (295-373), *The Letters of Saint Athanasius concerning the Holy Spirit*, translation with introduction and notes by C.R.B. Shapland, Epworth Press, London 1951, pp. 137-138]

## 2 – Our Father

(4) "This is why it is empty romanticism to plead: 'Spare us the dogmas, the Christology, the Holy Spirit, the Trinity! It suffices to proclaim God as Father and all men as brothers and to live this without any mystical theories. That is the only thing that matters!' This sounds very plausible, but does this really do justice to the complicated being called man? How do we know what fatherhood is or what it means to be brothers and sisters? What entitles us to put so much trust in these realities? There are indeed moving testimonies in early cultures to a pure trust in the 'Father' in the skies, but subsequent development mostly meant that religious attention very quickly moved away from him to concentrate on 'powers' that were much closer at hand; in the course of history, the image of man, and hence also the image of God, everywhere took on ambiguous traits. It is well known that the Greeks called their Zeus 'Father'. But this word was not an expression of their trust in him! Rather, it expressed the profound ambiguity of the god and the tragic ambiguity indeed, the terrible character of the world. (...)

People today bid farewell to the world of the fathers and sing the enthusiastic praises of 'brotherhood'. But in our de facto experience, is brotherhood really so unambiguous, so full of hope? According to the Bible, the first pair of brothers in world history were Cain and Abel; in Roman myth, we find the corresponding pair of Romulus and Remus. This motif is found everywhere and is a cruel parody – but one written by reality itself – of the hymn to 'brotherhood'. Have not our experiences since 1789 contributed new and even more dreadful features to this parody? Have they not confirmed the vision that bears the name 'Cain and Abel' rather than what the word 'brotherhood' promised us?

How, then, do we know that fatherhood is a kindness on which we can rely and that God, despite all outward appearances, is not playing with the world, but loves it dependably? For this, it was necessary that God should show himself, overthrow the images, and set up a new criterion. This takes place in the Son, in Christ. In his prayer, he plunges the totality of his life into the abyss of truth and of goodness that is God. It is only on the basis of this Son that we truly experience what God is". [Joseph Ratzinger, *The God of Jesus Christ. Meditations on the triune God,* Ignatius Press, San Francisco 2008, pp. 17-18]

**(5)** "Again, we find ourselves facing the question: what may we hope? A self-critique of modernity is needed in dialogue with Christianity and its concept of hope. In this dialogue Christians too, in the context of their knowledge and experience, must learn anew in what their hope truly consists, what they have to offer to the world and what they cannot offer. Flowing into this self-critique of the modern age there also has to be a self-critique of modern Christianity, which must constantly renew its self-understanding setting out from its roots. On this subject, all we can attempt here are a few brief observations. First we must ask ourselves: what does 'progress' really mean; what does it promise and what does it not promise? (...) To put it another way: the ambiguity of progress becomes evident. Without doubt, it offers new possibilities for good, but it also opens up appalling possibilities for evil – possibilities that formerly did not exist. We have all witnessed the way in which progress, in the wrong hands, can become and has indeed become a terrifying progress in evil. If technical progress is not matched by corresponding progress in man's ethical formation, in man's inner growth (cf. Eph 3:16; 2 Cor 4:16), then it is not progress at all, but a threat for man and for the world". [Benedict XVI, Encyclical Letter *Spe salvi* (2007) no. 22]

### 3 – Who art in heaven

**(6)** "Reason as such is open to transcendence and only in the encounter between transcendent reality and faith and reason does man find himself. So I think that the precise task and mission of Europe in this situation is to create this dialogue, to integrate faith and modern rationality in a single anthropological vision which approaches the human being as a whole and thus also makes human cultures communicable". [Benedict XVI, *Interview of Benedict XVI with the journalists during the flight to Portugal*. Apostolic Journey to Portugal (11 May 2010)]

**(7)** "Love is sufficient for itself; it gives pleasure to itself, and for its own sake. It is its own merit and own reward. Love needs no cause beyond itself, nor does it demand fruits; it is its own purpose. I love because I love; I love that I may love. Love is a great reality, and if it returns to its beginning and goes back to its origin, seeking its source again, it will always draw afresh from it, and thereby flow freely. Love is the only one of the motions of the soul, of its senses and affections, in which the creature can respond to its Creator, even if not as an equal, and repay his favor in some similar

275

way. (...) Now you see how different love is, for when God loves, he desires nothing but to be loved, since he loves us for no other reason than to be loved, for he knows that those who love him are blessed in their very love.

(...) The love of a bridegroom – or rather of the Bridegroom who is love – asks only the exchange of love and trust. Let the Beloved love in return. How can the bride – and the bride of Love – do other than love? How can Love not be loved?

Rightly, then, does she renounce all other affections and devote herself to love alone, for it is in returning love that she has the power to respond to love. Although she may pour out her whole self in love, what is that compared to the inexhaustible fountain of his love? The stream of love does not flow equally from her who loves and from him who is love, the soul and the Word, the Bride and the Bridegroom, the Creator and the creature – any more than a thirsty man can be compared to a fountain. Will the Bride's vow perish, then, because of this? (...) Although the creature loves less, being a lesser being, yet if it loves with its whole heart nothing is lacking, for it has given all". [Saint Bernard of Clairvaux (1090-1153), *Sermons on the Song of Songs*, Book II, no. 83, 4-6 (http://www.pathsoflove. com/bernard/songofsongs/sermon83.html, accessed in July 2014)]

**(8)** "We are now facing the question of how *truth* and *goodness* are related to one another. In God these two coincide with each other as well as with being. God knows and wills his being, and both his knowing and his willing are contained in his being. However, if we understand truth as being ordained to a finite, knowing intellect, and if we understand goodness as a being ordained to finite striving (or as a being-ordained of one existent to another existent to whose perfection the striving may contribute), truth and goodness are apart, although there persists a certain interconnection between them. (...) This latter relationship finds expression in the phrase 'a true good'. Only when the knowing of the existent as good is true, is the existent 'in truth' a good. This good is then not only congruent with the striving of some creature, but also with the will of the creator and – since in God knowledge and will coincide – simultaneously in accord with this good *archetype* [*Urbild*] in the divine intellect and this good is thus essentially true i.e., *true* in the sense of essential truth [*Wesenswahrheit*]". [Edith Stein (1891-1942), *Finite and eternal being: an attempt at an ascent to the meaning of being*, translated by Kurt F. Reinhardt, Washington Province of Discalced Carmelites, ICS Publications, Washington, DC 2002, pp. 311-312]

**(9)** "*2357*. Homosexuality refers to relations between men or between women who experience an exclusive or predominant sexual attraction toward persons of the same sex. It has taken a great variety of forms through the centuries and in different cultures. Its psychological genesis remains largely unexplained. Basing itself on Sacred Scripture, which presents homosexual acts as acts of grave depravity, [Cfr. Jn 19:1-29; Rm

1:24-27; 1 Co 6:10; 1 Tm 1:10] tradition has always declared that 'homosexual acts are intrinsically disordered' [Congregation for the Doctrine of the Faith, Dich. *Persona humana*, 8]. They are contrary to the natural law. They close the sexual act to the gift of life. They do not proceed from a genuine affective and sexual complementarity. Under no circumstances can they be approved.

*2358.* The number of men and women who have deep-seated homosexual tendencies is not negligible. This inclination, which is objectively disordered, constitutes for most of them a trial. They must be accepted with respect, compassion, and sensitivity. Every sign of unjust discrimination in their regard should be avoided. These persons are called to fulfill God's will in their lives and, if they are Christians, to unite to the sacrifice of the Lord's Cross the difficulties they may encounter from their condition.

*2359.* Homosexual persons are called to chastity. By the virtues of self-mastery that teach them inner freedom, at times by the support of disinterested friendship, by prayer and sacramental grace, they can and should gradually and resolutely approach Christian perfection". [*Catechism of the Catholic Church* nos. 2357-2359]

## 4 – Hallowed be thy name

**(10)** "The root reason for human dignity lies in man's call to communion with God. From the very circumstance of his origin man is already invited to converse with God. For man would not exist were he not created by God's love and constantly preserved by it; and he cannot live fully according to truth unless he freely acknowledges that love and devotes himself to His Creator. Still, many of our contemporaries have never recognized this intimate and vital link with God, or have explicitly rejected it. Thus atheism must be accounted among the most serious problems of this age, and is deserving of closer examination. The word atheism is applied to phenomena which are quite distinct from one another. For while God is expressly denied by some, others believe that man can assert absolutely nothing about Him. Still others use such a method to scrutinize the question of God as to make it seem devoid of meaning. Many, unduly transgressing the limits of the positive sciences, contend that everything can be explained by this kind of scientific reasoning alone, or by contrast, they altogether disallow that there is any absolute truth. Some laud man so extravagantly that their faith in God lapses into a kind of anemia, though they seem more inclined to affirm man than to deny God. Again some form for themselves such a fallacious idea of God that when they repudiate this figment they are by no means rejecting the God of the Gospel. Some never get to the point of raising questions about God, since they seem to experience no religious stirrings nor do they see why they should trouble themselves about religion. Moreover, atheism results not rarely from a violent protest against the evil in this world, or from the absolute character with which certain human values are unduly invested, and which thereby already accords them the stature of God. (...) For, taken as a whole, atheism is not a spontaneous development but stems from a variety of causes, including a critical reaction against religious beliefs, and in some places against the Christian religion in particular. Hence believers can have more than a little to do with the birth of atheism. To the extent that they neglect their own training in the faith, or teach erroneous doctrine, or are deficient in their religious, moral or social life, they must be said to conceal rather than reveal the authentic face of God and religion". [Vatican Council II, Pastoral Constitution *Gaudium et spes* no. 19]

**(11)** "Are we truly God's shrine in and for the world? Do we open up the pathway to God for others or do we rather conceal it? Have not we – the people of God – become to a large extent a people of unbelief and distance from God? Is it perhaps the case that the West, the heartlands of Christianity, are tired of their faith, bored by their history and culture, and no longer wish to know faith in Jesus Christ? We have reason to cry out at this time to God: 'Do not allow us to become a 'non-people'! Make us recognize you again! Truly, you have anointed us with your love, you have poured out your Holy Spirit upon us. Grant that the power of your Spirit may become newly effective in us, so that we may bear joyful witness to your message!'". [Benedict XVI, *Homily at Chrism Mass* (21 April 2011)]

**(12)** *"The right to religious freedom is rooted in the very dignity of the human person,* whose transcendent nature must not be ignored or overlooked. God created man and woman in his own image and likeness (cf. *Gen* 1:27). For this reason each person is endowed with the *sacred right* to a full life, also from a spiritual standpoint. Without the acknowledgement of his spiritual being, without openness to the transcendent, the human person withdraws within himself, fails to find answers to the heart's deepest questions about life's meaning, fails to appropriate lasting ethical values and principles, and fails even to experience authentic freedom and to build a just society". [Benedict XVI, *Message for the Celebration of the XLIV World Day of Peace* (8 December 2010)]

**(13)** "It is troubling that this service which religious communities render to society as a whole, particularly through the education of young people, is compromised or hampered by legislative proposals which risk creating a sort of state monopoly in the schools; this can be seen, for example, in certain countries in Latin America. (...) I exhort all governments to promote educational systems respectful of the primordial right of families to make decisions about the education of their children, systems inspired by the principle of subsidiarity which is basic to the organization of a just society. Continuing my reflection, I cannot remain silent about another attack on the religious freedom of families in certain European countries which mandate obligatory participation in courses of sexual or civic education which allegedly convey a neutral conception of the person and of life, yet in fact reflect an anthropology opposed to faith and to right reason". [Benedict XVI, *Address to the Members of the Diplomatic Corps* (10 January 2011)]

(14) "Adoring the God of Jesus Christ, who out of love made himself bread broken, is the most effective and radical remedy against the idolatry of the past and of the present. Kneeling before the Eucharist is a profession of freedom: those who bow to Jesus cannot and must not prostrate themselves before any earthly authority, however powerful. We Christians kneel only before God or before the Most Blessed Sacrament because we know and believe that the one true God is present in it, the God who created the world and so loved it that he gave his Only Begotten Son (cf. Jn 3: 16). We prostrate ourselves before a God who first bent over man like the Good Samaritan to assist him and restore his life, and who knelt before us to wash our dirty feet. Adoring the Body of Christ, means believing that there, in that piece of Bread, Christ is really there, and gives true sense to life, to the immense universe as to the smallest creature, to the whole of human history as to the most brief existence. Adoration is prayer that prolongs the celebration and Eucharistic communion and in which the soul continues to be nourished". [Benedict XVI, *Homily on the Solemnity of Corpus Christi* (22 May 2008)]

(15) "Through faith we are introduced to the mystery of love that is the Most Holy Trinity. We are in some sense embraced by God, transformed by his love. The Church is this embrace of God, in which men and women learn also to embrace their brothers and sisters and to discover in them the divine image and likeness which constitutes the deepest truth of their existence, and which is the origin of genuine freedom". [Benedict XVI, *Address during the visit to the Cathedral of Santiago de Compostela* (6 November 2010)]

(16) "He, Christ, who says of himself: 'I am the light of the world' (Jn 8:12), causes our lives to shine brightly, so that what we have just heard in the Gospel comes true: '*You* are the light of the world' (Mt 5:14). It is not our human efforts or the technical progress of our era that brings light into this world. Again and again we experience how our striving to bring about a better and more just world hits against its limits. Innocent suffering and the ultimate fact of death awaiting every single person are an impenetrable darkness which may perhaps, through fresh experiences, be lit up for a moment, as if through a flash of lightning at night. In the end, though, a frightening darkness remains.

While all around us there may be darkness and gloom, yet we see a light: a small, tiny flame that is stronger than the seemingly powerful and invincible darkness. Christ, risen from the dead, shines in this world and he does so most brightly in those places where, in human terms, everything is sombre and hopeless. He has conquered death – he is alive – and faith in him, like a small light, cuts through all that is dark and threatening. (...) In the final analysis, the world in which we live, in spite of its technical progress, does not seem to be getting any better. There is still war and terror, hunger and disease, bitter poverty and merciless oppression. And even those figures in our history who saw themselves as 'bringers of light', but without being fired by Christ, the one true light, did not manage to create an earthly paradise, but set up dictatorships and totalitarian systems, in which even the smallest spark of true humanity is choked.

At this point we cannot remain silent about the existence of evil. We see it in so many places in this world; but we also see it – and this scares us – in our own lives. Truly, within our hearts there is a tendency towards evil, there is selfishness, envy, aggression. Perhaps with a certain self-discipline all this can to some degree be controlled. But it becomes more difficult with faults that are somewhat hidden, that can engulf us like a thick fog, such as sloth, or laziness in willing and doing good. Again and again in history, keen observers have pointed out that damage to the Church comes not from her opponents, but from uncommitted Christians. 'You are the light of the world': only Christ can say: 'I am the light of the world'. All of us can be light only if we stand within the 'you' that, through the Lord, is forever becoming light. And just as the Lord warns us that salt can become tasteless, so too he weaves a gentle warning into his saying about light. Instead of placing the light on a lampstand, one can hide it under a bushel. Let us ask ourselves: how often do we hide God's light through our sloth, through our stubbornness, so that it cannot shine out through us into the world?

Dear friends, Saint Paul in many of his letters does not shrink from calling his contemporaries, members of the local communities, 'saints'. (...) There is no saint, apart from the Blessed Virgin Mary, who has not also known sin, who has never fallen. Dear friends, Christ is not so much interested in how often in our lives we stumble and fall, as in how often with his help we pick ourselves up again. He does not demand glittering achievements, but he wants his light to shine in you. He does not call you because you are good and perfect, but because he is good and he wants to make you his friends. Yes, you are the light of the world because Jesus is your light. You are Christians – not because you do special and extraordinary things, but because he, Christ, is your life, our life. You are holy, we are holy, if we allow his grace to work in us. (...) 'You are the light of the world'. Where God is, there is a future!". [Benedict XVI, *Address at Vigil with young people, Fair, Freiburg im Breisgau* (24 September 2011)]

## 5 – Thy Kingdom come (I)

**(17)** "We can put it even more simply: when Jesus speaks of the Kingdom of God, he is quite simply proclaiming God, and proclaiming him to be the living God, who is able to act concretely in the world and in history and is even now so acting. He is telling us: 'God exists' and 'God is really God', which means that he holds in his hands the threads of the world. In this sense, Jesus' message is very simple and thoroughly God-centered. The new and totally specific thing about his message is that he is telling us: God is acting now – this is the hour when God is showing himself in history as its Lord, as the living God, in a way that goes beyond anything seen before. 'Kingdom of God' is therefore an inadequate translation. It would be better to speak of God's being-Lord, of his lordship". [Benedict XVI, *Jesus of Nazareth*, Doubleday, New York 2007, pp. 55-56]

**(18)** "The generous and indissoluble love of a man and a woman is the effective context and foundation of human life in its gestation, birth, growth and natural end. Only where love and faithfulness are present can true freedom come to birth and endure. For this reason the Church advocates adequate economic and social means so that women may find in the home and at work their full development, that men and women who contract marriage and form a family receive decisive support from the state, that life of children may be defended as sacred and inviolable from the moment of their conception, that the reality of birth be given due respect and receive juridical, social and legislative support. For this reason the Church resists every form of denial of human life and gives its support to everything that would promote the natural order in the sphere of the institution of the family". [Benedict XVI, *Homily at Holy Mass with dedication of the Church of the Sagrada Familia and of the Altar* (7 November 2010)]

**(19)** "After affirming that man is the only creature on earth which God willed for itself, the Council immediately goes on to say that he *cannot 'fully find himself except through a sincere gift of self'*. This might appear to be a contradiction, but in fact it is not. Instead it is the magnificent paradox of human existence: an existence called *to serve the truth in love*. Love causes man to find fulfilment through the sincere gift of self. To love means to give and to receive something which can be neither bought nor sold, but only given freely and mutually. By its very nature the gift of the person must be lasting and irrevocable. The indissolubility of marriage flows in the first place from the very essence of that gift: *the gift of one person to another person*". [John Paul II, Letter to Families *Gratissimam sane* (1994) no. 11]

**(20)** "The Creator is he who 'calls to existence from nothing' and who establishes the world in existence and man in the world, *because he 'is love'* (1 Jn 4:8). We admittedly do not find this word love (God is love) in the creation account; nevertheless, that account often repeats, 'God saw everything that he had made, and indeed, it was very good' (Gen 1:31). Through these words we are led to glimpse in love the divine motive for creation, the source, as it were, from which it springs: *only love, in fact, gives rise to the good and is well pleased with the good* (see 1 Cor 13). As an action of God, creation thus means not only calling from nothing to existence and establishing the world's existence as well as man's existence in the world, but, according to the first account, bᵉrē',šît bārā', [*beresit bara*], it also signifies *gift*, a fundamental and 'radical' gift, that is, an act of giving in which the gift comes into being precisely from nothing.

Reading the first chapters of Genesis introduces us into the mystery of creation, that is, of the beginning of the world by the will of God, who is omnipotence and love". [John Paul II, *Man and Woman He Created Them. A Theology of the Body*, Pauline Books & Media, Boston, MA 2006, p. 180]

**(21)** "The fact that man 'created as man and woman' is the image of God means not only that each of them individually is like God, as a rational and free being. It also means that man and woman, created as a 'unity of the two' in their common humanity, are called to live in a communion of love, and in this way to mirror in the world the communion of love that is in God, through which the Three Persons love each other in the intimate mystery of the one divine life. The Father, Son and Holy Spirit, one God through the unity of the divinity, exist as persons through the inscrutable divine relationship. Only in this way can we understand the truth that God in himself is love (cf. 1 Jn 4:16). *The image and likeness of God in man*, created as man and woman (in the analogy that can be presumed between Creator and creature), thus also expresses the 'unity of the two' in a common humanity. (...) and is also a call and a task". [John Paul II, Apostolic Letter *Mulieris dignitatem* (1988) no. 7]

**(22)** "*Man became the image of God not only through his own humanity, but also through the communion of persons*, which man and woman form from the very beginning. (...) In fact, the gift reveals, so to speak, *a particular characteristic of personal existence*, or even of the very essence of the person. When God-Yahweh says, 'It is not good that the man should be alone' (Gen 2:18), he affirms that, 'alone', the man does not completely realize this essence. He realizes it only by existing *'with someone'* – and, put even more deeply and completely, by existing *'for someone'*. (...) Communion of persons means living in a reciprocal 'for', in a relationship of reciprocal gift. And this relationship is precisely the fulfillment of 'man's' original solitude. (...) The human body, with its sex – its masculinity and femininity – seen in the very mystery of creation, is not only a source of fruitfulness and of procreation, as in the whole natural order, but contains 'from the beginning' the 'spousal' attribute that is, *the power to express love: precisely that love in which the human person becomes a gift* and – through this gift – fulfills the very meaning of his being and existence. (...) this man cannot 'fully find himself except through a sincere gift of self' [*Gaudium et Spes*, 24:3]". [John Paul II, *Man and Woman He Created Them. A Theology of the Body*, Pauline Books & Media, Boston, MA 2006, pp. 163; 182; 185-186]

**(23)** "The contemporary family, like families in every age, *is searching for 'fairest love'*. A love which is not 'fairest', but reduced only to the satisfaction of concupiscence (cf. *1 Jn* 2:16), or to a man's and a woman's mutual 'use' of each other, makes persons *slaves to their weaknesses*. Do not certain modern 'cultural agendas' lead to this enslavement? There are agendas which 'play' on man's weaknesses, and thus make him increasingly weak and defenceless.

*The civilization of love evokes joy:* joy, among other things, for the fact that a man has come into the world (cf. *Jn* 16:21), and consequently because spouses have become parents. The civilization of love means 'rejoicing in the right' (cf. *1 Cor* 13:6). But a civilization inspired by a consumerist, anti-birth mentality is not and cannot ever be a civilization of love. (...) families cease to be witnesses of the civilization of love and can even become a negation of it, a kind of *counter-sign*. A broken family can, for its part, consolidate a specific form of 'anti-civilization', destroying love in its various expressions, with inevitable consequences for the whole of life in society". [John Paul II, Letter to Families *Gratissimam sane* (1994) no. 13]

## 6 – Thy Kingdom come (II)

**(24)** "Since that time, there has been a noticeable reduction in the wave of theologies of revolution that attempt to justify violence as a means of building a better world – the 'kingdom' – by interpreting Jesus as a 'Zealot'. The cruel consequences of religiously motivated violence are only too evident to us all. Violence does not build up the kingdom of God, the kingdom of humanity. On the contrary, it is a favorite instrument of the Antichrist, however idealistic its religious motivation may be. It serves, not humanity, but inhumanity". [Benedict XVI, *Jesus of Nazareth. Holy week: from the Entrance into Jerusalem to the Resurrection*, Part two, Ignatius Press, San Francisco 2011, p. 15]

**(25)** "Through the disciples and their mission, the world as a whole is to be torn free from its alienation, it is to rediscover unity with God. (...) That is precisely what Jesus' mission is. (...) leading 'the world' away from the condition of man's alienation from God and from himself, so that it can become God's world once more and so that man can become fully himself again by becoming one with God. Yet this transformation comes at the price of the Cross; it comes at the price of readiness for martyrdom on the part of Christ's witnesses". [Benedict XVI, *Jesus of Nazareth. Holy week: from* *the Entrance into Jerusalem to the Resurrection*, Part two, Ignatius Press, San Francisco 2011, pp. 100-101]

**(26)** "So indeed the Catholic school, while it is open, as it must be, to the situation of the contemporary world, leads its students to promote efficaciously the good of the earthly city and also prepares them for service in the spread of the Kingdom of God, so that by leading an exemplary apostolic life they become, as it were, a saving leaven in the human community". [Vatican Council II, Declaration *Gravissimum educationis* no. 8]

**(27)** "Educating, however, has never been an easy task and today seems to be becoming ever more difficult. Parents, teachers, priests and everyone who has direct educational responsibilities are well aware of this. Hence, there is talk of a great 'educational emergency' (...) Not even the greatest values of the past can be simply inherited; they must be claimed by us and renewed through an often anguishing personal option. When the foundations are shaken, however, and essential certainties are lacking, the impelling need for those values once again makes itself felt: thus today, the request for an education which is truly such is in fact increasing. Parents, anxious and often anguished about the future of their children, are asking for it; a great many teachers going through the sorrowful experience of their schools' deterioration are asking for it; society overall, seeing doubts cast on the very foundations of coexistence, is asking for it; children and young people themselves who do not want to be left to face life's challenges on their own are also asking for it in their inmost being. Those who believe in Jesus Christ, moreover, have a further and stronger reason for not being afraid: they know in fact that God does not abandon us, that his love reaches us wherever we are and just as we are, in our wretchedness and weakness, in order to offer us a new possibility of good". [Benedict XVI, *Letter to the Faithful of the Diocese and City of Rome on the urgent task of educating young people* (21 January 2008)]

**(28)** "It is therefore a service of love which we are all committed to ensure to our neighbour, that his or her life may be always defended and promoted, especially when it is weak or threatened. It is not only a personal but a social concern which we must all foster: a concern to make unconditional respect for human life the foundation of a renewed society.
We are asked to love and honour the life of every man and woman and to work with perseverance and courage so that our time, marked by all too many signs of death, may at last witness the establishment of a new culture of life, the fruit of the culture of truth and of love" [n. 77].
"The Gospel of life is for the whole of human society. (...) A society lacks solid foundations when, on the one hand, it asserts values such as the dignity of the person, justice and peace, but then, on the other hand, radically acts to the contrary by allowing or tolerating a variety of ways in

which human life is devalued and violated, especially where it is weak or marginalized. Only respect for life can be the foundation and guarantee of the most precious and essential goods of society, such as democracy and peace.

There can be no true democracy without a recognition of every person's dignity and without respect for his or her rights.

Nor can there be true peace unless life is defended and promoted. As Paul VI pointed out: 'Every crime against life is an attack on peace, especially if it strikes at the moral conduct of people... But where human rights are truly professed and publicly recognized and defended, peace becomes the joyful and operative climate of life in society'" [no. 101]. [John Paul II, Encyclical Letter *Evangelium vitae* (1995) no. 77; no. 101]

**(29)** "Tragically, above all in nineteenth century Europe, the conviction grew that God is somehow man's antagonist and an enemy of his freedom. As a result, there was an attempt to obscure the true biblical faith in the God who sent into the world his Son Jesus Christ, so that no one should perish but that all might have eternal life (cfr. Jn 3:16). The author of the Book of Wisdom, faced with a paganism in which God envied or despised humans, puts it clearly: how could God have created all things if he did not love them, he who in his infinite fullness, has need of nothing (cfr. Wis 11:24-26)? Why would he have revealed himself to human beings if he did not wish to take care of them? God is the origin of our being and the foundation and apex of our freedom, not its opponent. (...) Europe must open itself to God, must come to meet him without fear, and work with his grace for that human dignity which was discerned by her best traditions. (...) The cross and love, the cross and light have been synonymous in our history because Christ allowed himself to hang there in order to give us the supreme witness of his love, to invite us to forgiveness and reconciliation, to teach us how to overcome evil with good. (...) Blessed Cross, shine always upon the lands of Europe!". [Benedict XVI, *Homily at Holy Mass on the occasion of the Compostelian Holy Year, Plaza del Obradoiro, Santiago de Compostela* (6 November 2010)]

**(30)** "Coming forth from the eternal Father's love, founded in time by Christ the Redeemer and made one in the Holy Spirit, the Church has a saving and an eschatological purpose which can be fully attained only in the future world. But she is already present in this world, and is composed of men, that is, of members of the earthly city who have a call to form the family of God's children during the present history of the human race, and to keep increasing it until the Lord returns. (...) Pursuing the saving purpose which is proper to her, the Church does not only communicate divine life to men but in some way casts the reflected light of that life over the entire earth, most of all by its healing and elevating impact on the dignity of the person, by the way in which it strengthens the seams of human society and imbues the everyday activity of men with a deeper meaning and importance. Thus through her individual matters and her whole community, the Church believes she can contribute greatly toward making the family of man and its history more human". [Vatican Council II, Pastoral Constitution *Gaudium et spes* no. 40]

(31) "That there be peace on earth (cfr. Lk 2:14) is the will of God and, for that reason, it is a task given to man as well. The Christian knows that lasting peace is connected with men abiding in God's *eudokia*, his 'good pleasure'. The struggle to abide in peace with God is an indispensable part of the struggle for 'peace on earth' (...). When men lose sight of God, peace disintegrates and violence proliferates to a formerly unimaginable degree of cruelty. This we see only too clearly today". [Benedict XVI, *Jesus of Nazareth*, Doubleday, New York 2007, p. 85]

(32) "The Church forcefully maintains this link between life ethics and social ethics, fully aware that 'a society lacks solid foundations when, on the one hand, it asserts values such as the dignity of the person, justice and peace, but then, on the other hand, radically acts to the contrary by allowing or tolerating a variety of ways in which human life is devalued and violated, especially where it is weak or marginalized'". [Benedict XVI, Encyclical Letter *Caritas in veritate* (2009) no. 15].

(33) "Yet it should be added that, as well as religious fanaticism that in some contexts impedes the exercise of the right to religious freedom, so too the deliberate promotion of religious indifference or practical atheism on the part of many countries obstructs the requirements for the development of peoples, depriving them of spiritual and human resources. *God is the guarantor of man's true development*, inasmuch as, having created him in his image, he also establishes the transcendent dignity of men and women and feeds their innate yearning to 'be more' (...). When the State promotes, teaches, or actually imposes forms of practical atheism, it deprives its citizens of the moral and spiritual strength that is indispensable for attaining integral human development and it impedes them from moving forward with renewed dynamism as they strive to offer a more generous human response to divine love. In the context of cultural, commercial or political relations, it also sometimes happens that economically developed or emerging countries export this reductive vision of the person and his destiny to poor countries. This is the damage that 'superdevelopment' causes to authentic development when it is accompanied by 'moral underdevelopment'". [Benedict XVI, Encyclical Letter *Caritas in veritate* (2009) no. 29]

**(34)** "The 'types of messianism which give promises but create illusions' always build their case on a denial of the transcendent dimension of development, in the conviction that it lies entirely at their disposal. This false security becomes a weakness, because it involves reducing man to subservience, to a mere means for development, while the humility of those who accept a vocation is transformed into true autonomy, because it sets them free". [Benedict XVI, Encyclical Letter *Caritas in veritate* (2009) no. 17]

**(35)** "Now Kant considers the possibility that as well as the natural end of all things there may be another that is unnatural, a perverse end. He writes in this connection: 'If Christianity should one day cease to be worthy of love then the prevailing mode in human thought would be rejection and opposition to it; and the Antichrist would begin his – albeit short – regime (presumably based on fear and self-interest); but then, because Christianity, though destined to be the world religion, would not in fact be favoured by destiny to become so, then, in a moral respect, this could lead to the (perverted) end of all things'". [Benedict XVI, Encyclical Letter *Spe salvi* (2007) no. 19]

**(36)** "There is no doubt, therefore, that a 'Kingdom of God' accomplished without God – a kingdom therefore of man alone – inevitably ends up as the 'perverse end' of all things as described by Kant: we have seen it, and we see it over and over again. Yet neither is there any doubt that God truly enters into human affairs only when, rather than being present merely in our thinking, he himself comes towards us and speaks to us. Reason therefore needs faith if it is to be completely itself: reason and faith need one another in order to fulfil their true nature and their mission". [Benedict XVI, Encyclical Letter *Spe salvi* (2007) no. 23]

**(37)** "In order to protect nature, it is not enough to intervene with economic incentives or deterrents; not even an apposite education is sufficient. These are important steps, but *the decisive issue is the overall moral tenor of society.* If there is a lack of respect for the right to life and to a natural death, if human conception, gestation and birth are made artificial, if human embryos are sacrificed to research, the conscience of society ends up losing the concept of human ecology and, along with it, that of environmental ecology. (...) The book of nature is one and indivisible: it takes in not only the environment but also life, sexuality, marriage, the family, social relations: in a word, integral human development. Our duties towards the environment are linked to our duties towards the human person, considered in himself and in relation to others". [Benedict XVI, Encyclical Letter *Caritas in veritate* (2009) no. 51]

287

**(38)** "Yet the rationality of a self-centred use of technology proves to be irrational because it implies a decisive rejection of meaning and value. It is no coincidence that closing the door to transcendence brings one up short against a difficulty: how could being emerge from nothing, how could intelligence be born from chance? Faced with these dramatic questions, reason and faith can come to each other's assistance. Only together will they save man. *Entranced by an exclusive reliance on technology, reason without faith is doomed to flounder in an illusion of its own omnipotence. Faith without reason risks being cut off from everyday life*". [Benedict XVI, Encyclical Letter *Caritas in veritate* (2009) no. 74]

**(39)** "I understood that since the Church is a body composed of different members, the noblest and most important of all the organs would not be wanting. I knew that the Church has a heart, that this heart *burns with love*, and that it is love alone which gives life to its members. I knew that if this love were extinguished, the Apostles would no longer preach the Gospel, and the Martyrs would refuse to shed their blood... I understood that *love embraces all vocations, that it is all things, and that it reaches out through all the ages, and to the uttermost limits of the heart, because it is eternal.* (...) Yes, I have found my place in the bosom of the Church, and this place, my God, Thou hast Thyself given to me: in the heart of the Church, my Mother, I will be LOVE! ... Thus I shall be all the things...: thus will my dream be realized! (...) Yes, my Beloved, it is thus my short life shall be spent in Thy sight. The only way I have for proving my love is to strew flowers before Thee – that is to say, I will let no tiny sacrifices pass, no look, no word. I wish to profit by the small actions, and to do them for Love. (...) Jesus, Jesus! If the mere desire of Thy love awakens such delight, what will it be to possess it, to enjoy it for ever? (...) Why dost Thou not reserve these infinite longings to lofty souls, to the eagles that soar in the heights? Alas! I am but a poor little unfledged bird. I am not an eagle, I have but the eagle's eyes and heart! Yet, notwithstanding my exceeding littleness, I dare to gaze upon the Divine Sun of Love, and I burn to dart upwards unto Him! I would fly, I would imitate the eagles; but all that I can do is to lift up my little wings – it is beyond my feeble power to soar. What is to become of me? Must I die of sorrow because of my helplessness? Oh, no! I will not even grieve. With daring self-abandonment there will I remain until death, my gaze fixed upon that Divine Sun. Nothing shall affright me, nor wind nor rain. And should impenetrable clouds conceal the Orb of Love, and should I seem to believe that beyond this life there is darkness only, that would be the hour of perfect joy, the hour in which to push my confidence to its uttermost bounds. I should not dare to detach my gaze, well knowing that beyond the dark clouds the sweet Sun will shines". [Saint Thérèse of Lisieux (1873-1897), *History of a soul: The Authobiography of St. Thérèse of Lisieux with Additional Writings and Sayings of St. Thérèse* (http://

www.catholicbible101.com/St.%20Therese%20Story%20of%20 a%20soul. pdf, accessed in July 2014)]

## 7 – Thy will be done

**(40)** "'Thy will be done on earth as it is in Heaven': so that we may love Thee with (our) whole heart by thinking of Thee always, with (our) whole soul by desiring Thee always, with (our) whole mind directing unto Thee all our intentions, by seeking Thy honor in all things and with all our strength by expending all our strength and sense of soul and body in submission to Thy love (amor) and not in anything else; and may we love our neighbors even as our very selves by drawing all to Thy love to the extent of (our) strength, by rejoicing over the good things of others just as over our own and by compassionating (them) in evils and by giving offense to no one". [Saint Francis of Assisi (1182 ca. – 1226), *The Writings of St. Francis of Assisi. Translated from the Critical Latin Edition*, edited by Fr. Kajetan Esser, O.F.M., Franciscan Archive (http://www.franciscan-archive.org/patriarcha/opera/ preces.html, accessed in July 2014)]

**(41)** "Dear friends, before we say good-bye, and while the young people of Spain pass on the World Youth Day cross to the young people of Brazil, as Successor of Peter I entrust all of you present with this task: make the knowledge and love of Jesus Christ known to the whole world! He wants you to be the apostles of the twenty-first century and the messengers of his joy. Do not let him down! Thank you very much.

[*French*] *Chers jeunes de langue française, le Christ vous demande aujourd'hui d'être enracinés en Lui et de bâtir avec Lui votre vie sur le roc qu'il est Lui-même. Il vous envoie pour être des témoins courageux et sans complexes, authentiques et crédibles! N'ayez pas peur d'être catholiques, d'en témoigner toujours autour de vous avec simplicité et sincérité ! Que l'Église trouve en vous et en votre jeunesse les missionnaires joyeux de la Bonne Nouvelle!*

[My dear young people of the French-speaking world, today Christ asks you to be rooted in him and with him, to build your lives upon him who is our rock. He sends you out to be his witnesses, courageous and without anxiety, authentic and credible! Do not be afraid to be Catholic, and to be witnesses to those around you in simplicity and sincerity! Let the Church find in you and in your youthfulness joyful missionaries of the Good News of salvation!]

[*English*] I greet all the English-speaking young people present here today! As you return home, take back with you the good news of Christ's love which we have experienced in these unforgettable days. Fix your eyes upon him, deepen your knowledge of the Gospel and bring forth abundant fruit! God bless all of you until we meet again!

*[German] Meine lieben Freunde! Glaube ist keine Theorie. Glauben heißt, in eine persönliche Beziehung zu Jesus zu treten und die Freundschaft mit ihm in Gemeinschaft mit anderen, in der Gemeinschaft der Kirche zu leben. Vertraut Christus euer ganzes Leben an, und helft euren Freunden, daß auch sie zur Quelle des Lebens, zu Gott gelangen. Der Herr mache euch zu frohen Zeugen seiner Liebe.*

[My dear friends! Faith is not a theory. To believe is to enter into a personal relationship with Jesus and to live in friendship with him in fellowship with others, in the communion of the Church. Entrust the whole of your lives to Christ and bring your friends to find their way to the source of life, to God. May the Lord make you happy and joy-filled witnesses of his love.]

*[Italian] Cari giovani di lingua italiana! Vi saluto tutti! L'Eucaristia che abbiamo celebrato è Cristo risorto presente e vivo in mezzo a noi: grazie a Lui, la vostra vita è radicata e fondata in Dio, salda nella fede. Con questa certezza, ripartite da Madrid e annunciate a tutti ciò che avete visto e udito. Rispondete con gioia alla chiamata del Signore, seguiteLo e rimanete sempre uniti a Lui: porterete molto frutto!*

[My dear young Italians! Greetings to all of you. The Eucharist that we have celebrated is the risen Christ present and living in our midst: through him, your lives are rooted and built upon Christ, strong in faith. With this confidence, depart from Madrid and tell everyone what you have seen and heard. Respond with joy to the Lord's call, follow him and remain always united to him: you will bear much fruit!]

*[Portuguese] Queridos jovens e amigos de língua portuguesa, encontrastes Jesus Cristo! Sentir-vos-eis em contra-corrente no meio duma sociedade onde impera a cultura relativista que renuncia a buscar e a possuir a verdade. Mas foi para este momento da história, cheio de grandes desafios e oportunidades, que o Senhor vos mandou: para que, graças à vossa fé, continue a ressoar a Boa Nova de Cristo por toda a terra. Espero poder encontrar-vos daqui a dois anos, na próxima Jornada Mundial da Juventude, no Rio de Janeiro, Brasil. Até lá, rezemos uns pelos outros, dando testemunho da alegria que brota de viver enraizados e edificados em Cristo. Até breve, queridos jovens! Que Deus vos abençoe!*

[Dear Portuguese-speaking young people and friends, you have met Jesus Christ! You will be swimming against the tide in a society with a relativistic culture which wishes neither to seek nor hold on to the truth. But it was for this moment in history, with its great challenges and opportunities, that the Lord sent you, so that, through your faith, the Good News of Jesus might continue to resound throughout the earth. I hope to see you again in two years' time at the nest World Youth Day in Rio de Janeiro, Brazil. Till then, let us pray for each other, witnessing to the joy that brings forth life, rooted in and built upon Christ. Until we meet again, my dear young people! God bless you all!]

*[Polish] Drodzy młodzi Polacy, silni wiarą, zakorzenieni w Chrystusie! Niech owocują w was otrzymane w tych dniach od Boga talenty. Bądźcie Jego świadkami. Nieście innym orędzie Ewangelii. Waszą modlitwą i przykładem życia pomagajcie Europie odnaleźć jej chrześcijańskie korzenie.*

[Dear young Poles, strong in the faith, rooted in Christ! May the gifts you have received from God during these days bear in you abundant fruit. Be his witnesses. Take to others the message of the Gospel. With your prayers and example of life, help Europe to rediscover its Christian roots.]".
[Benedict XVI, *Angelus at Cuatro Vientos Air Base, Madrid* (21 August 2011)]

## 8 – On earth as it is in heaven (I)

**(42)** "Without their contribution it would truly be difficult to foster and strengthen understanding between nations, to breathe life into peace dialogues around the globe, to guarantee the primary good of access to information, while at the same time ensuring the free circulation of ideas, especially those promoting the ideals of solidarity and social justice. Indeed, the media, taken overall, are not only vehicles for spreading ideas: they can and should also be instruments at the service of a world of greater justice and solidarity. Unfortunately, though, they risk being transformed into systems aimed at subjecting humanity to agendas dictated by the dominant interests of the day. This is what happens when communication is used for ideological purposes or for the aggressive advertising of consumer products. While claiming to represent reality, it can tend to legitimize or impose distorted models of personal, family or social life. Moreover, in order to attract listeners and increase the size of audiences, it does not hesitate at times to have recourse to vulgarity and violence, and to overstep the mark. The media can also present and support models of development which serve to increase rather than reduce the technological divide between rich and poor countries". [Benedict XVI, *Message for the XLII World Communications Day* (24 January 2008)]

**(43)** "Hence it is appropriate that, as the Second Millennium of Christianity draws to a close, the Church should become more fully conscious of the sinfulness of her children, recalling all those times in history when they departed from the spirit of Christ and his Gospel and, instead of offering to the world the witness of a life inspired by the values of faith, indulged in ways of thinking and acting which were truly *forms of counter-witness and scandal*. (...) The Church (...) cannot cross the threshold of the new millennium without encouraging her children to purify themselves, through repentance, of past errors and instances of infidelity, inconsistency, and slowness to act". [John Paul II, Apostolic Letter *Tertio millennio adveniente* (1994) no. 33]

**(44)** Herebelow, for the sake of conciseness, are cited two of the seven *Confession of sins and asking for forgiveness* prayers expressed by the Holy Father at Holy Mass in the Vatican Basilica on 12 March 2000:

> *"The Holy Father: 'Lord, God of all men and women,*
> *in certain periods of history*
> *Christians have at times given in to intolerance*
> *and have not been faithful to the great commandment of love,*
> *sullying in this way the face of the Church, your Spouse.*
> *Have mercy on your sinful children*
> *and accept our resolve*
> *to seek and promote truth in the gentleness of charity,*
> *in the firm knowledge that truth*
> *can prevail only in virtue of truth itself.*
> *We ask this through Christ our Lord'".*
> *"The Holy Father: 'Lord of the world, Father of all,*
> *through your Son*
> *you asked us to love our enemies,*
> *to do good to those who hate us*
> *and to pray for those who persecute us.*
> *Yet Christians have often denied the Gospel;*
> *yielding to a mentality of power,*
> *they have violated the rights of ethnic groups and peoples,*
> *and shown contempt for their cultures and religious traditions:*
> *be patient and merciful towards us, and grant us your forgiveness!*
> *We ask this through Christ our Lord'".*

[John Paul II, *Universal Prayer: Confession of sins and asking for forgiveness during Holy Mass on First Sunday of Lent, Day of Pardon* (12 March 2000); see the whole text at http://www.vatican.va/news_services/liturgy/documents/ns_lit_doc_20000312_prayer-day-pardon_it.htm]

**(45)** "The summit and centre of the life and mission of every believer and every Christian community is the Eucharist, the sacrament of salvation in which Christ becomes present and gives his Body and Blood as spiritual food for eternal life. A truly ineffable mystery! It is around the Eucharist that the Church comes to birth and grows – that great family of Christians which we enter through Baptism, and in which we are constantly renewed through the Sacrament of Reconciliation. The baptised, through Confirmation, are then confirmed in the Holy Spirit so as to live as authentic friends and witnesses of Christ. The Sacraments of Holy Orders and Matrimony enable them to accomplish their apostolic duties in the Church and in the world. Finally, the Sacrament of the Sick grants us an experience of divine consolation in illness and suffering". [Benedict XVI, *Message on the occasion of the XXIV World Youth Day* (22 February 2009)]

**(46)** "I would like to reflect briefly on the need to lead Sacred Orders and Matrimony back to the one Eucharistic source. Indeed, both these states of life share the same root in the love of Christ who gives himself for humanity's salvation. They are called to a common mission: to witness to and make present this love at the service of the community in order to build up the People of God (cf. *Catechism of the Catholic Church*, n. 1534). (...) The family is a source of wealth for married couples, an irreplaceable good for children, an indispensable foundation of society and a vital community for the journey of the Church. (...)

The ministry that is born from the Sacrament of Matrimony is important for the life of the Church: the family is the privileged place of human and Christian education and remains, for this end, as the closest ally of the priestly ministry. It is a precious gift for the edification of the community. The priest's closeness to the family helps it in its turn to become aware of its own profound reality and its own mission, fostering the development of a strong ecclesial sensitivity. No vocation is a private matter, and even less so is the vocation to marriage, because its horizon is the entire Church. Thus an effort should be made in pastoral action to integrate and harmonize the priestly ministry with 'the authentic Gospel of marriage and of the family' (cf. *Direttorio di pastorale familiare*, Italian Episcopal Conference, 25 July 1993, n. 8) for an effective and fraternal communion. And the Eucharist is the centre and source of this unity that enlivens the whole of the Church's action.

Dear priests, because of the gift you have received in Ordination, you are called to serve as Pastors the ecclesial community, which is the 'family of families', and therefore to love each one with a paternal heart, with genuine detachment from yourselves, with full, continuous and faithful dedication. You are a living sign that refers to Jesus Christ, the one Good Shepherd. Conform yourselves to him, to his style of life, with that total and exclusive service of which celibacy is an expression. The priest also has a spousal dimension: to identify himself with the heart of Christ the Bridegroom, who gives his life for the Church his Bride (cf. Post-Synodal Apostolic Exhortation, Sacramentum Caritatis, no. 24). Cultivate deep familiarity with the Word of God, a light on your way. May the daily and faithful celebration of the Eucharist be the place in which to find the strength to give yourselves in the ministry every day and to live constantly in God's presence. He is your dwelling place and your heritage. You must be witnesses of this to the family and to every person. (...) Love your priests, tell them of your appreciation of the generous service they carry out. May you also be able to be supportive despite their limitations, without ever giving up asking them to be exemplary ministers among you who speak to you of God and lead you to God. Your brotherliness is a precious spiritual help to them and a support in the trials of life.

Dear priests and dear married couples, may you always be able to find in Holy Mass the strength to live belonging to Christ and to his Church in forgiveness, in the gift of yourselves and in gratitude. May the origin and centre of your daily activity be sacramental communion so that all things may be done for the glory of God". [Benedict XVI, *Address at meeting with families and priests in the Cathedral of Saint Cyriac for the Conclusion of the XXV Italian National Eucharistic Congress in Ancona* (11 September 2011)]

**(47)** "Yet there are shepherds who want to have the title of shepherd without wanting to fulfill a pastor's duties. (...) The Lord will help me to speak the truth if I do not speak on my own authority. For if I speak on my own authority, I will be a shepherd nourishing myself and not the sheep. However, if my words are the Lord's, then he is nourishing you no matter who speaks. (...) Who are they who nourish themselves? They are the shepherds the Apostle described when he said: They all seek what is theirs and not what is Christ's. (...) Many persons come to God as Christians but not as leaders. Perhaps they travel by an easier road and are less hindered since they bear a lighter burden. In addition to the fact that I am a Christian and must give God an account of my life, I as a leader must give him an account of my stewardship as well". [Saint Augustine (354-430), *Augustine's Sermon "On Pastors" – excerpts as found in the Liturgy of the Hours, Office of Reading,* Volume IV, Catholic Book Publishing Corp., New York 1975 (http://fathergilles.net/parishministry/On_Pastors_by_St_Augustine.pdf, accessed in July 2014)]

**(48)** "For he is the enemy of the Redeemer, who through the good works that he performs desires to be loved by members of the Church rather than by him. For indeed, a servant is guilty of adulterous thoughts if he desires to please the eyes of the bride when he is sent by the groom to offer gifts. And truly, when the mind of the spiritual director is seized by self-love, sometimes it carries him off to inordinate laxity, other times to undue austerity. (...) Thus it is well said through the prophet: 'Woe to them who sew cushions under every elbow and make pillows to place under the head of every age to catch souls.' (Ezek 13.18) To put cushions under every elbow is to cherish with bland flattery the souls that are slipping from their rectitude and reclining in the pleasures of the world. For it is as if a person reclined with a pillow under his elbow or a pillow under his head when the strict correction of sinners is withdrawn and replaced by the laxity of favor so that these sinners might rest in the softness of their error while no austerity of correction affects them.

But these directors clearly show themselves to be dubious when they fear to be caught in the pursuit of temporal glory. For those persons whom they perceive to hold no power over them, they always punish with a rigorous invective, never employing gentle correction. They choose to forget about the possibility of a pastoral touch and instead terrify them with their governing authority. Concerning this, the divine Voice rightly corrects through the prophet, saying: 'But you ruled over them with rigor and authority.' (Ezek 34.4) For loving themselves more than their Creator, they raise themselves proudly over the laity, thinking not about what they should do, but about what they can do. They do not fear the coming judgment, but glory impiously in temporal authority. It is pleasing for them to do what is illicit, and they revel that they laity cannot stop them. Therefore, the one who plans for evil behavior and yet expects others to be silent is a witness to the fact that he loves himself more than the Truth, which he does not wish to face.

　(...) But he who desires that the Truth is loved more than himself is he who does not wish to be spared before the Truth. Thus, Peter freely accepted the censure of Paul, and David humbly listened to the rebuke of his subordinate, because good spiritual directors, who know not self-love, believe the free word of sincerity from a subject to be the homage of humility (Cf. Gal 2.11 and 2 Sam 12.7). At the same time, it is necessary that the administration of spiritual direction be tempered by the great art of moderation so that the minds of the laity, when they are able to perceive some things rightly, should be able to offer a free voice, but one in which this freedom does not develop into pride. (...) It should also be known that good spiritual directors desire to please others, but this is to lead their neighbors by the sweetness of their own character to an affection for the Truth. It is not because they desire to be loved, but instead because they use affection for themselves as a sort of road to introduce the hearts of their audience to the love of the Creator. For it is certainly difficult for a preacher who is not loved, regardless of how well he speaks, to be heard. The one, then, who is set over others should study how to be endearing so that he may be heard, but not so that he can be loved for its own sake". [Saint Gregory the Great (540-604), *The Book of Pastoral Rule*, translation with introduction by G. Demacopoulos, St. Vladimir's Seminary Press, New York 2007, pp. 74-76]

**(49)** "Has not our modern world created its own idols? Has it not imitated, perhaps inadvertently, the pagans of antiquity, by diverting man from his true end, from the joy of living eternally with God? (...) The temptation to idolize a past that no longer exists, forgetting its shortcomings; the temptation to idolize a future which does not yet exist, in the belief that, by his efforts alone, man can bring about the kingdom of eternal joy on earth! Saint Paul explains to the Colossians that insatiable greed is a form of idolatry (cf. 3:5), and he reminds his disciple Timothy that love of money is the root of all evil. By yielding to it, he explains, 'some have wandered away from the faith and pierced their hearts with many pangs' (1 Tim 6:10). Have not money, the thirst for possessions, for power and even for knowledge, diverted man from his true Destiny, from the truth about himself? (...) Never does God, of whom the Apostle is an authorized witness here, ask man to sacrifice his reason! Reason never enters into real contradiction with faith! The one God – Father, Son and Holy Spirit – created our reason and gives us faith, proposing to our freedom that it be received as a precious gift. It is the worship of idols which diverts man from this perspective. Let us therefore ask God, who sees us and hears us, to help us purify ourselves from all idols, in order to arrive at the truth of our being, in order to arrive at the truth of his infinite being!". [Benedict XVI, *Homily at Holy Mass, Esplanade des Invalides, Paris* (13 September 2008)]

**(50)** "As we witness the abuse of economic power, as we witness the cruelties of a capitalism that degrades man to the level of merchandise, we have also realized the perils of wealth, and we have gained a new appreciation of what Jesus meant when he warned of riches, of the man-destroying divinity Mammon, which grips large parts of the world in a cruel stranglehold". [Benedict XVI, *Jesus of Nazareth*, Doubleday, New York 2007, p. 98]

**(51)** "In 1967, when he issued the Encyclical Populorum Progressio, my venerable predecessor Pope Paul VI illuminated the great theme of the development of peoples with the splendour of truth and the gentle light of Christ's charity. He taught that life in Christ is the first and principal factor of development and he entrusted us with the task of travelling the path of development with all our heart and all our intelligence, that is to say with the ardour of charity and the wisdom of truth. It is the primordial truth of God's love, grace bestowed upon us, that opens our lives to gift and makes it possible to hope for a 'development of the whole man and of all men'". [Benedict XVI, Encyclical Letter *Caritas in veritate* (2009) no. 8]

**(52)** "When, under the influence of the Paraclete, people discover this divine dimension of their being and life, both as individuals and as a community, they are able to free themselves from the various determinisms which derive mainly from the materialistic bases of thought, practice and related modes of action. In our age these factors have succeeded in penetrating into man's inmost being, into that sanctuary of the conscience where the Holy Spirit continuously radiates the light and strength of new life in the 'freedom of the children of God'. Man's growth in this life is hindered by the conditionings and pressures exerted upon him by dominating structures and mechanisms in the various spheres of society. It can be said that in many cases social factors, instead of fostering the development and expansion of the human spirit, ultimately deprive the human spirit of the genuine truth of its being and life – over which the Holy Spirit keeps vigil – in order to subject it to the 'prince of this world'". [John Paul II, Encyclical Letter *Dominum et vivificantem*, (1986) no. 60]

## 9 – On earth as it is in heaven (II)

**(53)** "The revealed Word, the humanity of Christ and his Church are the three supreme expressions of his self-manifestation and self-giving to mankind. As says Saint Paul in the second reading: 'Let each man take care how he builds. For no other foundation can anyone lay than that which is laid, which is Jesus Christ' (1 Cor 3:10-11). The Lord Jesus is the stone which supports the weight of the world, which maintains the cohesion of the Church and brings together in ultimate unity all the achievements of mankind. In him, we have God's word and presence and from him the Church receives her life, her teaching and her mission. The Church of herself is nothing; she is called to be the sign and instrument of Christ, in pure docility to his authority and in total service to his mandate. The one Christ is the foundation of the one Church. He is the rock on which our faith is built. Building on this faith, let us strive together to show the world the face of God who is love and the only one who can respond to our yearning for fulfilment. This is the great task before us: to show everyone that God is a God of peace not of violence, of freedom not of coercion, of harmony not of discord". [Benedict XVI, *Homily at Holy Mass with dedication of the Church of the Sagrada Familia and of the Altar* (7 November 2010)]

**(54)** "The Church accomplishes her mission by evangelization that passes on faith in Christ and by the quest for justice and peace that transform the world. Now, the Eucharist is the source and the summit of evangelization and of the world's transformation. The Church has the power to awaken in those tempted by despair the hope of eternal life. The Eucharist opens to sharing those who are tempted to close their hands. It highlights reconciliation instead of division. It puts life and human dignity at the centre of our faith commitment. In a society too often dominated by a 'culture of death', which the search for individual comfort, money or power only intensifies, the Eucharist reminds us of the rights of the poor and the necessity of justice and solidarity. It awakens the community to the immense gift of the new covenant that calls all humanity to go beyond itself". [Pontificial Committee for International Eucharistic Congresses, *The Eucharist: God's gift for the life of the world. Foundational theological document for the 49th International Eucharistic Congress of Quebec* (2008) no. 5-A]

**(55)** "Are contemporary development and progress, in which we take part, the fruit of an alliance with divine wisdom? (...) How does it come about that after some time man has found in all this gigantic progress a source of threat to himself? How and through what ways have we come to the fact that, at the very heart of modern science and technology, the possibility has arisen of mankind's massive self-destruction: the fact that daily life presents us with abundant evidence of the use, against man, of

297

that which should have been for his benefit and should have served him? How have we come to this? In his journey towards progress, hasn't man perhaps taken only the easiest path, forgetting his alliance with eternal wisdom? Hasn't he perhaps taken the 'wide road' and forgotten the 'narrow gate'? (cfr. Matthew 7)". [John Paul II, *Homily during Holy Mass at Le Bourget Airport*. Pastoral visit to Paris and Lisieux (1 June 1980); our translation]

**(56)** "Man's intimate relationship with God in the Holy Spirit also enables him to understand himself, his own humanity, in a new way. Thus that image and likeness of God which man is from his very beginning is fully realized. This intimate truth of the human being has to be continually rediscovered in the light of Christ who is the prototype of the relationship with God. There also has to be rediscovered in Christ the reason for 'full self-discovery through a sincere gift of himself' to others". [John Paul II, Encyclical Letter *Dominum et vivificantem*, (1986) no. 59]

**(57)** "Many people see only the outward form of the Church. This makes the Church appear as merely one of the many organizations within a democratic society, whose criteria and laws are then applied to the task of evaluating and dealing with such a complex entity as the 'Church'. If to this is added the sad experience that the Church contains both good and bad fish, wheat and darnel, and if only these negative aspects are taken into account, then the great and beautiful mystery of the Church is no longer seen.

It follows that belonging to this vine, the 'Church', is no longer a source of joy. Dissatisfaction and discontent begin to spread, when people's superficial and mistaken notions of 'Church', their 'dream Church', fail to materialize! (...) Thus the Church is God's most beautiful gift. Therefore Saint Augustine could say: 'as much as any man loves the Church, so much has he the Holy Spirit' (*In Ioan. Ev. Tract.* 32:8 [*PL* 35:1646]). With and in the Church we may proclaim to all people that Christ is the source of life, that he exists, that he is the great one for whom we keep watch, for whom we long so much. He gives himself, and thus he gives us God, happiness, and love. Whoever believes in Christ has a future. For God has no desire for what is withered, dead, *ersatz*, and finally discarded: he wants what is fruitful and alive, he wants life in its fullness and he gives us life in its fullness". [Benedict XVI, *Homily at Holy Mass, Olympic Stadium, Berlin* (22 September 2011)]

**(58)** "The proclamation of the Gospel is the particular task of the Bishop, who can say, with Saint Paul: 'If I preach the Gospel, that gives me no ground for boasting. For necessity is laid upon me. Woe to me if I do not preach the Gospel!' (*1 Cor* 9:16). To strengthen and purify their faith, the faithful need to hear the words of their Bishop, the catechist *par excellence*. (...) The Bishop's mission leads him to be the defender of the rights of the poor, to call forth and encourage the exercise of charity, which is a manifestation of the Lord's love for the 'little ones'. In this way, the faithful are led to grasp the fact that the Church is truly God's family, gathered in brotherly love; this leaves no room for ethnocentrism or factionalism, and it contributes towards reconciliation and cooperation among ethnic groups for the good of all". [Benedict XVI, *Address at Meeting with the Bishops of Cameroon, Church of Christ-Roi in Tsinga - Yaoundé* (18 March 2009)]

(59) "The *missionary* attitude always begins with a feeling of deep esteem for 'what is in man', for what man has himself. worked out in the depths of his spirit concerning the most profound and important problems. It is a question of respecting everything that has been brought about in him by the Spirit, which 'blows where it wills'. The mission is never destruction, but instead is a taking up and fresh building, even if in practice there has not always been full correspondence with this high ideal. And we know well that the conversion that is begun by the mission is a work of grace, in which man must fully find himself again. (...) This man is the way for the Church – a way that, in a sense, is the basis of all the other ways that the Church must walk – because man – every man without any exception whatever – has been redeemed by Christ, and because with man – with each man without any exception whatever – Christ is in a way united, even when man is unaware of it". [John Paul II, Encyclical Letter *Redemptor hominis* (1979) nos. 12-14]

(60) "Proclaiming Jesus Christ the one Saviour of the world 'constitutes the essential mission of the Church. It is a task and mission which the vast and profound changes of present-day society make all the more urgent' (Evangelii Nuntiandi, 14). Indeed, today we feel the urgent need to give a fresh impetus and new approaches to the work of evangelization in a world in which the breaking down of frontiers and the new processes of globalization are bringing individuals and peoples even closer. This is both because of the development of the means of social communication and because of the frequency and ease with which individuals and groups can move about today. (...) The present time, in fact, calls upon the Church to embark on a new evangelization also in the vast and complex phenomenon of human mobility. This calls for an intensification of her missionary activity both in the regions where the Gospel is proclaimed for the first time and in countries with a Christian tradition. (...) The current and obvious consequences of secularization, the emergence of new sectarian movements, widespread insensitivity to the Christian faith and a marked tendency to fragmentation are obstacles to focusing on a unifying reference that would encourage the formation of 'one family of brothers and sisters in societies that are becoming ever more multiethnic and intercultural, where also people of various religions are urged to take part in dialogue, so that a serene and fruitful coexistence with respect for legitimate differences may

be found', as I wrote in my Message last year for this World Day. (...) Here the Church is faced with the challenge of helping migrants keep their faith firm even when they are deprived of the cultural support that existed in their country of origin, and of identifying new pastoral approaches, as well as methods and expressions, for an ever vital reception of the Word of God. (...) The phenomenon of migration today is also a providential opportunity for the proclamation of the Gospel in the contemporary world. Men and women from various regions of the earth who have not yet encountered Jesus Christ or know him only partially, ask to be received in countries with an ancient Christian tradition. It is necessary to find adequate ways for them to meet and to become acquainted with Jesus Christ and to experience the invaluable gift of salvation which, for everyone, is a source of 'life in abundance' (cf. *Jn* 10:10). (...) Asylum seekers, who fled from persecution, violence and situations that put their life at risk, stand in need of our understanding and welcome, of respect for their human dignity and rights, as well as awareness of their duties". [Benedict XVI, *Message for the 98th World Day of Migrants and Refugees* (21 September 2011)]

**(61)** "So it is that genuine religious belief points us beyond present utility towards the transcendent. It reminds us of the possibility and the imperative of moral conversion, of the duty to live peaceably with our neighbour, of the importance of living a life of integrity. Properly understood, it brings enlightenment, it purifies our hearts and it inspires noble and generous action, to the benefit of the entire human family. It motivates us to cultivate the practice of virtue and to reach out towards one another in love, with the greatest respect for religious traditions different from our own.

Ever since the Second Vatican Council, the Catholic Church has placed special emphasis on the importance of dialogue and cooperation with the followers of other religions. In order to be fruitful, this requires reciprocity on the part of all partners in dialogue and the followers of other religions. I am thinking in particular of situations in some parts of the world, where cooperation and dialogue between religions calls for mutual respect, the freedom to practise one's religion and to engage in acts of public worship, and the freedom to follow one's conscience without suffering ostracism or persecution, even after conversion from one religion to another". [Benedict XVI, *Address to Clerical and Lay Representatives of other Religions, Waldegrave Drawing Room, St Mary's University College, Twickenham, London* (17 September 2010)]

**(62)** "In our increasingly secularized society, where even we Christians often find it difficult to speak of the transcendent dimension of our existence, we need to find new ways to pass on to young people the beauty and richness of friendship with Jesus Christ in the communion of his Church. (...) a new vision is needed, to inspire present and future generations to treasure the gift of our common faith. By treading the path marked out by the Gospel, by observing the commandments and by conforming your lives ever more closely to the figure of Jesus Christ, you will surely experience the profound renewal that is so urgently needed at this time. I invite you all to persevere along this path". [Benedict XVI, *Pastoral Letter to the Catholics of Ireland* (19 March 2010) no. 12]

**(63)** "I am certain that the rediscovery of Jesus Christ made flesh, our savior, will lead to a rediscovery of the personal, social and cultural identity of the faithful. Far from confusing the diversity and complementarity of the charisms and functions of ordained ministers and lay faithful, a reinforced Catholic identity will revive the passion for evangelization, which is proper to the vocation of every believer and of the nature of the Church (cf. Instruction *Le prêtre, pasteur et guide de la communauté paroissiale*, 23-24)." [Benedict XVI, *Address to the Bishops of the Episcopal Conference of Canada on their Ad Limina Visit* (20 May 2006); our translation]

**(64)** "But the relationship between faith and art is equally important because truth, the aim or goal of reason, is expressed in beauty and in beauty becomes itself, is proven to be truth. Therefore, wherever there is truth beauty must be born, wherever human beings are fulfilled in a correct and good way, they express themselves in beauty. The relationship between truth and beauty is inseparable and therefore we need beauty. (...) The Church was consequently a mother to art for centuries and centuries: the great treasure of Western art – music, architecture and painting – was born from faith within the Church. Today there is a certain 'dissidence' but this is bad for both art and faith. An art that lost the root of transcendence would not be oriented to God: it would be a halved art, it would lose its living root; (...) we must do our utmost to see that today too faith is expressed in authentic art". [Benedict XVI, *Interview with the journalists during the flight to Spain* (6 November 2010)]

**(65)** "New evangelization: (...) 'new' in ways that correspond with the power of the Holy Spirit and which are suited to the times and situations; (...) The Church is an immense force for renewal in the world. This is not, of course, because of her own strength but because of the power of the Gospel in which the Holy Spirit of God breathes, God Creator and Redeemer of the world. (...) Human beings of the third millennium want an authentic, full life; they need truth, profound freedom, love freely given. Even in the deserts of the secularized world, man's soul thirsts for God, for the living God. It was for this reason that John Paul II wrote: '(...) an overall view of the human race shows that this mission is still only beginning and that we must commit ourselves wholeheartedly to its service' (Encyclical Redemptoris Mission. 1)". [Benedict XVI, *Homily at First Vespers on the*

*Solemnity of the Holy Apostles Peter and Paul, Basilica of Saint Paul Outside the Walls* (28 June 2010)]

## 10 – Give us this day our daily bread

**(66)** "Work constitutes a foundation for the formation of *family life*, which is a natural right and something that man is called to. (...) Obviously, two aspects of work in a sense come into play here: the one making family life and its upkeep possible, and the other making possible the achievement of the purposes of the family, especially education. Nevertheless, these two aspects of work are linked to one another and are mutually complementary in various points. (...) In fact, the family is simultaneously a *community made possible by work* and the first *school of work*, within the home, for every person. (...) All of this brings it about that man combines his deepest human identity with membership of a nation, and intends his work also to increase the common good developed together with his compatriots, thus realizing that in this way work serves to add to the heritage of the whole human family, of all the people living in the world". [John Paul II, Encyclical Letter *Laborem exercens* (1981) no. 10]

**(67)** "In this regard it is useful to remember that while globalization should certainly be understood as a socio-economic process, this is not its only dimension. Underneath the more visible process, humanity itself is becoming increasingly interconnected. (...) The truth of globalization as a process and its fundamental ethical criterion are given by the unity of the human family and its development towards what is good. Hence a sustained commitment is needed so as to *promote a person-based and community-oriented cultural process of world-wide integration that is open to transcendence*. Despite some of its structural elements, which should neither be denied nor exaggerated, 'globalization, *a priori*, is neither good nor bad. It will be what people make of it'. We should not be its victims, but rather its protagonists, acting in the light of reason, guided by charity and truth". [Benedict XVI, Encyclical Letter *Caritas in veritate* (2009) no. 42]

**(68)** "Dear young people, listen closely to the words of the Lord, that they may be for you 'spirit and life' (*Jn* 6:63), roots which nourish your being, a rule of life which likens us – poor in spirit, thirsting for justice, merciful, pure in heart, lovers of peace – to the person of Christ. Listen regularly every day as if he were the one friend who does not deceive, the one with whom we wish to share the path of life. Of course, you know that when we do not walk beside Christ our guide, we get lost on other paths, like the path of our blind and selfish impulses, or the path of flattering but selfserving suggestions, deceiving and fickle, which leave emptiness and frustration in their wake.

(...) If you build on solid rock, not only your life will be solid and stable, but it will also help project the light of Christ shining upon those of your own age and upon the whole of humanity, presenting a valid alternative to all those who have fallen short, because the essentials in their lives were inconsistent; to all those who are content to follow fashionable ideas, they take shelter in the here and now, forgetting true justice, or they take refuge in their own opinions instead of seeking the simple truth.

Indeed, there are many who, creating their own gods, believe they need no roots or foundations other than themselves. They take it upon themselves to decide what is true or not, what is good and evil, what is just and unjust; who should live and who can be sacrificed in the interests of other preferences; leaving each step to chance, with no clear path, letting themselves be led by the whim of each moment. These temptations are always lying in wait". [Benedict XVI, *Address at Welcome Ceremony with young people on the occasion of the XXVI World Youth Day* (18 August 2011)]

## 11 – Forgive us our trespasses

**(69)** "The divine dimension of redemption is put into effect not only by bringing justice to bear upon sin, but also by restoring to love that creative power in man thanks to which he once more has access to the fullness of life and holiness that come from God. In this way, redemption involves the revelation of mercy in its fullness. The Paschal Mystery is the culmination of this revealing and effecting of mercy, which is able to justify man, to restore justice in the sense of that salvific order which God willed from the beginning in man and, through man, in the world". [John Paul II, Encyclical Letter *Dives in misericordia* (1980) no. 7]

**(70)** "In such a situation the obscuring or weakening of the sense of sin comes from several sources: from a rejection of any reference to the transcendent in the name of the individual's aspiration to personal independence; from acceptance of ethical models imposed by general consensus and behavior, even when condemned by the individual conscience; from the tragic social and economic conditions that oppress a great part of humanity, causing a tendency to see errors and faults only in the context of society; finally and especially, from the obscuring of the notion of God's fatherhood and dominion over man's life.

Even in the field of the thought and life of the church certain trends inevitably favor the decline of the sense of sin. For example, some are inclined to replace exaggerated attitudes of the past with other exaggerations: from seeing sin everywhere they pass to not recognizing it anywhere; from too much emphasis on the fear of eternal punishment they pass to preaching a love of God that excludes any punishment deserved by sin; from severity in trying to correct erroneous consciences they pass to a kind of respect for conscience which excludes the duty of telling the truth. And should it not be added that the confusion caused in the consciences of many of the faithful by differences of opinions and teachings in theology, preaching, catechesis and spiritual direction on serious and delicate questions of Christian morals ends by diminishing the true sense of sin almost to the point of eliminating it altogether?". [John Paul II, Apostolic Exhortation *Reconciliatio et paenitentia* (1984) no. 18]

**(71)** "Pope John Paul II, taking up the prophetic words of Pope Paul VI in the Apostolic Exhortation *Evangelii Nuntiandi*, had in a variety of ways reminded the faithful of the need for a new missionary season for the entire people of God.

At the dawn of the third millennium not only are there still many peoples who have not come to know the Good News, but also a great many Christians who need to have the word of God once more persuasively proclaimed to them, so that they can concretely experience the power of the Gospel. Many of our brothers and sisters are 'baptized, but insufficiently evangelized'. In a number of cases, nations once rich in faith and in vocations are losing their identity under the influence of a secularized culture. The need for a new evangelization, so deeply felt by my venerable Predecessor, must be valiantly reaffirmed, in the certainty that God's word is effective. The Church, sure of her Lord's fidelity, never tires of proclaiming the good news of the Gospel and invites all Christians to discover anew the attraction of following Christ". [Benedict XVI, Apostolic Exhortation *Verbum Domini* (2010) no. 96]

**(72)** "As the steward of the *Sacrament of Reconciliation*, the priest fulfills the command given by Christ to the Apostles after his Resurrection: 'Receive the Holy Spirit. If you forgive the sins of any, they are forgiven; if you retain the sins of any, they are retained' (Jn 20:22-23). The priest is the witness and instrument of divine mercy! How important in his life is the ministry of the confessional! It is in the confessional that *his spiritual fatherhood* is realized in the fullest way. It is in the confessional that every priest becomes a witness of the great miracles which divine mercy works in souls which receive the grace of conversion. It is necessary, however, that every priest at the service of his brothers and sisters in the confessional should experience this same divine mercy by going regularly to confession himself and by receiving spiritual direction. As a steward of God's mysteries, the priest is a special *witness to the Invisible* in the world". [John Paul II, *Gift and Mystery*, Doubleday, New York 1996, pp. 86-87]

**(73)** "And so the bridegroom is one with the Father and one with the bride. Whatever he found in his bride alien to her own nature he took from her and nailed to his cross when he bore her sins and destroyed them on the tree. He received from her and clothed himself in what was hers by nature and gave her what belonged to him as God. He destroyed what was diabolical, took to himself what was human, and conferred on her what was divine. (...) The Church is incapable of forgiving any sin without Christ, and Christ is unwilling to forgive any sin without the Church. The Church cannot forgive the sin of one who has not repented, who has not been touched by Christ; Christ will not forgive the sin of one who despises the Church. *What God has joined together, man must not separate. This is a great mystery, but I understand it as referring to Christ and the Church* [Mt. 19:6; Ep. 5:32]. Do not destroy the whole Christ by separating head from body, for Christ is not complete without the Church, nor is the Church complete without Christ". [Blessed Isaac of Stella, Abbot (1100 ca. – 1169), *Sermon 11, Liturgy of the Hours, Office of Readings, Friday, 23rd week, Ordinary Time* (http://www.liturgies.net/Liturgies/Catholic/loh/week23fridayor.htm, accessed in July 2014)]

**(74)** "Peter calls Jesus the 'chief Shepherd' (1 Pt. 5:4) because his work and mission continue in the Church through the apostles (cf. Jn. 21:15-17) and their successors (cf. 1 Pt. 5:1ff.), and through priests. By virtue of their consecration, priests are configured to Jesus the good shepherd and are called to imitate and to live out his own pastoral charity (...).

Jesus is the true bridegroom who offers to the Church the wine of salvation (cf. Jn. 2:11). He who is 'the head of the Church, his body, and is himself its savior' (Eph. 5:23), 'loved the Church and gave himself up for her, that he might sanctify her, having cleansed her by the washing of water with the word, that he might present the Church to himself in splendor, without spot or wrinkle or any such thing, that she might be holy and without blemish' (Eph. 5:25-27). The Church is indeed the body in which Christ the head is present and active, but she is also the bride who proceeds like a new Eve from the open side of the redeemer on the cross.

Hence Christ stands 'before' the Church and 'nourishes and cherishes her' (Eph. 5 :29), giving his life for her. The priest is called to be the living image of Jesus Christ, the spouse of the Church. Of course, he will always remain a member of the community as a believer alongside his other brothers and sisters who have been called by the Spirit, but in virtue of his configuration to Christ, the head and shepherd, the priest stands in this spousal relationship with regard to the community. 'Inasmuch as he represents Christ, the head, shepherd and spouse of the Church, the priest is placed not only in the Church but also in the forefront of the Church'. In his spiritual life, therefore, he is called to live out Christ's spousal love toward the Church, his bride. Therefore, the priest's life ought to radiate this spousal character, which demands that he be a witness to Christ's spousal love and thus be capable of loving people with a heart which is new, generous and pure - with genuine self - detachment, with full, constant and faithful dedication and at the same time with a kind of 'divine jealousy' (cf. 2 Cor. 11:2) and even with a kind of maternal tenderness, capable of bearing 'the pangs of birth' until 'Christ be formed' in the faithful (cf. Gal. 4:19)". [John Paul II, Apostolic Exhortation *Pastores dabo vobis* (1992) no. 22].

**(75)** "God does not fail to call men and women to his service. We must be grateful to the Lord for this, intensifying our prayers that he may continue to send workers to his harvest (cf. Mt 9: 37). A primary task of Bishops is the pastoral care of vocations and the human, spiritual and intellectual formation of candidates to the priesthood in seminaries and other formative institutes (cf. *Optatam Totius*, nn. 2,4). This formation must guarantee them the possibility of acquiring deep spirituality and rigorous philosophical, theological and pastoral preparation, also through the careful choice of educators and lecturers". [Benedict XVI, *Address to the Bishops of Episcopal Conference of Romania on their Ad Limina Visit* (12 February 2010)]

**(76)** "All priests should dedicate themselves with generosity, commitment and competency to administering the sacrament of Reconciliation. In this regard, it is important that the confessionals in our churches should be clearly visible expressions of the importance of this sacrament. I ask pastors to be vigilant with regard to the celebration of the sacrament of Reconciliation, and to limit the practice of general absolution exclusively to the cases permitted, since individual absolution is the only form intended for ordinary use. Given the need to rediscover sacramental forgiveness, there ought to be a *Penitentiary* in every Diocese. Finally, a balanced and sound practice of gaining *indulgences*, whether for oneself or for the dead, can be helpful for a renewed appreciation of the relationship between the Eucharist and Reconciliation. By this means the faithful obtain 'remission before God of the temporal punishment due to sins whose guilt has already been forgiven'". [Benedict XVI, Apostolic Exhortation *Sacramentum caritatis* (2007) no. 21]

**(77)** "We know that the faithful are surrounded by a culture that tends to eliminate the sense of sin and to promote a superficial approach that overlooks the need to be in a state of grace in order to approach sacramental communion worthily. The loss of a consciousness of sin always entails a certain superficiality in the understanding of God's love". [Benedict XVI, Apostolic Exhortation *Sacramentum caritatis* (2007) no. 20]

## 12 – As we forgive those who trespass against us

**(78)** "*As we ask forgiveness, let us also forgive.* This is what we say every day when we recite the prayer Jesus taught us: 'Our Father... forgive us our trespasses as we forgive those who trespass against us' (*Mt* 6:12). (...)

*Reconciliation* springs from forgiveness. This is our hope for every Ecclesial Community, for all believers in Christ and for the whole world.

Forgiven and ready to forgive, Christians enter the third millennium as *more credible witnesses to hope*. After centuries marked by violence and destruction, especially the last tragic one, the Church offers humanity, as it crosses the threshold of the third millennium, the Gospel of forgiveness and reconciliation, a prerequisite for building genuine peace". [John Paul II, *Angelus* (12 March 2000)]

**(79)** "Thus, mercy becomes an indispensable element for shaping mutual relationships between people, in a spirit of deepest respect for what is human, and in a spirit of mutual brotherhood. It is impossible to establish this bond between people, if they wish to regulate their mutual relationships solely according to the measure of justice. (...) Consequently, merciful love is supremely indispensable between those who are closest to one another: between husbands and wives, between parents and children, between friends; and it is indispensable in education and in pastoral work. (...) Society can become 'ever more human' only when we introduce into all the mutual relationships which form its moral aspect the moment of forgiveness, which is so much of the essence of the Gospel. Forgiveness demonstrates the presence in the world of the love which is more powerful than sin. Forgiveness is also the fundamental condition for reconciliation, not only in the relationship of God with man, but also in relationships between people. (...) For this reason, the Church must consider it one of her principal duties – at every stage of history and especially in our modern age – to proclaim and to introduce into life the mystery of mercy, supremely revealed in Jesus Christ. Not only for the Church herself as the community of believers but also in a certain sense for all humanity, this mystery is the source of a life different from the life which can be built by man, who is exposed to the oppressive forces of the threefold concupiscence active within him". [John Paul II, Encyclical Letter *Dives in misericordia* (1980) no. 14]

**(80)** "Man is called to a fullness of life which far exceeds the dimensions of his earthly existence, because it consists in sharing the very life of God. (...) At the same time, it is precisely this supernatural calling which highlights the relative character of each individual's earthly life. After all, life on earth is not an 'ultimate' but a 'penultimate' reality; even so, it remains a sacred reality entrusted to us, to be preserved with a sense of responsibility and brought to perfection in love and in the gift of ourselves to God and to our brothers and sisters.

The Church knows that this Gospel of life, which she has received from her Lord, has a profound and persuasive echo in the heart of every person – believer and non-believer alike – because it marvellously fulfils all the heart's expectations while infinitely surpassing them. Even in the midst of difficulties and uncertainties, every person sincerely open to truth and goodness can, by the light of reason and the hidden action of grace, come to recognize in the natural law written in the heart (cf. Rom 2:14-15) the sacred value of human life from its very beginning until its end, and can affirm the right of every human being to have this primary good respected to the highest degree. Upon the recognition of this right, every human community and the political community itself are founded.

In a special way, believers in Christ must defend and promote this right, aware as they are of the wonderful truth recalled by the Second Vatican Council: 'By his incarnation the Son of God has united himself in some fashion with every human being'. This saving event reveals to humanity not only the boundless love of God who 'so loved the world that he gave his only Son' (Jn 3:16), but also the incomparable value of every human person. (...) The Gospel of God's love for man, the Gospel of the dignity of the person and the Gospel of life are a single and indivisible Gospel". [John Paul II, Encyclical Letter *Evangelium vitae* (1995) no. 2]

**(81)** "God is infinite mercy, always, ready to forgive and to restore the sinner to righteousness. (...) It was as if Christ had wanted to reveal that the limit imposed upon evil, of which man is both perpetrator and victim, is ultimately Divine Mercy. Of course, there is also justice, but this alone does not have the last word in the divine economy of world history and human history. God can always draw good from evil, he wills that all should be saved and come to knowledge of the truth (cf. 1 Tim 2:4): God is Love (cf. 1 Jn 4:8). Christ, crucified and risen, just as he appeared to Sister Faustina, is the supreme revelation of this truth. (...) It was as if Christ had wanted to say through her: "Evil does not have the last word!" The Paschal Mystery confirms that good is ultimately victorious, that life conquers death and that love triumphs over hate". [John Paul II, *Memory and Identity*, Rizzoli International Publications, Inc., New York 2005, pp. 54-55]

**(82)** "The Church Appeals to the Mercy of God. (...) The more the human conscience succumbs to secularization, loses its sense of the very meaning of the word 'mercy', moves away from God and distances itself from the mystery of mercy, the more the Church has the right and the duty to appeal to the God of mercy 'with loud cries'. (...) Let us have recourse to God through Christ, mindful of the words of Mary's Magnificat, which proclaim mercy 'from generation to generation'. Let us implore God's mercy for the present generation. (...) This is, therefore, love of God, the insulting rejection of whom by modern man we feel profoundly, and we are ready to cry out with Christ on the cross: 'Father, forgive them; for they know not what they do'. At the same time it is love of people, of all men and women without any exception or division: without difference of race, culture, language, or world outlook, without distinction between friends and enemies. This is love for people – it desires every true good for each individual and for every human community, every family, every nation, every social group, for young people, adults, parents, the elderly – a love for everyone, without exception. This is love, or rather an anxious solicitude to ensure for each individual every true good and to remove and drive away every sort of evil". [John Paul II, Encyclical Letter *Dives in misericordia* (1980) no. 15]

## 13 – And lead us not into temptation (I)

**(83)** "According to Christian faith and the Church's teaching, 'only the freedom which submits to the Truth leads the human person to his true good. The good of the person is to be in the Truth and to *do* the Truth'.

A comparison between the Church's teaching and today's social and cultural situation immediately makes clear the urgent need *for the Church herself to develop an intense pastoral effort precisely with regard to this fundamental question*. This essential bond between Truth, the Good and Freedom has been largely lost sight of by present-day culture. As a result, helping man to rediscover it represents nowadays one of the specific requirements of the Church's mission, for the salvation of the world. Pilate's question: 'What is truth' reflects the distressing perplexity of a man who often no longer knows *who he is, whence* he comes and *where* he is going.

Hence we not infrequently witness the fearful plunging of the human person into situations of gradual self-destruction". [John Paul II, Encyclical Letter *Veritatis splendor* (1993) no. 84]

## 14 – And lead us not into temptation (II)

**(84)** "The evangelization of culture is all the more important in our times, when a 'dictatorship of relativism' threatens to obscure the unchanging truth about man's nature, his destiny and his ultimate good. There are some who now seek to exclude religious belief from public discourse, to privatize it or even to paint it as a threat to equality and liberty. Yet religion is in fact a guarantee of authentic liberty and respect, leading us to look upon every person as a brother or sister. For this reason I appeal in particular to you, the lay faithful, in accordance with your baptismal calling and mission, not only to be examples of faith in public, but also to put the case for the promotion of faith's wisdom and vision in the public forum. Society today needs clear voices which propose our right to live, not in a jungle of self-destructive and arbitrary freedoms, but in a society which works for the true welfare of its citizens and offers them guidance and protection in the face of their weakness and fragility. (...) Let the exhortation of Saint Paul in the first reading be your constant inspiration: 'Do not lag in zeal, be ardent in spirit, serve the Lord. Rejoice in hope, be patient in suffering and persevere in prayer' (cf. Rom 12:11-12)". [Benedict XVI, *Homily at Holy Mass, Bellahouston Park, Glasgow* (16 September 2010)]

**(85)** "The common practice today is to measure the Bible against the so-called modern worldview, whose fundamental dogma is that God cannot act in history – that everything to do with God is to be relegated to the domain of subjectivity. And so the Bible no longer speaks of God, the living God; no, now *we* alone speak and decide what God can do and what we will and should do. And the Antichrist, with an air of scholarly excellence, tells us that any exegesis that reads the Bible from the perspective of faith in the living God, in order to listen to what God has to say, is fundamentalism; he wants to convince us that only *his* kind of exegesis, the supposedly purely scientific kind, in which God says nothing and has nothing to say, is able to keep abreast of the times". [Benedict XVI, *Jesus of Nazareth*, Doubleday, New York 2007, pp. 35-36]

**(86)** "Yet another side of the 'lordship of God' (Kingdom) comes to light when Jesus makes the enigmatic statement that 'the kingdom of heaven has suffered violence, and men of violence take it by force' (Mt 11:12). It is methodologically illegitimate to admit only one aspect of the whole as attributable to Jesus and then, on the basis of such an arbitrary claim, to bend everything else until it fits. Instead we should say: The reality that Jesus names the 'Kingdom of God, lordship of God' is extremely complex, and only by accepting it in its entirety can we gain access to, and let ourselves be guided by, his message". [Benedict XVI, *Jesus of Nazareth*, Doubleday, New York 2007, p. 59]

**(87)** "But let us return to the third temptation. Its true content becomes apparent when we realize that throughout history it is constantly taking on new forms. The Christian empire attempted at an early stage to use the faith in order to cement political unity. The Kingdom of Christ was now expected to take the form of a political kingdom and its splendor. The powerlessness of faith, the earthly powerlessness of Jesus Christ, was to be given the helping hand of political and military might. This temptation to use power to secure the faith has arisen again and again in varied forms throughout the centuries, and again and again faith has risked being suffocated in the embrace of power. The struggle for the freedom of the Church, the struggle to avoid identifying Jesus' Kingdom with any political structure, is one that has to be fought century after century. (...) The tempter is not so crude as to suggest to us directly that we should worship the devil. He merely suggests that we opt for the reasonable decision, that we choose to give priority to a planned and thoroughly organized world, where God may have his place as a private concern but must not interfere in our essential purposes. Soloviev attributes to the Antichrist a book entitled *The Open Way to World Peace and Welfare*. This book becomes something of a new Bible, whose real message is the worship of well-being and rational planning.

(...) The Christian empire or the secular power of the papacy is no longer a temptation today, but the interpretation of Christianity as a recipe for progress and the proclamation of universal prosperity as the real goal of all religions, including Christianity – this is the modern form of the same temptation. (...) No kingdom of this world is the Kingdom of God, the total condition of mankind's salvation. Earthly kingdoms remain earthly human kingdoms, and anyone who claims to be able to establish the perfect world is the willing dupe of Satan and plays the world right into his hands". [Benedict XVI, *Jesus of Nazareth*, Doubleday, New York 2007, pp. 39-44]

## 15 – But deliver us from evil (I)

**(88)** "John Paul II, continuing the constant teaching of the Church, has reiterated many times that those who are directly involved in lawmaking bodies have a *'grave and clear obligation to oppose'* any law that attacks human life. For them, as for every Catholic, it is impossible to promote such laws or to vote for them. (...)

When political activity comes up against moral principles that do not admit of exception, compromise or derogation, the Catholic commitment becomes more evident and laden with responsibility. In the face of *fundamental and inalienable ethical demands,* Christians must recognize that what is at stake is the essence of the moral law, which concerns the integral good of the human person. This is the case with laws concerning *abortion* and *euthanasia* (not to be confused with the decision to forgo *extraordinary treatments,* which is morally legitimate). Such laws must defend the basic right to life from conception to natural death. In the same way, it is necessary to recall the duty to respect and protect the rights of the *human embryo.* Analogously, the *family* needs to be safeguarded and promoted, based on monogamous marriage between a man and a woman, and protected in its unity and stability in the face of modern laws on divorce: in no way can other forms of cohabitation be placed on the same level as marriage, nor can they receive legal recognition as such. The same is true for the freedom of parents regarding the *education* of their children; it is an inalienable right recognized also by the Universal Declaration on Human Rights. In the same way, one must consider *society's protection of minors* and freedom from *modern forms of slavery* (drug abuse and prostitution, for example). In addition, there is the right to *religious freedom* and the development of an *economy* that is at the service of the human person and of the common good, with respect for social justice, the principles of human solidarity and subsidiarity, according to which 'the rights of all individuals, families, and organizations and their practical implementation must be acknowledged'. Finally, the question of *peace* must be mentioned. Certain pacifistic and ideological visions tend at times to secularize the value of peace, while, in other cases, there is the problem of summary ethical judgments which forget the complexity of the issues involved. Peace is always 'the work of justice and the effect of charity'. It demands the absolute and radical rejection of violence and terrorism and requires a constant and vigilant commitment on the part of all political leaders". [*Congregation for the doctrine of the Faith, Doctrinal Note on some questions regarding the participation of Catholics in Political Life* (24 November 2002) no. 4]

**(89)** "If, on the one hand, the West continues to provide evidence of zealous evangelization, on the other hand anti-evangelical currents are equally strong. They strike at the very foundations of human morality, influencing the family and promoting a morally permissive outlook: divorce, free love, abortion, contraception, the fight against life in its initial phases and in its final phase, the manipulation of life. This program is supported by enormous financial resources, not only in individual countries, but also on a worldwide scale. It has great centers of economic power at its disposal, through which it attempts to impose its own conditions on developing countries. Faced with all this, one may legitimately ask whether this is not another form of totalitarianism, subtly concealed under the appearances of democracy". [John Paul II, *Memory and Identity*, Rizzoli International Publications, Inc., New York 2005, p. 48]

**(90)** "There exists something that is 'naturally' right, thanks to the compass provided by the creation, something that makes possible an international law that transcends the boundaries of those laws that are promulgated by individual states. There exists something that is naturally right, antecedent to our legislation, and hence it is simply impossible for *everything* that occurs to men to be 'right'. It is possible for laws to exist that are indeed valid legal statutes but are in fact injustice rather than 'justice'. Since it is God's creation, nature itself is a source of law. It indicates boundaries that must not be transgressed. The immediate relevance of this question is obvious: where the killing of innocent life is declared to be a 'right', injustice is made a law. Where the rule of law no longer protects human life, it is questionable whether it deserves the name of law. In saying this, I do not intend to impose a specifically Christian morality on all the citizens in a pluralistic society; no, what is involved here is *humanitas*, the 'specifically human quality' of man, who cannot declare the trampling underfoot of creation to be his own liberation without deceiving himself on a very profound level. (...) Is man free only once he has unchained himself from the creation and left it behind, as something that enslaved him? Or does he not thereby deny his own self?". [Joseph Ratzinger, *The God of Jesus Christ. Meditations on the triune God*, Ignatius Press, San Francisco, 2008, p. 23]

**(91)** "A positivist conception of nature as purely functional, as the natural sciences consider it to be, is incapable of producing any bridge to ethics and law, but once again yields only functional answers. (...) The positivist approach to nature and reason, the positivist world view in general, is a most important dimension of human knowledge and capacity that we may in no way dispense with. But in and of itself it is not a sufficient culture corresponding to the full breadth of the human condition. Where positivist reason considers itself the only sufficient culture and banishes all other cultural realities to the status of subcultures, it diminishes man, indeed it threatens his humanity.

(...) Man too has a nature that he must respect and that he cannot manipulate at will. Man is not merely self-creating freedom.

Man does not create himself. He is intellect and will, but he is also nature, and his will is rightly ordered if he respects his nature, listens to it and accepts himself for who he is, as one who did not create himself. In this way, and in no other, is true human freedom fulfilled. (...) The conviction that there is a Creator God is what gave rise to the idea of human rights, the idea of the equality of all people before the law, the recognition of the inviolability of human dignity in every single person and the awareness of people's responsibility for their actions. Our cultural memory is shaped by these rational insights. To ignore it or dismiss it as a thing of the past would be to dismember our culture totally and to rob it of its completeness". [Benedict XVI, *Address to the Federal Parliament in the Reichstag Building, Berlin* (22 September 2011)]

**(92)** "It is at the heart of the moral conscience that the eclipse of the sense of God and of man, with all its various and deadly consequences for life, is taking place. It is a question, above all, of the individual conscience, as it stands before God in its singleness and uniqueness. But it is also a question, in a certain sense, of the 'moral conscience' of society: in a way it too is responsible, not only because it tolerates or fosters behaviour contrary to life, but also because it encourages the 'culture of death', creating and consolidating actual 'structures of sin' which go against life. The moral conscience, both individual and social, is today subjected, also as a result of the penetrating influence of the media, to an extremely serious and mortal danger: that of confusion between good and evil, precisely in relation to the fundamental right to life. A large part of contemporary society looks sadly like that humanity which Paul describes in his Letter to the Romans. It is composed 'of men who by their wickedness suppress the truth' (1:18): having denied God and believing that they can build the earthly city without him, 'they became futile in their thinking' so that 'their senseless minds were darkened' (1:21); 'claiming to be wise, they became fools' (1:22), carrying out works deserving of death, and 'they not only do them but approve those who practise them' (1:32). When conscience, this bright lamp of the soul (cf. Mt 6:22-23), calls 'evil good and good evil' (Is

5:20), it is already on the path to the most alarming corruption and the darkest moral blindness". [John Paul II, Encyclical Letter *Evangelium vitae* (1995) no. 24]

**(93)** "(...) 'blasphemy' does not properly consist in offending against the Holy Spirit in words; it consists rather in the refusal to accept the salvation which God offers to man through the Holy Spirit, working through the power of the Cross. (...) We know that the result of such a purification is the forgiveness of sins. Therefore, whoever rejects the Spirit and the Blood remains in 'dead works', in sin. And the blasphemy against the Holy Spirit consists precisely in the radical refusal to accept this forgiveness, of which he is the intimate giver and which presupposes the genuine conversion which he brings about in the conscience. If Jesus says that blasphemy against the Holy Spirit cannot be forgiven either in this life or in the next, it is because this 'non-forgiveness' is linked, as to its cause, to 'non-repentance', in other words to the radical refusal to be converted.

(...) Blasphemy against the Holy Spirit, then, is the sin committed by the person who claims to have a 'right' to persist in evil – in any sin at all – and who thus rejects Redemption. One closes oneself up in sin, thus making impossible one's conversion, and consequently the remission of sins". [John Paul II, Encyclical Letter *Dominum et vivificantem* (1986) no. 46]

## 16 – But deliver us from evil (II)

**(94)** "Jesus' death is of a different kind. It is not the carrying out of a verdict that casts man back into the earth; rather, it is the action of a love that will not leave the others bereft of word, bereft of meaning, bereft of eternity. Jesus' death is to be understood, not in the context of the judicial sentence that expelled man from paradise, but rather in the light of the Songs of the Suffering Servant. Since his death takes place in the spirit of these words, it becomes a light for the peoples, a death in the context of his service of expiation, which desires to bring about reconciliation. And this means that his death puts an end to death". [Joseph Ratzinger, *The God of Jesus Christ. Meditations on the triune God,* Ignatius Press, San Francisco 2008, p.45]

**(95)** "The crisis of hope is more likely to affect the younger generations. In socio-cultural environments with few certainties, values or firm points of reference, they find themselves facing difficulties that seem beyond their strength. My dear young friends, I have in mind so many of your contemporaries who have been wounded by life. They often suffer from personal immaturity caused by dysfunctional family situations, by permissive and libertarian elements in their education, and by difficult and traumatic experience. For some – unfortunately a significant number – the

314

almost unavoidable way out involves an alienating escape into dangerous and violent behaviour, dependence on drugs and alcohol, and many other such traps for the unwary. Yet, even for those who find themselves in difficult situations, having been led astray by bad role models, the desire for true love and authentic happiness is not extinguished". [Benedict XVI, *Message on the occasion of the XXIV World Youth Day* (22 February 2009)]

**(96)** "For many people, especially the young, the city becomes an experience of rootlessness, anonymity and inequality, with the consequent loss of identity and sense of human dignity. The result is often the violence that now marks so many of the large cities (...): the city promises so much and delivers so little to so many. This sense of disappointment is also linked to *a loss of confidence in institutions* – political, legal and educational institutions, but also the Church and the family. (...) it becomes *a profoundly secular world*, a one-dimensional world which to many people can appear like a prison. In this 'city of man', we are called to build 'the city of God'. (...) there must be instead a new missionary outreach in the cities, with dedicated men and women, and young people, going forth in Christ's name to invite people into the community of the Church. (...) This will depend in large part upon the energy and dedication of *urban lay missionaries*, but they in turn will need the service of truly zealous priests who are themselves fired with the missionary spirit and who know how to kindle that spirit in others. It is vital that *seminaries and houses of formation be seen clearly as schools for mission* which train priests who can inspire the faithful to become the new evangelizers whom the Church now needs. (...) Not only the parishes, but also *Catholic schools and other institutions must be open to the pastoral imperative of evangelizing the city*". [John Paul II, *Address to the Bishops of the Episcopal Conference of Ontario (Canada) on their Ad Limina Visit* (4 May 1999)]

**(97)** "In this sense it is true that anyone who does not know God, even though he may entertain all kinds of hopes, is ultimately without hope, without the great hope that sustains the whole of life (cf. *Eph* 2:12). Man's great, true hope which holds firm in spite of all disappointments can only be God – God who has loved us and who continues to love us 'to the end', until all 'is accomplished' (cf. *Jn* 13:1 and 19:30). Whoever is moved by love begins to perceive what 'life' really is.

(...) Jesus, who said that he had come so that we might have life and have it in its fullness, in abundance (cf. *Jn* 10:10), has also explained to us what 'life' means: 'this is eternal life, that they know you the only true God, and Jesus Christ whom you have sent' (*Jn* 17:3). (...) If we are in relation with him who does not die, who is Life itself and Love itself, then we are in life. Then we 'live'. (...) Let us say once again: we need the greater and lesser hopes that keep us going day by day. But these are not enough without the great hope, which must surpass everything else. This great hope can only be God, who encompasses the whole of reality and who can bestow upon us what we, by ourselves, cannot attain. (...) God is the foundation of hope: not any god, but the God who has a human face and who has loved us to the end, each one of us and humanity in its entirety. His Kingdom is not an imaginary hereafter, situated in a future that will never arrive; his Kingdom is present wherever he is loved and wherever his love reaches us". [Benedict XVI, Encyclical Letter *Spe salvi* (2007) no. 27; no. 31]

## 17 – Betrayal

**(98)** "Precisely through this service man becomes in an ever new manner the 'way of the Church', as I said in the Encyclical on Christ the Redeemer and as I now repeat in this present one on the Holy Spirit. United with the Spirit, the Church is supremely aware of the reality of the inner man, of what is deepest and most essential in man, because it is spiritual and incorruptible. At this level the Spirit grafts the 'root of immortality', from which the new life springs. This is man's life in God, which, as a fruit of God's salvific self-communication in the Holy Spirit, can develop and flourish only by the Spirit's action. (...) Through the gift of grace, which comes from the Holy Spirit, man enters a 'new life', is brought into the supernatural reality of the divine life itself and becomes a 'dwelling-place of the Holy Spirit', a 'living temple of God'. For through the Holy Spirit, the Father and the Son come to him and take up their abode with him". [John Paul II, Encyclical Letter *Dominum et vivificantem* (1986) no. 58]

# Bibliography

## BIBLE

Scripture texts in this work are taken from the *New American Bible, revised edition*© 2010, 1991, 1986, 1970, Confraternity of Christian Doctrine, Washington, D.C.

## DOCUMENTS OF THE MAGISTERIUM

Magisterium texts in this work are taken from the Vatican institutional site www.vatican.va (© LIBRERIA EDITRICE VATICANA).

- CATECHISM OF THE CATHOLIC CHURCH.
- CATECHISM OF THE CATHOLIC CHURCH, *Compendium*.
- CONGREGATION FOR THE DOCTRINE OF THE FAITH, *Doctrinal Note on some questions regarding the commitment and participation of Catholics in political life*, 2002.
- PONTIFICAL COUNCIL FOR CULTURE, *Jesus Christ the Bearer of the Water of Life. A Christian reflection on the "New Age"*, 2003.
- PONTIFICAL COUNCIL FOR JUSTICE AND PEACE, *Compendium of the Social Doctrine of the Church*, 2004.
- PONTIFICIAL COMMITTEE FOR INTERNATIONAL EUCHARISTIC CONGRESSES, *The Eucharist: God's gift for the life of the world. Foundational theological document for the 49th International Eucharistic Congress of Quebec*, 2008.
- VATICAN COUNCIL II, Dogmatic Constitution on the Church *Lumen Gentium*, 1964.
- VATICAN COUNCIL II, Dogmatic Constitution on Divine Revelation *Dei Verbum*, 1965.
- VATICAN COUNCIL II, Declaration on Christian Education *Gravissimum educationis*, 1965.
- VATICAN COUNCIL II, Pastoral Constitution on the Church in the Modern World *Gaudium et spes*, 1965.

## Encyclical Letters

- BENEDICT XVI, *Deus caritas est*, 2005.
- BENEDICT XVI, *Spe salvi*, 2007.
- BENEDICT XVI, *Caritas in veritate*, 2009.
- JOHN PAUL II, *Redemptor hominis*, 1979.
- JOHN PAUL II, *Dives in misericordia*, 1980.
- JOHN PAUL II, *Laborem exercens*, 1981.
- JOHN PAUL II, *Dominum et vivificantem*, 1986.
- JOHN PAUL II, *Redemptoris Mater*, 1987.
- JOHN PAUL II, *Veritatis splendor*, 1993.
- JOHN PAUL II, *Evangelium vitae*, 1995.

## Apostolic Exhortations

- BENEDICT XVI, *Sacramentum caritatis*, 2007.
- BENEDICT XVI,*Verbum Domini*, 2010.
- BENEDICT XVI, *Africae Munus*, 2011.
- JOHN PAUL II, *Familiaris Consortio*, 1981.
- JOHNPAUL II, *Reconciliatio et paenitentia*, 1984.
- JOHN PAUL II, *Redemptoris custos*, 1989.
- JOHN PAUL II, *Pastores dabo vobis*, 1992.

## Apostolic Letters

- JOHN PAUL II, *Mulieris dignitatem*, 1988.
- JOHN PAUL II, *Tertio millennio adveniente*, 1994.

## Letters

- BENEDICT XVI, *Letter to the Bishops, Priests, Consecrated Persons and Lay Faithful of the Catholic Church in the People's Republic of China*, 2007.
- BENEDICT XVI, *Letter to the Faithful of the Diocese and City of Rome on the Urgent Task of Educating Young People*, 2008.
- BENEDICT XVI, *Letter to the President of the Pontifical Council for the Family on the occasion of the Seventh World Meeting of Families*, 2010.
- BENEDICT XVI, *Letter to the Catholics of Ireland*, 2010.
- JOHN PAUL II, Letter to Families *Gratissimam sane*, 1994.

## Messages

- BENEDICT XVI, *Message for the XLII World Communications Day*, 2008.
- BENEDICT XVI, *Message for the XXIV World Youth Day*, 2009.
- BENEDICT XVI, *Message for the Celebration of the XLIV World Day of Peace*, 2010.
- BENEDICT XVI, *Message for the Celebration of the XLV World Day of Peace*, 2011.
- BENEDICT XVI, *Message for the 98th World Day of Migrants and Refugees*, 2011.
- BENEDICT XVI, *Urbi et Orbi Message*, 2011.
- JOHN PAUL II, *Message to the Participants in the Plenary of the Pontifical Academy of Sciences*, 1996.
- JOHN PAUL II, *Message for the Celebration of the XXXV World Day of Peace*, 2001.

## Audiences

- BENEDICT XVI, *General Audience*, 3 February 2010.
- JOHN PAUL II, *General Audience*, 13 August 1986.
- PAUL VI, *General Audience*, 15 November 1972.
- PAUL VI, *General Audience*, 23 February 1977.

## Angelus

- BENEDICT XVI, *Angelus*, 18 February 2007.
- BENEDICT XVI, *Angelus at Cuatro Vientos Airport. Apostolic Journey to Madrid on occasion of XXVI World Youth Day*, 21 August 2011.
- JOHN PAUL II, *Angelus*, 12 March 2000.

## Prayers

- JOHN PAUL II, *Universal Prayer with Confession of sins and request for forgiveness during Eucharistic Celebration for the First Sunday of Lent, Day of Pardon*, 12 March 2000.

## Homilies

- BENEDICT XVI, *Homily during Pastoral Visit to the Roman Parish Church of "Santa Felicita e Figli Martiri"*, 25 March 2007.

- BENEDICT XVI, *Homily Solemnity of the Sacred Body and Blood of Christ*, 22 May 2008.
- BENEDICT XVI, *Homily at Holy Mass Notre Dame, Esplanade des Invalides, Paris. Apostolic Journey to France on the occasion of the 150th Anniversary of The Apparitions of the Blessed Virgin Mary at Lourdes*, 13 September 2008.
- BENEDICT XVI, *Homily at Holy Mass for the Priestly Ordination of the Deacons of the Diocese of Rome*, 20 June 2010.
- BENEDICT XVI, *Homily at First Vespers of the Solemnity of the Holy Apostles Peter and Paul in Basilica of Saint Paul Outside the Walls*, 28 June 2010.
- BENEDICT XVI, *Homily at Holy Mass in Bellahouston Park, Glasgow. Apostolic Journey to the United Kingdom*, 16 September 2010.
- BENEDICT XVI, *Homily at Eucharistic Celebration on the occasion of the Compostelian Jubilee Year at Plaza del Obradoiro at Santiago de Compostela*, 6 November 2010.
- BENEDICT XVI, *Homily at Holy Mass with dedication of the Church of the Sagrada Familia and of the Altar. Apostolic Journey to Santiago de Compostela and Barcelona*, 7 November 2010.
- BENEDICT XVI, *Homily at Chrism Mass*, 21 April 2011.
- BENEDICT XVI, *Homily at Holy Mass on the occasion of the National Day of Croatian Catholic Families in Zagreb Hippodrome. Apostolic Journey to Croatia*, 5 June 2011.
- BENEDICT XVI, *Homily Holy Mass at conclusion of XXV Italian National Eucharistic Congress in Ancona*, 11 September 2011.
- BENEDICT XVI, *Homily at Holy Mass in the Olympic Stadium, Berlin. Apostolic Journey to Germany*, 22 September 2011.
- JOHN PAUL II, *Homily Holy Mass at Le Bourget. Pastoral visit to Paris and Lisieux*, 1 June 1980.
- PAUL VI, *Homily Holy Mass for the conclusion of the Year of Faith*, 30 June 1968.

**Addresses and interviews**

- BENEDICT XVI, *Address at Papal Welcoming Ceremony on the Poller Rheinwiesen bank in Cologne on the occasion of XX World Youth Day*, 18 August 2005.
- BENEDICT XVI, *Address to Bishops of the Episcopal Conference of Atlantic Canada on their Ad Limina Visit*, 20 May 2006.
- BENEDICT XVI, *Address at Meeting with the Members of the General Assembly of the United Nations Organization, New York. Apostolic Journey to the United States of America*, 18 April 2008.

- BENEDICT XVI, *Address at prayer vigil with the young in front of Notre-Dame Cathedral, Paris. Apostolic Journey to France on the occasion of the 150th Anniversary of the Apparitions of the Blessed Virgin Mary at Lourdes,* 12 September 2008.
- BENEDICT XVI, *Address at Meeting with the Bishops of Cameroon at Christ-Roi Church in Tsinga, Yaounde. Apostolic Journey to Cameroon and Angola,* 18 March 2009.
- BENEDICT XVI, *Address at Meeting with the Bishops of Angola and Sao Tome. Apostolic Journey to Cameroon and Angola,* 20 March 2009.
- BENEDICT XVI, *Address to the Catholic religion teachers,* 25 April 2009.
- BENEDICT XVI, *Address to the Bishops of the Episcopal Conference of Romania on their Ad Limina Visit,* 12 February 2010.
- BENEDICT XVI, *Interview with journalists during the flight to Portugal. Apostolic Journey to Portugal,* May 11, 2010.
- BENEDICT XVI, *Address at Meeting with Clerical and Lay Representatives of other Religions in the Waldegrave Drawing Room of St Mary's University College in Twickenham, London. Apostolic Journey to the United Kingdom,* 17 September 2010.
- BENEDICT XVI, *Interview with journalists during the flight to Spain. Apostolic Journey to Santiago de Compostela and Barcelona,* 6 November 2010.
- BENEDICT XVI, *Address on visit to the Cathedral of Santiago de Compostela. Apostolic Journey to Santiago de Compostela and Barcelona,* 6 November 2010.
- BENEDICT XVI, *Address to Members of the Diplomatic Corps,* 10 January 2011.
- BENEDICT XVI, *Lectio Divina at Meeting with the Parish Priests of the Rome Diocese,* 10 March 2011.
- BENEDICT XVI, *Address at Welcome Ceremony with young people for XXVI World Youth Day. Apostolic Journey to Madrid,* 18 August 2011.
- BENEDICT XVI, *Address at Meeting with Families and Priest, Cathedral of Saint Cyriac for Conclusion of XXV Italian National Eucharistic Congress in Ancona,* 11 September 2011.
- BENEDICT XVI, *Address to the Federal Parliament, Reichstag Building, Berlin. Apostolic Journey to Germany,* 22 September 2011.
- BENEDICT XVI, *Address at Prayer vigil with the young people at the trade fair grounds of Freiburg im Breisgau. Apostolic Journey to Germany,* 24 September 2011.

- JOHN PAUL II, *Address to the Representatives of All Australian Institutions of Higher Learning*, Sydney, 26 November 1986.
- JOHN PAUL II, *Address to the Bishops of the Episcopal Conference of Ontario (Canada) on their "ad Limina" Visit"*, 4 May 1999.

## MONOGRAPHS

- St. ALPHONSUS LIGUORI, *On the Love of Christ, Liturgy of the Hours, Office of Readings for the Feast of St. Alphonsus Liguori* (http://www.liturgies.net/saints/alphonsusliguori/readings.htm, accessed in July 2014).
- St. ATHANASIUS, *The Letters of Saint Athanasius concerning the Holy Spirit*, translation with introduction and notes by C.R.B. Shapland, Epworth Press, London 1951.
- St. AUGUSTINE, *Confessions and Enchiridion*, newly translated and edited by Albert C. Outler, Westminster Press, Philadelphia 1955.
- St. AUGUSTINE, *Augustine's Sermon "On Pastors" – excerpts as found in the Liturgy of the Hours. Office of Reading*, Volume IV, Catholic Book Publishing Corp., New York 1975. (http://fathergilles.net/parishministry/On_Pastors_by_St_Augustine.pdf, accessed in July 2014).
- BENEDICT XVI, *Jesus of Nazareth*, Doubleday, New York 2007.
- BENEDICT XVI, *Jesus of Nazareth. Holy week: from the Entrance into Jerusalem to the Resurrection*, Part two, Ignatius Press, San Francisco 2011.
- St. BERNARD OF CLAIRVAUX, *From a Sermon by Saint Bernard, Liturgy of the Hours, Office of Readings, Wednesday, 23rd week, Ordinary Time* (http://www.liturgies.net/Liturgies/Catholic/loh/week23wednesdayor.htm, accessed in July 2014)
- St. BERNARD OF CLAIRVAUX, *Sermons on the Song of Songs* (http://www.pathsoflove.com/bernard/songofsongs/sermon83.html, accessed in July 2014).
- St. CATHERINE OF SIENA, *The Dialogue of Saint Catherine of Siena*, translated by Algar Thorold (https://www.ewtn.com/library/SOURCES/CATHDIAL.HTM, accessed in July 2014).
- St. CYPRIAN, *St. Cyprian on the Lord's Prayer. An English Translation, with Introduction*, by T. Herbert Bindley, Society for promoting Christian knowledge, London 1914.
- DENZIGER, HENRICUS & ADOLFUS SCHÖNMETZER (eds.), *Enchiridion Symbolorum*, Verlag Herder KG, Freiburg im Breisgau 1965.

- St. FRANCIS OF ASSISI, *The Writings of Saint Francis of Assisi. Translated from the Critical Latin Edition*, edited by Fr. Kajetan Esser, O.F.M., Franciscan Archive, 2000 (http://www.franciscan-archive.org/patriarcha/opera/preces.html, accessed in July 2014).
- St. FRANCIS OF ASSISI, *St. Francis' Letter to all the Faithful (2nd Version)* (http://totus2us.com/vocation/ saints/st-francis-of-assisi, accessed in July 2014).
- St. GREGORY THE GREAT, *The book of Pastoral Rule,* translation with introduction by G. Demacopoulos, St. Vladimir's Seminary Press, New York 2007.
- St. IGNATIUS OF ANTIOCH, *Epistles of St. Ignatius of Antioch*, (http:// www.catholicculture.org/culture/library/view.cfm?recnum=3836, accessed in July 2014).
- INTERNATIONAL DOCUMENTATION by FIAMC (World Federation of the Catholic Medical Association), *Forty Years of HUMANAE VITAE from a medical perspective* (http://www.fiamc.org/bioethics/humanae-vitae, accessed in July 2014).
- St. IRENAEUS BISHOP OF LYONS, *Against Heresies,* translated by J. Keble, James Parker and Co, London, Oxford and Cambridge 1872.
- Blessed ISAAC OF STELLA, Sermon 11, *Liturgy of the Hours, Office of Readings, Friday, 23rd week, Ordinary Time* (http://www.liturgies.net/Liturgies/Catholic/loh/week23fridayor.htm, accessed in July 2014).
- St. JOHN CHRYSOSTOM, *Homily by Saint John Chrysostom before he went into exile* (http://www.todayscatholicworld.com/homily-chrysostom.htm, accessed in July 2014).
- JOHN PAUL II, *Gift and Mystery*, Doubleday, New York 1996.
- JOHN PAUL II, *Memory and Identity. Conversations between Millenniums,* Rizzoli International Publications, Inc., New York 2005.
- JOHN PAUL II, *Man and Woman He Created Them. A Theology of the Body*, Pauline Books & Media, Boston, MA 2006.
- St. JOHN VIANNEY, *Catechism on Prayer* (http://saints.sqpn.com/stj18010.htm, accessed in July 2014).
- St. LEO THE GREAT, *From a Sermon on the beatitudes, Liturgy of the Hours, Office of Readings, Monday, 23rd week, Ordinary Time* (http://www.liturgies.net/Liturgies/Catholic/loh/week23mondayor.htm, accessed in July 2014).
- St. MAXIMILIAN KOLBE, *From a letter of Maximilian Mary Kolbe, Liturgy of the Hours, Office of Readings for the Feast*

*of St. Maximilian Kolbe* (http://www.liturgies.net/saints/kolbe/readings.htm, accessed in July 2014).

- St. POLYCARP, *The Epistle of Polycarp to the Philippians. The Greek and Latin Text of the Epistle, verse by verse, compiled by D.R. Palmer* (www.bibletranslation.ws, accessed in July 2014).
- RATZINGER, JOSEPH, *The God of Jesus Christ. Meditations on the triune God,* Ignatius Press, San Francisco 2008.
- STEIN, EDITH (St. Teresa Benedicta of the cross), *Finite and eternal being: an attempt at an ascent to the meaning of being,* translated by Kurt F. Reinhardt, Washington Province of Discalced Carmelites, ICS Publications, Washington, DC 2002.
- St. THERESE OF LISIEUX, *History of a Soul: The Authobiography of St. Thérèse of Lisieux with Additional Writings and Sayings of St. Thérèse* (http://www.catholicbible101.com/St.%20Therese%20Story%20of%20a%20soul.pdf, accessed in July 2014).

Printed in the United States
By Bookmasters